Marxist Introductions

General Editor
Steven Lukes

Also published in this series

Marxism and Anthropology   Maurice Bloch
Marxism and Philosophy   Alex Callinicos
Marxism and Law   Hugh Collins
Marxism and Ecology   Reiner Grundmann
Marxism and International Relations
    Vendulka Kubálková and Albert A. Cruickshank
Marxism and Morality   Steven Lukes
Marxism and Politics   Ralph Miliband
Marxism and Ideology   Ferruccio Rossi-Landi
Marxism and Literature   Raymond Williams

Marxism and the City

IRA KATZNELSON

CLARENDON PRESS · OXFORD
1993

Oxford University Press, Walton Street, Oxford OX2 6DP

Oxford New York Toronto
Delhi Bombay Calcutta Madras Karachi
Kuala Lumpur Singapore Hong Kong Tokyo
Nairobi Dar es Salaam Cape Town
Melbourne Auckland Madrid

and associated companies in
Berlin Ibadan

Oxford is a trade mark of Oxford University Press

Published in the United States by
Oxford University Press Inc., New York

First published 1992
Published in paperback 1993

British Library Cataloguing in Publication Data
Data available

Library of Congress Cataloging in Publication Data
Katznelson, Ira.
Marxism and the city / Ira Katznelson.
p. cm.—(Marxist introductions)
Includes bibliographical references and index.
1. Sociology, Urban. 2. Marxian school of economics. I. Title.
II. Series.
HT151.K334 1992 307.76—dc20 91-24863
ISBN 0-19-827924-8

10 9 8 7 6 5 4 3 2 1

Printed in Great Britain
on acid-free paper by
Bookcraft (Bath) Ltd
Midsomer Norton, Avon

'From now on, I'll describe the cities to you,' the Khan had said, 'in your journeys you will see if they exist.'

But the cities visited by Marco Polo were always different from those thought of by the emperor.

'And yet I have constructed in my mind a model city from which all possible cities can be deduced,' Kublai said. 'It contains everything corresponding to the norm. Since the cities that exist diverge in varying degrees from the norm, I need only foresee the exceptions to the norm and calculate the most improbable combinations.'

'I have also thought of a model city from which I deduce all the others,' Marco answered. 'It is a city made only of exceptions, exclusions, incongruities, contradictions. If such a city is the most improbable, by reducing the number of abnormal elements, we increase the probability that the city really exists. So I have only to subtract exceptions from my model, and in whatever direction I proceed, I will arrive at one of the cities which, always as an exception, exist. But I cannot force my operation beyond a certain limit; I would achieve cities too probable to be real.'

The Great Khan owns an atlas in which are gathered the maps of all the cities: those whose walls rest on solid foundations, those which fell in ruins and were swallowed up by the sand, those that will exist one day and in whose place only hares' holes gape . . .

The atlas has these qualities: it reveals the form of cities that do not yet have a form or a name. There is the city in the shape of Amsterdam, a semicircle facing north, with concentric canals—the princes', the emperor's, the nobles'; there is the city in the shape of York, set among the high moors, walled, bristling with towers; there is the city in the shape of New Amsterdam also known as New York, crammed with towers of glass and steel on an oblong island between two rivers, with streets like deep canals, all of them straight, except Broadway.

The catalogue of forms is endless: until every shape has found its city, new cities will continue to be born. When the forms exhaust their variety and come apart, the end of cities begins. In the last pages of the atlas there is an outpouring of networks without beginning or end, cities in the shape of Los Angeles, in the shape of Kyoto-Osaka, without shape.

(Italo Calvino, *Invisible Cities*, New York: Harcourt Brace Jovanovich, 1974, 69, 137–9)

Preface

DEFEATED in the East and discredited in the West, and lacking in knowledgeable or popular support, Marxism has broken down as an ideology and as a guide to governance. Why publish a book about it in the early 1990s? And even if Marxism remains an important analytical tool and critical resource in countries that are capitalist and democratic, why treat Marxism and the *city*? Over the time-span of its development as social and practical theory Marxism has had relatively little to say about cities. Moreover, in the late twentieth century the city itself has become more diffuse and imprecise (like the 'cities' on the last pages of the Great Khan's atlas), even, perhaps, to the point of not constituting a meaningful category at all.

The most important reasons I have had for writing *Marxism and the City* pivot on two hunches. The first is that for all its profound and infirming flaws as a total ensemble of understanding and governance, Marxism remains a vital tool for understanding and raising questions about key aspects of modernity. Moreover, in the aftermath of the conclusive triumph of liberal citizenship and markets over competing conceptions, the analytical and critical dimensions of Marxism, albeit in a manner far more modest than Marxists once hoped, may now find a new significance as a source of intellectual and political friction. The second hunch is that some of the key weaknesses in Marxism as social theory can be remedied by forcing it to engage seriously with urban-spatial concerns, particularly with regard to the relationship between structure and agency that is at the heart of all useful social theory. In short, I think this extended speculative essay on Marxism and the city can help produce a more capable, if more limited and modest, contribution by Marxism to the analysis of important dimensions of social, political, cultural, and economic life.

In part, too, my reasons for tackling the manifestly peculiar subject of Marxism and the city are personal and scholarly. When I started thinking about this book I had finished a volume on American cities and working-class formation. I was dissatisfied with the implicit, unexamined, not very rigorous *Marxisant* qualities of *City Trenches: Urban Politics and the Patterning of Class in the United States.* That book contributed indirectly to scholarly work on Marxism and the city, and it presented a sympathetic critique of then current work by scholars working on cities within a Marxist framework. The central thrust of *City Trenches*, however, concerned questions about class, politics, and collective action in the United States that are usually condensed under the label 'American exceptionalism', a focus that allowed me the luxury of indirection regarding some key issues in Marxist theory and urban studies.

As it turns out, the invitation to write *Marxism and the City* provided me with a chance to grapple with these questions at just the moment when Marxist scholarship was beginning to engage the city seriously as a constitutive element of social theory for the first time in its intellectual and doctrinal history. The focus from within Marxism on the city was initiated by the pioneering work of Henri Lefebvre in the 1960s. He began with a fundamental critique of the urban field as such, and moved on to various theoretical and empirical studies of the city. In the hands of such talented intellectual craftspeople as Manuel Castells, David Harvey, Chris Pickvance, Doreen Massey, John Lojkine, Sharon Zukin, Christian Topalov, and a host of other geographers, sociologists, historians, and political scientists, the new Marxist studies became the major source of innovation in the urban field. Relative newcomers to the journal collections of libraries—*Space and Society*, the *International Journal of Urban and Regional Research*, *Antipode*—took a leadership role in something approaching a paradigm shift in urban studies, at least for younger scholars. Today, after a period of robust creativity, the vitality of this scholarly effort has abated, or at least become more diffuse. While it is not entirely clear whether Marxist urban studies have reached a moment of closure or pause, either way this is a good time to take stock.

Marxism and the City is not principally a review essay,

however. The subject-matter of Marxism and the city holds out other promises. Cities have always been condensations of their civilizations. If their density distorts, so it also reveals. By focusing on cities as points in space, as places with determinate forms, and as *loci* for human activity, it is possible to illuminate from this vantage-point key aspects of history and the adequacy of alternative social theories. I think it possible to contribute towards an evaluation of Marxism's analytical capacities by focusing on the ways it can help explain the development of modern Western cities, and on how it can incorporate cities and city space into its analytical framework. I attempt to show how Marx's principal analytical projects are enhanced by incorporating an urban-spatial dimension; and, in turn, how some subjects of urban research and our understanding of cities are illuminated by their engagement with Marxism. At the same time, the encounter of Marxism with the city helps clarify some central issues of Marxist theory.

The character of *Marxism and the City* has been shaped by the lively scholarly climate at the Graduate Faculty of the New School for Social Research, New York, where colleagues have reminded me that scholarly work is balanced between private and collective acts. For reading an early draft of the manuscript and providing telling criticism I am especially indebted to Janet Abu-Lughod, Jeffrey Goldfarb, David Gordon, Norman Fainstein (now at the City University of New York), Anwar Shaikh, and Charles Tilly. For other contributions based on seminar discussions of chapters at the Center for Studies of Social Change and the General Seminar of the Graduate Faculty, I am grateful to Andrew Arato, Jerome Bruner, Eric Hobsbawm, Robert Heilbroner, Sonia Kruks (now at Oberlin College), Claus Offe, Ross Thomson, Louise Tilly, and Aristide Zolberg.

Outside the New School, Steven Lukes's valuable editorial comments prodded me to improve the manuscript. Shmuel Eisenstadt kindly took time out during a sabbatical visit to the Russell Sage Foundation to comment on draft chapters. My week-long stay at the A. E. Havens Center for the Study of Social Structure and Social Change at the University of Wisconsin proved particularly helpful. Its director, Erik Olin

Contents

1. Marxism and the City?   1
2. Themes in Marxist Social Theory   43
3. Towards a Respatialized Marxism:
   Lefebvre, Harvey, and Castells   92
4. Capitalism, City Space, and Class
   Formation:
   A Journey Organized by Friedrich Engels   141
5. From Feudalism to Capitalism:
   The Place of the City   157
6. Working Classes Map the City   203
7. Remapping the City   257

Select Bibliography   309
Index   313

1 Marxism and the City?

VENICE, Amsterdam, and Danzig (Gdansk) are canal towns built on or near the sea. Lucerne, Geneva, and Zurich are located at the end of a lake astride a river that drains into the lake. In what sense are all of these cities comparable objects of analysis? In what ways do each of these triplets, which I draw from Lucien Febvre's discussion of towns,[1] compose meaningful clusters of cities? How shall we understand similarities and divergencies in their character and personality?

Possible answers are self-evident only if we restrict ourselves to a classification and analysis of cities with respect to their natural locations. Writing about the city in 1898, Vidal de la Blache proposed that the central problems of urban geography were twofold: 'Nature prepares the site, and man organizes it in such fashion that it meets his desires and wants.' Febvre, citing this formulation, hastens to observe that at a minimum we need also to distinguish the genesis from the growth processes of towns to make sense of their development. Thus the physical location of cities must be considered a contributory factor to their founding, but immediately upon their formation, towns begin to develop divergent histories; for these, 'the physical peculiarity in question must have yielded place, in the development of these urban organisms, to factors of quite a different nature and of infinitely more importance: to factors of growth or . . . of enlargement'.[2]

---

[1] Lucien Febvre, *A Geographical Introduction to History*. London: Kegan Paul, Trench, Trubner, 1932, 338–41. Febvre opens his discussion of towns by appreciating the various typologies and classifications of geographers, but then moves quickly to question their depth and meaning: 'Not every comparison is valuable in itself,' he cautions, 'and to class the kings of France as fat and thin, tall or short, is not to contribute very effectively to a knowledge of their reign or character' (339).

[2] Ibid., 340–1. See also Febvre's discussion of historical and politi-

2 Marxism and the City?

Without a sustained and systematic consideration of such 'factors of quite a different nature', the city must remain an elusive object of study. If we think of the city, as Lewis Mumford does, as 'the point of maximum concentration for the power and culture of a community',[3] then the study of cities is no less than a particular kind of study of human civilization and its large-scale processes (such is the case even if the empirical range under consideration is limited in time and place, as it is with this book whose focus is oriented mainly to post-sixteenth-century cities in Western Europe and North America).[4] From this perspective, 'a city is a concrete

---

cal factors on p. 348. Lacking in this discussion is attention to the design of cities as a craft, and the connections between urban design and large-scale social processes. It is quite obvious that the design of the medieval town makes no sense without a focus on the role of religion, for example, or the 19th-century town without a consideration of the role of factory-based industry.

[3] Lewis Mumford, *the Culture of Cities*. New York: Harcourt Brace, 1938, 3. Whether cities are the hope or negation of civilization is a debate that has raged down through the ages. Each of these competing images is based on the shared view that cities, for good or ill, are particular kinds of condensations of human civilization.

[4] This limitation is not without costs. Through my omission of urban development in East and Central Europe and the Soviet Union, *Marxism and the City* reproduces the failure of recent Marxist work on the city to deal seriously and comparatively with patterns of urbanization in non-capitalist societies. This decision, which I have made both for reasons of focus and expertise, makes it more difficult to demarcate precisely the differences *capitalism* has made to post-feudal urbanization in contrast to other causes. As Murray and Szelenyi have put the point, 'The main weakness of the neo-Marxist position is that it lacks a theory of urbanization under socialism. As long as the new urban sociology will not provide us with a comprehensive theoretical explanation of the nature of urbanization under actually existing socialism it will always be doubtful to what extent they have the right to claim that the contradictions they discover in western cities can actually be related to the capitalist character of these societies.' Pearse Murray and Ivan Szelenyi, 'The City in the Transition to Socialism', *International Journal of Urban and Regional Research*, 8 (Mar. 1984), 93. This is an important point, but it is not as fundamental a criticism as this strong prose suggests because it accepts the mode of production as the basic tool for explicating history and composing units for comparative analysis.

manifestation of general social forces; but its identity stems from being a particular accommodation to them'.[5]

Given the immense scope of the project of urban analysis, it is hardly surprising that there is a vast array of definitions and typologies of the city, and a host of specifications of the objects of urban studies. Are cities agglomerations of population over a certain size, specific functions concentrated in space, juridical units, bounded enclaves, or all of these and more? Even in the hands of as brilliant a student of cities as Mumford, whose working definition of the city is a useful guide-post, definitional discussions of the city are studded with an extraordinary range of analytical, allusory, and metaphorical formulations: The city is the 'product of the earth', 'a product of time', 'a fact of nature, like a cave, a run of mackerel, or an ant-heap', 'a conscious work of art', the expression of 'man's social needs'.[6]

And yet, more than any I know, Mumford's summary discussion of the 'sociological concept of the city' provides a useful grip on the subject, even as it justifies and commands a range of inquiry as broad as that of the study of human civilization:

Once this critical judgement is made (itself, of course, open to question), the matter of how to conduct a research programme, and which comparative strategies to use, are important, but second-order questions. For many, perhaps most, of the questions raised by the engagement of Marxism and the city, comparisons with the Soviet and East European experiences are not germane; for others they are. Ivan Szelenyi has been both insistent and influential in widening the scope of urban inquiry to include the socialist experience. Three papers published in the early 1980s have been especially important in setting the agenda for his later work and that of others: Ivan Szelenyi, 'Structural Changes of and Alternatives to Capitalist Development in the Contemporary Urban and Regional System', *International Journal of Urban and Regional Research*, 5 (Mar. 1981); Szelenyi, 'Urban Development and Regional Management in Eastern Europe', *Theory and Society*, 10 (Mar. 1981); and Murray and Szelenyi, 'The City in the Transition to Socialism'.

[5] Eric Lampard, 'The History of Cities in the Economically Advanced Areas', *Economic Development and Cultural Change*, 3 (Jan. 1955), 84. Marxism represents one kind of working out of this relationship.

[6] Mumford, *The Culture of Cities*, 3–6.

4   Marxism and the City?

The essential physical means of a city's existence are the fixed site, the durable shelter, the permanent facilities for assembly, interchange, and storage; the essential social means are the social division of labor, which serves not merely the economic life but the cultural processes. The city in its complete sense, then, is a geographic plexus, an economic organization, an institutional process, a theater of social action, and an esthetic symbol of collective unity. On the one hand it is a physical frame for the commonplace domestic and economic activities; on the other, it is a consciously dramatic setting for the more significant actions and the more sublimated urges of a human culture[7]

In the face of such an encompassing, decentred subject, the vast majority of studies of the city divide it into manageable parts, studying this or that aspect of urban life: its architecture, its economics, its politics, its collective action, its life-styles, its symbolism. Virtually every review of scholarship in urban geography, urban sociology, urban politics, and urban economics laments this disorder and division. Well they should. For, as we will see in a moment, this fragmentation is rooted not only in the immensity of the subject, but in the theoretical grounding of most twentieth-century urban studies in a model of cities and society that underscores the real and perplexing complexity of modern industrial societies. Ever since the explosion of cities in the West since the middle of the nineteenth century, even social theorists who have tried to apprehend more than partial elements of the city have done so within an approach that treats modernity in terms of differentiation. If we are to understand the potential contribution of Marxism to urban studies, I believe it is with an understanding and critique of this tradition in social theory that we need to begin.[8]

[7] Ibid., 480.
[8] The fragmentation and growing sub-area specialization of disciplinary urban studies continues unabated. In a 1985 review essay, geographer J. W. R. Whitehand took note that 'within the English speaking world urban geography is showing further signs of separating into a number of specialisms: retailing, offices, residential mobility, public service provision and morphology'. A year later, he continued to discover ever 'increasingly specialized research, with precious few efforts that go only a small way towards linking individual strands of research'. J. W. R. Whitehand, 'Urban Geography: The City as a

Before moving to this consideration, however, there is a prior issue to be taken up. The immense variety of urban subjects, theories, classifications, and methods is symptomatic of a lack of certainty not only as to whether the social sciences possess the tools necessary to analyse cities, but as to whether the city, as both an empirical and a theoretical construct, constitutes a coherent entity to be studied.[9]

Philip Abrams argued influentially that it is precisely because 'the city is *not* a social entity' that urban analysts frequently fall victim to a misplaced concreteness; thus we should not be surprised that empirical studies in the various fields of urban studies 'have proved graveyards of actual generalizations about the town'. The central issue, he insisted, is the focus on urban entities as such:

the town is a social form in which the essential properties of larger systems of social relations are grossly concentrated and intensified— to a point where residential size, density and heterogeneity, the formal characteristics of the town, appear to be in themselves constituent properties of a distinct social order.[10]

Place', *Progress in Human Geography*, 9 (Mar. 1985), 85; Whitehand, 'Urban Geography: Within the City', *Progress in Human Geography*, 10 (Mar. 1986), 103. Likewise, Shefter has noted the diversity of conceptions of the city within political science. The city has been variously apprehended as a community, as a business, and as a competitive market; its content has been treated in diverse kinds of imagery: as a system, as a mechanism of social control, as an internal colony, as a seat of political chaos. Martin Shefter, 'Images of the City in Political Science', in Robert M. Hollister (ed.), *Cities of the Mind*. New York: Plenum, 1984.

[9] In part this fragmentation reflects the growing specialization and technical sophistication of the various disciplines, but I think this is a secondary feature. If one reads the various reports on subfields in geography, for example, that appear in the journal *Progress in Human Geography*, one is immediately made aware of the absence of coherence not only by the sheer number of such subfields (industrial geography, social geography, cultural geography, and so on), but also by how much the emphasis of what is significant in a given subfield varies from year to year and from author to author. This is the case especially for urban geography.

[10] Philip Abrams, 'Towns and Economic Growth: Some Theories and Problems', in Philip Abrams and E. A. Wrigley (eds.), *Towns in Societies: Essays in Economic History and Historical Sociology*.

Thus, there is a tendency to concentrate on urban form rather than on the substance of such key social processes as state-building or capitalist development that give cities shape and meaning.[11]

In further developing this argument, Peter Saunders has usefully pointed out that while the key founders of modern social theory—Marx, Weber, Durkheim—had a good deal to say about cities,

none of them considered it useful or necessary to develop a specifically urban theory . . . In other words, all three seem to have shared the view that, in modern capitalist societies, the urban question must be subsumed under a broader analysis of factors operating in society as a whole. While cities could provide a vivid illustration of fundamental processes such as the disintegration of moral cohesion (Durkheim), the growth of calculative rationality (Weber) or the

---

Cambridge: Cambridge University Press, 1978, 9, 10. An overview of the field that develops Abrams's perspective is R. E. Pahl, 'Concepts in Context: Pursuing the "Urban" of Urban Sociology', in Derek Fraser and Anthony Sutcliffe (eds.), *The Pursuit of Urban History*. London: Edward Arnold, 1983.

[11] We might wish to take preliminary note of two variants of the Abrams position. Peter Saunders concludes his *Social Theory and the Urban Question* (London: Hutchinson, 1981) with a chapter 'On the Specificity of the Urban'. He observes that urban sociology has been searching 'for a sociological phenomenon the source of which may be located in the physical entity of the city. It has been the history of an institutionalized sub-discipline in search of a subject.' He concludes that the city constitutes 'a valid object of analysis for the historian . . . and for the political economist . . . but that its significance for the sociologist is limited either to its usefulness as a social microcosm . . . or its importance in terms of the effects of moral density on social relationships'. He ends with a plea for the rejection of 'space as a defining feature of urban sociology', and with the exhortation that we develop 'a non-spatial urban sociology' (249, 250, 257, 258). Mark Gottdiener's *The Social Production of Urban Space* (Austin, Tex.: University of Texas Press, 1985) also argues for a revision of the role of space in urban studies, not by excising it, however, but by arguing that as a consequence of processes of deconcentration and metropolitanization, urbanization and urbanism have burst the bounds of the city. I do not agree that space can be displaced from the core of urban studies, nor with the suggestion that city boundaries no longer count. I return to these themes below in a fuller consideration of Gottdiener's book.

destructive forces unleashed by the development of capitalist production (Marx), they could in no way explain them. For all three writers, what was required was not a theory of the city but a theory of the changing basis of social relations brought about through the development of capitalism, and it was to the latter task that they addressed themselves.[12]

There is a considerable degree of ambiguity in Saunders's exegetical survey and Abrams's counsel: should studies of the city be reduced to an epiphenomenal status, or should they be more systematically joined to studies of large-scale social processes? Is the city—its built-environment and spatial relations—just a background or a stage for the play of these social processes, or a determined expression of them; or, much more interestingly, is their relationship more one of imbrication?

Abrams's point that the city is not a free-standing entity is well taken, even if generations of urbanists seem to have missed it. At the same time, as a formation of people, space, and activities with a distinctive legal as well as social status, the city, as David Harvey aptly put it, is a vantage-point from which to capture some 'salient features in the social processes operating in society as a whole—it becomes, as it were, a mirror in which other aspects of society can be reflected'.[13]

But even mirrors have a material existence. If the city concentrates and intensifies general processes, it does so in distinctive ways. Once accomplished, this concentration and

---

[12] Saunders, *Social Theory*, 12.

[13] David Harvey, *Social Justice and the City*. London: Edward Arnold, 1973, 16. For a discussion of the legal position of cities spanning feudalism to the present, see Gerald Frug, 'The City as a Legal Concept', *Harvard Law Review*, 93 (Apr. 1980). It might also be noted that virtually every civilization in human history has distinguished between 'city' and 'non-city'. This does not mean that there is an essentialist city with fixed form or content, only that the concentration of culture and economic and political power in cities has been one of the most consistent features of human existence, and certainly of modern Western history; this must not be flattened out or eliminated in a quest to understand the larger processes within which cities are embedded. Of course the way both cities and these processes have been apprehended has varied enormously. Cities have, for example, been seen as representing the extremes of both virtue and degradation.

intensification of social processes in urban space may itself become a constitutive element of these larger social processes. City space, at one and the same time, may be an objective construct, within which social relations are ordered, and what Harvey calls 'relational space', that is, 'space regarded, in the fashion of Leibnitz, as being contained *in* objects in the sense that an object can be said to exist only insofar as it contains and represents itself within relationships to other objects'.[14] Abrams's critique thus cannot be the last word, but it does point to a necessary and creative dialectic between such conceptions as these of urban space, and between city space and various social processes. This is what Italo Calvino tells us in different terms when he writes of the city as consisting of 'relationships between the measurements of its space and the events of its past'.[15]

---

[14] Harvey, *Social Justice*, 13. City space, like social space more generally, is both a material and a social matter. In a suggestive article, Jens Christian Tonboe discusses the debate between those who see such space as a reflection of social structures and those who see social structures and processes as products of material and spatial structures. Drawing on Danish discussions, he urges us not to choose between these polar positions: 'Space relates to something social just as much as to something material. On the other hand, space is not just a (passive) reflection of the social ("reflectionism").' He concludes: 'Space, as a material-geographic structure, can be found as product, object, mediator, resource, restriction and symbol as well as latent ("stored") and inert power in many socio-political processes and conflicts. However, it is never active, never a motor by itself. It is created and recreated, moved and adjusted only by human action, in the same way that political, economic, and social structures are. Its (societal) meaning and function is defined solely from its social setting in a specified time-space.' Jens Christian Tonboe, 'On the Political Importance of Space: The Socio-Spatial Relations of Trade Unions, Gender, and the Decentralized Danish Welfare State', *Acta Sociologica*, 29/1 (1986). Although I have some reservations about the terminology, which is borrowed from Giddens, it is this perspective on space that informs what I have written below.

[15] Calvino writes: 'I could tell you how many steps make up the streets rising like stairways, and the degree of the arcade's curves . . . but I already know this would be the same as telling you nothing. The city does not consist of this, but of relationships between the measurements of its space and the events of its past . . . As this wave from memories flows in, the city soaks it up like a sponge and

Marxism's claim to give shape and illumination to studies of the city is precisely that it possesses a distinctive way to make just this connection by utilizing the great span and comprehensiveness of Marxism's concepts and hypotheses about the shape of history. Rejecting the more common approach to urban studies developed in the late nineteenth and early twentieth centuries that was rooted in the problematic of differentiation, Marxism builds on the provocative historical correlation between shifts in the mode of production and the development of capitalism on the one hand and the growth of particular kinds of cities on the other.

Let us turn initially to the differences between Marxism and differentiation approaches to cities in the company of Max Weber, who had something of a split personality when it came to urban analysis. His first-hand reaction to the modern city was troubled wonderment at its fractionated qualities, and he came to think about cities in terms of differentiation. His urban scholarship, by contrast, was grounded in an analysis of the large-scale social processes that underpin urban development. It is this focus on social processes that he shared, at least in broad outline, with Marx, and that distinguished his writings on the city from those of most of his contemporaries.

I

Weber visited the United States in 1904. He had little to say as a social theorist about New York, Chicago, St Louis, and

---

expands . . . The city, however, does not tell its past, but contains it like the lines of a hand, written in the corners of the streets, the gratings of the windows, the banisters of the steps, the antennae of the lightning rods, the poles of the flags, every segment marked in turn with scratches, indentations, scrolls.' Italo Calvino, *Invisible Cities*. New York: Harcourt Brace Jovanovich, 1974, 10–11. In this statement, Calvino challenges us not only to make the kinds of connection between macroscopic processes and city space urged by Abrams, but between both and micro-level experiences of the city, and the character of the built-form, in the small as well as in the large. Calvino, of course, hardly exhausts the definitional problems associated with the term 'city'.

the other large cities he saw. But he made clear in his diary entries that these cities served as a metaphor for capitalist modernity: magnificently though frightfully fragmented, 'a mad pell-mell', extraordinarily unequal, characterized by 'a tremendous intensity of work', loosely integrated, composed of a mosaic of nationalities each in its own territory, yet marked by an uncaring individuality: 'undoubtedly one could take ill and die without anyone caring!' He was struck too by the way in which an unequal social structure was inscribed in space, and by the extent of the geographical divisions between work and home: 'When they finish work at five o'clock, people must often travel for hours to get home ... With the exception of the better residential districts, the whole tremendous city—more extensive than London!—is like a man whose skin has been peeled off and whose intestines are seen at work.'[16]

Like other figurative interpretations stressing that the city no longer possessed a consistent set of social, cultural, and political standards, Weber's shocked representation reflected, and his mapping and reading of urban space confirmed, a view of reality common to most of the leading social theorists of the late nineteenth and early twentieth centuries. The modern city was new, and terrifying.

The city as such was neither central in a descriptive sense, nor manifestly the main subject, of such great theorists as Marx, Durkheim, Weber, Toennies, and Simmel. Each dealt with the city, of course, but only as a small part of the larger project of coming to terms with an industrial, capitalist, state-centred modernity. Just the same, the large modern city was an inescapable and constitutive element of all their considerations of these hallmarks of the modern world.

Each understood in his own way a point made more recently by Raymond Williams, when he wrote that 'city life, until our own century, even in a highly industrialized society, was still a minority experience, but it was widely and accurately seen as a decisive experience, with much more than proportionate

---

[16] Citations from Marianne Weber, *Max Weber: A Biography*. New York: John Wiley, 1975, 285–7.

effects on the character of the society as a whole'.[17] The large city—as a central arena and symbol of modernity; as the product and locale of such fundamental social processes as state-making and capitalist development; and as the generative locale for the formation of collective identities and collective action—thus provided an inescapable setting and subject for nineteenth- and twentieth-century social theory, albeit a setting and subject usually only tacit or implicit.

The principal way students of the city constructed these analytical and cognitive maps suffered in part from an insufficient and distorted appreciation of space as an integral element of economic, social, and political life. The main source of this distortion has been a key strand of nineteenth- and twentieth-century social theory focusing on the connections between social differentiation and social order. The result has been a portrayal of the history of the modern city in terms of a rupture between pre-industrial cities characterized by a simple, integrated, homogeneous organization of space, and industrial, capitalist cities characterized by an unintegrated, heterogeneous, disorganized patterning of space.

An example of this kind of treatment can be found in Stephen Kern's volume, *The Culture of Time and Space, 1880–1918*. Using these two co-ordinates, he reconstructs the decomposition of certainty in the late nineteenth century. Kern understands space as consisting of three elements: form (an amalgam of shape and area), distance, and direction. In the four decades straddling the turn of the century, distances contracted, the city both spread and concentrated its direction, and its form altered in numerous ways. Kern shows how the humanities and the social sciences tried to come to terms with the resulting plurality of spaces. This attempt was exemplified by the Cubist movement in art which put the heterogeneity of space on to a single painting, and negated 'the traditional notion that the subject of a painting . . . is more important than the background'.[18] Within the city, the new organization

---

[17] Raymond Williams, *The Country and the City*. New York: Oxford University Press, 1973, 217.

[18] Stephen Kern, *The Culture of Time and Space, 1880–1918*. Cambridge, Mass.: Harvard University Press, 1983, 8.

of form, distance, and direction signified the demise of the traditional hierarchies of class and politics.

To understand why this kind of representation of the city has proved so alluring, it is useful to understand that the dramatic changes of the nineteenth century were themselves aspects of a larger story of post-sixteenth-century transformations. From the eleventh to the sixteenth centuries towns grew at a rather slow, quite even pace. They were nodes of trade and craft production within feudalism's system of parcellized sovereignty. Each town, like each of the basic units of feudalism, was a compound of political, economic, and symbolic power; in Max Weber's terms, a 'fusion of fortress and the market'. Each was an administrative centre, and a place where economic activities were based on principles of market exchange. Weber's examination of medieval cities provides a useful baseline.[19] Western cities, he showed, were characterized by an ordered quality that could not survive the transition from feudalism to capitalism through mercantilism.

The most important Baroque post-feudal cities were political capitals, the homes of royal courts: London, Paris, Amsterdam, Antwerp, Seville. Their fate was tied to absolutist states and to a mercantile international economic order. The societies in which they were embedded were characterized by a new division of property and sovereignty, and by a concentration of both in explosively growing urban centres. Indeed, it is this very feature that allows us to define the modern city in terms of the spatial implosion of (merchant and industrial) capital and of political power. We shall see that these most basic social processes of the post-sixteenth-century Western world have been fundamental to the creation of modern cities, and that these cities have been key elements in the reproduction of both capitalism and modern states.

In these cities the internal unity of the towns described by Weber was threatened not only by changes in size and density which breached the old walls and reorganized ancient quarters, nor only by more complicated relationships within the dominant classes now that political authority and private wealth-seeking were established as related but distinctly autonomous

---

[19]   Max Weber, *The City*. New York: Free Press, 1958.

activities. What also challenged the old unities was the beginning of new patterns, in space, relating to places of work and
places of residence. Joined in the workshops of the medieval
city, work and home began to separate for the political and
economic élites of the capital cities. Merchants who traded on
a world scale began to construct homes on the outskirts of the
city; in turn, state officials began to work increasingly in the
new offices of the crown at the city centre.

A second group of large modern cities, the industrial centres
built in the nineteenth century on the sites of old villages, like
Manchester, or on empty prairies, like Chicago, even more
dramatically altered the traditional organization of urban
space. The industrial cities were built as places of work
according to the logic of capitalist accumulation. And even in
the older mercantile centres and political capitals—London,
Paris, New York, Berlin—the pace and character of change
were astonishing.

What were the new cities of the nineteenth century like?
Consider the leading city of the United States, New York, a
city of bewildering alterations to established ways of life and
patterns of social relations. The city grew explosively, from
just 60,000 inhabitants in 1800 to over 1,100,000 by the eve of
the Civil War. New York began the period as a leading
commercial and trading centre, and it maintained that position. In addition, however, it became a major, and rapidly
growing, *locus* of manufacturing, using new industrial technologies. The nature of work and the labour process altered
radically, characterized by the decline of artisanship, a reorganization of skills, and the development of a modern, wage-
labour working class. The demand for unskilled labour was
fuelled by high rates of in-migration, so that by 1860, New
York was mainly a city of people who had been born elsewhere.
Further, New York was the site of growing and dramatic
inequality, with a new occupational structure that reflected a
new class and cultural division of labour.[20]

---

[20] For discussions of transformations of 19th-century New York,
see Ira Katznelson, *City Trenches: Urban Politics and the Patterning
of Class in the United States*. New York: Pantheon Books, 1981, esp.
ch. 3; Amy Bridges, *A City in the Republic: Antebellum New York*

Such dramatic changes in the city were embedded and expressed in a fundamental reorganization of the urban form, whose most emblematic shift was the accelerating and fundamental separation of wage work from the home, and, in turn, from the residential community. This division consisted of at least three interrelated and overlapping historical processes. First, the household ceased to be the main unit or location of production. Second, whole areas of large towns and cities came to be devoted *either* to residential use *or* to factory production. Third, the residential areas of the city became increasingly homogeneous in both the Marxist and Weberian senses of class. With the division of city space into separate districts defined by their functions, and with the growing homogeneity of the residential areas, the city came to be defined, and to define its residents, in terms of their connections to the now increasingly autonomous markets for labour and for housing. The job and the residence became distinctive commodities to be bought and sold by the discipline and logic of money and the market-place. Older bonds were no longer determinative.[21]

Within the built-form of the city patterns of daily life were

---

and the Origins of Machine Politics. New York: Cambridge University Press, 1984; and Elizabeth Blackmar, 'Re-walking the "Walking City": Housing and Property Relations in New York City, 1780–1840', *Radical History Review*, 21 (Mar. 1980).

[21] There is a massive literature on the separation of work and home, a theme to which I return in some detail below in Chapter 5. For now, I wish only to take note of two seminal articles by James E. Vance: 'Housing the Worker: The Employment Linkage as a Force in Urban Structure', *Economic Geography*, 42 (Oct. 1966), and 'Housing the Worker: Determinative and Contingent Ties in Nineteenth Century Birmingham', *Economic Geography*, 43 (Apr. 1967). The separation of work and home gave rise to a geographical sub-specialization on journeys to work. The basic data base for this mode of analysis is the journey to work matrix based on three kinds of information: the geography of the homes of members of the population in the active labour force, the geography of workplaces, and the number of trips between these units. A central characteristic of 19th- and 20th-century urbanization is the lengthening distance and growing frequency of these journeys. For a very useful overview, see Kevin O'Connor, 'The Analysis of Journey to Work Patterns in Human Geography', *Progress in Human Geography*, 4 (Dec. 1980).

shaped by a new transportation technology and new paths to and from work; by a centralization and demarcated definition of cross-class public space; indeed by the very emergence of class, in both the Marxist and Weberian senses of the term, at the workplace and in the residential community, as the building blocks of the urban, industrial, capitalist social structure.

In the embrace of these changes, the physical city began to define patterns and zones of activity, and in them, new spheres of freedom. For working people, the various separations of work and home made possible the development of a spatially bounded, institutionally rich, independent working-class culture in their neighbourhoods of the city, and, at the same time, they impelled cultural producers to create new commercial cultural forms capable of appealing to the various new social groups and classes of the industrial city. This was a culture of pastiche, which dramatized the varied tempo of city life, and which had the capacity to appeal in different ways to each class and stratum in the city's diverse population.

The consumption of this new mass culture went hand in hand with the development of segmented, regionalized group and class cultures. For if working people were free from property, they were now also free, once they had left the workplace, to create something of an autonomous culture. As the city was reorganized in space, the places where people lived became increasingly homogeneous. The capacity of people to buy or rent real estate determined where they might live. As a result, parts of the city became settlements of people sharing class attributes in Weber's sense of the capacity to consume goods and services offered in the market-place. From the more macroscopic perspective of the city as a whole, however, urban areas were now much more heterogeneous than they once had been.[22]

[22] For a stimulating consideration, see David Ward, 'Social Structure and Social Geography in Large Cities of the U.S. Urban-Industrial Heartland', *Historical Geography Research Series*, 12 (Dec. 1983). See also, Richard Dennis, *English Industrial Cities of the Nineteenth Century: A Social Geography*. Cambridge: Cambridge University Press, 1984.

It should not be surprising that the massive shifts in urban form and social geography, taken together, proved a puzzle for various social groups and classes, and for social theorists. Nor should it surprise us that the break-up of the more integrated city prodded many theorists to develop new principles of order, group cohesion, and social control. The main result of this quest was the paradigm of differentiation, which became the centrepiece of many major works of social theory in the late nineteenth and early twentieth centuries. This world-view was more than just one new cosmology: it provided the most important grammar and vocabulary for representing the new city and its new patterns of social space.

The results of massive shifts in the nineteenth-century city that so shocked such observers stimulated the interpretation that social differentiation is the hallmark and 'the inevitable product of social change'. According to this view, summarized but not held by Charles Tilly, 'the state of social order depends on the balance of forces between processes of differentiation and processes of integration and control; rapid or excessive differentiation produces disorder'.[23] From this vantage-point, rapid social change and its disorienting possibilities are the central general processes of modernity. This perspective is condensed in such dichotomous pairs as Maine's status and contract; Durkheim's mechanical and organic solidarity; and Toennies's *Gemeinschaft* and *Gesellschaft*.

To be sure, these antinomies are not identical. Toennies, for one, stressed the new importance of the market for urban differentiation. For him, the contrast between pre-capitalist and capitalist cities lay in the new pervasive *Gesellschaft*, which he conceived to be an

artificial construction of an aggregate of human beings which super-ficially resembles the *Gemeinschaft* in so far as the individuals live and dwell together peacefully. However, in the *Gemeinschaft* they remain essentially united in spite of all separating factors, whereas in the *Gesellschaft* they are essentially separated in spite of all the uniting factors ... everybody is by himself and isolated and there exists a condition of tension against all others ... nobody wants to

[23] Charles Tilly, *Big Structures, Large Processes, Huge Comparisons*. New York: Russell Sage Foundation, 1984, 50.

grant and produce anything for another individual, nor will he be inclined to give ungrudgingly to another individual if it not be in exchange for a gift or labour equivalent that he considers at least equal to what he has given.[24]

Durkheim, by contrast, referred to the new order in terms of the movement from relations of constraint ('mechanical solidarity') to relations that produce authentic forms of co-operation in the small-scale settings of the new differentiated city ('organic solidarity'). This solidarity is not based on shared values but on cohesion based on difference.

These positions, of course, need not be contradictory. The new urban neighbourhoods of nineteenth-century cities were profoundly shaped by market forces in real estate, for example, which often tore social bonds asunder. At the same time, many of the homogeneous neighbourhoods created as a result of the operation of local real-estate markets became homes to people who shared so many attributes that the development of quite dense and solidaristic networks of social organization was facilitated.

The treatments of differentiation by Toennies and Durkheim portray the community–interest association dichotomy in a manner that makes solidarity too automatic both in Toennies's *Gemeinschaft* and in Durkheim's situation of 'organic solidarity'. Calhoun captured this point well when he observed that Toennies's 'subjective community of "inner" relations . . . tends to discount the importance of the social bonds and political mechanisms which hold communities together and make them work'.[25]

---

[24] Ferdinand Toennies, *Community and Association*. London: Routledge and Kegan Paul, 1955, 64–5, 33–4; Emile Durkheim, *The Division of Labor in Society*. New York: Free Press, 1964.

[25] 'This discounting', Calhoun observes, 'also allows the proponents of idealized community frequently to underestimate the restraint which real community requires, the sacrifices which it demands, and the fears which enforce them.' He proposes instead, in a way quite consistent with my own treatment, that we see 'community as made up of social relations, and of their macrosocial organization, of which community may be a greater or lesser part'. Craig Calhoun, 'History, Anthropology, and the Study of Communities: Some Problems in Macfarlane's Proposal', *Social History*, 3 (Oct. 1978), 369–71.

From an analytical perspective, what is most striking is that both differentiation as *Gesellschaft* and differentiation as organic solidarity share a broad world-view, and an interpretation of what the massive changes in capitalism, the state, and the city meant. Tilly has enumerated the key principles of this perspective:

1 'Society' is a thing apart; the world as a whole divides into distinct 'societies,' each having its more or less autonomous culture, government, economy, and solidarity.

2. Social behavior results from individual mental events, which are conditioned by life in society. Explanations of social behavior therefore concern the impact of society on individual minds.

3. 'Social change' is a coherent general phenomenon, explicable *en bloc*.

4. The main processes of large-scale social change take distinct societies through a succession of standard stages, each more advanced than the previous stage.

5. Differentiation forms the dominant, inevitable logic of large-scale social change; differentiation leads to advancement.

6. The state of social order depends on the balance between processes of differentiation and processes of integration or control; rapid or excessive differentiation produces disorder.

7. A wide variety of disapproved behavior—including madness, murder, drunkenness, crime, suicide, and rebellion, results from the strain produced by excessively rapid social change.[26]

This orientation was given its greatest plausibility by the experienced changes in the city, which appeared to conform to this meta-description of reality. After all, the social and spatial differentiation of the city was manifest; what the new urban analysts sought to do was to read this differentiation in terms of a plausible account of the basic dynamics of industrial capitalist societies. This they did by the kind of simplification Tilly rightly criticizes, but in so doing some analysts, above all Georg Simmel, produced rich and perceptive treatments of the city. Simmel's corpus proved exceptionally important in the development of a differentiation approach to urban studies, especially in the Chicago School of the United States, and it is important for these reasons to dwell, if briefly, on his contribution.

[26] Tilly, *Big Structures*, 11.

Simmel's corpus was in part an attempt to come to terms with the metropolitan culture of Berlin. One of the best-known of his essays, 'The Metropolis and Mental Life', published in 1903, dealt with the impact of the city as such; and by his own testimony, his major works, including his first book, *Social Differentiation* (1890), and *The Philosophy of Money* (1900) were animated by shifts in the character of city life. 'Berlin's development from a city to a metropolis in the years around and after the turn of the century', Simmel observed, 'coincides with my own strongest and broadest development.'[27] Much more than his main contemporaries, Weber, Sombart, and Toennies, Simmel concentrated on contemporary experience, including that of the customer and the resident of the big city. His central questions concerned the elaboration of market relations in the differentiated city, and their effects on social relations.

In his first book, Simmel stressed how with increased differentiation the individual dissolves into elements; the result is the construction of human ties of a more varied sort with people who share partial traits and relationships. As a consequence, new group relations become possible, and there is an accelerated development of new forms of social interaction. A decade later, in *The Sociology of Money*, Simmel maintained this perspective, and, in an important addition, linked it explicitly to exchange relationships in urban society, a perspective developed even more fully as an urban analysis in 'Space and the Spatial Structures of Society', the penultimate chapter of Simmel's *Sociology* (1908). The themes in this chapter are also taken up in 'The Metropolis and Mental Life'.

---

[27] Cited in David Frisby, *Georg Simmel*. London: Tavistock Publications, 1984, 34. A comprehensive bibliography of books and articles by Georg Simmel can be found in Nicholas J. Spykman, *The Social Theory of Georg Simmel*. New York: Atherton Press, 1966, 274–86. An English version of 'Die Grosstadt und das Geistesleben', ('The Metropolis and Mental Life') can be found in Donald L. Levine (ed.), *Georg Simmel: On Individuality and Social Forms*. Chicago: University of Chicago Press, 1971, 324–39. Levine's introduction contains a fine discussion of the personal and intellectual relationship between Simmel and the Chicago School. See esp. pp. xlix–lvi.

In these works the key elements of a sociology of differentiation in space are elaborated. These include impersonality, detachment, isolation, segmented friendships, commodification of relationships, and, above all, the significance of boundaries. Perhaps the most brilliant contribution lies in Simmel's use of these elements to discuss alternative ways social relationships may get fixed in space. He contrasts the medieval city, which it was difficult to leave, with the residential mobility of the twentieth-century city. Although this freedom exists, Simmel observes, particular social groups become anchored to distinctive territories. These spaces tend to get named, thus individualized as separate; and each of these territories tends to have one or more special locations or buildings (a church, a market-place, a school, a transport centre) that gives it a focus, a hub of activity, an identity, and a boundary.

Simmel's work on the city thus brought together his interests in number and size, the division of labour, and the relationship between money and rationality and his interest in changing cultural forms in capitalism. He shows a keen appreciation of the ways in which capitalist development has reshaped each of these societal elements and their relationships; and yet, his work is rather more powerful as description and as a goad to questions than as an analysis of the processes that created this new plural reality.

Simmel's themes were developed most clearly with regard to their implications for a modern urban-based civilization in the political sociology of Louis Wirth, who, together with his Chicago School of Sociology colleagues, was deeply influenced by him. Wirth understood that Simmel's way of seeing urban space had profound implications for thinking about social and political order in society. For if society was internally divided, it had now to face basic new problems of social control. An integrated society could be self-regulating, but a differentiated one might dissolve into disconnected fragments. When Wirth wrote a preface to a revised edition of Robert Park's famous 1915 essay on the city, he singled out Simmel's 'The Metropolis and Mental Life' as 'the most important single article on the city from a sociological viewpoint', and Wirth's own 1938 essay, 'Urbanism as a Way of Life', resonates with Simmelian themes.[28] Unlike Simmel, who moved very fluidly, often without careful delineation, between urbanism and industrial capitalism because he saw the city as the centre of capitalist culture, Wirth sought rigorously to distinguish the two. He did so in order to make possible the development of an autonomous field of urban studies based on the human-ecological perspectives of the Chicago School, but such a distinction is also critical to any effort, which he did not undertake, to specify the character of the relationship between urban and capitalist development.

If Wirth's distinction between capitalism and urbanism elucidated Simmel's conflation of the two, though at a cost, Wirth's critique of the city unfortunately left out Simmel's insight that metropolitan differentiation made unparalleled individual and group self-development possible through the creation of new, relatively homogeneous, 'free' social areas. Instead, Wirth underscored the problems differentiation posed for social cohesion. According to him, the city was more than just a fragmented social and spatial order; it was also a divided and disorganized moral order. In this sociological analysis, Wirth highlighted an older, conservative lament. Thus, for example, Carlyle in 1831 had described industrial city dwellers as 'strangers . . . It is a huge aggregate of little systems, each of which is again a small anarchy, the members of which do not *work* together, but *scramble* against each other.'[29]

Wirth sided rather more with Toennies than with Durkheim. Primordial integrative ties had been replaced by artificial, secondary ones. Shared values had been shattered. The fragmentary and partial normative features of city life could not maintain social control (in the sense of the capacity of the society as a whole to regulate itself in accordance with shared aims). The consequences could be seen in political disorganization and an increase in such pathological behaviour as personality disorders, crime, and weakened family life. In this

---

[28] Louis Wirth, 'Urbanism as a Way of Life', *American Journal of Sociology*, 44 (July 1938). Wirth's assessment of the significance of Simmel can be found in the bibliographical essay he prepared for Robert E. Park, Ernest W. Burgess, and R. D. MacKenzie, *The City*. Chicago: University of Chicago Press, 1925, 219.

[29] Cited in Williams, *The Country and the City*, 215.

analysis Wirth presented in refracted form élite fears of contact with the new immigrant working-class masses, which were most often expressed in metaphors of health and disease.

Urban differentiation and its negative consequences were likely to get worse over time, Wirth thought, because spatial fragmentation and the collapse of a unified system of norms were driven by fundamental features of the new city: its density and its concomitant competition for scarce space, a competition that produced increasingly homogeneous districts, social boundaries, and the quest for social avoidance of the less desirable.

Wirth's response was to seek through the policies of municipal politics secondary, mechanical substitutes for the loss of primary mechanisms of social integration. He made a strong normative plea on behalf of rationality, planning, and social science as the vehicles for achieving at a secondary level the kind of societal co-ordination no longer available in the fragmented, differentiated city.

In conservative hands, this vision was a plea for the imposition of order by authoritative means if necessary. The differentiation perspective, however, was not just a reactionary position; it was equally the common sense of critics of capitalism on the left.[30] The differentiation perspective, in fact, has been less a subject for contest between right and left than the common-sense view of urban life, one that has been elaborated by geographers and sociologists, politicians and leaders of protest movements, novelists and artists. The portrait of differentiation versus order has provided the stock imagery of urban life.

---

[30] Engels, for one, heralded some of Simmel's and Wirth's themes when he wrote: 'the brutal indifference, the unfeeling isolation of each in his private interest becomes the more repellent and offensive, the more these individuals are crowded together, within a limited space. And, however much one may be aware that this isolation of the individual, this narrow self-seeking is the fundamental principle of our society everywhere, it is nowhere so shamelessly barefaced, so self-conscious as just here in the crowding of a great city. The dissolution of mankind into monads, of which each one has a separate principle, the world of atoms, is here carried out to its utmost extremes.' Cited in Williams, *The Country and the City*, 216.

This mode of representation has tended to confuse description and cause. The Chicago School and the ecological tradition it engendered have treated the expansion of the city as a *sui generis* natural process of urban development, without attending to the factors, processes, and interests that have shaped the ways in which urban space has been produced. It has been able to do so by inserting human ecology within a contentless structural functionalism.[31]

All this notwithstanding, the analytical tradition of differentiation and its depictions of cities and their spatial patterns have continued to prove immensely appealing, in part because they seem so readily to make sense of social reality. But this appearance is based on the quite flawed assumptions that the basic units of social analysis should be the individual and society; and that the ways society and the individual shape and constrain each other should provide the main objects of social science investigation.[32]

To look at society–individual interactions from the differentiation perspective is, first, to assume that society itself is a meaningful, independent entity; and, second, that its members internalize the norms of society. Human cognition, the formation of dispositions, and patterns of action are socially conditioned. Set within and against the social are individuals who are the carriers of societal patterns and values; hence the social can be apprehended through an analysis of the orientation of individuals to action, as well as their actual behaviour.

These assumptions may seem obvious—they are very deeply ingrained not only in our social science but in our culture—but they are unrealistic. It only makes sense to think of a unitary and coherent 'society' bounded in space if, taken together, its different aspects constitute a system. Yet, as an empirical matter society in the sense of a single, large-scale, interactive group never occurs. Much of the world is divided into national states with identifiable boundaries, but such processes and activities as family life, production, and communications either take place in social fields much smaller

---

[31] This critique is developed harshly in Tilly, *Big Structures*.
[32] For relevant critiques, see Saunders, *Social Theory*, chs. 2 and 3; and Gottdiener, *Social Production*, ch. 2.

than these units of citizenship or on a much larger, sometimes global, scale. When 'boundaries of different sorts of action do not *coincide*', Tilly writes, 'the idea of a society as an autonomous, organized, interdependent system loses its plausibility'. As an alternative to the reification of society as the pivotal unit of analysis, he proposes the adoption of the 'idea of multiple social relationships' of different scale.[33] At the other end of the continuum from 'society' is the individual as the irreducible unit of social analysis. People are meaningful as social actors only in so far as they *interact*. When Wirth borrowed from Simmel, it was this essential insight of Simmelian sociology that he neglected. In obvious ways, individuals are the basic integers of action, but only when joined in networks and relationships. Further, from the vantage-point of relational analysis of the kind Weber and Marx shared, the larger framework of action is provided not by society, but by such large-scale social processes as capitalist development and state-building that pattern ties between people in determinative ways.

From the vantage-point of the society–individual antinomy, the problem of differentiation appears as the problem of social order precisely because it becomes more difficult for individuals in a differentiated world to internalize societal values; differentiation produces a fragmentation of values. From the perspective of relationships and social processes, the descriptive portrait of modernity presented by the problematic of differentiation is itself irremediably flawed. Both the modern national state and modern capitalist production have been characterized by an increasing concentration (not differentiation or fragmentation) of sovereignty and capital.[34] Indeed, from this alternative vantage-point we see the history of

[33] Tilly, *Big Structures*, 23. I think this position, with which I agree, is agnostic about whether there is something like a structure at a deeper level that binds the various networks and social relationships together in some larger system. Certainly, at least some versions of Marxism require this assumption.

[34] There is a useful discussion of de-differentiation in Charles Tilly, 'Reflections on the History of European State-Making', in Tilly (ed.), *The Formation of National States in Western Europe*. Princeton, NJ: Princeton University Press, 1975.

modern cities not just in terms of their concentration of a new fragmented culture but also in terms of their development as a *locus* for the concentration of both capital and political power.[35] With regard to cities, in short, the differentiation perspective presents a plausible social and spatial representation, but at the considerable cost of closing off questions about key social processes that affect and shape city life, about the networks of relationships that, in their great variety, define urbanity, and about the enormous range of alternative spatial relations, patterns of class and group formation, and collective actions that characterizes modern cities.

Weber's *The City* provides a fine example of an alternative to the differentiation approach. Although he did not write a comparable analysis for nineteenth- and twentieth-century cities, the way he treated the subject of the medieval town shows the social process network alternative to advantage.[36] A central theme of his study is a contrast between the occidental and oriental city in terms of key differences in the nature of interactive groups: guilds and territorial associations in the West; clans and castes in the East; and between the ancient and medieval cities of the West in terms of the relative importance of military clans in the ancient city, and occupational associations in the medieval city. Further, Weber locates these groups and the networks in which they were embedded in terms of such basic social processes as the development of rational economic activity and the emergence of autonomous bases of political authority. What finally distinguished the medieval from the ancient city was the political triumph of those groups that were the carriers of rational, market-centred, capitalistic economic activity. Thus, for Weber, the sociological and historical dimensions of urban analysis fuse in a much more richly textured way than the simple dichotomies of the differentiation–order perspective could possibly allow.[37]

[35] This formulation leaves open the character of their relationship and the degree to which they are closely related.

[36] I draw in part in this analysis on Martin E. Spencer, 'History and Sociology: An Analysis of Weber's *The City*', *Sociology*, 3 (Sept. 1977).

[37] In an interesting treatment of Weber's theory of community, Gertrud Neuwirth shows just how sharply Weber broke with the

I do not mean to suggest that the issues that produced and gave force to the various differentiation approaches to social theory are no longer with us. They remain our issues: anonymity and alienation; how the city insinuates itself into intimate relations and civil society; the circulation of material goods and of images; the milling of crowds; the dissolution and construction of human bonds. We still want to ask if the city is a unified experience or a mere division and assemblage of disordered elements, and if these, separately and together, constitute a barbarism or an appealing spectacle or, more likely, an amalgam of both.[38]

---

differentiation perspective and an ecological framework. 'Ecological variables' for Weber, Neuwirth writes, 'assume importance only if, for instance, the choice of residential area by community members is an expression of their social power. Communities are defined in terms of the solidarity shared by their members, which forms the basis of their mutual orientation to social action. Solidarity is not seen as a function of ecological residence, but rather as a response to "outside" pressures. It is manifested in those relationships and communal actions which are relevant to the members' positions within the larger society or relative to other communities.' Gertrud Neuwirth, 'A Weberian Outline of a Theory of Community: Its Application to the "Dark Ghetto"', *British Journal of Sociology*, 20 (June 1969), 148–9. In stressing that power, not ecology, is at the core of Weber's approach to community, Neuwirth locates Weber on the social process–social relationships alternative to the differentiation approach, and in this way links Weber to Marx as a member of the same analytical family in spite of their differences. For a discussion of the ways in which Weber succeeds, and does not succeed, in moving between a problematic of the subject and a problematic of the analysis of large-scale structural processes, see Bryan Turner, 'The Structuralist Critique of Weber's Sociology', *British Journal of Sociology*, 28 (Mar. 1977). Turner takes issue, as I do implicitly, with the equation of Weber only with a sociology based on 'understanding'. To do so, Turner points out, is to concentrate on the works of the early Weber to the neglect of *Economy and Society*, within which his treatment of the feudal city is embedded. In *Economy and Society* the stress on meaning and individual actors is complemented (or supplanted, depending on one's reading) by the analysis of social structures and social relations. Max Weber, *Economy and Society: An Outline of Interpretive Sociology* (3 vols.). New York: Bedminster Press, 196.

[38] I have been informed in my own thinking about these questions

If these are still good questions, they cannot be confronted by the direct, common-sense route of the differentiation problematic. When we examine urban space, we must inquire after the social processes that produced the landscape we see, and about the various social relationships that bind the people in the factory, the office, the neighbourhood, the park, and the other arenas of city life. In so exploring, we will do better to recall the methods and perspective of Max Weber as the analyst of medieval towns than his horror-stricken jottings as a tourist in the New World.

II

If, by its stress on social processes and social relationships, the work of the Marxist tradition, like the Weberian, is counterposed to the differentiation problematic, what distinguishes Marxism from other alternatives, including Weberian ones? The answer lies in the specific content of Marxist social analysis, which has provided a systematic and coherent set of suggestions about the relationship of nature and society, and about which social processes count and how they should be studied.

Speaking at a symposium on the future of radical history, Perry Anderson observed that 'major historical problems always involve two kinds of intellectual difficulty: firstly the sheer multiplicity [and] complexity of the variables to be ascertained that bear on them, and secondly the identification of a defensible causal hierarchy within their interconnecting web'. Most historians and social scientists tackle these ques-

---

by two papers presented at a 1984 Wingspread Conference on the city. In the first, Ulf Hannerz used *smorgasbord* as 'a metaphor for an almost overwhelming diversity, and for an opportunity to pick and choose'. Cities are also characterized by serendipity, 'the experience of unanticipated discovery'. Ulf Hannerz, 'Smorgasbord and Serendipity: On Urban Cultural Process', unpublished, 1984. In the second, Albert Hunter assimilated Geertzian interpretation into the ecological and cultural traditions of the Chicago School. Albert Hunter, 'The Physics and Psychics of Community: Symbolic Ecology and the Chicago School', unpublished, 1984.

tions in *ad hoc* ways. Marxism, Anderson argued, enjoys a theoretical advantage (and, one might add, a moral vulnerability) because of 'its possession of a comprehensive and articulated set of concepts and hypotheses about the principal lines of historical development as a whole'.[39] At the centre of Marxist theory, of course, is the claim that the central organizing element of modern history is the mode of production. Utilizing this conceptual tool, Marxism has aimed at no less than the systematic comprehension of the basic elements of modern history in terms of past, present, and future constellations of the mode of production, as it has searched to find ways to shape the world's future course.

But if Marxism has been assertive to the point of great hubris about the most significant trends in human history, it played a very minor role in its first century in defining and shaping the analysis of cities. Urban phenomena were not captured for Marxist theory nor was Marxist theory used to explain problematical urban phenomena. I believe it is worth trying to remedy this dual silence both because Marxist theory would be improved, as I will seek to show, by attention to the city and because our understanding of how cities work can be enhanced by a considered application of Marxist questions and perspectives.

Marxism is on relatively secure terrain when it approaches the city. Its larger theoretical advantages are underscored by the provocative correlation between the temporal elaboration of various modes of production and the timing of the development of Western cities captured in familiar classifications of stages of urban development. It is common, with good reason, for analysts who differ about much else to distinguish between

---

[39] Perry Anderson, in Margaret C. Jacob, Ira Katznelson *et al.*, 'Agendas for Radical History', *Radical History Review*, 36 (1986), 33–4. Later in his remarks, Anderson took note of the central paradox of contemporary Marxism: 'Never has radical or socialist work—including a major, increasing corpus of Marxist historiography—enjoyed such authority in a common understanding of the past as in the last twenty-five years. But never too have radicals or socialists been more uncertain about the direction of the present, and diffident—even despondent—about the shape of the future than they are very widely today' (37).

feudal, mercantile, and industrial capitalist cities. Much urban literature is entirely intuitive about such classification, but this intuition about periodization has taken urban studies a long way.

The best recent empirical scholarship about the development of cities likewise reinforces the sense that there are strong warrants for thinking about urban history in terms suggested by Marx's quest for an understanding of epochal change. Jan de Vries's important study of the urbanization of Europe from the sixteenth to the nineteenth centuries, to which I return in Chapter 5, shows both the appropriateness and the suggestiveness of the Marxist world-view, and, in turn, challenges Marxist treatments of the mode of production to become more fine-grained by developing a richly textured object of analysis.[40] He demonstrates that as early as the sixteenth century there was an international network of towns and cities. The next 300 years were not simply an interregnum between feudal cities and the vigorous industrial urbanization of the nineteenth century. Broadly speaking, this period divides into three. In the first 150 years, from 1500 to 1650, most urban growth took place in smaller cities, and the overall number of towns did not increase beyond those of high feudalism. In the next 100 years, two monumental changes occurred. The growth of cities shifted in location and in scale, away from the Mediterranean to northern and western Europe, and away from smaller towns, which tended to stagnate, to a smaller number of large ports and political capitals. This pattern of very uneven growth altered dramatically after 1750. Thereafter, at least until the middle of the nineteenth century, growth in the very large cities was brought to a halt, and vigorous urban development took place once again in smaller cities and towns.

This portrait and periodization has the considerable merit of debunking such conventional ideas about urbanization as those associated with theories of modernization that imply either linear urbanization or a single rupture between traditional and modern cities. It also supports the view that city

[40] Jan de Vries, *European Urbanization, 1500–1800*. London: Methuen, 1984.

development followed a pattern that transcended national and local boundaries and that moved to a tempo and logic associated with very large-scale processes, coinciding at least in time with shifts from feudal to mercantile to proto-industrial capitalist development.

Marxism is also on secure ground because of its manifest appropriateness as a tool for trying to answer questions about some of the most important phenomena that any good account of cities must try to explain: the vast urbanization of the world since the 1820s, differences between capitalist and non-capitalist cities, transformations in land use and social geography, and cycles of urban decay and renewal. Thus, an obvious topic for a Marxist approach to cities might have been a systematic attempt to connect the fixing and concentration of capital and the urban implosion of industry in the nineteenth century as a ready way to enhance analyses of one of Marxism's central themes, the accumulation of capital.

Thus, it is not without irony that over the full span of its development Marxism has been very quiet about space and cities. It has had very little to say about whether and when urban space is consequential or trivial, though its silence has implied the latter. The city was virtually ignored in the development of Marxist theory for more than a century after the publication in 1845 of Engels's consideration of cities in the early development of the English working class.[41] The main exception until the 1960s was the debate in the Second and Third International about the relationship of the city and the countryside in the transition to socialism. These vigorous theoretical and practical discussions, based on Marx and Engels's various considerations of the division of labour in relationship to the characteristics of specific modes of production, had an anti-urban tinge, and they produced guidelines for the practices of regimes based on an understanding of Marxist principles (think of the brutal upheavals in the Soviet countryside some six decades ago, the forced evacuations from cities and towns by the Pol Pot regime, or anti-urban planning decisions by most Communist governments in East Europe)

[41] Friedrich Engels, *The Condition of the Working Class in England*. Stanford, Calif.: Stanford University Press, 1968.

that would surely have horrified Marx and Engels. This theoretical and political trend aside, for more than half of the twentieth century Marxists did not take up the great majority of questions central to urban research, including those that concern the connections between the spatial form of cities and their ties to large-scale social processes. Rather, Marxism remained stuck in the restricted pathway of the concept of the division of labour.[42]

It is this limitation that accounts to a considerable degree for the urban omissions within Marxism, and that has provided the theoretical warrants for the anti-urban policies of some Marxist regimes. Soja and Hadjimchalis are two of only a very small number of Marxist urbanists who have tried to explain the non-spatial character of Marxism. They have argued that the tradition's long silence was an unfortunate aberration as a result of the neglect of the spatial discussions in the *Grundrisse* because of its late publication, the failure of Marx to complete *Capital* so that we were left instead with a simplified model of a spaceless capitalism in a closed national economy, and the economism of the Second International.[43] I do not think this mix of contingent accident and the reductionist turn of late nineteenth-century Marxists will do as an explanation, for it misses the point that the failure of Marxism even to discuss space and the city was quite logical, given the

[42] Further, the neglect of the city by Marx as a proper analytic object was also the result of what might be called a technical determinism in his treatment of both the factory and the city as *loci* of production. Cities did not deserve their own independent treatment because they were regarded by Marx much as liberal economists considered them, as the most efficient, profit-maximizing means of organizing capitalist production. We shall see this reduction of the economic place of the city to an aspect of the technical division of labour as a complement to the subsumption of the city under the social division of labour (the town–country split) as a recurring element in later Marxist treatments of capitalist urbanization. I am indebted to David Gordon for this point, which he has developed in his essay 'Capitalist Development and the History of American Cities', in William Tabb and Larry Sawyers, *Marxism and the Metropolis*. New York: Oxford University Press, 2nd edn. 1984.

[43] Edward W. Soja and Costis Hadjimchalis, 'Between Geographical Materialism and Spatial Fetishism: Some Observations on the Development of Marxist Spatial Analysis', *Antipode*, 11/3 (1979).

character of Marx's consideration of the town–country split in the *Grundrisse* and elsewhere in his work as an aspect of the division of labour.[44]

We should recognize, however, that Marx's joining of urban development to the historical trajectory of the division of labour marked an important advance over the tendency of late nineteenth-century geographical studies, as they developed into an organized discipline, to legitimize colonialism by a kind of ecological determinism. As one geographer has observed, in this dominant form of geography,

If a region was highly developed economically, this fact was assigned to a favourable geographical environment and to the characteristics of its inhabitants. If, on the other hand, a region presented character-istics of underdevelopment, this was attributed to a poor geographical environment and the insufficient abilities or effort of its natives. Associated with these arguments went the theory of the *typical economic landscape*. This allocated to each space a particular eco-nomic landscape (sugar cane in Cuba, coffee in Brazil, etc.), attempt-ing to mystify by geographical determinism the spatial patterns imposed by colonial rule.[45]

Just as they corrected the asceptic and neutral character of the concept of the division of labour in classical political economy, so too with regard to the international division of labour Marx and Engels's grounding of space in social organization provided an important basis for a critique of social science as the servant of power.[46]

To be sure, although Marx and Engels did not manifestly make the city a theoretically central object of analysis, *within*

[44] I confess to a certain uneasiness about this line of explanation, for in explaining Marxism's silences I realize I have not accounted for what it was that various Marxist movements and intellectuals did focus on. Indeed, it is quite possible that the history of Marxism has been very little bound by the actual writings of Marx.

[45] Mario Rui Martins, 'The Theory of Social Space in the Work of Henri Lefebvre', in Ray Forrest, Jeff Henderson, and Peter Williams (eds.), *Urban Political Economy and Social Theory*. Aldershot: Gower Publishing, 1982, 163–4.

[46] Karl Marx, *Capital* 3 vols., New York: International Publishers, 1967, i. 72. Friedrich Engels, *The Housing Question*. Moscow: Pro-gress Publishers, 1979.

the problematic of the division of labour issues of urbanization and the city were quite important to their considerations of transformations in modes of production. 'The foundations of every division of labour that is well developed', Marx wrote in the chapter on 'Division of Labour and Manufacture' in Volume i of *Capital*, 'and brought about by the exchange of commodities, is the separation between town and country. It may be said, that the whole economic history of society is summed up in the movement of this antithesis.' He promptly added, 'We pass it over, however, for the present', never really to return.[47]

The centrality Marx here ascribed to the spatial division between town and country and the paucity of pages devoted to the subject is not quite the paradox it might seem. For both Marx and Engels, the opposition of town and country was epiphenomenal; urban or spatial forces have no independent standing within their treatment of the division of labour, because the split between the town and the countryside is the direct, unmediated result of the imperatives of the division of labour, understood at the level of the mode of production.

As such, the separation of different kinds of spaces and activities condensed a much larger story but was itself of no special interest. This 'larger story' encompassed both the internal division of labour of a given country into economic regions and a new international division of labour characteristic of modern capitalism. 'The further the separate spheres [nations], which act on one another, extend in the course of this development [of the division of labour], the more the original isolation of the separate nationalities is destroyed by the developed mode of production ... the more history becomes world history.'[48] Unlike Smith and Ricardo, from whom Marx borrowed the concept of the division of labour, he did not see its further elaboration as advantageous to all members of an industrializing capitalist society. On the contrary, both the internal and external divisions of labour were characterized by an inexorable uneven development, and by

[47] Marx, *Capital*, i. 352.

[48] Karl Marx, *The German Ideology*, in Robert Tucker (ed.), *The Marx–Engels Reader*. New York: Norton, 1972, 136.

growing class polarization. From this perspective, an anti-urban bias, such as that exhibited in Engels's *The Housing Question* (where he proposes that the crisis in housing provision cannot be addressed effectively by meliorist reforms, but only by a change in the mode of production that would permit the destruction of the large capitalist cities, and the more even distribution of the population over the whole territory of a country) and in the practice of deurbanization, zero urban growth strategies, and what Murray and Szelenyi call under-urbanization (whereby the rate of growth in industrial employment exceeds that of urbanization) pursued by various governing Communist parties, have been consistent with the theoretical emphasis by Marx and Engels on the division of labour.[49]

If Marx passed over the discussion of the town in *Capital*, it is worth recalling, none the less, that this was not a new theme for him. With Engels, he wrote in the *German Ideology* that 'The antagonism between town and country begins with the transition from barbarism to civilisation and runs through the whole history of civilisation to the present day'. The city, in that text, was presented as the foundation of class divisions rooted in the division of labour. In each mode of production, there has been a different and distinctive relationship of the city to society. Under capitalism, they wrote in the *Communist Manifesto*, 'the bourgeoisie has subjected the country to the rule of the towns'. In another, but equally underdeveloped passage in the *Grundrisse*, Marx argued:

The history of classical antiquity is the history of cities, but of cities founded on landed property and on agriculture; Asiatic history is a kind of indifferent unity of town and countryside (the really large cities must be regarded here merely as royal camps, as works of artifice ... erected over the economic construction proper); the Middle Ages (Germanic period) begins with the land as the seat of history, whose further development then moves forward in contradiction between town and countryside; the modern [age] is the urbanization of the countryside, not ruralization of the city as in antiquity.[50]

---

[49] Engels, *The Housing Question*; Murray and Szelenyi, 'The City in the Transition to Socialism', 93–100.

[50] Marx, *German Ideology*, 140; Karl Marx and Friedrich Engels,

Although there is a rich and provocative theoretical–historical construct in this passage, it is not one that Marx dwelt on very long, for in this text he quickly moves away from the medieval city, which he describes as 'a kind of independent organism', to a discussion of the new division of labour and labour markets characteristic of capitalism as such, which is entirely lacking in any specific reference to the city. As a result of this move, Marxism had to pay a considerable price with regard to areas central to its own concerns, for just the reasons Engels implicitly understood in his early writing on England when he made the emergence of new kinds of industrial cities the first focus of his treatment of working-class formation because that was where the new working classes could be found, and that was where their dispositions as members of a common class were forged.

Its urban omissions have hurt Marxism in other areas as well. Much of Marx's economics has implicit spatial elements:

in the determination of production prices through the uneven values of raw materials, labour and fixed capital over space; in the fixing of market prices, through the role of transport; in the determination of an average rate of profits through the spatial organization of the market. It is even possible to claim, based on the distinction between value and value-form, that the theory of labour-value requires for its full understanding the introduction of spatial considerations.[51]

Manifesto of the Communist Party, in Tucker, *Marx–Engels Reader*, 336; Karl Marx, *Grundrisse*. London: Penguin Books, 1973, 479. In spite of these resources in the Marxist tradition, and, as David Harvey observes, 'in spite of its evident theoretical, political and historical importance (under capitalism, for example, increasing proportions of the world's population have poured into urban centres and occupations and been exposed thereby to a distinctively urban politics and culture) the study of urbanization has not been in the forefront of Marxist concern. The neglect is all the more surprising since the urban basis of many revolutionary movements (from 1848 through the Paris Commune to the ghetto uprisings of the 1960's in the United States and the urban social movements which contributed so strongly to May '68 in Paris) is undeniable.' David Harvey, 'Urbanization', in Tom Bottomore, *et al.* (eds.), *A Dictionary of Marxist Thought*. Cambridge, Mass.: Harvard University Press, 1983, 503.

[51] Martins, 'The Theory of Social Space', 162–3.

By not taking up these matters within the framework of the spatial organization of cities within capitalism, Marx (and Marxism) missed the chance to make a specific link between the central economic features of the mode of production as he understood them and the texture of the organization of urban space.

Saunders, by contrast, argues, as part of his larger claim that concern with large social processes should be divorced from problems of urban space, that once capitalism was established urban matters ceased to be a concern for Marx and Engels because the mode of production permeated society and its relationships irrespective of the boundary of city and countryside. I think this a rather lame defence of the long silence about cities in the Marxist tradition, first because it celebrates a failure to specify the distinctively urban features of capitalism, and, second, because, as Saunders concedes, Marx and Engels made the *urban* working class the centrepiece of their hopes for social transformation. In all, the missed opportunity for urban analysis has left Marxist social theory in a weaker condition than was intrinsic to it. Rather than a despatialized Marxism, I will argue the virtues, if also the limits, of a respatialized Marxism.

One of the main aims of this book, in fact, is to create more of a balance between Marxism and the city, by counselling a less totalizing Marxism, and by exploring the possibilities, as well as the blunders, of Marxist contributions to an understanding of city space. It also seeks to recapture for Marxism some of the themes and analyses of urban space, understood both as objective construct and as relational space, pioneered by Engels in *The Condition of the Working Class in England*, and dwelt on in the *Communist Manifesto*'s congested discussion of the significance of the concentration of productive capital and the working class in large, explosively growing, nineteenth-century cities.[52] In this way, I argue, Marxism's

[52] Both Marx and Engels saw the city as a place of concentration and intensification of capitalist contradictions, and, as they wrote in the *Manifesto*, by the rescue of workers from rural life workers in cities now possessed the material conditions for collective action as a class.

three main analytical projects—the consideration of epochal change, the analysis of the process of accumulation within capitalist economies, and the development of a social theory capable of dealing with the full complexity of specific capitalist societies—can be advanced.[53]

Unlike the situation that prevailed only a quarter of a century ago, there is now a large body of work about the city within the Marxist tradition. The reinvigoration of an urban conversation within Marxism owed most in the first instance to the publication in the late 1960s and early 1970s of a series of important works by Henri Lefebvre, including *Le Droit à la ville*, *La Révolution urbaine*, and *La Pensée marxiste et la ville*,[54] and the publication in the early 1970s of landmark volumes by Manuel Castells and David Harvey, written in the context of the challenges posed both to authorities and to activists and scholars by the period's robust urban social movements.[55] Castells's *La Question urbaine* (1972) ushered in the development of an urban 'school' of structuralist Marx-

[53] In commenting on an earlier draft of this manuscript, David Gordon proposed to me that Marx had another distinctive project, that of method. I tend to think, rather, that the methodological goals of Marx were so deeply imbricated with the three substantive ones I enumerate that it is a mistake to separate them out. Of course, this is an arguable matter.

[54] Henri Lefebvre, *Le Droit à la ville*. Paris: Anthropos, 1968; *La Révolution urbaine*. Paris: Gallimard, 1971; *La Pensée marxiste et la ville*. Paris: Casterman, 1972.

[55] I do not wish to suggest that texts simply begat texts. I would stress that the urban character of so many of the movements of the 1960s, and their focus on such issues as race in the United States and local control of state services virtually everywhere in the West, concentrated the minds of left-oriented scholars, including Marxists. Some, like Castells and Touraine in France, found support in a nexus of funding that underpinned research contract-supported activism. Elsewhere, networks of urbanists sprang up like the one under the auspices of the Council for European Studies between 1974 and 1976 that linked together such figures as Robert Alford, Frances Fox Piven, Claus Offe, Manuel Castells (then at Berkeley), Roger Friedland, and David Gordon, among others. At the same time, I stress the relationship between various key books in the development of urban-centred Marxist work because a genuine intellectual conversation developed that did not require personal propinquity or a direct engagement with the movements on the ground.

ism, associated with Louis Althusser, which rediscovered the city as an object of attention for Marxism. There, Castells critically assimilated the insight of Lefebvre about the centrality of space and cities to the development of modern capitalism, but theoretically opposed Lefebvre's grounding of his studies in the theme of alienation taken from the early 'humanist' Marx. Likewise, Lefebvre's scholarship was a major source of inspiration for David Harvey's *Social Justice and the City* (1973). Harvey, already a geographer of significant reputation, organized this volume of essays along the fault-line of his rupture with liberal geography. The volume's 'socialist formulations' incorporated city space into analyses of patterns of capitalist accumulation, and put the relationship of analytical Marxism to the city at the centre of its concerns.[56]

One of the tasks of *Marxism and the City* is to evaluate the 'new urban sociology' for which the work of Lefebvre, Castells, and Harvey provided the point of departure, and in which Castells and Harvey proved the most durable figures throughout the 1970s and 1980s.[57] In particular, I want to make sense of what has happened to Marxism and to urban analysis when the two have been brought into relationship with each other. In an appreciation of the results of this interconnection, David Harvey has summarized the key themes and achievements this way:

Spurred on by events, Marxists turned to a direct analysis of urban issues in the 1960s. They sought to understand the economic and political meaning of urban, community-based social movements and their relation to work-based movements—the traditional focus of attention. The relations between production and social reproduction came under intense scrutiny as the city was variously studied as the locus of production, of realization (effective demand through consumption, sometimes conspicuous), of the reproduction of labour power (in which the family and community institutions, supported by physical and social infrastructures—housing, healthcare, educa-

[56] Manuel Castells, *La Question urbaine*. Paris: Maspero, 1972; published in English as *The Urban Question*. Cambridge, Mass.: MIT Press, 1977; Harvey, *Social Justice*.

[57] A useful overview, stressing the importance of the contributions of Castells and Harvey, is Sharon Zukin, 'A Decade of the New Urban Sociology', *Theory and Society*, 9 (1980).

tion, cultural life—played a key role, backed by the local state). The city was also studied as a built environment to facilitate production, exchange and consumption, as a form of social organization of space (for production and reproduction), and as a specific manifestation of the division of labour and function under capitalism (finance capital versus production, etc.) The overall conception which emerged was urbanization as the contradictory unity of all these aspects of capitalism.[58]

In assessing this body of work Harvey pronounced it very good. In spite of my criticisms in subsequent chapters, I agree with this evaluation. It was a striking reversal: had it not been for the recent contributions of Marxist urbanists, the field of urban studies would have had little definition or theoretical thrust.

As Marxist analysts began to grapple with the city in the terms suggested by *La Question urbaine* and *Social Justice and the City*, they found that the city became a graveyard of empirical generalizations for them just as it had for their differentiation model predecessors.[59] Further, much of the new urban research came to challenge the range of vision in the pioneer volumes of Castells and Harvey, and, in this way, stimulated others to question some of the basic tenets of Marxist theory.

The early 1980s work of Castells and Harvey was symptomatic of this varied and complicated reaction to the development of a Marxist urban research programme, to its lacunae, and to the theoretical and empirical problems it exposed. Read together, these books challenge us to consider the fruits of the engagement of Marxism with the city, and the different paths this rethinking may stimulate us to tread.

In his second landmark book, *The City and the Grassroots*,

---

[58] Harvey, 'Urbanization', 503–4.
[59] See e.g. the awkward fit of the case studies with the theoretical discussions in Castells, *La Question urbaine*, and his retrospective discussion concerning his empirical work and Marxist theory in *The City and the Grassroots: A Cross-Cultural Theory of Urban Social Movements*. Berkeley, Calif.: University of California Press, 1983. 'Our intellectual matrix, the Marxist tradition,' he wrote there, 'was of little help from the moment we entered the uncertain ground of urban social movements', (296).

published in 1983, Castells shifted the centre of his attention to problems of human agency in the history and struggles of urban social movements. *The City and the Grassroots* is remarkably different in organization, objects of analysis, narrative style, and theoretical ambition from *La Question urbaine*. The latter proceeds by way of a critique of urban sociology to develop a conceptual mapping of urban structure aimed at the creation of a grand Marxist theory of the city. The empirical materials in the book are used to illustrate the various theoretical claims. These specify the domain of urban studies as that of 'collective consumption', and present a formal structural theory of this domain. By contrast, *The City and the Grassroots* comes to a theoretical synthesis only after the presentation of very rich, textured case studies of urban movements of the past—including the Paris Commune and the Glasgow rent strike of 1915—and contemporary studies of Paris, San Francisco, Lima, Santiago, and Madrid. The emphasis is on context, contingency, culture, variability, and social meaning; themes almost wholly absent in the earlier work. Class struggle is no longer the only axis of social conflict and social change. Further, the theoretical conclusion is stated modestly, even tentatively. In this book, 'the theory is built as a carpenter builds, adjusting the measurements as he goes along', while in the earlier work theory is constructed 'as an architect builds, drawing first, building later'.[60]

If Castells stretched the bounds of his analysis so that its Marxism may no longer occupy the place of theoretical privilege, David Harvey continued to assert its centrality: 'I turned to the Marxian categories in the early 1970s, and reaffirm my faith in them here', he wrote in 1985, 'as the only ones suited to an active construction of rigorous, comprehensive, and scientific understandings of something as complex and rich as the historical geography of the urban process under capitalism.' Much of his effort in recent years has been devoted to 'the integration of the production of space and spatial configurations as an active element within the core of Marxian

---

[60] Arthur L. Stinchcombe, *Theoretical Methods in Social History*. New York: Academic Press, 1978, 122.

theorizing'.[61] Class struggle and capital accumulation remained at the very centre of Harvey's work.

And yet, like Castells, Harvey began to address new themes, well beyond his focus of the past decade on space and production, themes less directly grounded in canonical Marxist texts or on the hard rock of political economy. The second volume of his *Studies in the History and Theory of Capitalist Urbanization* is devoted to the ways the urban landscape produces and shapes consciousness and experience, and it proceeds at its core by way of a historical case study of these themes in the Paris of the second half of the nineteenth century. This new work is written in a different tone of voice, one more speculative, more contingent, at times even playful.[62]

The differences between the early and later work of both Castells and Harvey, as well as the differences between their bodies of work, may be variously apprehended: as defining a field of tension between a Marxism in which nothing is signified unless it is real (hence actors are deduced from structures) and a Marxism in which nothing is real unless it is signified (hence the focus on the production of meaning); or as defining the difference between a closed, hermetically sealed Marxism and a more open one; or, more radically, as the difference between a Marxist and a post- (even non-) Marxist analysis. Shall we fill Marxism's empty theoretical rooms, or must we build an altogether different house?

I wish to explore these issues with respect to the materiality and meaning of cities, urbanism, and space. I try to show how the engagement of Marxism with the spatial dimension of cities, and particular ways in which geographical space can be made interior to Marxist theory, significantly enhance the analytical capacities of Marxism, help solve some of its most pressing and glaring problems, and, at the same time, reveal very clearly some of the limits of Marxist theory. I set out on this journey in Chapter 3 with the help of Engels, Lefebvre,

[61] David Harvey, *The Urbanization of Capital: Studies in the History and Theory of Capitalist Urbanization*. Baltimore: Johns Hopkins University Press, 1985, pp. x, xi.

[62] David Harvey, *Consciousness and the Urban Experience: Studies in the History and Theory of Capitalist Urbanization*. Baltimore: Johns Hopkins University Press, 1985.

Harvey, and Castells. Before doing so, I propose to take a necessary, if winding, detour to examine some key aspects of Marxist social theory that will prove important when we arrive at the gates of the city.

2 Themes in Marxist Social Theory

INJURED and feeling betrayed by Leszek Kolakowski's having arrived at a 'point of negation' in his passage from a Marxist humanism to an anti-Marxism, Edward Thompson composed an open letter to Kolakowski in the early 1970s containing a spirited defence of Marxism as 'a plurality of conflicting voices which, nevertheless, argue within a common tradition'. The notion of a tradition, Thompson proposed, has the advantage of allowing for diversity by bringing all parts of the Marxist inheritance under scrutiny without dissolving Marxism into part of the common inheritance of all contemporary social theory and social science.[1]

In his polemic, Thompson usefully contrasted the idea of a tradition, drawn from literary criticism, with other ways the ideas offered by Marxism might be classified, especially the temptation of a self-contained, self-sufficient Marxism claim-

---

[1] Thompson chastised Kolakowski for stepping outside the bounds of the Marxist tradition, characterized by 'the very stature, universality, originality, and power of Marx's work; the disciplines he commanded and reshaped; his characteristic methods and preoccupations; the many voices added to the tradition since his death; and the extent of contemporary Marxist discourse. The tradition exists. It has defined itself in Marx's work and in the evolution (contradictory as that is) of his ideas. The point is (if one affirms this tradition as one's own) less to define the tradition than to define where one stands within it.' Here, for the moment, I am concerned more to define the elements, challenges, and problems of the tradition than to define where I stand with regard to it. E. P. Thompson, 'An Open Letter to Leszek Kolakowski', in Ralph Miliband and John Saville (eds.), *The Socialist Register 1974*. London: Merlin Press, 1974, 24–5. This essay has been reprinted in what may now be the more accessible source: E. P. Thompson, *The Poverty of Theory and Other Essays*. London: Merlin Press, 1978, 92–192. Embedded in this letter are some of Thompson's best discussions of such conceptual issues as the meaning of 'contradiction', 'law', 'logic of system', and 'reform' within Marxism.

ing to be the exclusive body of theory appropriate to the study of the modern world.[2] At the same time, Thompson cautions us to beware the reduction of Marxism to a contentless method or the too quick assimilation of Marxism into the common inheritance of Western thought, a caution well taken by adherents and detractors alike. At its most watered down, Marxism is a loose method of inquiry indisputably part of the shared heritage of all modern social theory and social science;

---

[2] I will argue later that aspects of the Marxist tradition are appealing precisely because they do not close in on themselves, but are open to other theoretical traditions. If such marriages are to take place (as between Weberian and Marxist treatments of politics, or between Marxism and choice theory) what counts, of course, is not whether such matches are desirable in principle, but the terms on which they are consummated. In any event, we should beware of Marxism at its worst: as a closed doctrine, based on approved texts, guarded by an ideological priesthood, and all too susceptible to the common plaints that Marxism tends to be monocausal, reductionist, mechanical, ahistorical, non-empirical, incapable of causal inference. To the extent that these familiar accusations hold Marxism is compromised at its core. I do not think they hold, or at least they need not.

There are secondary criticisms of Marx and Marxism which tend to confuse what is distinctive to this tradition from dilemmas, many irreconcilable, common to other theoretical traditions. These include: voluntarism versus structural constraints, class as against other bases of human motivation, tensions of theoretical and historical inquiry, and attempts to create general theories of human societies as opposed to theories that aim to explicate specific social formations.

At different times, and with different intensities, Marx was on different sides of all these issues. Perhaps more important, his work contains different resolutions of their relationships. In any event, as a result, there is certainly no single Marx, nor, to pick a more fashionable number, even two. With good textual warrants it is entirely possible to construct one's own preferred Marx (I will indulge myself a bit later on) and Marxism. Nevertheless, it should be said emphatically that there is no 'true' Marx, nor is there a single 'true' Marxism. And even if there were, should we care, except as a matter of intellectual accuracy? These issues are discussed by Daniel Bell in a justly stinging review of Michael Harrington's *The Twilight of Capitalism*. Daniel Bell, 'Review Essay: The Once and Future Marx', *American Journal of Sociology*, 83 (July 1977), 189. An earlier piece that heralds the critique here is Bell, 'The "Rediscovery" of Alienation: Some Notes Along the Quest for the Historical Marx', *Journal of Philosophy*, 56 (Nov. 1959).

'we pay our money in a footnote and all debts are met.' If this were all there were to Marxism, Thompson asks, why then 'should we concern ourselves further with the ardour and skill of the workman in his ill-lit workshop who first turned this product in his hands'?[3]

Why, indeed? Of what elements does a Marxist *tradition* consist?

I

Marx had a single orienting and overarching goal, from which he never wavered. This objective was no less than that of comprehending the entire sweep of Western history (with attention to its genesis and to comparisons with non-Western experiences), with the aim of affecting its course to produce a desirable post-capitalist world.[4]

---

[3] Thompson, 'An Open Letter', 22. In a useful review essay on 'Marxism and Sociology', Michael Burawoy poses just the choice I think we must avoid, a choice he characterizes in the following terms: 'Is Marx to be regarded as a grandmaster who shaped the development of sociology but whose thought has been assimilated into the main body of social theory? . . . Or, alternatively, is Marx the founder of an independent tradition which cannot be absorbed into the main body of social theory along with Durkheim and Weber without distortion?' Michael Burawoy, 'Marxism and Sociology', *Contemporary Sociology*, 6 (Jan. 1977), 9. Asking us to choose whether we are 'for Marx' or 'for sociology', Burawoy, in my view, implicitly asks us to select either a closed Marxism, with its own quite separate research programme that must live within Marxism's inherent limitations, of which I have more to say below, or a Marxism that becomes so permeable that it loses all its philosophical, theoretical, and methodological specificity. I suggest instead a strategy of engagement, in which non-Marxist work is assimilated into a Marxist frame, and Marxist scholarship into social science, in pursuit of an understanding of the large-scale social processes characteristic of modernity.

[4] Nothing of this sweep and character could have been attempted without a philosophy of history, and Marx had one centred on the identification and overcoming of alienation. Human history is the history of the 'subjugation of man by his own works, which have assumed the guise of independent things'. The transcendence of alienation requires the destruction of the order that generates it.

Marx sought to carry out this grand reconstruction of Western history through the elaboration of three distinctive, interrelated projects.[5] He sought, *first*, to construct a theory of history to account for change between epochs on the largest possible scale. Distinguishing between pre-class societies, pre-capitalist class societies, capitalist societies, and post-class, socialist and communist, societies, Marx explained this broad sweep of human history by focusing on struggles between social classes within the twin frame of the development of the technical characteristics of production (what he called the forces of production), and the nature of the relationships joining people in the social features of the production process (the relations of production), especially the unfolding separation of the direct producers from the means of their own labour, and from the means of their own reproduction. The central unit of analysis in this project is the mode of produc-

---

Unlike earlier modes of production, capitalism provides the instrument, in the proletariat, capable of achieving this most fundamental transformation to non-alienated human relationships.

If the development and destiny of capitalism constitutes the core of Marx's enterprise, his work necessarily entails both the ineseparability of theory and history, and a fluid movement between abstract structural and logical analysis and specific conjunctural studies. Leszek Kolakowski, *Main Currents of Marxism*, vol. i: *The Founders*. Oxford: Oxford University Press, 1978, 178. This paragraph draws liberally from his treatment of *The German Ideology* in chs. 8 and 9. See also Bertell Ollman, *Alienation: Marx's Conception of Man in Capitalist Society*. Cambridge: Cambridge University Press, 1971; and Shlomo Avineri, *The Political and Social Thought of Karl Marx*. Cambridge: Cambridge University Press, 1971.

[5] Useful aids to reading Marx include Allen Oakley, *The Making of Marx's Critical Theory: A Bibliographical Analysis*. London: Routledge and Kegan Paul, 1983; Tom Bottomore *et al.* (eds.), *A Dictionary of Marxist Thought*. Cambridge, Mass.: Harvard University Press, 1983; and Eric J. Hobsbawm (ed.), *The History of Marxism: Marxism in Marx's Day*. Bloomington, Ind.: University of Indiana Press, 1982. A bracing critique from the perspective of a radical version of methodological individualism is Jon Elster, *Making Sense of Marx*. Cambridge: Cambridge University Press, 1985. On the relationship between theory and history for Marx and Engels, see Philip Abrams, *Historical Sociology*. Ithaca, NY: Cornell University Press, 1982, ch. 3.

tion; the key issue the rules inherent in the basic dynamics of a given mode of production that govern the epochal shift from one mode of production to another.

The core idea of the mode of production is that of a long-term configuration of social organization, technology, property relations, class structure, and a distinctive patterning of the relationship between economics, politics, and society. The originality of this concept, Pierre Vilar notes, lies

in the fact that this was the first theoretical object which expressed *a social whole*, where earlier attempts at theory in the human sciences had been confined to the economy and had perceived social relations either as immutable (like the physiocrats' conception of landed property), or else as ideals to be attained (like the juridical liberty and equality of liberal thought). The second originality of the mode of production as a theoretical object is that it is a structure *of functioning development*, and as such is neither formal nor static. Its third originality is that such a structure itself implies the (economic) *principle* of the (social) *contradiction* which bears with it the necessity of its destruction as a structure, or its own *destructuration*.[6]

Each mode of production contains its own rules of transformation, inherent tendencies to crisis and change which are structural, and which manifest themselves in conflict between the social classes.[7] This first of Marx's projects is analytical, rather than chronological (except in the most obvious, sequential sense).[8]

[6] Pierre Vilar, 'Marxist History, a History in the Making: Towards a Dialogue with Althusser', *New Left Review*, 80 (July–Aug. 1983), 76.

[7] There is an important difference between the transformation rules for feudalism and for capitalism. While capitalism is sufficient to itself in the generation of its ultimate crisis, feudalism was not. It required an external impetus, such as merchant capitalism, to create the seeds of an alternative order.

[8] The best, and most rigorous, if highly contested, analytical treatment of this project is G. A. Cohen, *Karl Marx's Theory of History: A Defence*. Princeton, NJ: Princeton University Press, 1978. Cohen reads Marx as a technological determinist, and accords explanatory primacy to the forces of production. Andrew Levine and Erik Olin Wright have developed a pointed, if sympathetic, critique of Cohen's view of Marx. They argue that a Marxist analysis and politics require that a historical materialism based on this notion of primacy

Marx sought, *second*, to build a model of the economy within the capitalist epoch. Here, he tried to identify the dynamics of growth of the economy, its functioning on behalf of the accumulation of capital, its tendencies to crisis, and the mechanisms for overcoming them. That is, he sought to theorize the specifically economic components of the capitalist mode of production, including the growing divisions between capital and the proletariat, the concentration of property, the development of a reserve army of labour, the tendency of the rate of profit to fall, and the character of ever-deepening cyclical crises. In this project of the capitalist economy, Marx situated himself in opposition to the political economists, mainly Smith and Ricardo, because they saw capitalism as natural and eternal, and dealt with markets, which Marx saw as surface phenomena, rather than more basic, if less visible, economic forces; he also placed himself in opposition to the utopian socialists, including Proudhon and Fourier, because they failed to inquire into how capitalism actually works.[9]

---

must be supplemented by a consideration of class capacities, and, in particular, of hindrances to the development of working-class capacity posed by the state, by ideology, and by the social relations of production. Andrew Levine and Erik Olin Wright 'Rationality and Class Struggle', *New Left Review*, 123 (Sept.–Oct. 1980). In a similar vein, Ellen Meiksins Wood criticizes Cohen's technological determinism for reproducing the error of the classical political economists. Cohen, she writes, 'generalizes the particular historical experience of capitalism by abstracting the laws of capitalist production from their specific social determinations'. Ellen Meiksins Wood, 'Marxism and the Course of History', *New Left Review*, 147 (Sept.–Oct. 1984), 105. See also Wood, 'The Separation of the Economic and the Political in Capitalism', *New Left Review*, 127 (May–June 1981), 73.

[9] Marx never rejected the insights of the political economists. Rather, he incorporated their work within a larger frame; he thought their work not so much wrong as insufficient. By contrast, Marx was far more contemptuous of the utopian socialists, who, as he said of Proudhon, hear the bells ringing but do not know where.

There is, of course, an immense literature on Marx's economic analysis in *Capital*—on the character of his reasoning and concepts, including the much-contested labour theory of value and associated 'laws', such as the tendency of the rate of profit to fall. The best treatment I know of these issues is Daniel Little, *The Scientific Marx*. Minneapolis: University of Minnesota Press, 1986. I return to Little's

This is a distinctive project (whose key text is the three volumes of *Capital*) that cannot simply be subsumed into the first, the treatment of the sweep of history by the principles of a historical materialism. This first project, David Little observes, directed Marx 'to provide detailed studies of the economic structures of the various modes of production; but it does not provide guidance for conducting such an investigation, nor does it contain the concepts and theoretical tools necessary to formulate clear explanatory hypotheses in this area . . . *Capital* goes substantially beyond Marx's theory of historical materialism, both methodologically and substantively.' This elaboration of the capitalist economy is *not* just a work, however brilliant, of technical economics. Rather, this

---

work later when I discuss the relationship of structure and agency in Marx, and, in particular, alternative conceptualizations of the base in Marxist social theory. Useful complementary reading includes Ian Gough, 'Marx's Theory of Productive and Unproductive Labour', *New Left Review*, 76 (Nov.–Dec. 1972), an article that provides a fine summary of alternative possible readings; Erik Olin Wright, 'Alternative Perspectives in Marxist Theory of Accumulation and Crisis', *The Insurgent Sociologist*, 6 (Fall 1975), which likewise deconstructs the logical structure of a variety of Marxist views on patterns of capital accumulation and crisis; Wright, 'The Value Controversy and Social Research', *New Left Review*, 116 (July–Aug. 1979), an essay that takes up value theory not at the usual level of abstract debate but at the empirical level of research on the determination of profit; Amartya Sen, 'On the Labour Theory of Value: Some Methodological Issues', *Cambridge Journal of Economics*, 2 (June 1978), which distinguishes between three non-metaphysical interpretations of the theory (descriptive, predictive, and normative); Jon Elster, 'The Labor Theory of Value: A Reinterpretation of Marxist Economics', *Marxist Perspectives* (Fall 1978), which argues that value theory is sociological and normative, but not a contribution to economic theory; Geoff Hodgson, 'The Theory of the Falling Rate of Profit', *New Left Review*, 84 (Mar.–Apr. 1974), which provides a very helpful overview of alternative meanings of this 'law', and of their strengths and weaknesses; and the symposium, Bernard Elbaum *et al.*, 'The Labour Process, Market Structure and Marxist Theory', *Cambridge Journal of Economics*, 3 (Sept. 1979), in which the authors argue that even for the 19th century Marx underestimated four key elements of the labour process: new hierarchies at the workplace; inter-capitalist competition; divisions within the working class; and room for compromises between capital and labour.

second project is 'an integrated whole, not merely distinct pieces of economic analysis . . . the core of Marx's account has to do with the social institutions defining the capitalist mode of production, not the quantitative economic conclusions he reaches.'[10] This 'base' of the capitalist mode of production is an attempt to theorize the most important features of capitalism as an economic system, and to locate the role and place of other macrostructures, the most important being the state, in terms of their relationships with and roles within the capitalist mode of production. This project impresses a 'capital logic' on Western modernity. In carrying out the task of developing his own political economy, Marx remained within the spirit of classical political economy, which had embedded its economics in theories of human nature and in the analyses of complex social organizations, rather than in the spirit of modern economics, whose main hallmark is the attempt to simplify a complicated world by stripping away such considerations in order to treat economics as a set of calculations and exchanges as such.[11]

As in the first project, this treatment of capitalist economic development is not a theory of specific societies in their historical complexity, nor does it provide causal accounts of specific historical moments. Rather, it is a theory of economic structure that wilfully, for analytical reasons, makes claims for a logic of tendency inherent in the capitalist economy artificially removed, as it were, from actual time and place. History appears in the guise of anecdote and example. England was used by Marx in *Capital* as an expositional locale because, more than any other place, it exemplified the playing out of the structural character of capitalism; but nowhere did he provide a richly textured and contextualized history of capital-

[10]   Little, *The Scientific Marx*, 5–7.
[11]   The range of themes considered in *Capital* significantly transcends those that might be labelled narrowly economic. In addition to the abstract, logical model of accumulation and crisis, Marx presents quantitative and ethnographic descriptions of working-class life, at the workplace and away from work, and sociological and historical accounts of how the property relations of capitalism developed from the period of primitive accumulation forward, and how modern capitalist property relations are reproduced.

ist England, for his purpose was that of building a model, with illustrations.[12]

In this project, actors appear in ascribed roles. Capitalists, just as much as workers, are subjected to imperative laws. A capitalist is 'capital personified', who, though 'endowed with a consciousness and a will', must act independently of his 'control and conscious individual action'.[13] The model Marx developed in *Capital* is not a historical portrait in the ordinary sense. There is no analysis of class formation, since class only appears on the basis of criteria that are structural givens in this mode of production: capitalism's property relations define two sets of empty places, into one of which each member of the active labour force must fall. In offering various logics of tendency fundamental to the making of actual histories within capitalism, Marx presented history simultaneously at a very high level of generalization and at the level of rational actors pursuing strategies within structural limits that hold them in bondage.

The linkage between the two levels is provided by what Little calls a 'logic of institutions'. He writes, persuasively, that

Marx's construction in *Capital* is not a general system based on a few hypotheses; it does not unify all capitalist phenomena within a deductive system; it does not identify a set of 'laws of motion' that are genuinely analogous to laws of nature; and it makes use of

---

[12] Some commentators like to argue that *Capital* represents history in a deep sense of the term. I think this is a defence not necessary to mount. It is surely quite enough to construct a logical model of the main tendencies of economic development and crisis under capitalism. The degree to which Marx was successful is quite another matter, of course.

Colletti has observed that there is a double character to Marx's economic categories. They are at once regulative principles maintaining the equilibrium of the system, and also principles of contradiction. Lucio Colletti, 'The Theory of the Crash', *Telos*, 13 (Fall 1972).

[13] Karl Marx, *Capital*, i. New York: International Publishers, 1967, 152, 93. According to the fuller, more general formulation, 'In the form of society now under consideration, the behaviour of men in the social process of production is purely atomic. Hence their relations to each other in production assumes a material character independent of their control and conscious individual action.' Ibid., 92–3.

empirical evidence in a way quite different from that appropriate to the hypothetico-deductive model of justification.

Instead, he views Marx's account as 'a family of related explanatory arguments, bits of analysis, historical comments, and descriptive efforts loosely organized as a common perspective'; and as 'a selective description of certain fundamental features of the capitalist economy and an examination of the "logic of institutions" imposed by those features on the economy as a whole'.[14]

This conception of the logic of institutions is central to Little's reading. Within capitalism, the social relations of production as well as specific technical features of the economy constitute a system of motivations for capitalists as rational actors. Inside this motivational system, the representative capitalist—Marx's personification of capital—arrives at a particular strategy concerning capital accumulation, including matters of investment and labour relations. When capitalists act as representative capitalists, logically their behaviour *in aggregate* produces lawlike consequences, such as the tendency for the rate of profit to fall. In short,

a given feature of capitalism occurs because capitalists are rational and are subject to a particular set of incentives, prohibitions, and opportunities. When they collectively pursue the optimal individual strategies corresponding to these incentives, prohibitions, and opportunities, the explanans emerges as the expression or consequence of the resulting collective behavior.

The capitalist economy also establishes such motivational and conditioning circumstances for choice for workers. Further, the organization of choice for capitalists and workers is relational, involving a mix of domination and reciprocity, as each role is constituted by the other. Within this networked set of relationships embedded within the large-scale process of capitalism as an economic system the main social classes engage in a patterned process of strategic negotiation and struggle.[15]

[14] Little, *The Scientific Marx*, 12, 18.

[15] Ibid., 147; Karl Marx, *Grundrisse: Introduction to the Critique of Political Economy*. London: Penguin Books, 1973, 265. This perspective assumes a view of power that is connected to the intrinsic character of agents embedded within specific social structures and

Thus, within *Capital*, there is a working model of the relationship of structure and agency. The organizational structure of the capitalist economy 'is created by rational individuals pursuing independent ends under structured conditions of choice'. Individual capitalists and workers, alone or in combinations, act within this tightly defined system. Explanation 'consists in showing the process through which these conditions stamp the observable features of the capitalist system'. But this is not a model of naked individualism, nor of society as an entity. Rather it is a model of networks, relationships, and social processes. 'Society', Marx wrote, 'does not consist of individuals, but expresses the sum of interrelations, the relations within which these individuals stand.' Individuals are not to be understood atomistically, but as embedded within the social relations of the capitalist mode of production. At the same time, the source of social change is human agency.[16]

If Marx's first project sought to account for the origins and ultimate demise of capitalism, this second project of the analysis of the capitalist economy put content into the predictions of a transition beyond capitalism by specifying the transformation rules embedded in the logic of capitalism as a

---

institutional contexts rather than a behavioural view of power as compliance against one's will or interest. For a discussion, see Jeffrey Isaac, *Power and Marxist Theory: A Realist View*. Ithaca, NY: Cornell University Press, 1987. For his discussion of structured reciprocity and negotiation, see pp. 87–95. There is an important discussion of how capitalism establishes different logics of collective action for capitalists and workers in Claus Offe and Helmut Wiesenthal, 'Two Logics of Collective Action: Theoretical Notes on Social Class and Organizational Form', in *Political Power and Social Theory*, 1 (1980).

[16] Little, *The Scientific Marx*, 147–53. A complementary discussion has been provided by James Farr. Marx, he argues, 'was a scientific realist who rejected the Humean empiricist analysis of causes and laws. In substituting a realist analysis he provided a framework for understanding his own explanatory laws—the economic laws of motion of modern society. Yet Marx did not propose any so-called "natural laws of historical development". Rather he articulated what are more properly termed principles of historical interpretation. In method as in politics Marx thereby offered a genuine alternative to the dominant views of the day.' James Farr, 'Marx's Laws', *Political Studies*, 34 (1986), 202.

mode of production. Capitalism will necessarily be a transient mode of production both because the inherent logic of capital accumulation will produce a deep and unmanageable crisis of profitability (the result of a rise in the organic composition of capital at a faster rate than the exploitation of the working class), and as the result of class struggle. Although the history of capitalism is the history of a stepwise development marked by crises of accumulation and the discovery of mechanisms to surmount them[17]—and in this sense it is a system that works—capitalism continues to be undermined by its own internal contradictions, which, at some point, it will be unable to surmount:[18]

Taken together, Marx's first two projects provided a point of entry into historical processes, a guide to what is essential, a means of discovering a 'logic of process' in history, by means of his general principles concerning the centrality of productive activity in human social organization, the proposition that the 'innermost secret' of the social structure is the specific form in which 'surplus labor is pumped out of the direct producers,' and the generalization that up to now history since primitive communism has been the history of class struggle. And he provided a monumentally detailed and fruitful

[17] The metaphor of the staircase of capitalist development can be found in Henri Pirenne, 'The Stages in the Social History of Capitalism', *American Historical Review*, 19 (Apr. 1914).

[18] It is often noted that the linkage between crises of accumulation and class struggle is not very well specified by Marx, thus raising the issue, from the vantage-point of Marxism, of whether the pace of history can be forced. Colletti proposes the following solution regarding the relationship of factors of structure and agency in the transition from capitalism to socialism:

The falling rate of profit and the *quantitative* relation it expresses are considered as the way the historical and therefore transitory character of capitalism appears. Yet that way, and the 'purely economic way' in which it is expressed, are considered correlative to the 'bourgeois point of view', i.e., the viewpoint which remains 'within' the limitations of capitalist understanding,' the very viewpoint of capitalist production itself. Unless we are completely wrong, the fallibility of capitalism should not be seen by socialists as a theory of the crash, that is, in 'purely economic' terms.

In other words, objective tendencies such as the falling rate of profit make sense only to the extent that they appear as conditions and real premises of the class struggle, i.e., of the clash at a political and subjective level. Alone they have no decisive value. (Colletti, 'The Theory of the Crash', 45.)

specific application of these general principles to the analysis of capitalism, its particular development, and 'laws of motion'.[19]

Whether this achievement in fact offers a complete and comprehensive theory of the macroscopic tendencies in human history is surely a contested matter, to which I return, but no serious consideration of historical development today can go around it.

By trying to specify what all capitalist societies have in common in spite of their many dissimilarities, Marx established a framework and a starting point for a *third*, more complicated, less realized project: the attempt to construct a social theory capable of inventing explanations about specific capitalist societies (not just capitalism in general), understood as wholes (not just as economies) within the capitalist epoch. This third project demands a balance and clear terms of engagement between the structural and logical analyses characteristic of the first two projects, on the one hand, and grounded historical analysis, sensitive to variation, human agency, and contingency, on the other. For unlike the economic analysis of *Capital*, which does not present a theory of capitalist society as a whole, the content of the project of social theory is just that, and its main analytical problems concern the relationship between the economic 'base' and the 'superstructure': the character and explanatory power of capitalism as a structure, the primacy accorded to its causal capacities as opposed to those embedded in other structures, and an account of the ways in which the properties of capitalism as a mode of production are actualized in history. Most of this book focuses principally on the third of Marx's projects, but in so doing it perforce must also deal with the first two.[20]

---

[19] Wood, 'Marxism and the Course of History', 100.

[20] Marx also had a more speculative, even less fully developed project: the attempt to portray the structure, logic, actors, rationality, and norms of socialist and communist societies. Because Marx had to project forward, he focused on imputed similarities rather than on variations, and he did so without displaying any of the capacity for criticism he exhibited so fiercely in his work on capitalism. Although this socialist future might produce an efflorescence and a plurality of cultural and political forms of expression, it might also produce a flattening of society and a halt to creative self-development. The

It is not an exaggeration to say that arguably the most intractable analytical problems for the Marxist tradition have been the difficulties it has had, and the various solutions it has explored, regarding the incorporation of the logical–structural accounts of the first two projects of Marx into the third, concerned as it is with history, variation, and agency. The presentation of the capitalist mode of production in *Capital* is not concerned with any specific country at a specific historical moment; hence, by its choice of subject-matter, it is silent on the base–superstructure issues of determination. Marx's various historical works do deal with these matters in a highly place- and time-specific way, but without any attempt at explicit theorization. Marx's various texts, in short, provide hints and examples, but no positive specification of the mechanisms linking the base and superstructure.[21] Although much

---

ambivalence induced by the massive uncertainty about the leap beyond capitalism is compounded by the silences in Marx regarding the actual passage (or possible passages) from actual capitalisms described in his third project to actual socialisms. This silence is especially pronounced with respect to key political questions about the state in the phase of the dictatorship of the proletariat and questions of rights. The idea that a post-capitalist world is synonymous with an end to history, conflicts, contradictions, and scarcity has contributed to many of the deformations of today's Soviet-style socialist societies, and to the legitimation of their practices. For a recent discussion, see Steven Lukes, *Marxism and Morality*. Oxford: Oxford University Press, 1985.

Writing on 'History and the Future', Eric Hobsbawm takes note of just how difficult it is to project from current trends: 'I believe Marx discerned some basic tendencies with profound insight,' he writes, 'but we do not know actually what they will bring ... I am bound to say, however, that historians, like social scientists, are fairly helpless when confronted with the future, not only because we all are, but because they have no clear idea of what exactly the *ensemble* or system they are investigating is, and—in spite of Marx's superb pioneering—exactly how its various elements interact. What exactly is "society" (singular or plural) which is our concern?' Eric Hobsbawm, 'Looking Forward: History and the Future', *New Left Review*, 125 (Jan.–Feb. 1981), 18, 15–16.

[21] According to Gareth Stedman Jones, Marx's 'historical works were all written after the events they describe; they certainly contain important indications of the way in which political struggle and to a lesser extent ideological struggle relate to the material base or current

theoretical energy has been expended since Marx on the
antinomy of structure and agency and on questions of determination within the Marxist tradition, there have nevertheless
been 'two different planes of Marxist discourse, which nor-
mally lie at a considerable distance from each other'.[22] And
yet, like any meaningful body of social theory, Marxism can
only be fecund to the extent that it distinctively works within,
and manages the field of tension between, the structural and
the historical, the abstract and the concrete, the determined
and the contingent. Steven Lukes proposes terms for engaging
the problems of structure and agency this way:

The broad picture I am seeking to sketch here is of agents as
consisting in a set of (expanding and contracting) abilities, faced with
(expanding and contracting) opportunities. Together these constitute
structured possibilities which specify the powers of agents, varying
between agents and over time for any given agent ... On the view I
have advanced, social life can only properly be understood as a
dialectic of power and structure, a web of possibilities for agents,
whose nature is both active and structured, to make choices and
pursue strategies within given limits, which in consequence expand
and contract over time.

This formulation rejects explanations that focus only on
observed behaviour, because they exclude unrealized possibilities from the field of objects of analysis, and it insists we

---

combination of the forces and relations of production. But these
indications are never theorized as such: they have to be read *through*
the specific analysis of the historical events described. What emerges
from them, of course, is that the economy is in the last instance
determinant, and yet that superstructures possess a particular form of
causal efficacy which cannot simply be reduced to the economic base.
But the precise structural mechanism connecting the two is always
left unclear by Marx.' He then adds: 'The absence, on the theoretical
plane, of any mechanism to connect the determination in the last
instance by the economy and the relative autonomy of superstructures, was reproduced on the political plane in an inability to produce
a systematic theory of revolutionary politics.' Gareth Stedman Jones,
'Engels and the End of Classical German Philosophy', *New Left
Review*, 79 (May–June 1973), 31, 35.
   [22] Perry Anderson, *Lineages of the Absolutist State*. London: New
Left Books, 1974, 7.

discard undialectical theories and methodologies: 'No social theory merits serious attention that fails to retain an ever-present sense of the dialectic of power and structure.'[23]

This suggestive orienting formulation is silent, however, about the constituents of structure and the identities and motivations of agents. *Marxism's central theoretical claim is that it possesses the ability to delineate the contents at both poles of the dialectic: in its specification of structure through the conceptual and historical tool of the mode of production, and through its identification of class formation and class struggle as the pivots of agency.* Marxism's primary challenges are those of justifying and elaborating these choices, and suggesting in theory and in practice how to move between these stakes. Ironically, both Marx and the Marxist tradition have succeeded best in these respects when they have been most implicit: in historical writings about particular conjunctures embedded within assumptions about structure, causation, and the lawful quality of human relations. Marx's, and Marxism's, attempts to theorize the dialectic of structure and agency have either been too blunt and mechanistic, as in the famous passage developing the metaphor of base and superstructure in the *Preface to the Critique of Political Economy*, or divided between two quite different, and unsatisfactory, theoretical impulses.

Alvin Gouldner made this division the pivotal feature of his influential summary and analysis of the Marxist tradition. He claims that, over time, Marxism and its various projects have divided into two clusters of people and ideas. In *The Two*

---

[23] Steven Lukes, *Essays in Social Theory*. New York: Columbia University Press, 1977, 29. I should say that I am uneasy with Lukes's antinomy of structure and power, hence the contraction of power to agency. His essay argues that the notion of power structure is an oxymoron. Yet if we think of power as a set of capacities which agents have by virtue of their place and role within large-scale social structures, processes, and networks, and the exercise of power in the sense of agency as a utilization of these capacities within a framework of strategic negotiation, then power cannot be limited to one or another side of the ledger of structure and agency. For an additional illuminating discussion of structure–agency issues, see Sherry B. Ortner, 'Theory in Anthropology', *Comparative Studies in Society and History*, 26 (Jan. 1984).

Marxisms,[24] he presents a scorecard, complete with line-ups for each team. Lukács, Korsch, and the critical theorists of the Frankfurt School stand across a divide from Althusser, Balibar, and the *New Left Review*. Each group is committed to alternative solutions to the tension in Marx (indeed, in all social theory) between determinism and voluntarism.

'Marxism did indeed say', Gouldner writes, 'that capitalism was governed by blind and necessary laws to which persons were inescapably subject; it is also true that Marxism *treats* persons as free agents who will not only do what they must, but who can respond to appeals and be won over *even against their own class interests*.'[25] 'Critical' Marxism and 'scientific' Marxism, Gouldner claims, segregate these tendencies. The voluntary critical Marxists reject the base–superstructure metaphor in favour of a less well-defined totality.[26] They tend to be economic utopians who eschew economic analysis for political prescription. Their model of change tends to be abrupt and catastrophic. By contrast, scientific Marxists are more economistic in their analyses, more likely to be political utopians willing to wait out the play of inexorable economic laws, less apocalyptic in their visions of transition to socialism.

This dichotomous portrait is not unfamiliar. In similar, but more engaged, terms, Thompson devotes some two hundred furious pages to an attack on Althusser's 'orrery of errors' to distinguish it from a historical, libertarian, critical Marxism. 'There are two traditions,' according to Thompson. 'If I

---

[24] Alvin Gouldner, *The Two Marxisms: Contradictions and Anomalies in the Development of Theory*. New York: Seabury Press, 1980. Gouldner's posthumous volume, *Against Fragmentation: The Origins of Marxism and the Sociology of Intellectuals*. New York: Oxford University Press, 1985, is a complementary study. Here, Gouldner argues that Marxism is distinctively rooted in a new class of intellectuals, and that the doctrine's fate has been tied for better and for worse with this 'ecology'.

[25] Gouldner, *Two Marxisms*, 35.

[26] A grand reading of 20th-century Western Marxism in terms of the history of the development of 'totality' can be found in Martin Jay, *Marxism and Totality: The Adventures of a Concept from Lukács to Habermas*. Berkeley, Calif.: University of California Press, 1984.

thought that Althusserianism was the logical terminus of Marx's thought, then I could never be a Marxist.'[27]

For both Gouldner and Thompson, the roots of these divergent traditions can be found in Marx. Thompson contrasts the historical Marx, sensitive to variations between societies, with the Marx of the *Grundrisse* and *Capital*, who entered the world of political economy only to end up a prisoner of its categories. 'But what we have at the end', he wrote, 'is not the overthrow of "Political Economy" but *another* "Political Economy".' He continues:

Insofar as Marx's categories were anti-categories, Marxism was marked at a critical stage in its development, by the categories of Political Economy: the chief of which was the notion *of* the 'economic,' as a first-order activity, capable of isolation in this way, as the object of a science giving rise to laws whose operation would over-ride second-order activities.

As a result, Thompson argued, Marx's thought came to be 'locked inside a *static, anti-historical structure*'. History was thus reduced to 'the expression of ulterior laws', and historical evidence was used only to illustrate the operation of these laws.[28]

Likewise, Leonard Krieger's thoughtful, if neglected, essay of 1953 on 'Marx and Engels as Historians' contrasts the Marx

---

[27] Thompson, *The Poverty of Theory*, 381. Althusser's errors are identified, with more than a touch of demagoguery, with Stalinism, and the infamous events of 1956 and 1968. From 1956 'forward', he writes on the same page, 'it has been necessary, both within politics and within theory, to declare one's allegiance to one or the other. Between theology and reason there can be no room left for negotiation. Libertarian Communism, and the socialist and Labour movement in general, can have no business with theoretical practice except to expose it and drive it out . . . I declare unrelenting intellectual war against such Marxisms . . . how is it possible to say there are no such enemies, after the experience of high Stalinism, after Budapest 1956, after Prague 1968?' Surely it is possible to denounce Stalinism, totalitarianism, and Soviet imperialism without so thoroughgoing an association of Althusserianism with these political developments. A useful, fair-minded overview is provided in Steven B. Smith, *Reading Althusser: An Essay on Structural Marxism*. Ithaca, NY: Cornell University Press, 1984.

[28] Thompson, *The Poverty of Theory*, 253.

of *The Class Struggle in France* and *The 18th Brumaire*, who used categories that are 'social rather than metaphysical', with the Marx of *Capital*, 'where science in the sense of the precision of natural science is exalted to the position of the only possible method for penetrating to the essence of reality'. He complains that, as a consequence, 'one can no longer start with the empirical determination of the historical forms of "consciousness" and work down to "reality"; rather one must begin with a scientific analysis of "reality" and then work up to explain the forms of "consciousness"'. In the course of this development, Krieger argues, 'Marxism became a closed system . . . It now showed that it had digested its historical material and was completing the process of insulating itself from further convulsions conveyed by history.'[29]

Although there are many differences in their readings of the Marxist tradition and in their assessments of its value, for Gouldner, Thompson, and Krieger the punch-line is the same: given the development of 'two Marxisms', it is necessary to choose between them. They all choose the same way.

The very insistence on choice, however, is something of an analytical disaster. It wishes away the central intellectual tensions and promises of Marxism by definitional fiat.

This proposition that we choose reflects, in the first instance, a remarkable conflation of description and prescription. From the perspective of the history of ideas, Gouldner, Thompson, and Krieger are justified in dividing Marxism into two worlds. The theoretical tension between economic determination and voluntarism is not, as, for example, Lukács thought, simply a hallmark of 'bourgeois' thought. The split between 'scientific' and 'critical' camps *has* defined much of the development of Western Marxism and the self-identity of participants in Marxism's internecine disputes. But to their detriment. This intellectual and political division has been Marxism's central difficulty; to demand a choice between Marxism's divided trajectories is, simply, to reproduce the problem.

Further, this prescription is based on a basic confusion about

[29] Leonard Krieger, 'Marx and Engels as Historians', *Journal of the History of Ideas*, 14 (June 1953), 402.

the character and role of the three distinctive levels, or projects, in Marxist social theory, and thus about the conceptual requirements of each. Concretely, much of this confusion concerns Marx's attempt to identify the 'laws of motion' of capitalist economics, and thus to develop a logical theory of capital accumulation, and the relationship of this project to that of the analysis of capitalist societies as social wholes.

For its specific, central purpose of developing a model of the capitalist economy on its own terms, on the assumption that here lies the most important causally determinative feature of Western modernity, the closed system of *Capital* is deliberately and aptly closed. Its boundedness is essential to its task.[30]

---

[30] This project of Marx's is an example of what Anthony Giddens calls a methodological epoch, a deliberate theoretical abstraction in pursuit of identifying structures in a pure form. In his discussion, Jeffrey Isaac cites Nicos Poulantzas on this point ('The mode of production constitutes an abstract-formal object *which does not exist in the strong sense'*) and comments that, 'in other words, the concept of the mode of production is an abstraction denoting a complex social structure that is real, but that exists insofar as it is instantiated in the concrete practices of specific societies. Thus only social formations exist "in the strong sense," although these formations are structured by modes of production.' Isaac, *Power and Marxist Theory*, 118; the citation is from Nicos Poulantzas, *Political Power and Social Classes*. London: New Left Books, 1973.

Just as soon as Marxism moves to the empirical and historical analysis of the functioning of actual capitalist economies this closure is no longer apt. Indeed, the focus of analysis perforce instantly shifts to Marx's third project since in practice no capitalist economy can be understood, even minimally, without an account of the particular institutional configuration linking states and markets and the character of class formation within a particular country at a particular time (these are issues that need to be addressed even within the most orthodox versions of Marxism's third project). When Marxist economists mistake the second project of a closed theory for the third project they tend to produce a kind of blackboard economics divorced from matters of institutions and power. The result, typically, has been a combination of a reworking of conceptualizations of the economy at some distance from the empirical functioning of capitalist markets and a set of empirical failures, particularly concerning the claim that a capitalist crisis is inevitable, driven by an ineluctable increase in the organic composition of capital. At the same time, important attempts to remedy this situation by the elaboration of such conceptualizations as the social structure of accumulation by David Gordon

At the same time, this 'scientific' and 'economistic' aspect of Marxism has a potentially open role to play in the construction of social theory capable of illuminating actual history.

The central place Marx accords this closed structural analysis of capitalist accumulation takes its ontological justification from the *historical* fact that capitalism is differentiated from other systems precisely by the extent of the autonomy of the capitalist economy from the state and civil society.[31] The privileged place of the economy, and of the productive and market relations it embodies, Marx shows, is not natural or inevitable, but a distinctive and malleable human construct. This claim, of course, is not unique to Marxism (think of Polanyi and Schumpeter); in fact, the centrality of the economy is a much more contingent question for Marxism than it is in the naturalistic presentation of neo-classical economics.

When the logical model of capital accumulation is introduced as a core feature of a Marxist social theory of capitalist societies, the place of the model is transformed. In this analytical context the model makes no claim to be coextensive with history. Rather, capitalist accumulation is understood as the central, though not the exclusive, determinant of the structuring of life in different spheres of society. If the capitalists and workers of the scientific Marx are role categories, without reference to specific people—or to their lives, disposi-

---

and his colleagues are not, as they seem to claim, amendations of the second project of Marx but a shift to the level of the third, where they make an important contribution to the linkage between capitalist economics and questions of social and political organization.

[31] Unlike Cohen, but like Polanyi and Schumpeter, Ellen Meiksins Wood stresses the singularity of capitalism as the only mode of production to have a mechanism for filtering out unproductive economic arrangements. Capitalism produces its own economic dominance. She argues the need to 'distinguish fundamentally between any general tendency toward the improvement of productive forces . . . and the specific tendency of capitalism to revolutionize the forces of production . . . A stress on the uniqueness of capitalism and its development drive—and the denial of unilinearism that this implies—is therefore not an aberration or a momentary, if fatal, lapse in Marxism. It is deeply embedded in and intrinsic to Marx's own analysis from the start.' Wood, 'Marxism and the Course of History', 97–9.

tions, and actions—in this context *the same categories* contribute to an understanding of social experience, not outside history, but within it.

In short, *in the shift from the second of Marx's projects to the third, the meaning and status of the economic model alters.* On its own, the theory of capitalist accumulation, and its attendant laws of motion, can be evaluated as a closed operative system.[32] Joined to the project of a social theory of capitalist societies new questions are posed about the relationship of logical and chronological time, materialism and determination, structure and agency.

The realization of Marx's third project of a social theory appropriate for the analysis of capitalist societies depends on a shift in focus away from the epochal discontinuities in the mode of production and economic model-building on a grand scale characteristic of each of Marx's first two projects to an engagement with *variations* within the capitalist mode of production. Marx's historical writings did not shy away from making this shift, but these occasional pieces are few in

---

[32] I use the word 'operative' in the sense of the distinction introduced by Boudon between what he calls an 'intentional definition' of structure, which *describes* an object as a system in order to show that 'one is dealing with a group of interdependent variables', and 'an operative definition ... characterized by the incorporation of the concept of structure within a theory attempting to account for the systematic nature of an object'. Raymond Boudon, *The Uses of Structuralism*. London: Heineman, 1971, 16. I would claim that only in his second project did Marx achieve the development of an operative structural analysis. A central issue of his third project of social theory of capitalist societies is a very great degree of ambiguity about whether he sees the relationships between the parts of such societies, and especially their connections to the economy, as constituting a system in the more modest sense of defining a field of interrelationships, or in the stronger sense of being able to provide a theory to account for the specificity of this interdependence. There is a symmetrical relationship between these two moments of structural analysis identified by Boudon and G. A. Cohen's discussion of functionalism in which he distinguishes between functional hypotheses that make for plausible accounts of provocative correlations between variables and second-order elaborations of these accounts by the specification of intentional or non-purposive mechanisms. Cohen, *Karl Marx's Theory of History*, ch. 9.

number and implicit in theory as compared to his mature, systematic, voluminous economic thought. Further, Marxism in this century, on *both* sides of Gouldner's divide, has shared in an unfortunate tendency to construct social theories of capitalist societies *without* making this shift.[33]

It may seem self-evident that such has been the case with 'scientific' Marxists (such as Althusser, whose back-of-the-hand dismissal of history so infuriated Thompson), but it is certainly not true of this group alone. Consider Georg Lukács's *History and Class Consciousness*, a text central to the tradition of critical Marxism. For Lukács, the totality of capitalist reality is determined by the diffusion of the commodity principle to all spheres of life. The fetishism of commodities produces reification, which becomes ever more elaborated with the development and growing complexity of modern capitalism. Through reification, the relationships between people appear as relationships between things; people lose their agency and their autonomous consciousness to the mechanistic fragmentation of the zones of social existence.[34]

[33] Raymond Williams comments: 'But one thing that is evident in the best Marxist cultural analysis is that it is very much more at home in what one has to call *epochal* questions than in what one has to call *historical* questions.' Raymond Williams, 'Base and Super-structure in Marxist Cultural Theory', *New Left Review*, 82 (Nov.–Dec. 1973), 8.

[34] George Lukács, *History and Class Consciousness: Studies in Marxist Dialectics*. Cambridge, Mass.: MIT Press, 1971. One of the more influential features of this text has been its identification of analytic rationality with capitalist reification. This strain of anti-scientific romanticism is foreign to Marx. As Agnes Heller has pointed out, Marx was a pre-eminently modern thinker, whose orientation was dynamic and pointed to the future, who saw capitalist industrialization as a motor of historical progress, and who replaced religion with science as the appropriate basis for securing a knowledge-based foundation for knowing and acting. Agnes Heller, 'Marx and Modernity', *Thesis Eleven*, 8 (Jan. 1984). Lukács, by contrast, presented the battleground between capitalism and socialism as in part one of the methodological division between scientific rationality and totality understood in terms of the diffusion of the commodity principle. This antinomy has been a central feature of critical Marx-ism; exemplary discussions can be found in the writings of Herbert Marcuse and Lucien Goldmann.

This is an entirely ahistorical portrait with regard both to the base and superstructure of Marxist theory. Capitalism as a mode of production, and specific societies as complicated amalgams of overlapping modes of production, are missing themes in Lukács. But further, as Stedman Jones observes,

it is not simply the economic history of modes of production—the 'base'—which is etherialized virtually out of existence by Lukács. The whole complexity of differential political and culture systems in the *superstructure* is contracted into a few wooden leitmotifs. For Lukács, the thesis that the dominant ideology in any social formation is the ideology of the ruling class is interpreted as the saturation of the social totality by the ideological essence of a pure class subject. But it is important to notice that this domination has virtually no *institutional* apparatus whatsoever. It is simply 'pure ideology'—the unseen rays of a hidden centre of the universe: commodity fetishism. Thus in *History and Class Consciousness*, Lukács's whole account of bourgeois ideological domination is reduced to the invisible emanations of reification from commodities, which radiate to bleach the consciousness of the inhabitants of capitalist society.[35]

For Lukács, there is no empirical, only a potential, proletariat, as the extension of commodity fetishism beyond the economic, productive realm creates a fissure between its imputed consciousness and 'the real, psychological thoughts of men about their lives'.[36] As a consequence, social change is a dichotomous all or nothing proposition; the 'all' being a revolutionary socialist practice, where the proletariat, having achieved at last its theoretically imputed consciousness, and its potential to overcome the division between object and subject, appears at long last on the historical stage to transcend capitalism.

Lukács's voluntarism is divorced from real actors. His proletariat has nothing to do with actual working-class people. Indeed, the great weight of the analysis in *History and Class Consciousness* explains why, in the fetishized and reified world of the capitalist mode of production, the working class is incapable of becoming a proletariat. The logic of commodity fetishism is that of atomization. Even at moments of economic crisis, the fate of workers is perceived as an individualized crisis, and 'the reified mind is unable to perceive a pattern in this "chaos"'.

And yet Lukács develops a myth of a transition to socialism in which, at the end of capitalist history, the working class will in fact seize its world-historical role as a proletariat. Its objective possibilities will be realized, as the boundary between imputed and actual consciousness disappears, and its consciousness will become 'deed'. In that magical moment of the fusion of being and consciousness socialism will arrive as the people's choice. This myth has no grounding whatsoever in Lukács's assessment of capitalist society.[37] Rather, it provides a justification of the role of a vanguard party, whose 'organization is the form of mediation between theory and practice'.[38]

---

[37] The only partial exception is the role Lukács ascribes to the impact of the final economic crisis of capitalism on the transformation of potential to actual consciousness within the working class. It might be underscored that although Lukács's politics were abstract, they were not reformist.

Lukács, in short, obliterates the divide between the real and the ideal. He 'does this', Isaac writes, 'by positing a teleology, whereby those in a subordinate position are either actually or immanently in opposition to the existing system of power . . . One consequence of this teleological treatment of the problem of interests is that discrete acts of resistance, and more ordinary forms of negotiation and conflict, are inaccurately interpreted as signs of movement toward social transformation. This mistake leads toward the moralizing of theoretical analysis, and a failure to acknowledge the coherence and stability of social forms. A second consequence of this is inattention to real normative questions. Insofar as change is seen as immanent, it becomes less imperative to figure out why change is justified and how the future should be better organized.' Isaac, *Power and Marxist Theory*, 106–7.

[38] Lukács, *History and Class Consciousness*, 105, 178, 299. Stedman Jones's essay concludes with a useful discussion of Lukács's theory of the state and of political action. Stedman Jones, 'The Marxism of the Early Lukács', 57.

We may well ask, in parenthesis, why so much of Western Marxism avoids coming to grips with the central problems of social theory and history by remaining aloof at the level of the mode of production. I am drawn to Perry Anderson's diagnosis that Western Marxism has

To focus for the moment on Lukács is not to argue for the superiority of the camp of scientific Marxism. Rather, it is to underscore that the very division of Marxism into two groups along the lines delineated by Gouldner severely weakens Marxism as a social (and practical) theory, and that it produces a basic misunderstanding of the status of Marx's different analytical projects. For if we move from the level of the mode of production to social formation; and from Marx's second, logical–economic project to his third, that of the social theory of capitalist societies, at issue is not whether to link the logical and the chronological, or structure and agency, but how.

Of all the leading figures of twentieth-century Marxism, Antonio Gramsci made the fullest and most fruitful attempt to assay these issues. Curiously, far too much of the scholarship concerned with his prison notebooks and other writings debates whether he is one of Gouldner's scientific Marxists or a critical Marxist, or even whether he departed in a fundamental way from original Marxism.[39]

---

above all been the Marxism of defeat. Whether it be Althusser on ideology, Marcuse on sexuality, Adorno on nature, Sartre on scarcity, or Gramsci on hegemony, he observes, all, 'no matter how otherwise heteroclite . . . share one fundamental emblem: a common and latent *pessimism*', and it is not hard to work out why this should be so. Perry Anderson, *Considerations on Western Marxism*. London: New Left Books, 1976, 88. Indeed, each of the themes or concepts of these 20th-century Marxists can be read as an attempt to account for the failure of the working class to make the leap from Lukács's actual consciousness to his imputed consciousness. There is also an academic side to this characteristic concern of modern Marxism, the extent to which Marxism is a closed theory. This is a difficult subject to explore because, as Gouldner observed, 'Marxism established itself by accentuating those of its doctrines that separate and distinguish it from adversaries *and* from its competitors, while at the same time glossing over or remaining silent about doctrines it may *share* with them. It thereby established [a] distinguishable identity for itself, enabling it to make claims, and seek resources and commitments in its own name. It is neither just research nor facts and logic, then, that shape the character of a theory; the identity of a theory is shaped *also* by the politics and the political economy of the intellectual life.' Gouldner, *Against Fragmentation*, 89.

[39] Among others, the first position is argued by Chantal Mouffe ('Hegemony and Ideology in Gramsci', in Mouffe (ed.), *Gramsci and*

Debates of this kind do not take us very far. For just the reasons why I reject Gouldner's dichotomy in its prescriptive aspect, all these positions are either wrong or beside the point. They try to squeeze Gramsci into the mould of traditional debates where he does not fit, or they miss his bid to transcend the two camps of Marxism. Gramsci's great strengths are his refusal to choose between the critical and scientific tendencies, and his attempt to work with and through the inherent tensions of joining a theoretical project to a historical one, in his case the study of the terrain of Italian society, in order to understand, while sitting in Mussolini's gaol, the immensity of the defeat of the Left.

The key to Gramsci's work is his effort to capture and incorporate the state and civil society as objects of analysis for Marxism. He recognized that both are massive, complex, and highly differentiated in modern capitalist societies; and that their characteristics vary considerably from place to place and from time to time. It was from this orienting perspective that Gramsci tried to make sense of the peculiarities of Italian

---

Marxist Theory. London: Routledge and Kegan Paul, 1979); the second by Gouldner. The debate shows just how stylized the base–superstructure discussion has become within Marxism. Norberto Bobbio, for example, claims that Gramsci inverted the thought of Marx and Engels in two key respects: by stressing the importance of the superstructure over the economic base; and within the superstructure by giving primacy to ideological and cultural rather than institutional arrangements. Bobbio, 'Gramsci and the Conception of Civil Society', in Mouffe, *Gramsci and Marxist Theory*. Jacques Texier, by contrast, argues that Gramsci's work, though completely silent about economic questions, takes orthodox Marxist economics for granted, and is concerned to discover how and under what terms the base actually penetrates and shapes the superstructure. Texier then restates the issue as if he has solved its key problems, when in fact he has merely highlighted them: 'In fact, for Gramsci,' Texier writes, 'the infrastructure is indeed "primary" and "conditioning" and in this he is a Marxist. But this in no way means that the superstructures are not active at all times, nor even that men's superstructural activity does not become determinant in relation to the infrastructure when a period of social revolution commences, this is when relations of production have become irrational.' Jacques Texier, 'Gramsci, Theoretician of the Superstructures', in Mouffe, *Gramsci and Marxist Theory*, 58–9.

history—particularly the role of Catholicism and the north–south split—within an open, contingent, but not relativistic Marxist framework.[40]

Of course what is most interesting in Gramsci is not his break with the mechanical determinism of the Marxism of the Second International, but the character of this break, which seems to me entirely consistent with Krieger's description of Marx's historical writings:

Not only the history itself but the agents of the history were endowed with a twofold existence. When Marx emphasized how much 'in historical struggles must one distinguish the phrases and fancies of the parties from their real organism and their real interests, their conception of themselves from their reality,' he was not in any historiographical sense seeking to separate truth from illusion, but rather to order two diverse elements within the field of history along the lines of what amounted to a kind of subject–object relationship. However hierarchical their arrangement, 'subjective' ideas and actions on the one hand and 'objective' historical law and the situation which it produced on the other were distinct forces by reason of their imperfection and were necessary to each other for the making of history. Fundamentally, this is the familiar idea of the 'superstructure' but what makes it significant for our purposes is that in Marx's approach to history it was not simply a device to deprecate ideologies but also a means of accepting into his account actions and ideas which were not in full harmony with the 'objective' social process.[41]

[40] Antonio Gramsci, *Selections from the Prison Notebooks*. New York: International Publishers, 1971; Gramsci, *Letters from Prison*. New York: Harper and Row, 1973; Gramsci, *Selections from Political Writings, 1910–1920*. New York: International Publishers, 1977. Useful secondary treatments include Leonardo Salamini, *The Sociology of Political Praxis: An Introduction to Gramsci's Theory*. London: Routledge and Kegan Paul, 1981; John M. Cammett, *Antonio Gramsci and the Origins of Italian Communism*. Stanford, Calif.: Stanford University Press, 1967; Antonio Pozzolini, *Antonio Gramsci: An Introduction to his Thought*. London: Pluto Press, 1970; Carl Boggs, *Gramsci's Marxism*. London: Pluto Press, 1976; Boggs, *The Two Revolutions: Gramsci and the Dilemmas of Western Marxism*. Boston: South End Press, 1984; Ann Showstack Sassoon (ed.), *Approaches to Gramsci*. London: Writers and Readers, 1982; and Perry Anderson, 'The Antinomies of Antonio Gramsci', *New Left Review*, 100 (Nov. 1976–Jan. 1977).

[41] Krieger, 'Marx and Engels as Historians', pp. 386–7.

By developing a series of specific sociological and political concepts—the most important being 'hegemony' and 'historical bloc' (the specific historical situation in which an 'essential class' exercises hegemony)—and by creating a political sociology of conflict capable of dealing with the complexities of the modern state and civil society, Gramsci elaborated on the most promising lines of inquiry embedded in Marx's historical writings. In this elaboration, the base–superstructure distinction is developed as a complex web of relations in which the economic, political, and cultural elements of a situation are interconnected, and in which the historicity of social structure is made central. The different dimensions in any specific society do not move in sealed, logically determined orbits, as in the Althusserian formulation, but they interconnect in a single historical rhythm. Thus, for Gramsci, variations in the content and rules of political conflict and in the outcomes of political struggles cannot be explained in terms of disappointment as against theoretically derived expectations, but what actually did occur must be made the object of explanation. In making this effort to develop a Marxist political sociology, Gramsci was thus radically anti-reductionist. Further, as his debt to Croce makes clear, Gramsci's Marxism was developed in a dialogue with non-Marxist scholarship.

With this achievement, all serious attempts within Marxism to deal with the base–superstructure problem became overtly or implicitly Gramscian. Before returning to the city in Chapter 3, I should like to explore these issues of Marxist social theory in the work of Edward Thompson, Raymond Williams, Eric Hobsbawm, and G. A. Cohen because they demonstrate the repertoire of alternative theoretical moves Marxists sensitive to these questions have made since Gramsci. The capacity of Marxism to provide an attractive alternative to the differentiation problematic in studies of the city hinges on the character and persuasiveness of these linkages. In the chapter's concluding discussion, I will return to the issue of the capaciousness of Marxist theory.

II

The subject-matter of Edward Thompson's work—working-class values and political culture, the significance of law, moral choices, and expectations—in the determinate location of eighteenth- and nineteenth-century England, as well as his self-conscious identification with a particular reading of the Marxist tradition, locates his work at the heart of Marx's third project. Because this aspect of Marx's contribution was so much less well developed than studies at the level of the mode of production, Thompson has chosen to develop the

real silence in Marx, which lies in the area that anthropologists would call value systems ... There is a silence as to cultural and moral mediations, as to the ways in which the human being is imbricated in particular, determined productive relations, the way these material experiences are handled by them in cultural ways, the way in which there are certain value-systems that are consonant with certain modes of production and productive relations which are inconceivable without consonant value-systems.[42]

In so doing, he has sought to move Marxism to studies of capitalism rather than the logic of capital, and he has broken with base–superstructure formulations as hopelessly mechanical. Writing more than a half-decade before the publication of *The Making of the English Working Class*, Thompson argued the inadequacy of this metaphor in these terms:

In all their historical analysis Marx and Engels always kept in view the dialectical interaction between social consciousness ... and social being. But in trying to explain their ideas they expressed them as a make-belief model ... in fact, no such basis and superstructure ever existed; it is a metaphor to help understand what does exist—men, who act, experience, think, and act again.[43]

[42] 'Interview with E. P. Thompson', in Middle Atlantic Radical Historians' Organization, *Visions of History*. New York: Pantheon Books, 1984, 20.

[43] E. P. Thompson, 'Socialist Humanism', *New Reasoner*, 1 (1957), 111–13. Later in this essay, Thompson identified the base–superstructure metaphor with Stalinism in these terms: 'Stalinism converted the concepts of "reflection" and of the "superstructure" into mechanical operations in a semi-automatic model. The

The central conceptual contribution of Thompson is to suggest how 'experience', located at the juncture of social being and social consciousness, provides a means of linkage between structure and agency. As Perry Anderson has pointed out, 'experience' has a double meaning, referring both to a set of subjective perceptions of reality and to a more active sense of a process of learning, potentially leading to action to modify reality; and, further, there is no perfect symmetry between determined experience and self-determination within the realm of experience.[44] The duality of 'experience' sets out a domain for inquiry, but unless the duality is explored in its full complexity the fertile possibilities suggested by Thompson's work cannot be realized.

The clearest statement Thompson makes about the nature of the connections between social theory and history in Marxism can be found in 'The Poverty of Theory'. There, he defends 'historical materialism' against both anti-historicist Marxists and non-Marxist historians by arguing that the ontological status of the past cannot be affected by historiography ('The object of historical knowledge is "real" history'); by claiming that historical knowledge is provisional, incomplete, selective, and limited by the questions historians pose (but for none of these reasons untrue); by insisting that the claim of historical materialism is not its epistemological distinctiveness, but its procedures, hypotheses, categories, and concepts; and by arguing that such concepts as exploitation, class struggle, mode of production, and hegemony do not constitute rules of history but expectations. These are not ideal types that are fulfilled in the passage of historical time, but are

---

conscious process of intellectual conflict were seen not as agencies in the making of history but as an irritating penumbra of illusions, or imperfect reflections, trailing behind economic forces' (129). This indictment of Stalinism is surely apt, and so is the cautionary warning that the division of the world into base and superstructure is a construction, not a report of historical reality. But such is the case with theories of all kinds, and they are not the less valuable, or more capable of being dismissed as useful tools to apprehend social reality, for this reason alone.

[44] Perry Anderson, *Arguments within English Marxism*. London: Verso Books, 1980, 26–7.

whole families of special cases, families which include adopted orphans and the children of typological miscegenation. History knows no regular verbs ... History is not rule-governed, and it knows no sufficient causes ... For historical explanation discloses not *how* history must have eventuated but why it eventuated in this way and not in other ways; that process is not arbitrary but has its own regularity and rationality; that certain kinds of event (political, economic, cultural) have been related, not any way one likes, but in particular ways and within determinate fields of possibility.[45]

These propositions fall into three categories: a spirited endorsement of the historical craft, understood in quite traditional naturalistic ways,[46] a set of claims about the construction and utilization of concepts, and an approach to the issue of determination.

From within this perspective Thompson himself presents a glaring 'silence': on the ontological and determinative status he wishes to accord to the structure of capitalist accumulation. If history is 'real', and the concepts best used to explicate this reality are the Marxist ones of exploitation and class analysis, what precise assessment does Thompson wish to make about the centrality Marx accorded the analysis of political economy? Nowhere in *The Making of the English Working Class* does Thompson tackle this question systematically. And nowhere in 'The Poverty of Theory' does Thompson do more than exhort a 'supercession' of *Capital* by historical materialism. If Thompson's work 'stresses the importance of cultural

---

[45] Thompson, 'The Poverty of Theory', in *The Poverty of Theory*, 231–42.

[46] History, he writes, 'does not of course actually exist, like some plasma adhering to the facts, or as some invisible kernel within the shell of appearances. What we are saying is that the notion (concept, hypothesis as to causation) has been brought into a disciplined dialogue with the evidence, and it has been shown to "work"; that is, it has not been *dis*proved by contrary evidence, and that it successfully organizes or "explains" hitherto inexplicable evidence; hence it is an adequate (although approximate) representation of the causative sequence, or rationality, of these events, and it conforms (within the logic of the historical discipline) with a process which did in fact eventuate in the past. Hence it exists simultaneously both as a "true" knowledge and as an adequate representation of an actual property of those events.' Ibid., 235–6.

resources and human intervention for social change and class politics', a recent sympathetic critique asks:

where is the reciprocal analysis of social change—the structured, material limits within which the English working class had to make itself? The absence of any systematic discussion of the ways in which English industrialization concretely affected the given patterns of class and community relations makes it appear that history did not in any way happen behind the backs of the English working class. In his zeal to correct the 'objectivist' biases of economic historians and more orthodox Marxists, Thompson fleshed out only one side of the full dialectic of being and consciousness.[47]

It is just this absence of reciprocation that allows Anderson his most telling rejoinder to Thompson. If, for Althusser, experience is merely illusion, for Thompson, by contrast, there is only the inversion of this limitation. 'What is needed', Anderson persuasively argues, 'beyond the abstract counter-position of these two poles is *conceptual* clarification of the very different senses and forms of "experience", and *empirical* study of the respective historical variations encompassed by each.'[48] In the end, Thompson stops short of such a project, because in his spirited defence of history he developed a deep aversion to theory.

It is not difficult to understand, even to sympathize, with Thompson's aversion. Marx's theoretical work on political economy fails to examine systematically the reproduction of the working class (labour power) itself. Instead of treating working people as subjects, the theory treats them almost exclusively as the objects of capital. Yet, no working class is

---

[47] Ellen Kay Trimberger, 'E. P. Thompson: Understanding the Process of History', in Theda Skocpol (ed.), *Vision and Method in Historical Sociology*. New York: Cambridge University Press, 1984, 224. Another reading of the same issue concludes that Thompson's lack of direct consideration of relations of production produces the paradox that he might in fact concede too much, at least implicitly, to economic productivism and determination. Ellen Meiksins Wood, 'The Politics of Theory and the Concept of Class: E. P. Thompson and his Critics', *Studies in Political Economy*, 9 (Fall 1982). See also Gregor McLennan, *Marxism and the Methodologies of History*. London: Verso Books, 1981.

[48] Anderson, *Arguments within English Marxism*, 57–8.

constituted automatically, nor does any working class live in, or struggle with, capitalism in general.[49]

But the inability to deduce history from theory does not provide grounds for the rejection of Marx's project of political economy. Though analytical and structural rather than chronological, this closed system was constructed in a profoundly historical way, based on deep learning about the actual trajectory of capitalist development in Britain.[50] Attempts such as Thompson's or Krieger's to shower praise on the historical Marx while displaying an aversion towards Marx the economic analyst miss just how much the former is embedded in the latter.

Nevertheless, as Christian Topalov cautions, 'the construction of theory from history does not guarantee that theory will allow an understanding of historical phenomena. For this to be possible a proper place in the conceptual system must be given to social relations which are the driving force in the whole affair.'[51] The shift from the project of political economy to the project of social theory thus entails a movement from role categories to actual relationships between people; in the Marxist construction, to members of social classes in struggle. To understand these relations we should be just as wary of leaving structural determinations behind too quickly as we must be about allowing such determinations to replace concrete histor-

[49] As Topalov notes, there is a keen theoretical cost to this omission: 'To build a theory of these social relations in capitalism is in my view necessary not only to understand history and not abandon it to empiricism, but also to avert the danger of an economistic derailment of a marxism which forgot that capital is the relation of capital to non-capital. Which is, after all, the fundamental limit to capital.' Christian Topalov, 'Capital, History, and the Limits of Economics', *International Journal of Urban and Regional Research*, 7 (Dec. 1983), 607.

[50] For a warm appreciation of the quality of Marx's learning, see Charles Tilly, 'Karl Marx, Historian', *Michigan Quarterly Review*, 22 (1983).

[51] Topalov, 'Capital, History', 605–6. For a fuller elaboration of these points, theoretically and substantively, see Christian Topalov, 'Social Policies from Below: A Call for Comparative Historical Studies', *International Journal of Urban and Regional Research*, 9 (June 1985).

ical analysis. In any event, to put social relations at the centre of the analysis requires that we return to Thompson's junction point of being and consciousness, and, in so doing, that we take up the core problem of determination.

Thompson is emphatic in his rejection of the base–superstructure metaphor, but what in his mood of theoretical *ressentiment* does he suggest be put in its place? Thompson comes closest to suggesting an answer in the concluding pages of *Whigs and Hunters*. There, he presents a marvellously dialectical and suggestive discussion of law.

He takes aim at a mark no different than the target of 'The Poverty of Theory': the mechanical determination of such superstructural elements as the law by the economic base. From this standpoint the rule of law is the rule of the ruling class. Of course much of Thompson's empirical work demonstrates just this class-boundedness of eighteenth-century law. At the same time, he pleads for a rejection of reductionism and of 'superior and inferior' structures.[52]

His attempt at an alternative (on 'the narrowing ledge of traditional middle ground') first establishes the irreducibility of the law, which has 'its own logic, rules, and procedures' that cannot be subsumed into the dominant class; second, that the distinction between base and superstructure is infirmed when we actually examine the constitutive role of law in

---

[52] E. P. Thompson, *Whigs and Hunters: The Origins of the Black Act*. New York: Pantheon Books, 1975, 260. For an example of a mechanical application of the base–superstructure metaphor to legal matters, see Alan Stone, 'The Place of the Law in the Marxian Structure–Superstructure Archetype', *Law and Society Review*, 19/1 (1985). Stone writes: 'To summarize so far, paying attention to the Marxian idea of structure and superstructure allows us to understand how the economic structure and the activities of judicial decision-makers are linked to the making of specific decisions that constitute and maintain the mode of production. Linkages move along the following path: structure→essential legal relations→derivative sub-relations→particular rules ... Thus, without resorting to crude instrumentalism, this construction shows how legal agents act to support capitalist social relations, and at the same time it accords with the manner in which legal decisions are made. Moreover, it allows us to detect signals indicating when the mode of production is being seriously challenged. When an economy's essential legal relations are openly challenged, we know that this is the case' (59–60).

production; and, third, that the law expresses and represents norms, albeit contested ones, held by the whole community. Thompson does not wish to be misunderstood: the law is used to impose class power, but the law is not simply a pliant tool; it possesses its own substantial existence, and even the use of the law by the dominant class has to adapt and work through the institutions and ideology of the law, and in so doing the class is constrained by the law. Further, the very existence of the rule of law, however class-biased, is the outcome of much popular struggle, and the mediation of class rule by the law represents a significant mitigation of class domination in so far as it deflects unmediated force.[53]

This discussion is immensely suggestive, but imprecise— not about the law (the subject of this densely textured volume), but about the terms of relationship, in both historical and theoretical terms, between the productive economy and the law. What is not clear from Thompson's discussion of the ways the law is imbricated in production is whether he wishes to do away entirely with the agenda of issues concerning determination suggested by the metaphor of the base and the superstructure. Surely, at a minimum, there is some tension between the argument that law has an autonomous substantiality and the claim that the boundaries between the law and production are impossible to discern. If the meaning and role of the law within capitalism cannot be apprehended by a

[53] Thompson, *Whigs and Hunters*, 260–9. An exceptionally interesting supplement to *Whigs and Hunters* is David Sugarman's 'Law, Economy, and the State in England, 1750–1914', in Sugarman (ed.), *Legality, Ideology, and the State*. New York: Academic Press, 1983. Especially interesting are his discussions of the rise of the legal profession, the relationship between landed property and the law, the tensions between absolute and more qualified property rights, conflicts over the plurality of possible legal forms, including procedures for establishing facts and for enforcement, and, most notable, the development of what he calls facilitative laws that straddle the divide of public and private law. Such laws are agencies of state policy in that they define permissible conduct, but at the same time they are instruments through which individuals may expand their autonomy from the state. Sugarman argues that such facilitative laws as those governing companies and contracts allow capitalists, and capitalism, to manage the contradictory features of the law noted by Thompson.

recourse to mechanical formulae, then what, instead, are the determinate and dialectical features governing their relationship?

In the discussion of determination in 'The Poverty of Theory', Thompson exhorts us to 'observe in the laboratory of events the evidence of determination, not in its sense as rule-governed law but in its sense of the "setting of limits" and the "exerting of pressures"'.[54] He draws this formulation from Raymond Williams's chapter on determination in *Marxism and Literature*.

There, Williams emphatically and persuasively argues that 'A Marxism without some concept of determination is in effect worthless', yet 'A Marxism with many of the concepts of determination it now has is quite radically disabled'.[55] His discussion is subtle and illuminating. It has two key elements, each of which establishes and maintains a certain necessary intellectual tension.

The first element concerns determination as the setting of limits. As such, the term appears to imply a sense of external-ity, beyond and outside a field of action. This Williams calls 'abstract determinism'. Within the capitalist mode of produc-tion the 'strongest single reason for the development of abstract determinism is the historical experience of large-scale capitalist economy, in which many more people than Marxists concluded that control of the process was beyond them, that it was at least in practice external to their wills and desires, and that it had therefore to be seen as governed by its own "laws"'. Williams sees this impulse as bitterly ironic, because it transforms a critical doctrine into a recipe for passivity. But there is a second sense of determination as the setting of limits, that which Williams calls 'inherent determinism . . . in which the essential character of a process or the properties of its components are held to determine (control) its outcome: the character and properties are then "determinants"'.[56] In this

---

[54] Thompson, 'The Poverty of Theory', 241–2.

[55] Raymond Williams, *Marxism and Literature*. Oxford: Oxford University Press, 1977, 83.

[56] Ibid., 86, 84, 85.

inherent sense of the term, agency is reintroduced, but within qualifying conditions; hence the setting of limits.

The second element concerns determination as the exertion of pressures. Inherent determination is more than negative determination; it is also the exertion of pressures against and within existing limits:

> 'Society' is then never only the 'dead husk' which limits social and individual fulfilment. It is also always a constitutive process with very powerful pressures which are both expressed in political, economic, and cultural formations and, to take the full weight of 'constitutive', are internalized and become 'individual wills'.

Determination in this sense is located not outside but within social processes, which are themselves a combination of 'an active and conscious as well as, by default, a passive and objectified historical experience'.[57]

Determination in this formulation is a complex process. Although Williams discards the abstract determination of enclosed domains implied by some of the more mechanical renderings of base and superstructure, he does not reject the metaphor *tout court*. Instead, to his discussion of internal determination he adds two further critical elements: a widening of our understanding of the base, and a multifaceted reading of how the base and superstructure may be connected. In so doing, he is far more permissive about the use of analytical categories than Thompson; at the same time he cautions against the unnoticed shift from analytical constructs to substantive description. Use the metaphor to illuminate fundamental questions about social processes, but beware of

---

[57] Ibid., 87, 88. A similar discussion of determination is provided by John McMurtry, who distinguishes determination as a blockage of possibilities, 'a setting of limits', and determination as 'mapping' in a particular setting. This sense 'refers to the *mapping*, so to speak, that takes place between a specific Economic Structure and the particular legal, political, and ideological phenomena of a society'. Such a sense of determination refers to content as well as to limits. Alas, Marx gives no rules whereby such a "mapping" proceeds, but he frequently discusses, describes, and alludes to cases of its occurrence.' John McMurtry, 'Making Sense of Economic Determinism', *Canadian Journal of Philosophy*, 3 (Dec. 1973), 258.

being seduced into thinking that base and superstructure are hermetically sealed entities.

Much recent attention within Marxism, Williams observes, has been dedicated to an elaboration of the substantive complexity and autonomy of the superstructure. These considerations have included such modifications to analysis as the ideas of temporal lags, mediation, and corresponding or homologous structures. Instead, or at least as a complement, he urges a reconsideration of the base and its reduction to economistic understandings of modes of production, or, within capitalism, to the laws of motion of capital. Even if limited to the ambit of economics as in the second project of Marx, the base is 'very much more active, more complicated and more contradictory' than most orthodox renditions. The base is a process, not a fixed state. He proposes, however, that with regard to what I have identified as Marx's third project, the idea of the base be extended beyond the production of capitalist economic relationships to 'the primary production of society itself, and of men themselves, [to the] material production and reproduction of real life'.[58]

In this way, Williams sharply expands the content of the base within traditional Marxist theory. He proposes 'the radical move' of 'making cultural history material' in order to capture 'the full possibilities of the concept of culture as a constitutive social process, creating specific and different "ways of life", which could have been remarkably deepened by the emphasis on a material social process'. He does so by incorporating language and consciousness 'into the material social process itself'.[59] Culture, especially hegemony, which he understands as a selective tradition of dominant meanings and values, is materially produced, and the product mediates being and consciousness.

I think this radical expansion of the meaning of 'base' is extremely problematical because to accept it is to erode two great strengths of Marxist theory. The first of these is the

[58] Williams, 'Base and Superstructure', 4, 5, 6.

[59] Williams, *Marxism and Literature*, 19, 61. For other treatments of these topics by Williams, see his 'Problems of Materialism', in his *Problems in Materialism and Culture*. London: Verso Books, 1980, and *Culture*. London: Fontana Books, 1981.

specificity of Marxism's direct engagement with the development of capitalism as one of the central hallmarks of modernity in the West. Its explanatory claim that capitalist economics is the centrepiece of the modern Western experience may be contested, but that this claim is basic to Marxism cannot. Marxism is the most coherent body of theory we possess about the development of capitalism as an economic system. To expand the concept of the base so that it loses this specificity is to lose the tight linkage between Marxism's central ontological claim and its theoretical apparatus.

The second strength of Marxism put at risk by Williams's expansion of the base to encompass all kinds of productive activity is the possiblity of achieving clarity about Marxism's propositions concerning determination (in the very terms clarified by Williams). More precisely, I think it an important project to inquire about the causal power of capitalist accumulation, its setting of limits and exertion of pressures. In *Capital*, Marx presents a very high level of historical generalization and abstraction about the dynamics of capitalist economics. As we shift our focus to a lower level of generalization in treating particular societies, and towards a treatment of the totality of social relations, not just the economic ones, Marxism poses the question as to whether and to what extent we should understand non-economic relations in specific times and places as economically determined. This we cannot do once the base is expanded to include elements, whether cultural, political, or spatial, which in theoretical terms are *potentially* superstructural.

Questions about determination are issues about the autonomy and contingency of the superstructure. To say, for example, that the state, or urban space, is autonomous may have one of two meanings: in the weaker form, that it is not epiphenomenal; in the stronger form, that it has its own interior logic. To say that something is contingent is to say in the weaker form that the given theory cannot explain it, or in the stronger form that it cannot be explained (fully or partially) even if embedded within a broader and wider version of the theory.[60]

---

[60] I am indebted to Peter Railton of the University of Michigan for these formulations.

In short, I think it desirable to separate Williams's important guiding discussion of determination from his costly attempt to make the notion of the base more capacious. In making this distinction, we may be guided by Hobsbawm's approach to the base and G. A. Cohen's approach to the superstructure.

Hobsbawm's attempt to define the content of the base is more traditional than that of Williams, but more expansive than economic production very narrowly conceived. He accepts Eric Wolf's formulation that the base is 'the complex set of mutually dependent relations among nature, work, social labor and social organization'.[61] In this, Hobsbawm parallels Little's rejection of the quite common treatment of the economic base in naturalistic terms, as consisting of mechanisms underlying the accumulation process that require hypothetical and theoretical reasoning to be discovered.

Hobsbawm then demarcates the domain of determination between base and superstructure by characterizing the base in terms of the 'materialist conception of history', which, within capitalism, gives a privileged status to the trajectory of economic production as 'the *basis* of historical explanation', though it is 'not historical explanation itself'. It could not be, because 'History is not like ecology: human beings decide and think about what happens'. In terms of the distinctions between Marx's various projects, Hobsbawm is proposing that the key questions of determination in capitalist societies lie at the junction of an expanded notion of capitalist accumulation, on the one side, and actual history, with all its attendant variations, on the other: 'Thus we know of societies which have the same material base but widely varying ways of structuring their social relations, ideology, and other superstructural features.'[62]

If such is the case, however, we are left with the puzzle of how to account for such variations, and in so doing whether there is much point to the base–superstructure distinction. More precisely, in Williams's terms, if the base sets limits on

[61] Eric Wolf, *Europe and the People without History*. Berkeley, Calif.: University of California Press, 1983, 74.

[62] Eric Hobsbawm, 'Marx and History', *New Left Review*, 143 (Jan.–Feb. 1984), 42, 43, 44.

variations, does it also exert pressures on outcomes? If so, how, and in interaction with what other social processes that are not part of the base but conceived in terms of the social organization of economic production? These are issues basic to the evaluation in subsequent chapters of Marxist work on the city.

Hobsbawm deals with them by arguing, first, that historical analysis should begin with, and exhaust the limits of, the base—the mode of production understood as a combination of the technical level of the forces of production and 'the social arrangements by which labour is mobilized, deployed, and allocated'. He allows for contingency and variation, however, by arguing, second, that 'not all non-economic phenomena in history can be derived from specific economic phenomena, and particular events or dates are not determined in this sense'.[63] In this way, Hobsbawm adopts a restricted definition of the superstructure much like Cohen's, as 'those non-economic institutions whose character is explained by the nature of the economic structure'.[64] In this construction the superstructure is not simply synonymous with all non-economic institutions, nor is it necessarily the case that most non-economic institutions are superstructural. In this formulation, considerations of base and superstructure *must* open up to domains of causal explanation in which Marxism can claim neither ontological nor epistemological privilege. It is a paradox that Williams extends the bounds of Marxism so much that in his formulation it can achieve its ambitions of being an inclusive social theory, whereas the more orthodox approaches of Cohen and Hobsbawm necessarily lead to a less bounded Marxism.[65]

[63] Ibid., 43.

[64] Cohen, *Karl Marx's Theory of History*, 216, 217.

[65] Two other formulations of issues of determination which, though useful, are more opaque than those of Williams, Hobsbawm, and Cohen are those of Helmut Fleischer and R. F. Atkinson. Fleischer argues that 'the relationship between the sphere of economic production and all the rest is not to be understood as a causal relationship . . . all that Marx claims here is that changes [in the superstructure] correspond to changes in the sphere of production', both in the sense that some superstructural elements require a certain economic level

To pursue the latter course is thus preferable for more than one reason: first, it promises a tighter Marxism whose very exaggerations and enthusiasms make it possible to illuminate key features of a very complex social reality. The more firm and cohesive the Marxism, the better its carrying capacities can be judged. Second, the kind of lean Marxist theory suggested by Cohen and Hobsbawm, precisely because of its coherent approach to a definition of the base and questions it invokes about the relationship of these particular foundations to superstructural features of society, invites us to explore whether side by side with capitalism we may discover other large-scale social processes that have likewise had a fundamental impact in shaping the modern world. The main candidates for such a parallel status, deserving of comparable theoretical treatment, are the development of coherent national states and the emergence of networks of relationships in civil society with a high degree of autonomy from both the economy and the state in the West since the sixteenth century.

By proceeding in this manner, it is possible to maintain the integrity and specificity of the Marxist tradition, as Thompson insists we must, and yet also to apply its analysis of capitalism as a mode of production in tandem with analyses of the causal contributions of other key processes, like those of the state, without forcing a priori choices about a hierarchy of social processes. Marxism, to be sure, does possess such a causal hierarchy, but its utility to social and historical analysis need

---

as a necessary condition, and in the sense that economic interests are always involved in superstructural relations, even if they are not the exclusive interests so involved. Helmut Fleischer, *Marxism and History*. New York: Harper and Row, 1973, 109–10. Atkinson makes the point that the determinism–freedom problems of Marxism are not especially acute, but they appear so because of 'the absence of a clear and accepted account in Marxist writings of the "mechanism" by which the economic structure determines the other levels of social life . . . Though there does not have to be a mechanism for the theory to be true—correlation would suffice—it is not altogether unnatural to think that there is a gap in the theory, and some consequent tendency to imagine a purely deterministic filling for it.' R. F. Atkinson, 'Historical Materialism', in G. H. R. Parkinson (ed.), *Marx and Marxisms*. Cambridge: Cambridge University Press, 1982, 64.

not depend on an acceptance of its distinctive explanatory claims about the relative causal importance of economic structures. Put another way, the causal power of Marxism is considerable whether or not the analysis of capitalism as an economic system is accorded as much weight *vis-à-vis* other macrostructures as the Marxist tradition insists it must.[66]

Likewise, with such an approach to Marxism's third project of social theory, it is possible to ask whether Marxism's failure to sketch a coherent, substantive, and persuasive approach to determination and to the linkage of structure and agency can be remedied. Even in Marx's historical writings, as Gareth Stedman Jones observes, where 'the economy is in the last instance determinant, and yet the superstructures possess a particular form of causal efficacy which cannot be simply reduced to the economic base . . . the precise structural mechanism connecting the two is always left unclear by Marx'. Although Engels in his own mature work took up this task, he did so either with a lack of clarity, or by leading Marxist theory into mechanical formulations of problems of determination.[67] In consequence, the project of a social theory for capitalist societies remained undeveloped, full of puzzles and false moves about base and superstructure, determination, theory and history, and the relationship to non-Marxist scholarship. Is it possible to do better?

---

[66] Thus, for example, far better than the incorporation of ideology and culture into the Marxist base, as proposed by Williams, is the proposal of Sewell that we accord ideology the constitutive status of a distinctive 'anonymous and collective, but transformable, structure'. By proceeding in this manner, Sewell observes in his critique of Theda Skocpol, it is also possible to identify the causal importance of various autonomously determined macrostructures to the history of particular times and places. In her own work on revolutions, he comments appreciatively, 'Skocpol manages to specify the distinct causal contributions of class, state, and international structures and processes to the outbreak and outcome of revolutions, while at the same time respecting the unique and unfolding concatenation of causal forces in each of the revolutions she studies'. William H. Sewell, Jr., 'Ideologies and Social Revolutions: Some Reflections on the French Case', *Journal of Modern History*, 57/1 (1985), 61, 58.

[67] Gareth Stedman Jones, 'Engels and the End of Classical German Philosophy', *New Left Review*, 79 (May–June 1973), 31, 32.

Two alternative approaches commend themselves. The first, of which there is more than one variant, tries to overcome these difficulties by eliminating the very tension inherent in holding structure and agency apart as analytically distinct. Influential efforts along these lines have recently been made by Anthony Giddens and Ernesto Laclau with Chantal Mouffe. Giddens, who works alongside rather than within Marxism (and who is impressed that Marx's structural account of modern capitalism 'remains the necessary core of any attempt to come to terms with the massive transformations that have swept through the world since the eighteenth century'[68]), treats structures and the activity of subjects as so tightly intertwined that both must be examined simultaneously to avoid the cost of an artificial duality. For their part, Laclau and Mouffe now reject Marxism because they think it inherently incapable of apprehending the open and contingent qualities of social relations and human agency. Their solution is a mirror image of orthodox Marxism. They lean very heavily (though not entirely) in the direction of agency, making what remains of structure epiphenomenal of the discursive practices of subjects and their articulations. A second approach, which I prefer, and which I explore in the remaining chapters by way of a consideration of cities and space, insists on the analytical distinctness of structure and agency in order to make possible an examination of their complex and contingent interconnections.[69]

Giddens's 'theory of structuration' has the principal aims of finding a way to avoid leaning too hard towards objectivism or subjectivism and of showing just how deeply social structures and human activity are intertwined. Social structure and agency cannot exist apart from each other. In that social structures enable human action and, at once, are the effects of

---

[68] Anthony Giddens, *A Contemporary Critique of Historical Materialism*. Berkeley, Calif.: University of California Press, 1981.

[69] This is an alternative to solutions that have the effect of 'withdrawing any autonomy or independence from one of them, if not from both'. Margaret S. Archer, *Culture and Agency: The Place of Culture in Social Theory*. Cambridge: Cambridge University Press, 1988, p. xiii. This book, which rejects the conflation of structures and subjects, has influenced my thinking a good deal. I return to it in Chapter 7.

such action, the usual structure–agency dichotomy is profoundly misleading. Social structure does not exist apart from practices, nor practices without an embeddedness in structured relations. Social structures contain rules, concepts, and norms that provide idioms of human action; in turn, because people have at least a working knowledge of social structures through their experience with the institutions of day-to-day life, their very action shapes and composes the social structure at the same moment that the actions of people in their routine conduct reproduce those structures.[70] According to Perry Anderson, this is less an attempt 'to strike a just balance between structure and agency in social explanation' than an effort to reject decisively the duality itself.[71]

Anderson upbraids Giddens for leaning too hard in the direction of agency and for understating the pressures of social determinations. In this I think he does not get it quite right. For what Giddens is after, and in this he succeeds brilliantly, is a probing of the mutually constitutive aspects of structure and agency. However, to the extent to which he goes further to imply a conflation of structure and agency within a theory of structuration, he makes it impossible to hold them apart, in the kind of semi-artificial tension that is needed to explicate the terms of their relations. If Giddens usefully and suggestively stresses the complexity of the engagement of structure and agency, a complete rejection of the dualism would not only understate, as Anderson insists, the ways in which structural relations 'are not simply rules and resources for actors to employ: they are also forces that shape the nature and aims of actions themselves', but would also diminish the underdetermined aspects of human agency.[72]

Laclau and Mouffe, who recoil in their *Hegemony and*

---

[70] Anthony Giddens, *New Rules of Sociological Method*. New York: Basic Books, 1976, and *Central Problems in Social Theory: Action, Structure, and Contradiction in Social Analysis*. Berkeley, Calif.: University of California Press, 1979. See also Giddens's essay, 'On the Theory of Structuration', in his collection, *Studies in Social and Political Theory*. New York: Basic Books, 1977.

[71] Perry Anderson, 'A Culture in Contraflow—I', *New Left Review*, 180 (Mar.–Apr. 1990), 54.

[72] Ibid.

Socialist Strategy from the essentialism they see as inherent in Marxism, push as hard as one reasonably can in the direction of agency, virtually to the point of arguing that the construction of identities and interests occurs within an unconstrained field of possibilities. They resolve the problems of Marxist social theory by leaving Marxism, and, indeed, causal social science, in favour of a view of the world as constituted by complex discourses.[73] As Isaac points out, their appreciation of matters of structure and constraint in their development of their key concepts of hegemony and articulation is more subtle than their harshest critics allow; none the less, they come very close to an 'indeterminist analysis of agency'. At a minimum, they are not clear about 'whether there are . . . real structural determinants operative in social life, determinants that both set limits and provide enablements to our social and political activity, including our discursive interventions'.[74] Most of the time Laclau and Mouffe come very close to saying that it is only our language and our theories that make the world; the kind of project with which Marxism is engaged in its social theory is therefore both beside the point and necessarily teleological and reductionist. In so doing, they give up on the very notion of grappling with the complex issues of determination and the mutual constitution of structure and agency.[75]

[73] Ernesto Laclau and Chantal Mouffe, *Hegemony and Socialist Strategy: Towards a Radical Democratic Politics*. London: Verso Books, 1985. Two of their harshest critics have been Ellen Meiksins Wood, in her *The Retreat from Class: A New 'True' Socialism*. London: Verso Books, 1986, a disappointing restatement of orthodoxy that demonstrates what Laclau and Mouffe see as so wrong in the Marxist tradition, and the more sophisticated, if also more nasty and *ad hominem*, review by Norman Geras, 'Post-Marxism?', *New Left Review*, 163 (May–June 1987).

[74] Isaac, *Power and Marxist Theory*, 217, 215.

[75] A penetrating critique of the linguistic approach is provided in the chapter on 'Structure and Subject' in Perry Anderson, *In the Tracks of Historical Materialism*. London: Verso Books, 1983. He points out the tension between the fact that linguistic structures, among human institutions, change very slowly and unconsciously, yet the subjects within language in post-structuralist analysis are accorded very great freedom. 'For utterance has no *material* constraint whatever: words are free in the double sense of the term. They cost

Thus, each in their own way, Giddens and Laclau and Mouffe put some of the most important issues of Marxist social theory aside, either by eliding them or by rejecting their significance. I suggest they cannot be sidestepped so easily— not because Marxism's particular solutions to structure–agency questions have been unusually compelling but for two other reasons. The conflation of structure and agency, or a decisive bias in either direction, makes it impossible to explore some of the most vexatious questions about the social world which require that they be kept in tension as analytically distinct; and, second, because Marxism, with all its shortcomings, compels our attention to the extent that we see capitalism as at least one of modernity's great macrostructures. In what follows I approach the significance and capacities of Marx's, and Marxism's, project of social theory with an agnostic and critical frame of mind. I examine the status of Marxism in relationship to theories of large-scale historical processes and the social-theoretical issues of structure, agency, and determination by bringing Marxist theory to bear on the city and by bringing urban-spatial issues to bear on Marxism.

In spite of the fact that, with the exception of Giddens, virtually all the key discussions of Marxist social theory written by scholars who are not urbanists are spaceless,[76] this

---

nothing to produce, and can be multiplied and manipulated at will, within the laws of meaning.' Thus the subjects within the structure of language can have little or no effect on it. Not so within economic or political structures, where the subjects have such collective character as classes, nations, or groups, rather than being individuals as in speech structures, and 'the agency of these subjects is capable of effecting profound transformations of these structures'. It is this distinction, he claims, that provides 'an insurmountable barrier to any transportation of linguistic models to historical processes of a wider sort'. The aggrandizing claims of language produce 'a contraction of language into itself', thus severing 'any possibility of truth as a correspondence of propositions to reality' (44–6).

[76] For reviews of Giddens's ideas on time–space, see Jens Christian Tonboe, 'On the Political Importance of Space: The Socio-Spatial Relations of Trade Unions, Gender, and the Decentralized Danish Welfare State', *Acta Sociologica*, 29/1 (1986); Alan Pred, 'Production, Family, and Free-Time Projects: A Time-Geographic Perspective on the Individual and Societal Change in Nineteenth Century U.S.

city-centred strategy is plausible for two reasons. First, the civilizational qualities of cities underscored by Mumford and the deeply intertwined history of capitalism and cities since the sixteenth century make it reasonable to wager that the history of urban development constitutes something of a critical case for Marxism, and its grand reach. Second, the complex character of city space as a combination of landscape, areal diversity, built-environment, and social geography invites us to explore how specific spaces have been shaped and, in turn, how their existence provides resources for, and restrictions on, human activity. More precisely, we can ask how well Marxism accounts for key features of urban history and class formation, and how an elucidation of these phenomena sheds light on the adequacy of the theory itself. I propose to begin this examination with the most important urban studies within Marxism since the 1960s.

Cities', *Journal of Historical Geography*, 7 (Jan. 1981); Nicky Gregson, 'On Duality and Dualism: The Case of Structuration and Time Geography', *Progress in Human Geography*, 10 (June 1986); and Alex Callinicos, 'Anthony Giddens: A Contemporary Critique', *Theory and Society*, 14 (Mar. 1985).

3 Towards a Respatialized Marxism: Lefebvre, Harvey, and Castells

WITH our detour at an end, let us cross the threshold of the city in the company of Henri Lefebvre, David Harvey, and Manuel Castells, the three most influential recent students of Marxism and the city.[1] Through the study of the city, each has introduced space into the core of one or more of Marxism's projects. By examining their work, it is possible to assess the current status of the respatialized Marxism they have tried to fashion. This post-1960s Marxism of the city has shown how Marxist theory can powerfully illuminate things urban, and also how an explicitly urban focus can strengthen Marxism as social and empirical theory. But the fitful attention urbanists have paid to different aspects of Marxist theory has produced a lumpy legacy.

The work accomplished in the past quarter-century has treated Marx's project of understanding epochal change mainly as background to more current events. By contrast, it has successfully elaborated and deepened his project of the analysis of capitalism as an economic system, but, in spite of much effort, it has contributed only unsteadily to his project of a social theory for capitalist societies. The limitations of Marxist urban studies to date have been due principally to a certain narrowness of subject-matter, a lack of engagement with history, and a restrictive treatment of the issues central to, but

[1] The discussion in this chapter of attempts to link Marxism and the city in the 1970s and 1980s is not a comprehensive review. I am silent about much of the great outpouring of work in this vein, principally by sociologists, geographers, and planners. The main features of this intellectual landscape are my concern here, less so its nuanced contours. To discern these, the best guides are the pages of three young journals: *Antipode*, the *International Journal of Urban and Regional Research*, and *Society and Space*.

difficult for, Marxist social theory: base and superstructure, structure and agency, and causal determination.

A second wave of books by Harvey and Castells in the early 1980s tackled just these topics, but in this work the interlacement of Marxism with the city reached something of an impasse. Harvey tried to bypass the obstacles by staying wholly within the Marxist maze, Castells by constructing new exits. Neither, I argue, discovered a persuasive solution. After developing this appraisal later in this chapter, I will counsel, in the next, that we can best deal with this situation by leaving, and then re-entering, the city by a road Marxism could have taken but did not—blazed not by Lefebvre, Harvey, or Castells, but by the young Friedrich Engels. As we turn into the city now, however, in our first reconnoitre, Lefebvre must be placed at the head of the queue, because it was he who first showed Marxism the way back to the city.

I

In the early 1970s, when David Harvey and Manuel Castells emerged as the two most influential urbanists seeking to return Marxism to urban concerns, they focused inescapably on Lefebvre's writings. At the time, only he had broken the silence in Marxism about the city. Thus, when Harvey raised the question in the summary chapter of *Social Justice and the City*, 'What insights and revelations do we gain through the use of Marx's method in the investigation of urban phenomena?', he opened his response by observing that 'The only other work I can call upon is that of Henri Lefebvre'. Harvey had just made the intellectually audacious move of leaving behind the comfortable habitat of mainstream geography to explore whether and how Marxist theory might provide a framework within which to connect the analysis of social processes and spatial forms. With the exception of Lefebvre's work (especially his 1970 volume, *La Révolution urbaine*, which utilized Marxism to analyse post-war urbanism, and *La Pensée marxiste et la ville*, published in 1972), Harvey could find no other models or guides within Marxism. Likewise, Castells oriented the theoretical development of *La Question urbaine* to 'the urbanistic thinking of one of the greatest theoreticians of contemporary Marxism, Henri Lefebvre', whose work 'is no doubt the profoundest intellectual effort that has been made towards understanding the urban problems *of the present day*'.[2]

Lefebvre's growing interest in the city coincided with his break with the French Communist Party in the late 1950s and early 1960s, and his search for a way to explain the non-fulfilment of Marx's prediction of the ultimate capitalist crisis.[3] 'Marxism', he told an interviewer in 1987,

---

[2] Harvey wrote, 'There are parallels between his concerns and mine and there are similarities in content (which is reassuring) and some differences in interpretation and emphasis (which is challenging). Lefebvre's work is more general than my own but it is also incomplete in certain important respects. Nevertheless, I feel more confident in appealing to [it].' David Harvey, *Social Justice and the City*. London: Edward Arnold, 1973, 302–3. Manuel Castells, *The Urban Question: A Marxist Approach*. London: Edward Arnold, 1977 (trans. by Alan Sheridan of *La Question urbaine*. Paris: Maspero, 1972), 86–7. Henri Lefebvre, *Le Droit à la ville*. Paris: Anthropos, 1968; *Du rural et de l'urbain*. Paris: Anthropos, 1970; *La Révolution urbaine*. Paris: Gallimard, 1970; *La Pensée marxiste et la ville*. Paris: Casterman, 1972. See also his 'Reflections on the Politics of Space', *Antipode*, 8 (May 1976), and Gallia Burgel *et al.*, 'An Interview with Henri Lefebvre', *Society and Space*, 5 (Mar. 1987). In my discussion of Lefebvre, I treat this corpus as a unity at the price of moving too rapidly over differences in these texts and losing much of the nuance in the argument. I think this is a justifiable approach because, as will be apparent quite soon, I think Lefebvre should be quickly left to his place of honour, more as a pioneer who raised and pursued long-dormant questions than as an analyst who succeeded in putting answers to them.

Lefebvre's work has secured little notice in the Anglo-American world. Few of his texts have been translated into English, in part because his work is in many respects an immanent critique of French society (new forms of planning, the fascination with technology for its own sake, the rigidities of the PCF) and of French intellectual currents (especially the scientific Marxism of the Althusserian structuralists).

[3] Lefebvre was arguably the most important philosopher–theorist in the post-war PCF. Until his formal break with the Party, his relationship with its political leadership was strained. In 1949, he was castigated for comparing Marxism to sociology. After 1956, he was a member of the editorial group of *Arguments*, a dissident journal.

is, above all, a method of analysing social practices; it is not a series of assumptions, postulates, or dogmatic propositions ... By 1960, something extraordinary happened which I wanted to explain as a Marxist. The Revolution had failed; it had not taken place. There had been two world wars. What had occurred in Russia had given rise to Stalinism ... There was the enormous massacre of the Second World War, and, with the Liberation, one expected a major event and a renewal; but that did not happen either. So, by 1960, there was an emptiness. The Reconstruction was complete, so what filled the gap?[4]

Marx, he argued, failed to anticipate the triumph of science and the technological revolution, and Marxists have taken these into account insufficiently. This profound change, characterized by the rise of a new technocratic class, the expansion of the scale of the market to encompass the whole world, and new discoveries like the mathematical theory of information of the 1950s, superseded traditional capitalism; it was 'a replacement for the unfinished social and political revolution'.[5] The effects of the explosion of knowledge and its impact on production and human relations have included the refashioning of space, the autonomous assertion of the urban, and the planned development of cities as new kinds of fields of invention, production, and play. This basic change has invalidated the traditional Marxist view of how human liberation might occur, but it did not negate either the idea or the possibility of such liberation. A decisive shift had occurred. The vision of a non-exploitative society must now focus on the city and on urban relationships, not, as before, principally on the ownership or organization of industrial production.

Lefebvre turned to urban research in part as an aspect of his departure from orthodox Marxism, and in part as a result of his observations, in the early 1960s, of a new, and, he thought, potentially felicitous, merging of spatial planning and a liberatory praxis in the construction of the new town of Lacq-

---

He was expelled after the 1958 publication of *Problèmes actuels du marxisme* (Paris: PUF, 1958), accused of factionalism.

[4] Burgel *et al.*, 'An Interview with Henri Lefebvre, 29.

[5] Ibid.

Mourenx in the Atlantic Pyrenees, and in the work of DATAR (Délégation à l'Aménagement du Territoire et à l'Action Régionale). 'After all,' he reflected some two decades later, 'the creation of new towns and the redevelopment of existing ones was quite a new approach compared with the classic descriptions of urban phenomena. However, my initiation was neither from the point of view of philosophy, nor sociology, though these were present implicitly, nor was it historical or geographical. Rather, it was the emergence of a new social and political practice.'[6]

Lefebvre's work on the city was original and bold. He sought to establish the emergence of a new, post-industrial, urban stage in human history; and within this framework, he tried to make sense of all the basic questions about differentiation, social cohesion, and urban meaning that had been so important to late nineteenth- and early twentieth-century students of the city. In this quest, he developed a theory of space, and he introduced into urban discourse the analysis of the state, and the role of the political in shaping people's dispositions about the city.

Lefebvre's scheme hinged on a separation of the city and urbanism as theoretical and empirical constructs. The city is an arrangement of objects in space; urbanism a way of life. In our times, Lefebvre claimed, urbanism has transcended the city to pattern daily existence across the once-meaningful urban–suburban–rural divides. Moreover, urbanism has spread over much of the globe to produce ever more homogeneous aspirations and styles of living. Although Lefebvre claimed that 'there is not a strict correspondence between modes of production and the spaces they constitute', he argued none the less that 'each epoch produces its own space'. For the period from the 1960s on, a new kind of space—joined to a new kind of urbanism—had been created: 'it was at a world-scale, based on aeroplanes, motorways, suburbs, peripheries, the destruction of historic centres and conurbations.'[7]

This portrait of the recent past is part of a periodicity of cities developed by Lefebvre. Within this schematic, he explained the disappearance of the city from Marxism as an

[6] Ibid., 28.   [7] Ibid., 31.

accurate reflection of the place the city actually occupied within industrial capitalism. In the pre-industrial, agrarian phase of human history, according to Lefebvre, the city was removed from the core of production. Towns performed only a superstructural role *vis-à-vis* the mode of production, that of the political city aptly characterized by Max Weber's treatment of the city in the Occident. The political city was overtaken by the mercantile city. Lefebvre interpreted this transformation as a change within cities rather than as a change in their contextual environment. The city maintained its medieval political functions, but added a trading function in order to serve its growing population base.

A critical transformation occurred with the shift from the mercantile to the industrial city. Now, rather than the city being a generative force for change, industrializing factors exogenous to cities reshaped their size, form, and function. The city became a wholly dependent entity. Encapsulated by the logic of capitalist accumulation, the city ceased to be a worthy object of independent study. From this perspective, Marx was wholly correct in treating the city only in so far as it was a marker of the division of labour.

But now, in the twentieth century, the urban moment has come, or, at least, has begun. Industrial capitalist society has been transcended, in dialectical fashion, by urban society. Industrialization no longer produces urbanization as its servant; just the reverse. We are living through the moment of transition, when the capitalism of which Marx wrote in *Capital* is becoming a historical artefact. The driving forces of the new order are urban, and these are liberating humankind from capitalism's constraints. In Marxist economic terms, the secondary circuit of capital, concerned not with the production of surplus value in industrial activity as is the first, but with its creation through finance and speculation, has become dominant.

The urban age promises the possibility of a new humanism. Urbanism, now transcending the city, reorganizes social relations in a revolutionary way. Initially, the city is a key actor, for by concentrating human relations in non-repressive ways it frees the possibility of self-organization. In this model, working-class agency is no longer required, for the class structure loses its traditional specificity. Capitalism is ending, but not in the way Marx anticipated.

This consideration of the urban moment is a combination of description and prescription. Spatial relations provide a field of praxis. Space is not just a built-environment but a force of production and an object of consumption. It is also an object of political struggle, because space is an instrument of control by the state. Within industrial capitalism, space divided and fragmented, and became disarticulated from society and its needs. The urban moment constitutes an opportunity to achieve a new phase in human history by the reappropriation of the 'right' to use space to serve human purposes and to reassert the meaning and dignity of everyday life far more in harmony with nature than industrial capitalism could permit.

This is a deliberately utopian vision, and a strategic intervention. Traditional notions of socialist revolution concentrating on the ownership of the means of production cannot produce liberation in the new age of urbanism. What is required instead is a radical shift in focus to the way in which human life is organized and lived in social space.

Though he provided a touchstone for the early, influential work of Harvey and Castells, each responded to Lefebvre in a different way.[8] Harvey sought to show that Lefebvre was premature in his jettisoning of capitalism as the frame for his urban inquiries, and that he was mistaken in treating cities as wholly dependent entities within the capitalist mode of production. Rather, they are essential to capitalist accumulation and integral to it: they are constitutive elements of the capitalist base. Castells, by contrast, broadly accepted Lefebvre's historical chronology, the limited place of the city

---

[8] The best sympathetic interpretation of Lefebvre's work on space and the city can be found in Mark Gottdiener, *The Social Production of Urban Space*. Austin, Tex.: University of Texas Press, 1985, esp. ch. 4. He argues that many of the criticisms of Castells and Harvey were based on the writings of Lefebvre available in the early 1970s, and that he overcame many of their objections in his volume, *La Production de l'espace*. Paris: Anthropos, 1974, whose more mature treatment of space did not supplant the class struggles of traditional Marxism, but complemented them with a strategy of spatial liberation.

in past capitalist development, and the importance of the urban as a distinctive site of conflict and change. However, he thought Lefebvre's 'urban' bordered on a kind of spatial fetishism and lacked a theoretical specificity within the framework of Marxism, which he sought to provide. In so doing, Castells argued that the city constitutes a distinctive domain of consumption, reproduction, and collective action.

Harvey argued that the hypothesis that urban society now dominates industrial capitalism, and that there has been a massive, even revolutionary, shift in social organization as a consequence, rests more on dialectical metaphysics than on empirical work. Lefebvre's claim that 'contradictions between urbanism as a structure in the process of transformation and the internal dynamic of the older industrial society are usually resolved in favour of the former' is not realistic, for 'in certain important and crucial respects industrial society and the structures which comprise it continue to dominate urbanism'. Harvey rests this claim on three bases: first, the created space of cities does not spring forth from the interior logic of the urban; rather, 'It is industrial capitalism that is creating space for us—hence the frequently expressed sense of alienation with respect to created space'. Second, urbanization continues to proceed within the requirements of the reproduction of capital for the creation of needs and the creation of effective demand. 'Urbanization provides the opportunity for industrial capital to dispose of the products it creates. In this sense the urbanization process is still being propelled by the requirements of industrial capitalism.' Third, 'the production, appropriation, and circulation of surplus value have not become subordinated to the internal dynamic of urbanism, but continue to be regulated by conditions derived from industrial society'. The second circuit of capital has not replaced the first. So, he concludes,

Where does this leave us with respect to Lefebvre's thesis? To say that the thesis is not true at this juncture of history is not to say that it is not in the process of becoming true or that it cannot become true in the future. The evidence strongly suggests the forces of urbanization are emerging strongly and moving to dominate the centre stage of world history ... Lefebvre is describing some dominant trends. Lefebvre can also be interpreted as presenting a hypothesis concerning the possibilities immanent in the present. Many hopeful and utopian things have been written about the city throughout its history. We now have the opportunity to live many of these things provided we can seize upon the present possibilities. We have the opportunity to create space, to harness creatively the forces making for urban differentiation. But in order to seize these opportunities we have to confront the forces that create cities as alien environments, that push urbanization in directions alien to our individual or collective purpose.

But, Harvey adds, 'To confront these forces, we must understand them.' To that task, he has devoted the past two decades.[9]

Castells tackled Lefebvre's work on cities and space from a different, complementary, but even more basic angle. He upbraided Lefebvre for creating an independent theory of cities and space—'the crisis of urban reality is the most important, more central than any other'—thus forgetting that 'there is no theory of space that is not an integral part of a general social theory'. With this lapse, Castells argues, Lefebvre left behind the social process–social relationships camp to which Marxism belongs to join the differentiation perspective of mainstream urban sociology as exemplified by the Chicago School. The 'urban' for Lefebvre is 'nothing more than emancipated creative spontaneity' produced 'not by space or by time, but by a form which, being neither object nor subject, is defined above all by the dialectic of centrality, or of its negation (segregation, dispersal, periphery). What we have here is something very close to Wirth's thesis concerning the way social relations are produced.'[10]

The result, Castells insists from the perspective of an Althusserian Marxism, is a metaphysical and ideological analysis that accords complete spontaneity to human action in creating urban forms, and by giving central causal power to the forms thus created. Together with the supercession of class conflict, these moves by Lefebvre have left him with a utopia bereft of a strategy to achieve it.

There is a sense in which these critiques of Harvey and

Castells talk past Lefebvre. They were concerned with how to utilize Marxism, in quite orthodox ways, to generate new theoretical perspectives on the city. Lefebvre, however, was concerned more with creating an animating utopia as a goad to political practice. His work both anticipated, and was embedded in, the Marxist humanism of the New Left.

Nevertheless, Harvey and Castells were both on the mark. Lefebvre's chronology of urban development was merely asserted, and in important respects, as we shall see in Chapter 5, not very well elaborated. It was certainly not based on careful empirical scholarship. He accepted (as did Harvey and Castells) the disappearance of the city as both subject and object from Marxism during the period of industrial capitalism. The realization of urban possibilities seemed almost entirely a matter of voluntary praxis; causal constraints were noted, but forgotten in the interest of exhortation. In all, Lefebvre (re-)created an idolatry of the city by his combination of an asserted historical progression and his assertion that urbanization and its attendant spatial relations together provide the new master processes of modernity.

Lefebvre may have shown Marxism the way back to the city, but having reached its gates, he entered by bidding Marxism's project of social theory farewell. Lefebvre's work illustrates the pitfalls of staying entirely on the 'critical' side of Gouldner's dichotomy. Like Lukács, Lefebvre apprehended the totality of society through a single integrating mechanism—in his case, that of urban spatial relations that encompass all of everyday life:

The urban . . . is perhaps a form, that of the encounters and gathering of *all* the elements of the social life, from the fruits of the earth . . . to the symbols and so-called cultural works . . . There is no urban reality without a centre; commercial, symbolic, of information, of decision, etc. In this form the urban has a name: it is simultaneity.[11]

---

[11] Lefebvre, *Le Droit à la ville*, 206; translation from Mario Rui Martins, 'The Theory of Social Space in the Work of Henri Lefebvre', in Ray Forrest, Jeff Henderson, and Peter Williams (eds.), *Urban Political Economy and Social Theory: Critical Essays in Urban Studies*. Aldershot: Gower Books, 1982, 170–1.

By developing a terminology and analysis of this simultaneity, together with his rejection of the continuing relevance of capitalist accumulation as the centrepiece of modernity, Lefebvre presents a Marxism bereft of the central challenges of structure and agency. Indeed, this tendency in Lefebvre's work accentuated over time, so that his writings of the late 1970s and early 1980s turned increasingly phenomenological.[12]

According to the very logic of Lefebvre's schematic history of the city, Marxism can take us up to the urban moment, not into it. In the urban period, balanced between the atomization of space—when 'social space became a *collection of ghettos* . . . of the élite, of the bourgeoisie, of the intellectuals, or the immigrant workers, etc . . . [that] are not juxtaposed . . . [but] hierarchical, spatially representing the economic and social hierarchy, dominant and subordinated sectors'[13]—and the new possibilities of a liberatory practice in which space is reappropriated for play and human self-actualization, traditional Marxism no longer has anything to say. By contrast, Harvey and Castells carried Marxist theory with them as they passed the portals of the city. How did they, and Marxism, fare in this reunion?

It is no exaggeration to say that the double critique of Harvey and Castells fundamentally shaped the new discourse

[12] Martins and Gottdiener have both argued that Castells's critique of Lefebvre did not (quite obviously) take his post-1972 writings into account, and that these are more refined and developed both in their presentation of his macroscopic chronology, culminating in the urban period, and in the analysis of capitalist space as increasingly homogeneous, fragmented, and hierarchical. Martins, 'The Theory of Social Space'; Gottdiener, *The Social Production of Urban Space*, ch. 4. On the contrary, I think Lefebvre's departure from the interesting terrain of Marxism has become more pronounced in his turn to phenomenology, and his growing interest in 'mental space'. On the other hand, there are important and suggestive discussions in the later Lefebvre on the role of the state in integrating the increasingly fragmented and 'ghettoized' spaces of the late 20th-century city. Interestingly, this theme of the role of the state as a force for spatial integration recurs in Castells.

[13] Lefebvre, *De l'état*. Paris: Union Générales des Editions, 1978, 309–10; trans. in Martins, 'The Theory of Social Space', 179.

of the city within Marxism.[14] The main elements of the new Marxist work of the 1970s and 1980s have been, first, a concern to understand the city as a *capitalist* city, whose main contours have been determined by large-scale economic forces dictated by the rhythms of capital accumulation, investment strategies, and the provision of a supply of labour, and, second, the effort to specify the character and emancipatory possibilities of urban social movements, either as supplements to, or as replacements for, such traditional *loci* of working-class insurgency as trade unions and political parties.[15]

II

In 1969, when he was a young English expatriate assistant professor of geography at Johns Hopkins University, David Harvey published a massive and influential methodological treatise, *Explanation in Geography*. In that book's concluding comment, he tried to set the agenda for the coming decade, as a move away from issues of technique and the methodological issues he had just been treating towards what he called both a philosophy and a theory of geography. Harvey wrote:

It should be clear, therefore, that an adequate methodology provides a *necessary* condition for the solution of geographical problems; philosophy provides the *sufficient* condition. Philosophy provides the

[14] Not everyone interested in critical work on the city welcomed these new departures or judged their influence positively. The most vituperative criticism came from Ruth Glass: 'For the past few years, an intinerant band of Castells' disciples, often accompanied by the master himself, have been prominent in international and north American sociological conferences. The literature of and around Castells' *œuvre* has grown in bulk; a cult has developed; and some obtuse references to it have become obligatory in trendy sociological circles . . . This awful verbal pollution spreads: it saps sense and energy, (in Castells' code it is called ideological purity). In the products of that language shoddiness is built in.' Ruth Glass, 'Verbal Pollution', *New Society*, 29 Sept. 1977, 667–8. This was verbal overkill. Many of Glass's substantive criticisms have since been acknowledged by Castells, but they were overstated, and she was certainly wrong to argue in this review that his work represented nothing new.

[15] The best short review of this literature is Sharon Zukin, 'A Decade of the New Urban Sociology', *Theory and Society*, 9 (1980).

steering mechanism, methodology provides the power to move us closer to our destination. Without methodology we will lie becalmed, without philosophy we may circle aimlessly without direction. I have mainly been concerned with the nature of the power devices which are available to us. But I would like to close by returning to the interface between methodology and philosophy . . .

Without theory we cannot hope for controlled, consistent, and rational, explanation of events. Without theory we can scarcely claim to know our own identity. It seems to me, therefore, that theory construction on a broad and imaginative scale must be our first priority in the coming decade. It will take courage and ingenuity to face up to this task. But I feel confident that it is not beyond the wit and intelligence of the current generation of geographers. Perhaps the slogan we should pin up on our study walls for the 1970s ought to read: 'By our theories you shall know us.'[16]

In the ensuing four years, Harvey found such a theory, Marxism, and an object of analysis for this theory within geography, the city.

He signified this discovery and this focus in his brilliant collection, *Social Justice and the City*. The book is divided between essays Harvey calls liberal formulations, concerned with such staples of geography as spatial differentiation and distributions of populations and activities in space, and those he calls socialist formulations, rather more concerned with connections between spatial phenomena and modes of production. In making this shift, Harvey sought to reject the narrow morphological character of his discipline, its radical separation of fact and value, its obsession with problems of data and measurement, and its fragmentary qualities. Like Castells's work, which I discuss below, Harvey's book had an immediate and stunning effect on urban studies. With great rigour, it broadened the domain of geography, redefined the objects of urban analysis, and opened up a host of new questions. *Social Justice and the City*, in short, was a foundational text.[17]

[16] David Harvey, *Explanation in Geography*. Baltimore: Johns Hopkins University Press, 1979, 482, 486.

[17] I had a small role to play in its US publication, having served as an anonymous reader for Johns Hopkins University Press. I remember reading this dense and difficult manuscript in just two very long sessions, because I literally could not put it down, so profound and basic did it seem.

Above all, the book, in both its liberal and socialist parts, sought to demonstrate how it was possible to bring social processes and spatial forms together both analytically and as a guide to action, and to show their interpenetration. In this volume, spatial forms incorporate social processes; and all social processes are inherently spatial. Joining both sections are four key themes: the nature of theory (in which Harvey seeks to break what he sees as an artificial separation between methodology and philosophy, and in which he tries to make the reader self-conscious about the act and consequences of categorization); the nature of space (in which he replaces the familiar question, 'what is space?', with the question, 'how is it that different human practices create and make use of distinctive conceptualizations of space?'); the nature of social justice (which he moved from 'a predisposition to regard social justice as a matter of eternal justice and morality' to regard it as 'something contingent upon the social processes operating in society as a whole'); and the nature of urbanism (seen not as a thing in itself, but as providing a line of sight into society). He turned to Marxism to deal with these issues, which span the book's 'liberal' and 'socialist' moments, not on a priori grounds, but because it permitted these tasks to be accomplished.[18]

The way in which Harvey proceeded, we have seen, was inspired by Lefebvre yet it rejected completely the independent determinative centrality Lefebvre had attributed to spatial relations. For Harvey, space is not an ontological category as such, but a social dimension that both shapes and is shaped by human agency: 'Spatial forms are ... seen not as inanimate objects within which the social process unfolds, but as things which "contain" social processes in the same manner that social processes *are* spatial.'[19]

The various essays in *Social Justice and the City* still repay careful reading; in the first part, for their Rawlsian perspective on urban spatial relations with regard to urban planning and income distribution (as in his discussion of 'territorial justice', and the balance between centralized and decentralized gover-

---

[18] Harvey, *Social Justice and the City*, 10–17.
[19] Ibid., 10–11.

nance), and, in the second part, for their specification of a Marxist research agenda on the city concerned with reinterpreting the sweep of urban history in terms of the integration of the economy and the circulation of surplus in different modes of production. The wonderful sensibilities about space and meaning systems that Harvey exhibited in the early 'liberal' formulations have continued to animate his work since his turn to Marxism. These include a concern with the texture of the relationship between individuals, groups, and their social space, the connections between different kinds of human activities and their distinctive spaces, architecture and urban landscape as markers of the social order, the work–home linkage, the place of functionalism in urban analysis, and the limits on the capacity of the state in a market society.[20]

The second half of *Social Justice and the City* was an early, and in some respects a very preliminary and schematic attempt, lurching at times between the scientific and critical Marxist camps. This Marxist section includes a paper that demonstrates how ghetto housing for American blacks is underpinned by a 'blameless' entrepreneurial set of initiatives, and, an important paper on the theory of urban land use, focusing on the 'catalytic moment' of collision between the use and exchange values of land. This powerfully utilizes long-neglected discussion in Marx about rent and the micro-economics of land and space which show how rent is a rationing device for land as a permanent and immovable commodity required by all, open to multiple uses and meanings, which changes hands infrequently but decisively. It also includes a sweeping macroscopic overview of urban development throughout human history by contrasting different mechanisms of generating and deploying the social surplus. Here, the city is conceptualized historically as 'a pivot around which a given mode of production is organized, as a centre of revolution against the established order, and as a centre of power and privilege (to be revolted against)'. Cities are formed 'through the geographic concentration of social surplus product, which the mode of economic integration must therefore be capable of producing and concentrating'. Utilizing Karl Polanyi's cat-

---

[20] Ibid., chs. 1–3.

egories of economic co-ordinating mechanisms—reciprocity, redistribution, and market exchange—together with Marx's concept of the mode of production, Harvey presents the city as contained within a field of relations between the social surplus, the dominant mode of economic organization, and the spatial organization of society. Within capitalism, the city is both a *locus* and a stabilizer of accumulation and its contradictions.[21]

Social Justice and the City shines with insights and challenges to research. But above all, these essays remain important as markers in the rediscovery of the city for Marxism, and Marxism for the city. In the subsequent two decades, Harvey has worked carefully, steadily, but also selectively, through the research agenda of *Social Justice and the City*. Throughout, his central goal has been very clear: to expand and extend Marx's work on capitalist accumulation to give it an explicit spatial dimension.

While criticizing academics who inhabit the diverse worlds of ecology, Weberian analysis, neo-classical economics, *and* Marxism for their intellectual fragmentation and for their failure to take account of each other and their themes, Harvey has been insistent throughout about the status of Marxism as the master theoretical analysis of modernity because of the privileged causal place of capitalism. Reflecting on academic fragmentation, Harvey asks, 'Does this mean we have to abandon Marx for some eclectic mix of theoretical perspectives? Not at all. If capitalism persists as the dominant mode of production, then it is with the analysis of that mode of production that we have to start.'[22]

Harvey did so most fully in *The Limits to Capital*.[23] In the concluding pages of *Social Justice and the City*, Harvey had judged his preliminary foray into the analysis of cities in terms of the circulation of surplus value to have been inadequate:

[21] Ibid., 203, 216.
[22] David Harvey, *The Urbanization of Capital: Studies in the History and Theory of Capitalist Urbanization*. Baltimore: Johns Hopkins University Press, 1985, 263–4.
[23] David Harvey, *The Limits to Capital*. Chicago: University of Chicago Press, 1982.

To understand the circulation of surplus value is in fact to understand the way in which society works. Unfortunately, we do not possess the kind of insight into the structure of this circulation to make definitive statements about it . . . It would require a work of at least the magnitude and insight of Marx's *Capital* to unravel all of the complexities.[24]

The Limits to Capital was an attempt to supply this missing text. Here, his main aim was to reconstruct Marx with space built in. His argument has the following elements: the various units of Marx's logical analysis of the capitalist economy— labour, capital, and money—all move in and through space. The spatial organization of capitalism is not merely a reflection of capital accumulation (think of the variations in the organization of space and cities from place to place and from time to time). 'Location is socially produced. The production of spatial configurations can then be treated as an "active moment" within the overall temporal dynamics of accumulation and social reproduction.'[25] This task requires not only a review of all the main elements of Marxist economics, but the highlighting and development of themes that only play a secondary and tertiary role for Marx: issues of finance capital and rent in particular.

The Limits to Capital makes important contributions to Marxism and the study of cities in a number of respects by developing the suggestive but underdeveloped passages in *Capital* that deal with rent, and by directly introducing spatial elements into the analysis of the process of capital accumulation. By making these moves, *The Limits to Capital* makes stronger Marx's second project of the analysis of capital accumulation.

The circulation of capital through the use of land, which Harvey sees as performing an important co-ordinating function for capitalism, helps account for the remarkable historical geography of capitalist cities: 'Factories and fields, schools, churches, shopping centres and parks, roads and railways litter a landscape that has been indelibly and irreversibly carved out according to the dictates of capitalism.' The theoretical

---

[24] Harvey, *Social Justice and the City*, 312.
[25] Harvey, *Limits to Capital*, 374.

concept through which Marxist political economy can comprehend this spatial organization is rent.[26]

Capital ends with a fragment on 'Classes'. At the conclusion of three volumes dealing with the relationship between two social classes, capital and labour, Marx surprisingly wrote that capitalism is characterized by 'three classes—wage labourers, industrial capitalists, and landowners constituting together, and in their mutual opposition, the framework of modern society'. The latter class earns ground rent, which Marx here describes as that 'form in which property in land . . . produces value'.[27] Questions of land and rent, of course, are central to patterns of urban development, since cities represent one kind of location for investments of capital that simultaneously modify the ownership and the usage of land and in so doing alter the configuration of urban space.

The core of Harvey's contribution to the theory of rent is to 'define a coherent theory of ground rent within the framework of value theory itself', and in this way to transcend the traditional treatment of rent in classical political economy as a matter of distribution rather than production. 'But distribution relations', he writes suggestively,

can . . . occupy strategic co-ordinating roles within the capitalist mode of production. The circulation of interest-bearing capital does not produce value directly but it helps to co-ordinate the production of surplus value (replete, of course, with all of its contradictions). Could it be, then, that the circulation of capital in search of rent

[26] Ibid., 373. Harvey's work is one of the very few attempts to develop the concept of rent within the framework of Marxist political economy. The best technical, critical assessment of Harvey's treatment of rent is Steven Katz, 'Towards a Sociological Definition of Rent: Notes on David Harvey's *The Limits to Capital*', *Antipode*, 18 (Apr. 1986). Katz's central complaint is that Harvey restricts his definition of rent to 'a system of intracapitalist coordination and competition. Harvey both downplays, and is unable to integrate, the historical reality of worker struggle into the logic of capitalist rent.' Katz calls for 'not only the reproduction of historical and sociological analysis into political economy, but a reconceptualization of both rent and space as the objects and locations of cross-class struggle' (65–6).

[27] Karl Marx, *Capital* (3 vols.). London: Penguin Books, 1981, iii. 1023.

performs an analogous co-ordinating role? ... a positive answer to this question lies deeply buried within Marx's writings, that the 'proper' circulation of capital through the use of land and therefore the whole process of fashioning an 'appropriate' spatial organization of activities (replete with contradictions) is keyed to the functioning of land markets, which in turn rest upon the capacity to appropriate rent.[28]

In his analysis of 'the production of spatial configurations', Harvey takes as his centrepiece the idea that as capitalism has developed the pace of the circulation of capital has increased in extraordinary ways, facilitated by massive and accelerating shifts in transportation and communications technologies. This acceleration, Harvey acutely observes, has occurred not only in time but through space; and, by the late nineteenth century, by means of increasingly important ways through urban space. It is the built-form of the city—the created space of the capitalist city—that makes the acceleration of capital possible, and that provides capitalism with such other functional requisites as a place to invest surplus capital and a *locus* for the reproduction of the labour force. Such investment opportunities present capital with a 'spatial fix' to deal with crises of cycles, surplus, and underinvestment.

Capitalist production is inherently anarchic. The collective interest of capitalists lies in a balance between production and consumption, but the rationality of capitalist competition and technological development makes such a balanced expansion of the economy almost impossible to achieve. The result is crises of overproduction. These may be displaced in the first instance by the artful use of the credit system, but only for a time. There may yet be a further displacement—this is Harvey's signal contribution to Marxist accumulation theory— through the manipulation of geography and space: the spatial fixes of imperialism and the reorganization of the built-environment within the core capitalist countries.[29]

[28] Harvey, *Limits to Capital*, 333, 331. He adds, 'Like interest bearing capital, rental appropriation has both positive and negative roles to play in relation to accumulation. Its co-ordinating functions are bought at the cost of permitting insane forms of land speculation' (331).

[29] The sequence of 'fixes' for capitalism in Harvey's work is more

The built-environment itself is thus necessary to capitalism and to its accelerated development. At times, however, it may also become an impediment, because a built-environment is fixed; it is 'a vast humanly created resource system, comprising use values embedded in the physical landscape, which can be utilized for production, exchange and consumption'. As such, it can never change as fast as the tempo of economic development demands. One result is the accelerated destruction and rebuilding of the built-form of the capitalist city in a process analogous to Schumpeter's notion of creative destruction. The city is forever being developed and redeveloped at quickening rates to keep up with the new tempo and rhythms of accumulation. This is neither an abstraction, as any resident of a major city knows first-hand, nor is it only a current event, as the massive rebuilding of nineteenth-century Paris and Vienna attests.[30]

To further this perspective, Harvey developed in very fecund detail a Marxist theory of finance capital and rent, as well as, less successfully, a functionalist account of the state, in order to understand how through a mix of markets and steered co-ordination the reorganization of the built-form constantly recurs. These discussions in *The Limits to Capital* are very

---

asserted than demonstrated. Nevertheless, it is usefully suggestive in the ways in which it makes geography and space on different scales, from the urban to the global, integral to Marxism's analysis of capital accumulation. For a discussion of these issues, see Gerry Kearns, 'Making Space for Marx', *Journal of Historical Geography*, 10 (Oct. 1984).

[30] Harvey, *Limits to Capital*, 233. In a review of *La Question urbaine*, Stephen Elkin upbraided Castells for a lack of specificity regarding the claim that 'urban arrangements are so fundamental to accumulation, consumption and reproduction of the social order that any breakdown in them would in fact constitute a crisis for the larger political economy. The difficulty in judging the claim is precisely the difficulty of knowing in what sense urban units contribute to the functions enumerated. If we knew how the parts, including the urban parts, fit together then we might well conclude with Castells that the "slack" couldn't be taken up by other arrangements.' It is the great merit of Harvey's work on space and accumulation that he tries to provide just such a missing specification. Stephen L. Elkin, 'Castells, Marxism, and the New Urban Politics', unpublished MS, 1979.

important because they leap well beyond the various locational analyses of mainstream geography and neo-classical economics, even as Harvey was able to incorporate them in his illuminating discussions of location, forms of rent, distributional struggles between capitalists and landlords, land markets, transportation, the mobility of capital, spatial infrastructure, and uneven urban development.[31]

III

If these various themes in the first decade of David Harvey's work in a Marxist vein influenced and reflected one of the two main focuses of the new urban Marxism, work on the city concerning the accumulation of capital, the second dominant theme, the emergence and political potential of urban social movements, was mainly influenced by, and reflected in, the work of Manuel Castells.

La Question urbaine opens with a devastating critique of traditional urban sociology, especially as exemplified in the Chicago School, for fetishizing space, and, in the precise sense of Althusserian terminology, for producing ideology. The various mainstream approaches to the study of the city made the error of treating urban developments in an immanent fashion, thus obscuring their dependent relationship with capitalism

---

[31] Some of the best parts of Harvey's more recently published two volumes of *Studies in the History and Theory of Capitalist Development*, which I discuss later in this chapter, extend and refine these discussions. The first volume, *The Urbanization of Capital*, contains essays on finance capital, land rent, residential differentiation, uneven development, planning, and, as in *Social Justice and the City*, a macroscopic historical treatment of urban development from a Marxist perspective. Overall, this volume is a recursive look at the themes raised in *Social Justice and the City*, and, given the range of time over which the individual essays were drafted, both an anticipation and a retrospective on *The Limits to Capital*. The continuities and persistence of Harvey's research project within Marxism are impressive. In the second volume, *Consciousness and the Urban Experience*, Harvey breaks new ground, by inquiring into the questions of disposition, language, meaning, culture, and agency he had left behind in the early chapters of *Social Justice and the City*.

as a mode of production. As against this work, the main aim of *La Question urbaine* was that of finding a scientifically justifiable object of analysis for cities.

Specific processes do take place in cities, Castells argues, including a distinctively urban kind of organization of social relationships in space as well as patterns of consumption organized collectively by the state. With regard to both, the defining characteristic of the city is the use of space and its social relationships and processes to reproduce the labour power necessary for capitalist production. The spatial differentiation of the city stressed by the Chicago School, and the focus on everyday life emphasized by Lefebvre, find meaning within this framework. For Castells, each moment of the capitalist mode of production requires a reciprocal organization of urban space in order to facilitate the reproduction and consumption processes appropriate to a given level of production. If capitalist production was the formative element for Harvey in the making and remaking of urban space, for Castells the formative element was the requirement that capitalism reproduce the supply of labour through the process of consumption. In the coincidence of the spatial and social units of advanced capitalism in collective consumption, Castells found the scientific definition of the urban lacking in mainstream work.

In advanced 'monopoly' capitalism, the state increasingly intervenes in the consumption process by the provision of collective goods and services to ensure that capitalism has the level and character of urban space and consumption that it requires.[32] One result is the growth of a direct, unmediated linkage between urban dwellers where they live and the state as the provider of such consumption goods as housing, transportation, education, and social services. These interventions by the state have the double effect of reproducing the capitalist order, and, at the same time, of creating basic contradictions

---

[32] Castells carried out a large-scale empirical treatment of this proposition in his study of state planning in the reshaping of the Dunkirk region, where the state intervened to create a built-environment appropriate to the production and consumption requirements of monopoly capitalism. M. Castells and F. Godard, *Monopolville: l'enterprise, l'état, l'urbain*. Paris: Mouton, 1974.

that provide new bases of conflict and new possibilities for social transformation.[33]

The new urban social movements that appeared in the 1960s, according to Castells, were a reflection of the new linkages between city space and an interventionist state. Because of the pivotal role of this relationship for capitalist accumulation, urban social movements—in tandem with the unions and political parties of the working class—have the potential to affect the trajectory of capitalist development and the possibilities of a transition to socialism just as surely as the older workplace-based conflicts between labour and capital. Urban movements thus represent a powerful and promising *locus* of anti-capitalist working-class struggle.[34]

[33] A trenchant critique of 'collective consumption' was provided by R. E. Pahl, who, in the past decade, has produced some of the best commentary on the new urban Marxism from a neo-Weberian perspective. His main objection is that in Castells's 'discussions of the nature, role, and importance of "collective consumption", a number of analytically separate issues are sometimes mistakenly elided together . . . issues are combined together without separate consideration and without elaborating the arguments which justify such a combination: (a) The Socialization of the Consumption Process; (b) The Role of the State in the Socialization of Consumption; (c) The Distributional Consequences of (b); (d) The Level of Provision.' Additionally, Pahl persuasively upbraids Castells for moving too quickly to assume that the increasing management of daily life by the state must necessarily lead to the mobilization of urban social movements. This is a contingent matter. R. E. Pahl, 'Castells and Collective Consumption', *Sociology*, 12 (May 1978), 309–10, 314. He also reviewed *La Question urbaine* in *Progress in Human Geography*, 2 (Mar. 1978).

[34] It is possible to read this discussion without attention to the impact of May 1968 and the need for orthodox Marxism to try to assimilate the new movements into its analysis of capitalist development and transformation. More generally, the new urban sociology can be understood as an attempt to discover new bearers of agency at a time when the traditional blue-collar social base has eroded. Marxists have grappled with the post-industrial phase of capitalism in other ways, too, of course, including definitional strategies that expand the working class beyond its industrial base, and attention to cross-class coalitions in the logic of social democratic politics. The coping strategies have been of one of two kinds: new mappings of the working class or an insistence on the plasticity of class and group formation.

Castells's position on urban social movements underwent refinement and development in the 1970s, especially in the 'Afterword' to the English edition of *La Question urbaine* and in his essays, *City, Class and Power*. In these essays, reflecting the then promising possibilities of Eurocommunism, he argues, first, that urban struggles need not be linked directly or necessarily to working-class unions and parties, but, independent of those class-specific organizations, may open up the possibility of cross-class alliances; second, that social divisions based on collective consumption develop a growing degree of independence from the traditional class structure; and, third, that, as a consequence, they have an autonomous role to play in anti-capitalist struggles. Over time, consumption becomes the fulcrum of capitalism; hence the state–neighbourhood relationship pivoting on collective consumption increases in its importance for the reproduction of the capitalist economic and social order. This work of the later 1970s presaged Castells's later argument in *The City and the Grassroots* that urban movements are not to be considered an integral aspect of the class struggle between labour and capital, but as independent social forces that sit side by side with traditional class-based conflict. In this revision of orthodox Marxism, consumption is given parity with production.[35] In the later work, in a move that can only be considered ironic in the light of his early critique of mainstream urban sociology, Castells further developed the idea of the autonomy of the urban, but now as a context for the generation of symbols and social meaning. To that intellectual and political shift, I return below.

[35] Castells, *City, Class and Power*. London: Macmillan, 1978. This book, and the earlier *La Question urbaine*, evince no interest in the historical development of the city, nor in historical questions of class formation. Writing from a vantage-point of a Marxism at least as orthodox as that of Castells's first book, the historian John Foster regretted that these analytical characteristics make class struggle 'purely formal' in Castells's analysis. John Foster, 'How Imperial London Lost its Slums', *International Journal of Urban and Regional Research*, 3 (Mar. 1979).

IV

The themes central to the early work of David Harvey and Manuel Castells, as well as the strengths and limitations of the new urban sociology they promoted, can be discerned if we attend briefly to three representative collections of papers written in the 1970s that reflect the frisson of intellectual excitement that attended the rediscovery of the city by Marxism. The first, *Captive Cities: Studies in the Political Economy of Cities and Regions*, consists of papers presented in the early years of the Research Committee on the Sociology of Urban and Regional Development of the International Sociological Association. These essays nicely capture the simultaneous emergence of Marxist and Weberian critiques of urban sociology, both of which reject the differentiation perspective and the naturalization of space that had been its chief characteristics. They also exhibit the sharpening divide between Marxist and Weberian work. The Marxist papers focus on accumulation and social movements; the Weberian, on the autonomous role of the state. There is little dialogue in the book between the two positions.[36] Subsequently, as the new

[36] Michael Harloe (ed.), *Captive Cities: Studies in the Political Economy of Cities and Regions*. London: John Wiley, 1977. In introducing the volume, Harloe wrote: 'In the past few years the ideological nature of much sociology and the uncritical role of the sociologist in the developed societies has been challenged. Many sociologists adopted new theoretical and political positions and some of those who were concerned with urban studies started to reevaluate their branch of the discipline. This activity began in a number of different countries and was carried out by sociologists with widely differing approaches, but a number of them came together at the Seventh World Congress of Sociology at Varna in 1970 to start a discussion of their work and an exchange of ideas and experiences. A new Research Committee of the International Sociological Association was established, the Research Committee on the Sociology of Urban and Regional Development. This book contains revised versions of a series of papers, most of which were presented to sessions of the Committee held between 1970 and 1974, although this introduction contains some references to material which has been published more recently' (p. 1).

The Research Committee has flourished. In September 1987 it held

Marxist work gained confidence and momentum—in large measure under the tutelage of Castells, in search of a scientific Althusserian Marxism, and of Harvey, keen to demonstrate the privileged capacity of Marxism in opposition to liberal positions—it interacted even less with other analytical traditions.

In their pioneering efforts, the book's essays share a number of other revealing, and limiting, traits that have continued to characterize the new Marxism of the city. They are sublimely uninterested in history. They eschew comparative analysis. As a consequence, they either utilize their cases to illustrate theoretical points, or they treat the single-country case materials as adequate to generate theory. And the theory they generate tends to be highly schematic and formalistic.

The second collection, *Urban Sociology: Critical Essays*, which appeared roughly simultaneously with the first, sought 'to make available to English-speaking readers a sample of recent French-language writings on urban sociology by authors adopting a historical materialist, or Marxist, viewpoint'.[37] This collection of translations, which predated by one year the appearance in English of Castells's *La Question urbaine*, made accessible an emerging body of work by Lamarche, Lojkine, and Olives, in addition to three papers by Castells.

Here, too, none of the essays has a historical orientation; all focus on contemporary cities and current struggles. Their main questions concern the specification of a theoretically-grounded object of analysis for urban studies; the dialectical relationship between the way the economic base is spatially structured and the consequences of capital accumulation for urban space (with particular emphasis on property development, planning, and the circulation of money created by collective consumption of state-provided goods and services); and the develop-

---

its sixth conference on 'Urban Change and Conflict'. Although the current events that have shaped these conferences have changed over time (the 1987 meeting focused principally on economic restructuring in the age of Thatcherism and Reaganism and the new global world economy), the durability of themes and participants has been notable.

[37] C. G. Pickvance (ed.), *Urban Sociology: Critical Essays*. London: Methuen, 1976, 1.

ment of social movements and patterns of conflict between groups created and shaped within this dual system of capital accumulation and urban space.

Like *Captive Cities*, the third collection, *City, Class and Capital*, published papers presented to the Regional and Urban Research Section of the International Sociological Association; it represents the development of the field by the late 1970s, as well as the new depth and density of work by Harvey and Castells. By this date, the specific case studies had grown more nuanced, and the theoretical work less schematic, but the overall profile of the positive and limiting features of the new Marxist scholarship remained. On the positive side: a radical break with the differentiation problematic, the attempt to spatialize Marxism's logical theory of capital, acute analyses of current problems, and an appreciation of the specificity of urban bases of conflict. On the limiting side: an exclusive focus on the present, the failure to conduct comparative research, a flat and functionalist view of the state, and a tendency to theoretical autarchy. The main lacuna in this work was the absence of more than mechanical treatments of the connections between the economic–spatial 'base' of late twentieth-century cities and the dispositions and collective action of the social movements these studies chronicled so well. In short, the Marxist project of social theory languished.[38]

[38] Michael Harloe and Elizabeth Lebas (eds.), *City, Class and Capital: New Developments in the Political Economy of Cities and Regions*. New York: Holmes and Meier, 1982.
Much of the scholarship produced under the label of Marxist urbanism in the 1970s, inspired by Harvey and Castells, was considerably more crude in its handling of social theory than the works discussed here. For an example of the former, which argues without any nuance or attention to the specificity of things urban that the 'contemporary urban form is the superstructural manifestation of bourgeois social relations', see Larry Sawyers, 'Urban Form and the Mode of Production', *Review of Radical Political Economics*, 7 (Spring 1975).
The major exception to the lack of interest by the new Marxist urbanism in history, and in Marx's first project of epochal change, is Michael Durnford and Diane Perrons, *The Arena of Capital*. London: Macmillan, 1983. A synthetic study focusing empirically on the development of the economy of Britain from 1066 to the present, the book aims to show how the joining of spatial analysis and Marxist

It was precisely to these issues that both Harvey and Castells addressed their work of the early and middle 1980s; Harvey in *Consciousness and the Urban Experience*, Castells in *The City and the Grassroots*. Both are attempts to advance the social-theoretical engagement of Marxism with the city. Their objects of analysis are similar: the emergence of a distinctively urban consciousness and pattern of collective action in nineteenth- and twentieth-century cities, and the growing importance of planned state interventions as shapers of the built-environment and social life in cities and as targets of mass protest. In these objects, they returned to the terrain of Lefebvre, in an explicit engagement of the city with classical Marxism. Their strategies and conclusions, however, could not have been more different.

V

'Capitalism', Harvey wrote, 'has produced a "second nature" through urbanization and the creation of built-environments of extraordinary breadth and intricacy. It has also produced a new kind of human nature through the urbanization of consciousness and the production of social spaces and a particular structure of interrelations between the different loci of consciousness formation.'[39] We have seen how Harvey's early work was concerned principally to explain how and why this 'second nature' of urban space was produced. Here, he extends this analysis by further tracing the interconnections between urban development and the motion of capital, and, more important, by tracing the linkages between this urban structure and the patterning of group and class formation.

---

historical materialism can make this grand story, including its urban parts, more comprehensible. This ambitious book relies, at key moments of the presentation, rather more on economically rooted argumentation than on the development of space-specific formulations. The sweep is grand, but the quest to make space a constitutive element of economic change is more asserted than achieved.

[39] Harvey, *Consciousness and the Urban Experience*, 273.

Harvey made a number of substantive forays into this social-theoretical project. The longest section of *Consciousness and the Urban Experience* is devoted to the redevelopment of Paris between 1850 and 1870 under Baron Haussman's tutelage. There is a wonderful small essay on the construction of the Basilica of Sacre-Coeur. Three theoretical essays—'Money, Time, Space, and the City', 'Class Struggle and the Built Environment', and 'The Urbanization of Consciousness'—map the themes underpinning the case studies. Throughout, Harvey is emphatic that the modern city is, above all, a *capitalist* city:

A city is an agglomeration of productive forces built by labor employed within a temporal process of circulation of capital. It is nourished out of the metabolism of capitalist production for exchange on the world market and supported out of a highly sophisticated system of production and distribution organized within its confines. It is populated by individuals who reproduce themselves using money incomes earned off the circulation of capital (wages and profits) or its derivative revenues (rents, taxes, interest, merchants' profits, payments for services). The city is ruled by a particular coalition of class forces, segmented into distinctive communities of social reproduction, and organized as a discontinuous but spatially contiguous labor market within which daily substitutions of job opportunities against labor power are possible and within which certain distinctive quantities and qualities of labor power may be found.[40]

Given the capitalist character of the city, Marxism is its privileged interpreter. Criticizing work by neo-classical economists, Weberian analysts of power, feminist students of patriarchy, and analysts working in an ecological tradition, Harvey found them all to be 'tragic reflections of an urbanized consciousness; they reflect surface appearances, do little to elucidate inner meanings and connections, and do much to sustain the confusions by replicating them in learned terms'. Marxism, by contrast, can penetrate to the essence of the capitalist mode of production. His goal, therefore, was not to join Marxism to other perspectives that have paid more attention to specifically urban phenomena, but 'to build into the Marxist perspective the kinds of detailed sophistication that

[40] Ibid., 250.

writers like Simmel and Wirth achieved. The urbanization of consciousness has to be understood in relation to the urbanization of capital.'[41]

The 'urbanization of consciousness' is shorthand for the formation of individual and group dispositions based not on class but on a multiplicity of identities—of territory, gender, ethnicity, race—and the broader conceptualization of community. These, he argues, echoing Castells, usually reflect a relationship between people in a given place to each other and to the state. Places of residence, as opposed to locales of work, he affirms begrudgingly, order 'status, position and prestige in ways that made Weberian concepts of consumption classes look legitimate.'[42]

The urbanization of consciousness thus poses a basic challenge to an autarchic Marxism because its patterning of dispositions and collective action does not emerge in unmediated ways from the accumulation process, nor does it reflect traditional Marxist class categories. The entire volume by Harvey wrestles with this dilemma within the self-imposed limitation of not moving outside the boundaries of a self-sufficient Marxism.

Much of Harvey's earlier work stressed how the development of the city in the capitalist epoch temporarily resolved the crisis tendencies of the system and facilitated an enhanced process of capital accumulation. Here, he is compelled to focus on the consequences of this history of city development as a mediator between structure and agency within the capitalist mode of production. Capitalist cities, he concedes, have produced a new differentiated urban consciousness, unanticipated by Marx, based on the complexity of its actors and their positions in space and in spatially defined relations with political authorities. To explain this development, Harvey attempts two interrelated tasks that demonstrate a deep ambivalence and an unresolved tension. He seeks to show how capitalist development convenes the spatial relationships that make this new consciousness possible, and he tries to demonstrate, in a strained affirmation of orthodoxy, that the non-class relationships it expresses are fundamentally fictitious,

[41] Ibid., 252.   [42] Ibid., 255.

because the only irreducible social relations in a capitalist mode of production are those of capital and labour:

Increasing urbanization makes the urban the primary level at which individuals now experience, live out, and react to the totality of transformations and structures in the world around them . . . It is out of the complexities and perplexities of this experience that we build an elementary consciousness of space and time; of social power and its legitimations; of forms of domination and social interaction; of the relations to nature through production and consumption; and of human nature, civil society, and political life.

Curious kinds of consciousness arise out of the confusions of that experience. The modes of thinking and acting cannot be captured directly by appeal to polarized or even complex class structures. With a real material basis in daily urban life, the modes of consciousness cannot be dismissed as false, although I shall insist that they are necessarily fetishistic. The replication in thought of the intricate material patternings of surface experience obscures the inner meanings, but the surface appearance is real enough.[43]

The line of reasoning is clear: capitalism creates the city; the city creates a consciousness that reflects its varied reality; yet that consciousness deflects attention away from the primal forces of the capitalist mode of production that underlie the production and functioning of cities. This is the great secret of the capitalist social order. Not only does the city give the accumulation process the capacity to secure a spatial fix, it also misshapes class struggle by deflecting it into 'fetishistic' dimensions.

Harvey tells this story concretely, with great verve, in his case study of Paris between 1850 and 1870. It details how the physical city was altered radically, and how this dramatic morphological change produced new patterns of group formation. His strategy is that of elucidating 'a spiral of themes . . . starting with the comparative statics of spatial relations [which], moves through distribution (credit, rent, taxes), production and labor markets, reproduction, and consciousness formation to set the space in motion as a real historical geography of a living city'.[44]

---

[43] Ibid., 251.   [44] Ibid., 69.

Harvey treats the reconstruction of Paris by Baron Hauss-man under the sponsorship of Louis Napoleon only months after the declaration of the Empire, not as an aspect of state formation, but as a concrete instance of the spatial fix strategy he had proposed in *The Limits to Capital*. The massive public works that reshaped the city were undertaken, in this account, to overcome 'the first great crisis of capitalism' by 'the long-term application of capital to the reorganization of space relations'.[45]

Haussman, Harvey claims, understood the deeply capitalist character of the city, and the economic and spatial processes already under way within it; thus he saw his builder's role as that of accommodating and accelerating those trends. To be sure, the Emperor and Haussman 'wanted to make Paris a capital worthy of France, even of Western civilization', but

to his credit, Haussman well understood his limited role. For though he had authoritarian power and frequent delusions of grandeur, he also recognized that he had to liberate more than just the flow of goods and people from their medieval constraints if Paris was to be transformed. The force he had to mobilize, and in the end the force that mastered him, was the circulation of capital.

The consequence was that 'in the end he simply helped make it a city in which the circulation of capital became the real imperial power'.[46]

The massive construction projects begun in 1851 resolved the capitalist crisis by absorbing available surpluses of capital and labour, to be sure, but we should be more careful than Harvey not to confuse consequence and motive. Nevertheless, even if we were to prefer a less economy-centred interpretation of the genesis of the rebuilding of Paris, there is no denying that what was at stake was a massive economic undertaking with profound consequences for French capitalism. Harvey presents the various aspects of this story in fascinating detail: dramatic changes in rent and property, shifts in credit markets,

[45] Ibid., 70. On the face of it, this is an extraordinarily unbalanced argument, unsupported by careful empirical evidence. It is sympto-matic of Harvey's devaluation of the independent importance of the state and the interests and perspectives of its officials.

[46] Ibid., 76.

the emergence of a pro-development coalition of financial and real-estate interests, the rationalization of land use, and the massive mobilization of labour power.

What of the consequences for urban consciousness? The reorganization of space, Harvey tellingly observes, had a contradictory result. The deindustrialization of the city centre, the new separation of work and home, and the growing residential segregation of the city fundamentally changed the geography of class struggle by creating spaces within which the working class had a relatively free existence; in their faubourgs workers became hard to monitor. Dense sociability had long been characteristic of the neighbourhoods of Paris, and they had served in the eighteenth as well as the nineteenth centuries as locales of class formation.[47] But after the Haussmanization of Paris, long-established ties of family, work, and living places were sundered, the cross-class patterns of daily interaction in the residential communities were diminished, and more fine-grained distinctions developed between different quarters. Although Paris had long been segregated,

within the overall pattern there had been considerable spatial mixing. Dismal slums intermingled with opulent town houses; craft workers and artisans intermingled with aristocratic residences on the Left Bank and in the Marais; and the celebrated vertical segregation (rich bourgeois on floor above the boutique and worker families in the garret) did bring some social contact between the classes. Masters and employees in industry and commerce had also traditionally lived close to each other.

Haussman did not create residential segregation, but, together with the effects of rent in the housing market, his public works created a city whose social space was much more clearly defined:

Slum removal and building speculation consolidated bourgeois quarters to the west, while the separate system of land development in the northern and eastern peripheries produced tracts of low-income housing unrelieved by any intermingling with the upper classes. Land-use competition also consolidated the business and financial

---

[47] For a marvellous treatment of 18th-century Paris, see David Garrioch, *Neighbourhood and Community in Paris, 1740–1790*. Cambridge: Cambridge University Press, 1986.

quarters, while industrial and commercial activities also tended toward a tighter spatial clustering in selected areas of the center— printing on the Left Bank, metal working on the inner northeast, leather and skins around Arts et Metiers, ready-to-wear clothing just off the *grands boulevards* . . . Zones and wedges, centers and peripheries, and even the fine mesh of quarters were much more clearly class-determined or occupationally defined in 1870 than they had been in 1848.[48]

But if the new spatial configuration of Paris was conducive to a developed, elaborated, and protected sphere of working-class formation on a class basis, it also, in contradictory fashion, promoted the development of new kinds of consciousness based not on class but on community. This sometimes reinforced class identities, but at other times either superseded or cross-cut them to produce a jumbled consciousness that divided, weakened, and made incoherent the possibilities and politics of the working class. The climax of Harvey's story, an all too brief and schematic discussion of the Paris Commune, exhibits this double trend. This extraordinary urban revolt reflected the contradictory aspects of the new Paris:

Splits between radical bourgeois, each armed with his own splendid theory of revolution, between practical patriots and peddlers of rhetoric and dreams, between workers bewildered by events and leaders of craft unions trying to render consistent and compelling interpretations, between loyalties to *quartier*, city, and nation, between centralizers and decentralizers, all gave the Commune an air of incoherence and a political practice riddled with internal conflict.[49]

In spite of the protean force of capital harnessed to the rebuilding of Paris, and even at a revolutionary moment, the resulting politics did not have the simple power of labour confronting capital, and thus did not conform to the clear fault-lines of a Marxist model of class struggle. In this, the Commune implicitly represents a key moment of transition, when the diversity of the differentiated city overtook the simplifications of the class structure of capitalism to give shape to a multifaceted urban consciousness. Here, in this

---

[48] Harvey, *Consciousness and the Urban Experience*, 167.
[49] Ibid., 218.

analysis, Harvey marries his scientific Marxism of accumulation to an analysis of consciousness that, perhaps unwittingly, joins together key aspects of the work of Lefebvre and Lukács. As for Lefebvre, the urban realities of modern capitalist societies organize a crucible of sentiment, dispositions, and political culture. As for Lukács, the new society is inherently atomizing; it renders class consciousness of a revolutionary kind virtually impossible. The new urban consciousness, in this presentation, is something of a phoney and a sham, if not quite fully *false* consciousness. In an ultimate sense, this consciousness reflects the antinomy of labour and capital, because the city that produces urban consciousness is fundamentally a creature of capitalism. But the linkage between capitalist structure and a working-class transformative agency is sundered by the new urbanization:

Once institutionalized and reified, these relations ... [geographical configurations of physical and social relations] are transformed into complex codes of urban living that have their own significations and rigidities. The semiotic of the city reinforces the structurations of physical and social space, and so enters directly into the urbanization of consciousness.[50]

Just as for Lukács the only retort to reification caused by the extension of the commodity principle to all of society was an all or nothing revolutionary politics, so Harvey concluded with a ringing but rather unspecific injunction

to put the urbanization of revolution at the center of our political strategies ... Any political movement that does not embed itself in the heart of the urban process is doomed to fail in advanced capitalist society. Any political movement that does not secure its power within the urban process cannot long survive. Any political movement that cannot offer ways out of the multiple alienations of contemporary urban life cannot command mass support for the revolutionary transformation of capitalism.

This political advice, he admits, is 'ambiguous', but he insists this is a matter of preference: 'But I prefer to leave it so.'[51] For my part, I do not think this ambiguity is a matter of volition, for his analysis forces him from the field of concrete

---

[50] Ibid., 265.   [51] Ibid., 276.

political engagement to a utopian revolutionary politics deeply embedded in the silences of his presentation and in his treatment of Marxist social theory.

Specifically, there are two clusters of limitations in *Consciousness and the Urban Experience*. The first concerns the book's failure to develop a perspective on class and group formation within Marxism that transcends a simple kind of reflectionism based on the operative assumption of correspondence between structure and meaning. The second concerns the inherent limits of a closed Marxism. Let us look at each in turn.

Like many Marxists, Harvey treats class formation in a bimodal way: it exists or it does not. The problem with urban consciousness is that it masks and deflects class formation. Even though 'conflicts in the living place are ... mere reflections of the underlying tension between capital and labor ... they stand between capital and labor and thereby shield the real source of tension from view. The surface appearance of conflicts around the built environment ... conceals a hidden essence that is nothing more than the struggle between capital and labor.' As a consequence, urban conflicts have a hidden potential of joining with workplace conflicts to produce a more complete challenge to capitalism, but as to how and under what conditions community-based mobilizations might achieve this potential Harvey is completely silent.

In part this silence is the result of his treatment of group formation in terms of correspondence: union consciousness reflects the capitalist workplace; urban consciousness the capitalist residential community. This is impoverished social theory that begs the interesting questions about how capitalism as an economic order sets limits and exerts pressures, and about the various dimensions of class and group formation.

These problems manifest themselves at four levels. The first concerns Harvey's treatment of the capitalist base, especially in *The Limits to Capital*. In some respects, *Consciousness and the Urban Experience* is a rejoinder to critics of that book who upbraided Harvey for his separation of theory and history, and for his strategy of developing theory by the elaboration of the conceptual apparatus of *Capital*.[52] This line of attack is as misplaced as the criticism of *Capital* I discussed in Chapter 2 for developing a closed logical theory of capital accumulation. As with Marx's work, Harvey's treatment of accumulation is appropriately closed for its purpose of making space a constitutive element of accumulation. But, as with Marx, the meaning of the treatment of the capitalist base must change when it is inserted into the project of social theory capable of illuminating whole societies and their histories.

However, unlike Marx's treatment of the base, Harvey's elaboration of the motion of capital lacks an inherent tie between structure and agency. We saw in the last chapter how Marx connected a very high level of generalization about capitalist production to a coherent account of action by rational agents. What Little calls the 'logic of institutions' of the capitalist mode of production provides a motivational structure within which capitalists act; in turn, their activities (re-)create the organizational structure of the capitalist economy. By contrast, Harvey's portrait is a naturalistic one; *Capital* is understood as 'a unified deductive theory in which a small number of theoretical principles serve to unify the empirical phenomena of capitalist society'.[53] These centre on the labour theory of value and the production of surplus value. From this perspective, the empirical consequences of the abstract model of capitalism can be worked out in advance as predictions about many matters, including patterns of class formation. This treatment of Marx's analysis as analogous to some theories in the natural sciences creates a capitalist base that is all structure and no agency. For Harvey, the result, as one critic has put it, is the 'failure to specify how the system's requirements of capitalism are identified by agents competent to undertake the social, political and economic management that Harvey sees those requirements as calling forth'.[54] For

[52] Two examples are Kearns, 'Making Space for Marx', and Christian Topalov, 'Capital, History and the Limits of Economics', *International Journal of Urban and Regional Research*, 7 (Dec. 1983).

[53] Daniel Little, *The Scientific Marx*. Minneapolis: University of Minnesota Press, 1986, 16. See also the discussion below, in Chapter 2.

[54] Kearns, 'Making Space for Marx', 413.

Harvey, one of these requirements is the city because it is needed to provide a spatial fix. But who are the agents who understand this functionalism, and make it work? If capital as an economic and social force is understood, as Harvey presents it, as an abstract and singular entity, then what joins together the different fractions of finance capital, *rentiers*, and manufacturers into a coherent, unified agent?[55]

If the first problem of social theory for Harvey lies in this conceptualization of the capitalist base, the second is the ontological status he confers on urban space in capitalist cities. Though he acknowledges that a key feature of nineteenth- and twentieth-century industrialization in the West has been the spatial separation of work and residence, he insists the former be accorded primary status, the latter only a secondary one; do not workplaces necessarily belong to the base and residential communities to the superstructure? At one stroke, this intellectual move in the name of Marxist orthodoxy vitiates Harvey's own key insight that the growth of the capitalist city *changes* the character of the 'base'. For if we are interested in the social organization of society, that is, the ways of life of actual people in real social formations, then there is no warrant for giving a privileged place to the workplace in the analysis of group and class formation, 'for with the separation of work and home, and between social classes in space, class relations are lived and experienced not only at work, but also off work in residence communities'.[56] If we are interested in how social classes in cities are formed as groups sharing dispositions, then we must attend to how they construct maps of their social terrain in both domains, and to how they do, or do not, link them.

These are not all or nothing matters, but contingent questions. Given the complicated separations and interrelations of work and residence, alternative kinds of group and class formation are neither more real nor more natural than others.

[55] I am indebted to Charles Tilly for this point.
[56] Ira Katznelson, 'Working-Class Formation: Constructing Cases and Comparisions', in Ira Katznelson and Aristide Zolberg (eds.), *Working Class Formation: Nineteenth Century Patterns in Western Europe and the United States*. Princeton, NJ: Princeton University Press, 1986, 16.

This, then, is the third problem in Harvey's social theory. Rather than ask under what conditions class emerges as the unifying cognitive map for a working class in a capitalist city, and why it is that different groups of working people are formed as different kinds of working classes in very similar capitalist and urban settings, he instead elides these issues by his reflectionist strategy of correspondence. Capitalism produces city spaces which disorganize the working class by creating 'urban consciousness', a term lacking in precision that he uses as a kitbag within which to gather all non-class bases of shared dispositions.

The fourth shortcoming of Harvey's social theory is the absence of any consideration of problems of collective action. He appears to assume, without discussion, that each kind of consciousness—class consciousness and urban consciousness—produces its own kind of collective action unproblematically. But groups of people sharing life situations and dispositions may or may not act collectively to transform their dispositions into behaviour. Such collective action connotes more than unselfconscious shared behaviour which exists whenever people have certain traits in common. The links between the social organization of classes and groups, their dispositions, and their patterns of collective action must be at the very centre of studies of class and group formation, but Harvey's approach to the subject, a simple class in itself–for itself formulation, makes all such considerations superfluous. As a consequence, Harvey's history of nineteenth-century Paris has more in common analytically with the ahistorical Marxism of Lukács than with the work of the Marxist historians who have written on this period, including that of Engels.

If limitations of social theory vitiated Harvey's attempt to link theory and history, so too did his insistence on a closed Marxism. The costs are most apparent in his flat and functional treatment of the state and its role in shaping the built-environment, which gives to the state only a second- or third-order co-ordinating role. He assumes that the development of cities—even in cases like that of the massive, state-directed reconstruction of Paris—is principally, almost exclusively, the product of the logic of capital; and that the state is merely its instrument.

Harvey does take the state seriously. Beginning with the convincing observation that 'much of the recent Marxist theorizing on the state is rather badly informed when it comes to understanding the relation between the state and the money and credit systems', he contributes to a remedy by focusing on central banks as pivots of modern credit, and as points of central control within the modern state.[57] He argues, provocatively, that money is not an exclusive instrument of capital or of the state but a key element securing their interrelationship. And, following Marx, Polanyi, and Simmel, he shows how a money economy characterized by the hegemony of price-setting markets constitutes a distinctive kind of human community within capitalism.[58]

Alas, Harvey takes the state seriously only as an instrument for the functional reproduction of capital:

The proper conception of the role of the state in capitalist society is controversial. I shall simply take the view that state institutions and the processes whereby state powers are exercised must be so fashioned that they, too, contribute, insofar as they can, to the reproduction and growth of the social system. Under this conception we can derive certain basic functions of the capitalist state:
1. help to stabilize an otherwise rather erratic economic and social system by acting as a 'crisis manager';
2. strive to create the conditions for 'balanced growth' and a smooth process of accumulation;
3. contain civil strife and factional struggles by repression (police power), cooperation (buying off politically or economically), or integration (trying to harmonize the demands of warring classes or factions).[59]

In this view, the state possesses only that degree of autonomy it needs to perform these functions. States, and state-located actors, have no independent interests. The state as an independent macrostructure has no unconfined or self-motivated standing, and hence is not a worthy object of the construction of theory.

Even in the domain of central banking and monetary policy so basic to the history of state-making and to the capacity of

---

[57] Harvey, *Limits to Capital*, 282.
[58] Harvey, *Consciousness and the Urban Experience*, 2–6.
[59] Harvey, *The Urbanization of Capital*, 174–5.

national states, Harvey locates the only motor of development within the functional requirements of capital. 'The reasons for such a high degree of state involvement' in credit and banking, he writes, 'are not hard to pin down. Accumulation requires a free, untrammeled and continuous flow of interest-bearing money capital. This flow has to be sustained in the face of over-speculation, distortion, and all the other "insane forms" that the credit system inevitably spawns.' Thus, if the circulation of capital is to be free from disruption, regulation of the credit system is necessary. Money capitalists cannot provide it because of the dynamics of competition; hence state intervention.[60]

Harvey's treatment of the state suffers serious problems of chronology, since, for him, capitalism is always the first cause. Unfortunately, the history of modern state-making will not accommodate this fiction. His discussion of the state is also weakened by all the familiar defects of functionalist analysis unaccompanied by the specification of mechanisms (whether purposive or not) that sustain the imputed functional relationship. The state for Harvey is always the passive actor, determined by other forces (for example: 'The French state at mid-century was in search of a modernization of its structures and practices that would accord with contemporary needs'[61]), which, on discussion, prove to be the needs created by capitalist economic crises. Further, by working only at the level of the mode of production and by making the a priori assumption that the state in capitalism is necessarily class-biased in all its activities, Harvey makes a strategic politics about space and cities impossible. The only choices are the status quo or revolutionary practice.

Each of the key themes of Harvey's work suffers as a consequence of his closed Marxism, and his failure to grant an ontological independence to states, state-building, and politics.

---

[60] Harvey, *Limits to Capital*, 281. Harvey's arguments about the state always take this form of simple functionalism. He treats planners and planning as the intelligence function of capital within the state; imperialism as a mechanism of spatial fix for capital; urban politics as the quest for a cross-class alliance that can protect capital, and so on.

[61] Harvey, *Consciousness and the Urban Experience*, 96.

His conflation of the state and capitalism into the single jumbo macrostructure of the capitalist mode of production eliminates some of the most important questions about urban development, the shaping of the built-environment, the role of planning, the expansion of governmental services, and the defining of class and group formation. The centrepieces of Harvey's work—the analysis of land use, rent, and the adaptation of the urban environment to accommodate the accelerated pace of the circulation of capital—cannot possibly be developed without an elaboration of the interests and actions of local officials, and government bureaucrats who, together with lawyers, landlords, developers, and bankers are enmeshed in a politics of property.[62]

That the state is a key actor in capitalist cities is scarcely surprising. Modern capitalism, after all, is instantiated by sets of rules in law and in policy established by and through the state to regulate and steer markets and to mitigate the effects of economic forces in distribution. These rules, laws, and policies are shaped and contested by interested state officials, and by citizens who act in and through a variety of alternative possible identities and institutions: those of class, ethnicity, gender, territory, and locality; and through political parties, social movements, *ad hoc* groups, bureaucratic agencies, and interest associations.

The necessary and simultaneous growth of large-scale urban centres as implosions of capital was also the moment when state actors began to acquire a growing significance on the urban scene. Think of health and safety regulations, the mapping of street grids, the construction of public spaces, and the creation of transportation networks. To be sure, at every moment there has been an intertwining of government and capital, but the story of urban development can be told only in caricature as a tale of capitalist requirements achieved

[62] A brilliant discussion of these issues and of the ways in which a politics of property helped shape Liberal–Conservative national politics is Avner Offer, *Property and Politics, 1870–1914: Landownership, Law, Ideology and Urban Development in England*. Cambridge: Cambridge University Press, 1981. Unfortunately, this book, published in an expensive edition and written in an austere style that makes no concessions to the reader, has found only a small audience.

unimpeded and unresisted, or as the story of actors bearing the 'real' names of labour and capital.

VI

Harvey's weaknesses are Castells's emphases, but not always his strengths. His massive landmark study of social movements, *The City and the Grassroots*, is richly concerned with variation and contingency, with actors and the autonomous role of the state, with gender and ethnicity, with history and problems of collective action. He rejects understandings of meaningful social change as consisting only of moments of apocalyptic, epochal rupture. He insists on the singularity of each context, from sixteenth-century Spain to late twentieth-century San Francisco. And he stresses that much of what goes on in cities must be understood as conflicts about the very definition of rules of the urban economic, social, and political game, as much as instances of play within those rules.

The book is constructed as a series of fine case studies of social movements, past and present. A first part shows how popular movements by citizens since the sixteenth-century have been directed at transforming the city, and how varied the bases of such collective action have been, from the 1520–22 *Comunidades* of Castilla, which challenged the absolutist monarchy, to the Paris Commune, the Glasgow rent strike of 1915, which helped give birth to public housing, the tenants' movement in Veracruz in 1922, and the ghetto revolts of the 1960s in American cities. In these brief, but lovingly etched, treatments, Castells seeks to recapture the role of ordinary citizens for studies of urban history, and to demonstrate that across an immense variety of contexts the agency of ordinary people has shaped the development of cities.[63] From these studies he draws a number of lessons for

[63] As Norman Fainstein has pointed out, there is also a cost to this strategy. Castells's history lacks the narrative depth that comes with sticking to a time and place. His is the history of the ideal–typical case, chosen to make an analytical point; thus, inevitably, it is history with many of the complexities left out. Fainstein also usefully calls into question Castells's working assumption that mass urban

his more contemporary work: most urban struggles are not class-based, and their central *locus* of organization and goals has been grass-roots democracy; the movements were not only rooted in cities, but took specifically urban problems as their objects of conflict; for all, space was an important expression of social organization; in each, women played a significant role. Taken together, these points constituted a powerful rejoinder to the view of Harvey that an urban consciousness is at best an indirect expression of the conflict between capital and labour, and at worst an instance of false consciousness.

For Castells, by contrast, these movements are deeply rooted in the materiality of modern cities, across time and place, a position he forcefully develops in the centrepiece contemporary studies of *The City and the Grassroots*: of urban trade unionism and collective consumption in Paris; of cultural expression by gays and Latinos in San Francisco; of the urban populism of squatters in Santiago; and of the interaction of each of these dimensions in Madrid.

The organizing principle of these studies is what Castells calls the production of urban *meaning*. Such, in fact, is his definition of the city:

Cities, like all social reality, are historical products, not only in their physical materiality but in their cultural meaning, in the role they play in the social organization, and in peoples' lives. The basic dimension in urban change is the conflictive debate between social classes and historical actors over the meaning of urban, the significance of spatial forms in the social structure, and the content, hierarchy, and destiny of cities in relationship to the entire social structure. A city (and each type of city) is what a historical society decides the city (and each city) will be ... We therefore define as *urban form the symbolic expression of social meaning and of historical superimposition of urban meanings (and their forms) always determined by a conflictive process between historical actors.*[64]

___

movements are always inherently progressive, and, implicitly, the corollary that the state is inevitably not a progressive actor but an agent of capital, order, and control. Norman Fainstein, 'Class and Community in Urban Social Movements', *Urban Affairs Quarterly*, 20 (June 1985).

[64] Castells, *The City and the Grassroots*, 302–3.

He gives primacy to urban meaning because its definition expresses interests, arrays urban functions in a hierarchy, and gives form to the development of cities by symbolically expressing the values and priorities of a distinctive urban civilization.

Thus, for Castells, social change in cities is above all concerned with the alteration of urban meaning. The process is inherently conflictual, and the sources of conflict are plural. At some moments, urban concerns and effects are by-products of transurban groups and struggles, such as the activities of capital stressed by Harvey in the interest of facilitating the accumulation of capital. At others, they are the result of self-conscious *urban* social movements, whose targets are collective consumption, political self-management, and cultural expression in the city. Although such movements rely on other actors, such as the mass media, political parties, and technically competent professionals, to secure their goals, they remain urban social movements only in so far as they maintain independence. The precise content of these movements, their various substantive emphases, their definitions of urban meaning, and their linkages to other actors cannot be deduced from a single, unified theory of urban relations. Rather, the great range of urban movements can be interrogated and understood using this matrix.

In all, this is a remarkably suggestive performance. The range of learning and empirical work in *The City and the Grassroots*, the willingness to rethink fundamental questions, and the striking advances in formulation as compared to his early work are immensely appealing.

What a long way Castells had come from the Althusserian structuralism of *La Question urbaine*. Now, Castells had this to say about Marxism:

Our intellectual matrix, the Marxist tradition, was of little help from the moment we entered the uncertain ground of urban social movements . . . [There was] a reduction of Marxist thought, even for Marx and Engels, because pressured by the urgent task of providing theoretical tools for the labour movement and popular insurrections, they were compelled to place the accumulation of capital and domination by the state at the forefront of their work as revolutionary intellectuals . . .

In any case, such a reduction had its lasting effects on any effort to renew Marxist thought on urban problems. When, in the late 1960s, both Lefebvre and ourselves called attention, on different and even opposite lines, to the need to introduce a class conflict analysis into the new realm of problems identified as urban, so developing the heritage of Marxist theory, we were delighted to observe the expansion, first in France, later in other countries, of a major research effort in that direction. This did not happen necessarily because our call was so powerful or influential, but rather because the time was right. The growing urban contradictions and conflicts in advanced industrial societies required a refurbishing of the prevailing currents of urban theory.

Yet, with some fortunate exceptions, Marxism as a whole has been unable to stand up fully to the challenge ... To the physical determinism of human ecologists, or to the cultural idealism of the Wirthian tradition, Marxists tended to respond by reducing the city and the space to the logic of capital ...

But how is the connection established between the structure and the practices, between the mode of production and the historical process of class struggle? According to Marx, through class formation and class consciousness: a class in itself becomes a class for itself. But how does this occur? Marx has no answer ... By definition, the concept of social movement as an agent of social transformation is strictly unthinkable in the Marxist theory.[65]

About this movement from orthodoxy to scepticism he was not only entirely self-conscious, but exemplary in the clear and direct exposition of the causes and character of the massive shifts in his thinking. In a review and critique of his own earlier work which chronicles this intellectual and political passage, Castells stood by the devastating criticisms of urban sociology in his first book, but wisely recanted its formalism and what he now saw as its serious theoretical errors. These he identified as thinking of a system without the actors, and thus deducing them from structures; economism and the assertion of the primacy of productive forces; unresolved tensions in the position that sees the transition to socialism as the result of a structural crisis and the position that sees it as the consequence of class struggle; and a crude functionalist analysis of the state. In all, Castells averred, he

[65]   Ibid., 296–300.

had moved from prescribing revolutionary transformations from the asceptic world of deductive theory to a concern with transforming the 'real world by understanding the actual, substantive dynamics of social change'.[66]

He attributed the shifts in his position principally to his experiences as an empirical analyst of urban social movements, and as an active participant in the Citizen Movement in Madrid in post-Franco Spain and an observer of the Gay Movement in San Francisco. The struggle of the Citizen Movement to define its independence from the Spanish Communist Party impelled Castells to break with the Leninist tradition. And the terrain of struggle by homosexuals around San Francisco convinced him that there are important bases of conflict about urban meaning before which Marxism must stand mute.[67]

What did Castells make of the massive amount of empirical material for the making of social theory appropriate to the

[66] Manuel Castells, 'From the Urban Question to the City and the Grassroots', Working Paper 47, Urban and Regional Studies, University of Sussex, Aug. 1985. This paper is an edited transcript of a talk given by Castells at the Fifth Urban Change and Conflict Conference at the Universty of Sussex in April 1985.

For a review that places the shifts in Castells's thinking in terms of changes in French urban sociology more generally, stressing a movement 'away from general objects of study toward microsociology', see Jean-Claude Kaufman and Monique Laigneau, 'French Urban Sociology: Problems and Prospects', *Urban Affairs Quarterly*, 19 (Mar. 1984).

[67] My own impression is that Castells's move to the University of California, Berkeley, and his growing familiarity with the United States, was an even more decisive influence than he acknowledges in this paper. For one of the hallmarks of class and group formation in the United States since the ante-bellum period has been the radical separation between the politics of the workplace and the politics of community; and a second has been the absence of a working-class socialist or labourist political party.

In *The City and the Grassroots* Castells generously notes that my 'sharp criticism of our theory . . . in his [my] last book provided the groundwork for the attempt to integrate the general characteristics of urban social change and the historical context in which movements develop' (300). He has pointed out to me, after reading an early draft of this chapter, that I am now taking him to task for having followed my earlier advice too assiduously!

analysis of the city, and for Marxist theory in particular? Here, the book proved disappointing. If for Harvey (and for the Castells of *La Question urbaine*) agency disappeared except as a reflection of structure, in *The City and the Grassroots* structure disappeared in the face of the great variety of human agency.

In the name of historicity and contingency, Castells abjures entirely discussions of causality and determination. There is no hierarchy of causal factors in this work, either with regard to a specific set of social processes in the world or with regard to a set of theoretical tools at various levels of abstraction to apprehend cities and urban social movements, and their contingent consequences. Everything has become relative: capital accumulation and other social processes; Marxism and other social theories. The rich presentation of various urban social movements is at the expense of what could loosely be called structured contextual characteristics; there are only movements across space and time. And because there is no context, there is no provision for influence by the movements over some structural characteristics.[68]

Like Harvey, but from a very different path, Castells returned to the urbanism of Lefebvre: the specificity of the urban, the focus on space and meaning, and, in the end, the quest for 'the theory of the good city and a good theory of the city'. He concludes, in words that might have been written by Lefebvre, 'Our hope and bet is that, notwithstanding the threatening storms of the current historical conflicts, humankind is on the edge of mastering its own future, and therefore of designing its good city. At last, citizens will make cities.'[69]

---

[68] A recent illuminating, if highly polemical, exchange on the research possibilities and directions suggested by *The City and the Grassroots* focuses on the issue of context and social movements. Chris Pickvance, 'The Rise and Fall of Urban Movements and the Role of Comparative Analysis', and Manuel Castells, 'Commentary on C. G. Pickvance's "The Rise and Fall of Urban Movements"', *Society and Space*, 3 (Mar. 1985). Also useful are Patrick Mullins, 'Community and Urban Movements', *Sociological Review*, 35 (Mar. 1987), and R. R. Hall, D. C. Thorns, and W. E. Willmott, 'Community, Class and Kinship: Bases for Collective Action Within Localities', *Society and Space*, 2 (June 1984).

[69] Castells, *The City and the Grassroots*, 336, 337.

VII

Each in his own way, applying the thumb of structure or the fingers of agency, Harvey and Castells abandoned the project of Marxist social theory, whose central questions concern the joining together of structure and agency in a single hand. Where does this leave Marxism and the city? Has their engagement come to an end in the formulism of Harvey and the pluralism of Castells?

I think not. Much would be lost in such an abandonment, including the valuable insights into both structure and agency by each of these theorists.

In the remainder of *Marxism and the City* I sketch an alternative programme that, unlike the work of Castells, does not see marxism as only one of a larger number of plausible theories, but, unlike the work of Harvey, rejects the hubris of a closed Marxism and identifies mechanisms connecting structure and agency. To develop this alternative, I first return to the early work on cities by Friedrich Engels in *The Condition of the Working Class in England*. In his compressed discussion of Manchester and other early industrial revolution urban centres, Engels blazed a road that, regrettably, has not been travelled either by Marxism or by students of the city. Thus, in Chapter 4, we begin a new journey back to the city on this road not yet taken.

4 Capitalism, City Space, and Class Formation: A Journey Organized by Friedrich Engels

WITH the assistance of the young Engels, who journeyed to England in 1842, this chapter begins a consideration of three interrelated questions: the determinations that have shaped urban space; the spatial organization of cities within the limitations imposed by these structural determinations at given historical moments; and the contingent and variable patterning of group and class formation within this spatial repertoire. I take up these issues not just to end a long silence within Marxism or to provide an alternative to the recent terms of engagement of Marxism with the city, but also because this subject provides a marvellous, though unrealized, chance to address basic problems of Marxist social and political theory.

If, for Marxism, the accumulation of capital defines the structuring content of the capitalist mode of production, the formation of the working class and its capacity to transform the social order is at the heart of its understanding of agency. Capitalist accumulation and working-class formation, together, delineate a field of analytical and political tension that has challenged, and haunted, Marxism from the start. Although there is no more fundamental question for Marxism than the relationship between capitalism understood abstractly as a system of production, whose organizing principle masks exploitation at the moment of its occurrence, and the identities, dispositions, and activities of actual working people in specific places at given historical moments, these two dimensions of capitalism have been juxtaposed awkwardly and unsurely within Marxist theory.

Too frequently, Marxism has traversed the distance between the poles of structure and agency by lurching from one to the other or by invoking very simple ideas about unmediated determination. Its politics equally have lacked a sure footing. Given the failure of its expectations for the working class, Marxist activists have either placed their ideological and organizational trust in a vanguard or created a politics indistinguishable from other left-of-centre statist orientations. Discussions within Marxism of the transition to socialism have oscillated between a focus on insurmountable economic crises and on class struggle without providing a persuasive account of their interconnections.

The new Marxist work on the city succeeded, at times brilliantly, in broadening the substantive content of Marxism beyond accumulation and beyond the workplace, and this work has certainly tried to come to grips with new kinds of collective identity and activity that have developed in late twentieth-century Western cities. Yet its social theory has failed to advance beyond stale formulas about determination and about how to connect structure and agency, or it has given up trying. We have seen how David Harvey, as an example of the first kind, remained committed to a reflectionist epistemology that ultimately reduces questions concerning the agency of class actors to issues of capitalist production and reproduction. For him, the distinctively urban aspects of the consciousness of working people are anomalous interpositions between the revolutionary potential inherent in capitalism and its realization. Manuel Castells's early work even more thoroughly treated the linkage between capitalist accumulation and class struggle in a formalistic and reductionist way. His more recent writing, by insisting that Marxism has nothing distinctive to say about the connections between the trajectory of capitalist economic development and group identities, meaning, and collective action, effectively abandoned the project of Marxist social theory.

The theoretical and strategic promise of an interaction of Marxism with the city, and the city with Marxism, thus remains unachieved. And yet, Marxism and the city is not a subject that can be put aside. After all, since the early nineteenth-century, Western working classes have in the main been urban. Within the workplaces, residential communities, and public spaces of cities, working people have experienced capitalism. I mean this in both senses of 'experience': the working classes of Western Europe and North America have had their lives, possibilities, and world-views decisively shaped by capitalism as a large-scale historical process in the settings provided by urban locations; in the same cities, they have made sense of, and have learned how to deal with, capitalist realities. Capitalist cities have provided the concrete lived worlds, at work and at home, that working people have been forced to map cognitively. Out of this urban-centred engagement with capitalism working classes have been constituted as social actors. If the term 'class struggle' is to have any meaning it must be rooted in this process of class formation, and in the variety of resulting outcomes.

I

With the exception of Engels's *Die Lage der arbeitenden Klasse in England*, published in Leipzig in 1845, Marxism has not pursued the agenda of linking capitalist development, city space, and working-class formation.[1] Engels was very young, just 22, when he came to Manchester to work in a branch of his father's textile firm of Ermen and Engels. He experienced the 'shock city'[2] of industrial capitalism at a time when he was already committed as a Left Hegelian to the prospect of revolutionary change and to the likelihood of England being its first venue. In Manchester, he had access to all the social classes and to their ways of life. For nearly two years, he utilized his fresh and keenly observant mind to assess developments in the leading textile city of the English industrial revolution.

[1] Marxists long neglected Engels's 'pre-Marxist' book. Furthermore, more than four decades passed before translations were available. An American edition was first published in 1887, an English one in 1892. A second exception worth noting is work by David Gordon. See esp. his 'Capitalist Development and the History of American Cities', in William Tabb and Lawrence Sawyers (eds.), *Marxism and the Metropolis*, 2nd edn. New York: Oxford University Press, 1984, a promissory note on a book put aside.

[2] The phrase is Asa Briggs's in *Victorian Cities*. London: Penguin Books, 1968.

The book is flawed. Its ideological commitments biased the use of evidence, at times in a heavy-handed way. Manchester was not a representative city. The portrait of Manchester, and the other 'great towns', is something of a cartoon. The industrial city was more varied as a social and spatial place than the book's portrait allows. Engels's picture of a division between two starkly differentiated classes in a segregated landscape of great wealth and unrelieved misery was overstated even in Manchester, the country's most class-divided setting.[3]

No matter, because this caricature captured precisely the chief emergent features of the burgeoning capitalist city. Manchester may not have been typical, but it was archetypical. We may quibble with the details but not the essentials of Engels's social geography. Writing at the precise branching moment of the emergence of the modern industrial capitalist city, he connected the development of this new urban form to the epochal changes of the industrial revolution; he showed how changes in the organization of city space affected social relationships within and between classes; and he tied this social geography to the suffering and coming to consciousness of the new proletariat.

His basic research strategy, like that Marx would use later, was that of finding the critical case (England, and Manchester

---

[3] The literature on Manchester is immense. See e.g. Alan J. Kidd and K. W. Roberts, *City, Class and Culture: Studies of Social Policy and Cultural Production in Victorian Manchester*. Manchester: Manchester University Press. 1985; Gary Messinger, *Manchester in the Victorian Age: The Half-Known City*. Manchester: Manchester University Press, 1985; P. H. Abell, *Transport and Industry in Greater Manchester*. Rotheram: Eastwood Press, 1978; François Vigier, *Change and Apathy*. Cambridge, Mass.: MIT Press, 1970; and G. F. Chadwick, 'The Face of the Industrial City: Two Looks at Manchester', in H. J. Dyos and Michael Wolff (eds.), *The Victorian City*, London: Routledge and Kegan Paul, 1973, i. A fascinating report on Manchester, and on the condition of its working class, virtually contemporaneous with that of Engels, was published in a series of articles in the *Morning Chronicle* in October and November 1849: Angus Bethune Reach, *Manchester and the Textile Districts in 1849*, ed. C. Aspin. Helmshore: Helmshore Local History Society, 1972. Engels's treatment may also be compared to that of L. Faucher, *Manchester in 1844*. London: 1969 (originally pub. 1844).

within it) that heralded new developments that would later become more commonplace. 'Today England', he wrote,

is a unique country with a capital city of 2½ million inhabitants, with huge factory towns; with industries which supply the needs of the whole world, making practically everything by means of the most complicated machines. England has an industrious, intelligent and dense population, two-thirds of which is engaged in industry. The population is composed of quite different classes than it used to be and these social groups make up quite a different sort of nation, with new customs and new needs. The Industrial Revolution has been as important for England as the political revolution for France and the philosophical revolution for Germany. The gulf between the England of 1760 and that of 1844 is at least as great as that between France under the *ancien régime* and the France of the July Revolution. The most important result of this Industrial Revolution has been the creation of the English proletariat.[4]

What was the possibility, he wanted to know, that this new working class might become a revolutionary actor? Rather than begin with work-centred relationships, which later provided the *locus* of most Marxist reflections on this question, Engels took it up from the vantage-point of the new industrial towns.

Engels wrote near the end of a five-decade period of remarkable urbanization. None of the ten largest cities in England less than doubled in population between 1801 and 1851 (compared with only one of the top French cities of the same period). At this moment of astounding growth, Leeds and Birmingham tripled in size; Manchester and Liverpool quadrupled. All of the ten largest cities had populations of over 100,000 by 1851, with Liverpool and Manchester well over 300,000.

In the face of this unprecedented concentration of people and functions, Engels asked four broad questions: How did these towns originate? What mechanisms embedded in capitalist accumulation sustained their growth? What were their most important spatial and human characteristics? How might

---

[4]   Friedrich Engels, *The Condition of the Working Class in England*, trans. W. O. Henderson and W. H. Chaloner. Stanford, Calif.: Stanford University Press, 1968, 23–4, 29.

these features affect class formation? He treated city space and social relations as the key mediators between the explosive growth of capitalist production and the coming to consciousness and political possibility of the working class.

Industry and commerce attain their highest stage of development in the big towns, so that it is here that the effects of industrialisation on the wage earners can be most clearly seen ... The vast majority of the inhabitants of these towns are the workers. We propose to discuss their condition and to discover how they have been influenced by life and work in the great factory towns.[5]

Engels provides an account of the new urbanization by locating its principal impetus in changes in manufacturing dating from the mid-eighteenth-century. These shifts in technology and social organization required the centralization and concentration of capital, factories, and people.

Big industrial establishments need many hands massed together in one building. They have to live together and the labour force of even a relatively small factory would populate a village. Others are attracted to the vicinity of the factory to satisfy the needs of the operatives and these include such craftsmen as tailors, shoe-makers, bakers, builders and joiners.

With this initial concentration, a new dynamic is created that leads to further city growth:

The inhabitants of the new industrial village, particularly the younger generation, become skilled factory workers and become accustomed to a new way of life. There generally comes a time when the first factory cannot employ all the workers in the

---

[5] Ibid., 29. Useful treatments of this work can be found in Steven Marcus, *Engels, Manchester and the Working Class.* New York: Random House, 1974; Gertrude Himmelfarb, *The Idea of Poverty: England in the Early Industrial Age.* New York: Vintage Books, 1985, ch. 11; and Gareth Stedman Jones, 'Engels and the Genesis of Marxism', *New Left Review*, 106 (Nov.–Dec. 1977).

Note that three of Engel's questions are versions of each of Marx's three theoretical projects: dealing with epochal change on a grand scale, but focusing on the transition from feudalism to capitalism; developing an account of the accumulation of capital within the capitalist epoch; and constructing a social theory capable of analysing whole societies in the period of capitalism.

industrial village. This leads to a fall in wages which in turn attracts industrialists to the district. In this way a village grows into a little town and a little town expands into a city. The more the town grows the greater are the advantages which it has to offer industrialists. It has railways, canals and roads and there is an ever-growing variety of skilled labour available. Competition between local builders and engineers reduces the cost of building new factories to a level below what has to be paid when a factory is built in a remote spot to which timber, machinery, building operatives and industrial workers have to be transported. The new town has its market and its exchange, which are crowded with buyers. It is in direct contact with the sources of raw materials and with markets in which manufactured goods can be sold. All this explains the remarkably rapid expansion of the great industrial towns.

Rural wages, however, remain lower than city pay scales, and the countryside continues to compete for industrial investment. But this route, too, invokes the process of urbanization, once a factory is located in the countryside. Rural industrialization thus 'does not lessen the tendency toward industrial centralisation and every new rural factory carries within it the seed of a future factory town. If it were possible for this furious expansion of industry to continue unchecked for another century every manufacuring district in England would become a single large factory town.'[6]

This account of competition, labour markets, locational advantages, sunk costs, and transaction costs is strikingly modern. It not only identifies the new cities as capitalist ones, but specifies mechanisms for their creation and growth. But it was not here that Engels made his most important and suggestive contributions. Rather, it was in his accounts of the connections between the social structure of capitalism and the spatial structure of the town, and between this social geography and working-class formation. He develops these themes in his brief surveys of London, the lace production city of Nottingham, the port of Liverpool, the textile towns of Leeds and Bradford in the West Riding of Yorkshire, and finally in a more expanded discussion of Manchester, the city Engels explores in closest detail, 'the classic type of modern industrial

---

[6] Engels, *Condition of the Working Class*, 28–9.

town . . . the regional capital of South Lancashire, and . . . the classic home of English industry. This is the masterpiece of the Industrial Revolution and at the same time the mainspring of all the workers' movements.'[7]

Modern Manchester grew from the base of a small medieval town. As late as 1775, it was not a manufacturing city but a commercial centre for the surrounding countryside, where such manufacturing as existed in the district was located. Its area was very small, comprising a circle with a radius of only 1,200 feet (120 metres). With the revolutionary changes in cotton production in the later decades of the eighteenth century, the town began its period of explosive population growth from a base of just 22,000 in 1775. In 1790, there were still only two cotton mills in the city, employing 1,240 workers; just thirty years later, the city was home to 66 mills employing 51,800 people; and population density had grown from 15 to over 65 people per acre (0.4 hectares). By mid-century, Manchester could no longer be crossed easily by foot (by 1890 it had nearly doubled its diameter and population once again).[8]

Engels argues that the principal characteristics of Manchester and the other cities he studied were new kinds of segregation and division in space, and a profound social isolation and indifference between the classes. The 'one community' paternal ethos of eighteenth-century England had come to an end with great abruptness.

In all the industrial towns, 'the workers are segregated in separate districts where they struggle through life as best they can out of sight of the more fortunate classes of society'. In twenty-five pages of thick description, Engels takes us into these various working-class residential neighbourhoods of Manchester. He walks us through the most densely populated neighbourhoods, with jumbled thoroughfares, inadequate sanitation, and tumbledown houses. He makes us see the homeless. He also shows how the newly developed building

[7] Ibid., 50–1. 'I know Manchester as well as I know my native town and I know more about it than most of its inhabitants.'

[8] This information is drawn from Vigier.

industry and its logic of profitability have helped craft this new built-environment. This combination of ethnography and analysis is gripping.

In the book's most important passage Engels steps back from his pointillist portraits of the working-class districts of Old Town and New Town, Ancoats and Hulme, to present a remarkable overview of the spatial design of the city as a whole. Here, he confronts the striking paradox of the orderly way the social classes are arrayed in space in spite of the absence of planning. The market-places of industrial location, house-building, and retailing had produced a layout of the city whose main features included a commercial core, where the classes did not so much interact as pass each other by ('Yet they rush past each other as if they had nothing in common. They are tacitly agreed on one thing only—that everyone should keep to the right of the pavement so as not to collide with the stream of people moving in the opposite direction. No one even thinks of sparing a glance for this neighbor in the streets'); radial avenues linking the centre to the outskirt suburban residences of the bourgeoisie ('by the time Ardwick Green is reached, the street has changed its character yet again and is flanked with residences occupied by the upper and middle classes. Beyond Ardwick Green lie the big gardens and the country villas of the wealthier factory owners and merchants'); petty bourgeois retail shops lining these avenues ('Even the less pretentious shops adequately serve their purpose of hiding from the eyes of wealthy ladies and gentlemen with strong stomachs and weak nerves the misery and squalor which are part and parcel of their own riches and luxury'); and behind them, the teeming and desperate living quarters of the industrial working class ('On reaching them one meets with a degree of dirt and revolting filth, the like of which is not to be found elsewhere').[9]

Although each element of this description of segmented city space and cross-class isolation might have been something of an exaggeration for the fifth decade of the nineteenth century,

---

[9] Engels, *Condition of the Working Class*, 31, 55, 56, 58. The first citation in parentheses refers to London, not Manchester.

as some of Engels's critics have charged,[10] it brilliantly cap-
tures the main lines of spatial development not only for the
early industrial cities, but for the century to come. The classic
passage of his analytical description of Manchester, which
presages most of the main themes of twentieth-century urban
geography and sociology, deserves extended quotation:

Owing to the curious lay-out of the town it is quite possible for
someone to live for years in Manchester and to travel daily to and
from his work without ever seeing a working-class quarter or coming
into contact with an artisan. He who visits Manchester simply on
business or for pleasure need never see the slums, mainly because the
working-class districts and the middle-class districts are quite distinct
. . . In those areas where the two social groups happen to come into
contact with each other the middle classes sanctimoniously ignore
the existence of their less fortunate neighbours. In the centre of
Manchester there is a fairly large commercial district, which is about
a half mile long and a mile broad. The district is almost entirely given
over to offices and warehouses. Nearly the whole of this district has
no permanent residents and is deserted at night, when only policemen
patrol its dark, narrow thoroughfares with their bull's eye lanterns.
This district is intersected by certain main streets which carry an
enormous volume of traffic. The lower floors of the buildings are
occupied by shops of dazzling splendour. A few of the upper stories of
these premises are used as dwellings and the streets present a
relatively busy appearance until late in the evening. Around this
commercial quarter there is a belt of built up areas on the average
one and a half miles in width, which is occupied entirely by working
class dwellings. The area of workers' houses includes all Manchester
proper, except the centre, all Salford and Hulme, an important part of
Pendleton and Chorlton, two-thirds of Ardwick and certain small
areas of Cheetham Hill and Broughton. Beyond this belt of working-
class houses or dwellings lie the districts inhabited by the middle
classes and the upper classes. The former are to be found in regularly
laid out streets near the working-class districts—in Chorlton and the
remoter parts of Cheetham Hill. The villas of the upper classes are
surrounded by gardens and lie in the higher and remoter parts of
Chorlton and Ardwick or on the breezy heights of Cheetham Hill,
Broughton and Pendleton. The upper classes enjoy healthy country
air and live in luxurious and comfortable dwellings which are linked

---

[10] See e.g. David Ward, 'Victorian Cities: How Modern?', *Journal
of Historical Geography*, 1/9 (1975).

to the centre of Manchester by omnibuses which run every fifteen or thirty minutes ... These plutocrats can travel from their houses to their places of business in the centre of the town by the shortest routes, which run entirely through working-class districts, without even realising how close they are to the misery and filth which lie on both sides of the road. This is because the main streets which run from the Exchange in all directions out of the town are occupied almost uninterruptedly on both sides by shops, which are kept by members of the lower middle classes.[11]

In this account of the social morphology of Manchester, Engels pioneered in the analysis of the spatial structure of the city, including its zones and radial axes; the geography and condition of housing; public transportation and the journey to work; the development of suburbs and central business districts; the relationship between work and residence; and the arrangement in space of social interactions within and between classes.[12] But unlike the way these issues have been treated subsequently in various academic studies, Engels consciously linked their origins to the large-scale development of industrial capitalism and their consequences to the emergence of class consciousness.

For Engels, it was not only the concentration of workers in the factory that facilitated the development of such mass working-class movements as trade unionism, Chartism, and socialism, but also the concentration of workers in autonomous working-class communities, where, free from the direct supervision of their employers or the state, they could create such institutions as reading rooms, and working men's clubs and societies. The organized working-class movement utilized the semi-free space of the neighbourhoods to meet (in the pubs, friendly societies, and other venues), to proselytize, to organize. In the sharply class-divided spaces of cities like Manchester, workers become 'conscious of the fact that they form a separate class, and have their own interests, policies

[11] Engels, *Condition of the Working Class*, 54–5.
[12] In enumerating these topics, I have deliberately repeated some of the chapter titles from Richard Dennis, *English Industrial Cities of the Nineteenth Century: A Social Geography*. Cambridge: Cambridge University Press, 1984. Dennis utilizes the recent work of geographers to go over much the same ground as Engels.

and points of view, which are opposed to those of the capitalist property owners. Above all they are conscious of the fact that on their shoulders rests the real power of the nation and the hope of its future progress.'[13]

II

There are considerable limitations to Engels's analysis. Like Edward Thompson's *The Making of the English Working Class*, the great twentieth-century work on working-class formation in this period, *The Condition of the Working Class in England* is too quick to assume as natural and inevitable the passage from the misery and segregation of the working class to its formation as a class with revolutionary potential. The emergence of class as a social construction capable of mapping the new social geography of urban capitalism as a matter of class, not just at work but also away from work, was a highly uncertain and contingent matter, as, for example, the experience of the United States has shown.[14] But even if Engels

[13] Engels, *Condition of the Working Class*, 273.

[14] I have discussed these issues in Ira Katznelson, *City Trenches: Urban Politics and the Patterning of Class in the United States*. New York: Pantheon Books, 1981; 'Working Class Formation: Constructing Cases and Comparisons', in Ira Katznelson and Aristide Zolberg (eds.), *Working Class Formation: Nineteenth Century Patterns in Western Europe and the United States*. Princeton, NJ: Princeton University Press, 1986; and 'Working Class Formation and the State: Nineteenth Century England in American Perspective', in Peter B. Evans, Dietrich Rueschemeyer, and Theda Skocpol (eds.), *Bringing the State Back In*. Cambridge: Cambridge University Press, 1985. Richard Harris has rooted this contingency in space by constructing a dialectic of space and class formation. He shows how, on the one hand, because the city is a place that offers proximity to working people it provides a material basis for consciousness and collective action; but the segregation of the working class at the same time may promote intra-class rather than inter-class bases of consciousness and mobilization. See Richard Harris, 'The Spatial Approach to the Urban Question: A Comment', *Society and Space*, 2 (Mar. 1983); and Harris, 'Residential Segregation and Class Formation in the Capitalist City: A Review and Directions for Research', *Progress in Human Geography*, 8 (Mar. 1984).

was wrong to think that the English model of class formation provided the single possible trajectory and that the activity of the working classes in the 1840s heralded an imminent revolutionary practice ('The revolution *must* come. It is now too late for a peaceful outcome to the affair'),[15] his placement of city space at the centre of his consideration of the meaning of industrial capitalism, and his strikingly prescient treatment of urban issues, did open an exceptionally fertile avenue of inquiry about city space, capitalist development, and class formation. Unfortunately, Marxism did not take it up.

To be sure, some of the propositions that later emerged as centrepieces in the development of classical Marxism first surfaced in this book by Engels: the focus on production rather than market competition as capitalism's central motor; the novel features of industry, including the reserve army of labour and crises of overproduction; the formation of the working class into a proletariat capable of challenging the capitalist order; and the distinction between artisan radicalism and working-class socialism.[16] Yet just as it is important to give *The Making of the English Working Class* its due within the history of Marxist theory, so it is also important to underscore that in the subsequent elaboration of these themes Marxists, including Engels, dropped the urban emphasis and the spatial elements from their work. As a result, they needlessly denied themselves important resources capable of contributing to the development of social theory.

Engels, in short, showed how Marxism might incorporate the city into its social theory in order to create an account of the emergence of different kinds of working-class subjectivity. In pursuit of this aim, he also introduced urban space, albeit in a very condensed way, into the core of Marx's macroscopic historical materialism and into Marx's account of the logic of capitalist accumulation by utilizing the organization and reorganization of the urban built-form to show how city space defines a dynamic, changing terrain: the city appears at once

---

[15] Engels, *Condition of the Working Class*, 335.
[16] For a discussion, see Stedman Jones, 'Engels and the Genesis of Marxism', 102. See also his essay, 'Engels and the End of Classical German Philosophy', *New Left Review*, 79 (May–June 1973).

in his work as absolute space (as a given environment and as a framework), as relative space (in which people and activities are in patterned interaction with each other), and as relational space (in which the spatial dimension is interiorized in objects and social processes).[17] In Engels's formulation, the city has a certain shape within which people live their lives and conduct their activities; this space helps impel these activities, and these activities contain spatial elements within them. The dispositions and behaviour of city dwellers are lived in and through such spatial processes as the journey to work, the relatively autonomous operation of housing and labour markets, the degree of differentiation between work and home, the extent of segregation between groups and social classes, the ease of movement between places in the city and between the city and other places, and the relationship of the private and public domains. In his treatment of such matters in *The Condition of the Working Class in England*, Engels was the foremost pioneer in the analysis of what David Cannadine, echoing Engels, has called the 'links between the shapes on the ground—the physical form which the evolving city took— and the shapes in society—the nature of the social relationships between people who lived in the towns'.[18]

Just the same, even if Marxism would profit by travelling down the road blazed by Engels, the promises of the city for Marxism, and of Marxism for analyses of the city, we will see, can be redeemed only if this road is widened to place the story of state-making and states alongside the histories of feudalism and capitalism. I attempt to show in subsequent chapters how, in this way, it will be capable of managing more traffic: a better chronology, and account of the causes, of post-feudal urbanization; a more specific treatment of the content of the built-form of the city, especially as it concerns the separation of work and home; and a more contingent analysis of class formation. On this enhanced route, the city can be treated

[17] These distinctions are drawn from David Harvey, *Social Justice and the City*. London: Edward Arnold, 1973.

[18] David Cannadine, 'Residential Differentiation in Nineteenth Century Towns: From Shapes on the Ground to Shapes in Society', in James H. Johnson and Colin G. Pooley (eds.), *The Structure of Nineteenth Century Cities*. London: Croom Helm, 1982, 235.

better both as *explicans* and *explicandum*; and, too, both as a point in space and as a place with a distinctive social and spatial organization.[19]

The broadening of Engels's road implies two major changes to the central analytical projects of Marx. First, instead of treating the transition from feudalism as a single movement towards capitalism, the transition can more fruitfully be viewed as a twinned, and intertwined, shift from the medieval system of parcellized sovereignty (in which each unit of feudal society, whether rural or urban, fused property and power), to a system that separated newly concentrated political sovereignty from private property. Second, within the capitalist epoch, instead of focusing exclusively on the logic of the process of capitalist accumulation, we need also to work with a parallel 'logic of institutions' for the history of state-making and the functioning of states.[20]

On this broadened road, Marxism can help contribute to an understanding of how the city is constituted by, and helps constitute, capitalism and state-making. Post-feudal urbanization in the West has been the nucleated location for states of power and capacity, administration, information-gathering, and decision-making; just as it has been the nucleated location for private capital and its process of accumulation. These patterns of concentration, and their interrelationships, have varied over time, and have been expressed in and through changing configurations of urban space. Cities as points and as places can thus be defined in terms of this double coalescence.[21]

---

[19] Note that this agenda, in its attention to history and to the project of social theory, is considerably broader than that tackled to date by the new Marxist urbanism.

[20] Rather than search for a once and for all hierarchy of relations between capitalist and state development, or for the competing capacity of each to shape the modern world, we need to find a reading of history in order to know first how in some times and places each might have had its moment of dominance or truth; and to show that at all times there is a complicated exchange between them, even if the principles of this exchange may vary over time. The study of cities can help facilitate this theoretical enterprise. For an important orienting discussion, see Aristide R. Zolberg, 'Origins of the Modern World System: A Missing Link', *World Politics*, 33 (Jan. 1981).

[21] Cities are both economic units and legal–political entities

The provocative union of Marxism and the city proposed by Engels addressed only part of this agenda because he had nothing to say in this early work about the history, character, and activities of national states. Engels's contribution lies in the way he raised fundamental, and still challenging, questions in three dimensions that correspond to each of Marx's theoretical projects which, alas, have been developed by Marxism without exploiting these lines of development: (1) questions about the linkages between large-scale processes, principally the development of capitalism, and the emergence of the modern capitalist city (what was the role of the city in the development of modern capitalism, and how, in turn, did capitalism inform the development of the urban system?); (2) questions about the linkages between the city as a point in the accumulation process and its internal forms (how has the city contributed to the process of capitalist accumulation, as well as to its contradictions, and how, in turn, has capitalism as a system of economic production and reproduction helped determine the contours of urban space?); and (3) questions about the linkages between these forms and the development of class and group consciousness (how have the various spatial developments of cities within capitalism affected patterns of group and class formation, and, in turn, what role have these actors had in shaping the urban built-environment?). These are the tasks entailed in joining Marxism and the city, and these are the questions I explore in the remaining chapters.

---

within states. The boundaries of the city are thus the objects of contest. These are political struggles about where the implosion of capital and power will take place, who the players in urban conflicts will be, what identities they will assume, and what institutional vehicles will decide these questions.

5 From Feudalism to Capitalism: The Place of the City

ONE area where Marxism has dealt with the city is the transition from feudalism to capitalism. This discussion has been satisfactory only in part. Too much is compressed in the very idea of this epochal transformation. Marxism's conception of feudalism has been too narrow: it has treated some 500 years of history in terms of a single direction of change, and it has flattened the dimensions and varieties of transition. Further, Marxism's insistence on parallel treatment as modes of production for feudalism, which fused sovereignty and property, and for capitalism, which did not, is misplaced. And yet, even if Marxism's discussion of the transition has been flawed, it is here that we can find some of the most important attempts to make cities a constitutive part of a key historical and theoretical problem. In this chapter, I should like to broaden and shift the terms of this engagement of Marxism with the city. By so doing, it is possible to shed some light on the impact cities had on large-scale change in early modern Europe, and, in turn, on the ways cities as places were altered by the demise of feudalism.[1]

[1] This account is indebted to David Gordon's insistence that an earlier draft was unsatisfying in its approach to feudalism and in its failure to provide enough material to consider the relationship of cities and the creation of a post-feudal order; and to Charles Tilly who found its sketch of the feudal state and its relation to cities unsatisfactory for implicitly creating France and Britain as if they represented all of medieval Europe and for asserting, on the basis of this reduced scale, that medieval urban growth was even and stable. In revising this chapter with these criticisms in mind I have especially profited from the book Tilly has since published, *Coercion, Capital, and European States, AD 990–1990.* Oxford: Basil Blackwell, 1990, and from the suggestive portrayal of 'State and Class in European Feudalism' by Herbert Gintis and Samuel Bowles in Charles Bright and Susan Harding (eds.), *State-Making and Social Movements.* Ann

I

The historical transformation from feudalism to capitalism occupies a tremendously important place in Marxism's project of developing a historical materialism capable of explaining major qualitative changes in the social organization of Western societies. As Heinz Lubasz points out, it 'is the *only* transition from one socio-economic formation to another which Marx ever purports to have found, the one and only transition, therefore, which he can cite in support of the view that, as feudalism generated capitalism so capitalism is bound to generate communism'.[2] And yet, as I noted in Chapter 2 there

---

Arbor, Mich.: University of Michigan Press, 1984. The chapter's geographical focus remains much as it was, however, in part because I am self-consciously reading backwards, as Marx did, from the outcomes of the 18th and 19th centuries with respect to the *loci* of capitalist development and in part because of the need to simplify this discussion. Thus, I am deliberately not concentrating on the 'exterior states, such as Sweden and Russia, that went through their formative years with relatively large concentrations of coercion and relatively small concentrations of capital', or on 'interior states, such as Genoa and Holland, for which the opposite was true'. Rather, I focus on the 'intermediate states, such as England and France, in which concentrations of capital and of coercion grew up side by side'. These intermediate states were those characterized by the most symmetrical balance between states, as *loci* of coercion, and cities, as *loci* of capital, in the feudal epoch. Tilly, *Coercian, Capital*, 64.

   [2] Heinz Lubasz, 'The Transition from Feudalism to Capitalism: Marx's Two Theories of Social Development', unpublished MS, 1982. In a challenge to Marxist understandings of the transition from feudalism to capitalism centring on producive relations and the appropriation of surplus, Immanuel Wallerstein has distinguished between three levels of this shift in social organization: the transformation of a redistributive world system to a capitalist world economy; the incorporation of outside systems into this market system; and the processes of commercialization and proletarianization within these societies. Even if one dissents from the causal hierarchy proposed by Wallerstein, these distinctions between levels are useful analytically. None the less, they lead us away from a consideration of the traditional Marxist issues of transition, and they have no place, except a functional one, for one of the hallmarks of the transition to a post-feudal order, that is, the centralization of states

is an important difference between the mechanisms for the demise of feudalism and capitalism. In Marx's analysis, the tendencies to crisis and system-change are internal to the core logic and functioning of capitalism as a system of accumulation, and they presage the form of post-capitalist social organization; by contrast, the system of surplus extraction within feudalism contains no such structural necessity. As a consequence, Marxism has lacked the tools required to account simultaneously for the demise of feudalism and the development of early capitalism in the same manner as its analysis of the crisis tendencies of capitalism seeks to account for the emergent features of a post-capitalist world.

It is the absence of an internal dialectic within Marxism's treatment of feudalism that brought into question the purported homology in the transformation rules of feudalism and capitalism. Needing to discover a solution to this incommensurability, especially for England, the 'classical' home of capitalist development, Marxism has pursued two main possibilities. One has been a search to discover 'laws' of development for the feudal mode of production analogous to those elaborated by Marx for capitalism.[3] Another has been

---

and state capacity. Immanual Wallerstein, 'From Feudalism to Capitalism: Transition or Transitions?', paper presented to a meeting of the American Historical Association, Dec. 1974

[3] Robert Brenner's now classic (and contested) articles on the late feudal countryside have placed class struggle, and the capacity for collective action of the peasantry at the local village level, at the heart of an explanation as to why the landed aristocracy successfully reimposed serfdom in Eastern Europe, but not in Western Europe, where peasants had a greater capacity to resist such a reimposition. Robert Brenner, 'Agrarian Class Structure and Economic Development in Pre-Industrial Europe', Past and Present, 70 (Feb. 1976), and 'The Agrarian Roots of European Capitalism', Past and Present, 97 (Nov. 1982). These contributions, as well as critical essays and Brenner's response, have been collected in T. H. Aston and C. H. E. Philpin (eds.), The Brenner Debate: Agrarian Class Structure and Economic Development in Pre-Industrial Europe. Cambridge: Cambridge University Press, 1983. Brenner has also written a critique of Paul Sweezy and Immanuel Wallerstein's account of the development of capitalism out of feudalism. He argues that they place too much stress on market forces and too little on production and class

the identification of an external force within the confines of feudalism capable of providing a beach-head for the successor form of social organization, capitalism.

Medieval towns provided Marxism with its most plausible candidate for the second solution. Characterized by secular rationality and materialism, they have been identified as 'non-feudal islands in the feudal seas', and as 'a foreign body in feudal society', necessary perhaps to the trading aspects of feudalism, but deeply antagonistic and subversive to it. Henri Lefebvre argued that this position—first elaborated by Adam Smith in his discussion of cities and the creation of modern capitalism in book 3 of *The Wealth of Nations*—was also adopted by Marx, for whom 'the dissolution of the feudal mode of production and the transition to capitalism is attached to a *subject*, the town. The town breaks up the medieval system (feudalism) . . . the town is a "subject" and a coherent force, a

---

relations; he criticizes the view that the growth of trade gives rise to an increased division of labour, rising labour productivity, and a smooth transition to a self-generating process of capitalist expansion; and he demurs from the view that capitalist class relations are a result, rather than a cause, of capitalist development. A more recent, and very suggestive, formulation, which focuses on England and builds on the work of Brenner, but tries to improve on his comparison of England and France, is Richard Lachmann, *From Manor to Market: Structural Change in England, 1536–1640.* Madison, Wis.: University of Wisconsin Press, 1987. Lachmann treats the development of capitalist-type relations in rural England in terms of a game of three sets of élite actors: the gentry, the crown, and the clergy. Both the creation of a rural proletariat and the development of landed private property, he argues, were the results of strategic action by the gentry. In order to protect their own control over the coveted agricultural surplus, they successfully acted to proletarianize peasant labour and make it subject to labour markets and they generated a market in land. In this way, they precluded either the clergy or the crown from appropriating the surplus through the use of feudal mechanisms. An account that focuses more on the economic dynamics of change within feudalism, and that adopts a careful view about the significance of class struggle (wisely noting that the determinants of an outcome are not necessarily the same as the causes of a conflict), is Edward Nell, 'Economic Relationships in the Decline of Feudalism: An Examination of Economic Interdependence and Social Change', *History and Theory*, 6/3 (1967).

partial system which attacks the global system and which . . .
destroys it.'[4] This position, which was developed later as the
historiographical common wisdom outside of Marxism by
Henri Pirenne, Max Weber, and Lewis Mumford, was initially
incorporated to serve this purpose into post-Second World War
Marxism by Paul Sweezy in his critique of the work of Maurice
Dobb.[5].

Dobb had analysed the various crisis points within feudalism, and had argued that capitalism arose when feudalism
could no longer contain and resolve crises of demography
(brought on in part by disease), stagnating trade, the blood-
letting of war, and landlord–peasant class struggle, and when
various solutions to these crises, including absolutism and the
reimposition of serfdom, failed to resolve them. Sweezy's
critique was based on the point that arguments such as these
may well account for the decline of feudalism but have little
to say about the genesis of the successor mode of production.
He argued that feudal cities were the 'prime mover' *both* for
the decomposition of feudalism and for the rise of capitalism
precisely because they constituted an 'external' proto-capital-
ist agent of dissolution within the ambit of the feudal mode of
production. Cities, as relatively autonomous and free zones of
merchant activity, represented a negation of the immobile
patron–client ties of the feudal countryside. These were transcended by the capacity of merchants to redirect production
away from the local markets of towns and their immediately

---

[4] M. M. Postan, *The Medieval Economy and Society: An Economic
History of Britain in the Middle Ages.* London: Weidenfeld and
Nicolson, 1972, 212. Marc Bloch, *Feudal Society.* London: Routledge
and Kegan Paul, 1965, 444. Henri Levebvre, *La Pensée marxiste et la
ville.* Paris, Casterman, 71; trans. in R. J. Holton, *Cities, Capitalism
and Civilization.* London: Allen and Unwin, 1986, 30.

[5] The Dobb–Sweezy debate, together with relevant commentaries,
has been collected in Rodney Hilton (ed.), *The Transition from
Feudalism to Capitalism.* London: New Left Books, 1976. A useful
summary, as well as a critique, of Marx's and other urban-centred
views of the transition to capitalism can be found in Holton, *Cities,
Capitalism and Civilization.* The view of the world market as both
cause and consequence of capitalist development has been elaborated
by Immanuel Wallerstein, *The Modern World System.* New York:
Academic Press, 1974, 1980, i and ii.

surrounding regions to trade on a much wider scale. In turn, once the various urban nodal points of the market became intertwined in a larger market system, which included overseas trade, the new world system became self-reinforcing, and capitalist production and exchange came to be elaborated on an ever-larger scale.

There are considerable warrants for this city-centred position. There was an obvious contrast between the functionally undifferentiated countryside and the economic specialization of the craft and trade activities centred in the towns. The autonomy of the towns allowed them to have their own legal codes and local governments, and to provide a free refuge to serfs who sought to escape from manorial servitude. There was a provocative correlation, Holton notes, between 'the upswing of the European economy between 1000–1300 in terms of population growth, increasing production and the development of new markets, [and] a process of urban expansion'. Further, as he observes, the towns provided a location for 'the development of autonomous *Burgertum* involving association between individuals, rather than exclusively ascriptive ties based on kinship or personal dependence'.[6]

It may well be, as Perry Anderson stresses, that 'a *dynamic opposition* of town and country was alone possible in the feudal mode of production: opposition between an urban economy of increasing commodity exchange, controlled by

---

[6] Holton, *Cities, Capitalism and Civilization*, 64. See also 30. Holton's book is directed toward a criticism of these positions. By contrast, Ivan Szelenyi sides with Weber and the neo-Smithian Marxists in arguing, in an essay comparing the East European and West European experiences, that things urban had an independent causal status *vis-à-vis* the creation of capitalism because cities as market-places were decisively implicated in the development of modern capitalism. '"Urban" is at least a relatively distinct phenomenon analytically, as much producing capitalism as it is its product.' Ivan Szelenyi, 'Urban Development and Regional Management in Eastern Europe', *Theory and Society*, 10 (Mar. 1981), 174. My own position, as will be clear in a moment, *contra* Holton, is that cities did in fact play an important role in the demise of feudalism and in the development of early capitalism, but, *contra* Szelenyi, that this role was rather different from that mooted by the usual town-centred portraits of this epochal transformation.

merchants and organized in guilds and corporations, and a rural economy of natural exchange, controlled by nobles and organized in manors and strips'—a separation made possible by the unusual autonomy of medieval towns from external political authority and supervision, an independence signified and protected by their physical ramparts. Nevertheless, the argument that the city in this opposition provided an *exogenous* instrumental agent that made the long-term reproduction of feudalism impossible cannot be sustained, certainly not in the elegant, simple form proposed by Sweezy.[7]

Marxism has been unable to build a persuasive urban-centred account of the transition from feudalism to capitalism based on the town's alien and upstart qualities. The urban solution to a search for feudalism's transformation rules is undermined by the town's integral place within feudal law and social organization, and by the character of its ties to the countryside within feudalism both as a system of production and as a system of rule. The medieval town must be placed in its context, and that context was feudalism. The relationship between the town and feudalism was mainly one of synergism, not contrariety. The principles undergirding feudalism—principles of political authority, hierarchy, regulation, and space—included and incorporated the towns. Further, patterns of identity, fealty, and collective activity within the urban spaces of medieval Europe bore a striking identity with those of the countryside.

None the less, I will argue, urban locations did have a pivotal role to play both in the demise of feudalism and in the rise of capitalism, one quite different from that of the linear developmental trajectory ascribed to it by Sweezy. The resources of capital ('tangible mobile resources, and enforcible claims on such resources'[8]) that were concentrated in late medieval towns and cities played a key role in shaping the character and activities of mercantilist states and economies. In particular, urban-based economic resources made possible the vast absolutist concentrations of sovereignty that marked the end of

[7] Perry Anderson, *Lineages of the Absolutist State*. London: New Left Books, 1974, 148.

[8] Tilly, *Coercion, Capital*, 17.

the more fragmented and less capable feudal states. Moreover, the highly stylized and regulated economic environments of feudal towns tended to deflect economic innovation to the countryside, where it had the effect of diluting feudal relations, and where new investments of capital created a less concentrated production-based urbanization as a counterpoint to the large Baroque cities that were the *loci* of interdependent mercantile activity and state power. Further, political developments in feudal towns provided an administrative model that acted as a demonstration effect for the creation of increasingly capable, centralized states. In turn, these transformations reshaped the system of cities. The economic activities of the new commercial capitalism were located in big city trading sites and small city centres of proto-industrialization. The towns that had served as trading relay points and as *loci* for craft production during the feudal epoch stagnated and many contracted. At the same time, some, but only a few, of the older urban centres burgeoned into mammoth concentrations of people, power, and property, as centres of kingship and overseas trade. Within these cities the spatial arrangements that developed located commercial, artisanal, and state activities in a new post-medieval urban form.[9]

II

Feudalism is an immensely condensed term, both in the range of types and in the characteristics that compose the family of instances. Feudalism's rich complexity as a form of social organization cannot be accommodated even by a term as complex as 'mode of production' because it understates feudal society's juridical elements. By attempting to incorporate the legal and political elements into the conception of the feudal mode of production, Perry Anderson demonstrated just how

[9] An important discussion of the spatial organization of these cities can be found in Lewis Mumford, *The City in History*. New York: Harcourt, Brace, and World, 1961. I take up issues of the social geography of feudal towns and Baroque cities in my *City Trenches: Urban Politics and the Patterning of Class in the United States*. New York: Pantheon Books, 1981, ch. 2.

difficult a task this is. Contrary to traditional Marxist approaches that make the economic relationship of lords and serfs the defining characteristic of feudalism, he insisted that feudalism cannot be defined except via its 'political, legal and ideological superstructures' since these specify the 'type of extra-economic coercion' that distinguishes feudalism from other kinds of pre-capitalist modes of production.[10] Though Anderson thus placed state-centred matters at the heart of his analysis of the distinctiveness of feudalism, he did so in the manner of a closed Marxism. As Gintis and Bowles observe, 'to remain faithful to the traditional notion of property-based extraction as an essential core, with respect to which surrounding social forms are but embellishments and instruments of reproduction, Anderson is impelled to consider the feudal state as "superstructural," and hence derivative of class relations.'[11] This move fails to capture the ways in which feudalism's complicated relationship of property and sovereignty makes it necessary to put aside this assumption of an economic, as distinguished from a political, base in order to explore the specific terms of engagement between feudalism's forms of state and authority and its mechanisms of production and extraction.

Feudalism organized agricultural and urban production within the framework of a fragile state system and the integrating values of Christendom. In pre-state kinship systems, space is organized through family ties; in state systems, however basic, society is organized within territorial boundaries defined by political power and control, rather than by societal self-organization. In this sense, feudal societies were spaces ruled over by kings who did not preside 'over tribes or kinsmen but over a territory and its people'.[12] But unlike modern national states they did not govern 'multiple contiguous regions and their cities by means of centralized, differentiated, and autonomous structures',[13] and unlike modern

---

[10] Anderson, *Lineages of the Absolutist State*, 404.

[11] Gintis and Bowles, 'State and Class', 22.

[12] Robert A. Dodgshon, *The European Past: Social Evolution and Spatial Order*. London: Macmillan, 1987, 130.

[13] Tilly, *Coercion, Capital*, 2.

nation states, they did not rule over nations, understood as primordial entities, but over kingdoms that 'comprised and corresponded to a "people" (gens, natio, populus), which was assumed to be a natural, inherited community of tradition, custom, law, and descent'. Kingdoms were collective entities in a given territory that were 'the highest, most honourable, and most perfect of all secular communities'.[14]

The pioneering anthropological work on early state systems and cities by Robert McCormick Adams, based on studies of Mexico and Mesopotamia, stressed that the replacement of kinship by state systems entailed a growing specialization of administration and rule in increasingly complex societies in areas larger than those that could be integrated and governed on principles of kinship. Dodgshon maintains that this development is essential to an understanding of feudalism because of its new interrelationships of society, authority, and territory. According to now conventional portraits by anthropologists, kinship systems presided over by chiefs have an inherent tendency to division as a part of their demographic and political dynamics. Each new unit reproduces the characteristics of that from which it emerged. In more elaborate systems of chiefdoms, the different units of the larger structure reproduce the essential elements of the centre. States, by contrast, according to this literature, solve the problem of fission by a more complicated organizational structure that makes the parts of the system dependent on the centre, and which makes each part of the larger system less self-sufficient and less complete, and thus more dependent on the legal, administrative, and normative features of kingship.[15]

Seen in these terms, the many feudal states were something of a hybrid. On the one hand, their territorial organization was not a reflection of kinship; rather, kingdoms organized society

<hr>

[14] Susan Reynolds, *Kingdoms and Communities in Western Europe, 900–1300*. Oxford: Oxford University Press, 1984, 250.

[15] Robert McCormick Adams, *The Evolution of Urban Society*. Chicago: Aldine Books, 1966; R. Cohen and E. R. Service, (eds.), *Origins of the State: Anthropology of Political Evolution*. Philadelphia: Institute for the Study of Human Issues, 1978; H. J. M. Claesen and P. Skalnik (eds.), *The Early State*. The Hague: Mouton, 1978; Dodgshon, *The European Past*, 130–2.

in space. On the other hand, the units of feudal society were not functionally differentiated. On the contrary, 'although having an internal differentiation of role and function, the lordships which emerged as the building blocks of the feudal state still tended to replicate the role and functions of the royal centre above them'. Rather than being an integrated and differentiated system, the feudal kingdom was a system in which the king franchised his authority downwards 'as a system of government. The whole style of feudalism, with kings conceding not just land but powers of lordship to their major vassals, meant that the latter could behave, within their fiefs, like little kings.' Not surprisingly, this kind of arrangement was beset with deep problems of integration since it reproduced some of the main decentralized characteristics of complex chiefdoms.[16]

'European feudalism', Gintis and Bowles write, 'may be represented as (a) a form of property-based production and extraction, (b) a form of state, and (c) a specific articulation of the two.' The complex feudal state established the framework for feudalism as a system of rural and urban production through the intermixture of two competitive but mutually dependent juridical principles:

Royal sovereignty, the first of these competing forms of state, exhibited in prototypical form the modern system of unitary administration, justice, and military organization. Feudal suzerainty, the second of these forms, was marked by the liege–vassal relationship, fragmented jurisdiction, and the hierarchical layering of authority. The unity of the feudal state lay precisely in the dynamic underlying the contrast of sovereign and suzerain principles of concentrating power and distributing the prerogatives of office.[17]

Feudal states with these characteristics, as successors to the Roman Empire, were numerous and fragile,[18] but it would be

16 Dodgshon, *The European Past*, 132–3.
17 Gintis and Bowles, 'State and Class', 20–1.
18 Of his baseline year, Tilly writes of the 'enormous fragmentation of sovereignty then prevailing throughout the territory that would become Europe. The emperors, kings, princes, dukes, caliphs, sultans, and other potentates of AD 990 prevailed as conquerers, tribute-takers, and rentiers, not heads of state that durably and densely regulated life within their realms.' Further, within a 'ring formed by these sprawl-

too blunt to describe them, as they commonly are, as weak. Rather, they were very supple decentralized organizational instruments of rule which, through their systems of delegation and patron–client ties, integrated once-autonomous households and kin systems into a coherent pattern of authority, however loosely coupled.

The feudal state had a tense double aspect. Even though it was fragmented, and the presence of the sovereign limited in many areas, 'the principle of suzerainty itself was always complemented by a web of royal institutions operating under the aegis of the highest among the feudal suzerains—the monarch—and his administrative staff'. In the German principalities, but especially in England and France, the monarchy was more than just the highest level of suzerainty; it represented a distinctive claim to authority, rule, and the administration of justice, with the king as the overlord of all lords. Further, within this aspect of the framework of the state, the concept of private property took shape, at odds with the notion that fiefs were inalienable. The idea of private property developed within the framework of feudalism, achieving 'its legal substance only on the basis of royal law and courts, which were thus woven into the very fabric of feudal society'.[19] At

---

ing, ephemeral states sovereignty fragmented even more, as hundreds of principalities, bishoprics, city-states, and other authorities exercised overlapping control in the small hinterlands of their capitals'. A half-millennium later, around the periphery of Europe, there were rulers 'who dominated substantial territories: not only the Ottoman Empire, but also Hungary, Poland, Lithuania, Muscovy, the lands of the Teutonic Order, the Scandinavian Union, England, France, Spain, Portugal, Naples'. Encircled by this zone, much of the centre of Europe was still divided into 'hundreds of formally independent principalities, duchies, bishoprics, city-states, and other political entities that generally could use force only in the immediate hinterlands of their capitals'. Europe in 1490, with some 80 million people, 'divided into something like 500 states, would-be states, statelets, and statelike organizations . . . Europe remained a land of intensely fragmented sovereignty.' Tilly, *Coercion, Capital*, 39–42. This discussion of the feudal state, while bearing mainly on France and England, also holds in terms of the principles of rule for the Germanic zone between France, Hungary, Denmark, and Italy.

[19] Gintis and Bowles, 'State and Class', 23–5.

the same time, the state had a different aspect as it was deeply enmeshed in the system of suzerainty. From this vantage-point, the king stood at the top of the feudal hierarchy and his position 'was necessarily different not in kind, but only in degree, from the subordinate levels of lordship beneath it. The monarch, in other words,' Anderson writes, 'was a feudal suzerain of his vassals . . . not a supreme sovereign set above his subjects.'[20]

The king of a feudal state can thus be seen as an element in the form of social organization that has variously been described as one of 'parcellized sovereignty'[21] and as a system in which 'most social relationships were extremely localized, intensely focused on one or more of a number of cell-like communities—the monastery, the village, the manor, the castle, the town, the guild, the brotherhood, and so forth'.[22] If Christendom and the state provided the overarching values and practices of hierarchy giving a place to these units, each, at the same time, possessed a relatively high degree of institutional completeness and autonomy. Each, too, whether a rural fief or a walled town, fused property and sovereignty:

At the base of the feudal state hierarchy the fief tended in general to coincide with the manor (or union of manors), the site of the direct confrontation of lord and subordinate peasantry. This particular articulation of feudal state with feudal agricultural production gave rise to the most critical of the specific defining characteristics of the feudal social formation: *the fusion of the elementary unit of the suzerain state and the basic unit of agricultural production.*[23]

[20] Anderson, *Lineages of the Absolutist State*, 151.
[21]   To my knowledge, the phrase 'parcellized sovereignty' was coined by Perry Anderson in *Lineages of the Absolutist State*. It is developed as part of a framework for understanding the feudal town in the important essay by John Merrington, 'Town and Country in the Transition to Capitalism', *New Left Review*, 93 (Sept.–Oct. 1975).
[22] Michael Mann, *The Sources of Social Power: A History of Power from the Beginning to* A.D. *1760.* Cambridge: Cambridge University Press, 1986, 376–7.
[23] Gintis and Bowles 'State and Class', 27. They continue: 'This fusion can be understood only by recognizing that in feudalism, as in other social formations, class relations possess a political structure distinct from the state. The feudal fusion is in fact expressed by two unities, one institutional and the other political. First, the basic unit

The fragmentation of political authority within feudalism thus took a specific form, that of its delegation to people who possessed private means of surplus appropriation. The units of property and political authority within feudalism were thus identical. 'Each basic "fragment" of the state', Ellen Meiksins Wood has observed, 'was at the same time a productive unit in which production was organized under the authority and for the benefit of a private proprietor ... The essential characteristic of feudalism, then, was a privatization of political power which meant a growing integration of private appropriation with the authoritative organization of production.'[24] Control over the means of production and the means of coercion were fused, and the activities of producing and maintaining order were interdependent in each of the squares of the feudal chequerboard.[25]

Urban centres were integral parts of this system. Braudel, representing a more common position, has argued to the contrary that medieval towns 'made themselves into autonomous worlds, city-states, buttressed with privileges (acquired or extorted) like so many juridical ramparts ... The miracle of the first great urban centuries in Europe was that the town ... was able to lead a completely separate life for a long time.' Further, 'capitalism and towns were basically the same thing in the West'.[26] This formulation is doubly misleading. For the towns were inherently feudal in just these characteristics: in their ramparts, their juridical privileges, even their economic functions as crossroads and as relay points of exchange. Like the other units of feudal society, the towns were collective

---

of the state (the fief) coincides with the basic unit of production (the manor). Second, the apex of the political structure of the basic unit of the state coincides with the apex of the political structure of the unit of production, as incarnated in the person of the lord of the manor.'

[24] Ellen Meiksins Wood, 'The Separation of the Economic and Political in Capitalism', New Left Review, 127 (May–June 1981), 88.

[25] Nell, 'Economic Relationships in the Decline of Feudalism', 330.

[26] Fernand Braudel, Capitalism and Material Life, 1400–1800. New York: Harper and Row, 1973, 398, 400. The case for the feudal qualities of the town, by contrast, has been assertively put by Yves Barel, La Ville medievale: Système social, système urbaine. Grenoble: Presses Universitaires de Grenoble, 1977.

corporate bodies that shared in feudalism's characteristics of delegated authority and the integration of property and power. Even where 'extorted', the town's privileges of autonomy were secured by hierarchical grants of charters and were safeguarded by the logic and operation of feudalism as a parcellized system, and the town's relationship to territorial authorities always remained 'a precarious balance of autonomy and dependence'.[27] Even more, the ability of the towns to function as economic units within the medieval world depended on the inherently feudal division of kingships into segmented units. Thus, urban-based trade existed within the interstices of feudalism. Only when the larger system began to change in the fourteenth and fifteenth centuries did the towns begin to alter as well.[28]

The recent pioneering study of Susan Reynolds, focusing on the horizontal bonds and patterns of lay collective activity in Western Europe between 900 and 1300, strongly supports the view of the town as a principal part of the feudal mode of production. She shows, first, 'that there was much less difference in social and political organization—not least in its collective manifestations—between different parts of western Europe than seems to be generally thought', and, second, that there was much less difference between urban and rural communities than is commonly argued. She concedes, of course, that 'At first sight, with their republican constitutions, mercantile rulers, industrial conflicts, and personally free populations, towns seem an anomaly in the monarchical,

[27] Paul H. Hohenberg and Lynn Hollen Lees, *The Making of Urban Europe, 1000–1950.* Cambridge, Mass.: Harvard University Press, 1985, 43. In a balanced summary, they also reject the 'tempting oversimplification to see cities only as an alien growth in the medieval cultural body, a breeding ground of "modern" secular values and ideas. As we have noted, the medieval church was increasingly urban, and it was in the cities that its major unifying and civilizing missions for the system as a whole were worked out. In other words, cities were integral to the pursuit of medieval social ideals even though they also harbored the practices and reflections that would challenge prevailing values' (40).

[28] I took up these issues, with a similar orientation but different emphasis, in *City Trenches,* ch. 2. This formulation as regards change is an inversion of Braudel's discussion of cause and effect.

seigniorial, and agricultural middle ages'. But this apparent contrast is deceptive in the main not only because the town found its place within the macro-characteristics of feudalism, but because the institutions and patterns of life in towns were quite similar in many respects to non-urban institutions and patterns.[29]

Reynolds's argument about towns is implanted within her densely documented claims about the robust collective habits of medieval life. She shows how horizontal ties of community were made possible by the parcellized features of feudalism, and how both custom and law provided a framework for the corporate body—including urban ones—as the basic frame-work of action. Once the force and commonality of the collective activities of lay society are taken into account, our understanding of the towns as 'internal' or 'external' entities within feudalism tilts decisively in the direction of the former. This is the case for the origins, institutions, and autonomy of medieval towns.

Much effort has been expended to explain the origins of the clustering in the tenth and eleventh centuries of people whose occupations were primarily not agricultural and who formed urban social units they and others understood to be distinct. In his summary of competing perspectives, Harold Carter usefully distinguishes between mercantile settlement theory (a view associated with Henri Pirenne which argues that towns grew when merchants involved in long-distance trade settled at crucial locations in the major lines of movement); market theory (which stresses the town as a nodal point of local rather than long-distance trade); artisanal theory (which stresses production, not exchange, with the argument that towns originated when craftsmen clustered as part of a growing division of labour; for obvious reasons, many Marxists have found this version congenial); guild theory (which emphasizes

---

[29] Reynolds, *Kingdoms and Communities*, 156. On the integrative role of kingship and Christendom, see also Maurice Keen, *The Pelican History of Medieval Europe*. London: Penguin Books, 1968, chs. 1 and 4. There were recurring tensions between the principles of secular rule and the church, of course, yet at the same time, as the sacrament of coronation showed, there was a substantial religious element to medieval kingship.

the legal rights secured by associations initially created for religious or social reasons); military theory (which sees the agglomeration of people and activities in terms of the need to establish garrisons); ecclesiastical theory (which sees the agglomeration as caused by the rights, privileges, and immunities of the church); free village theory (which sees the new towns as extensions of already autonomous smaller villages); and Romanist theory (which treats feudal towns as direct successors of Roman cities). These alternatives are not of course mutually exclusive, and some combinations may be more persuasive for some places than others. Whether or not the initial foundation of a feudal town was the Roman *castrum*, a fortified residence or castle, or an ecclesiastical centre, these would have remained only isolated points 'unless they were translated into towns by the active influence of trade and commerce which created the second element which was grafted onto the pre-existing nuclear strong-point'.[30] As such, all medieval towns were either central places servicing the economic requirements of their regions or points in more fluid and sometimes larger-scale networks of trade, or both.[31]

Reynolds does not so much disagree with the various accounts of the origins of medieval towns as think the search for an independent theory of urban origins is vitiated by the inherent place of towns in all feudal relations from the start. At the outset of the feudal era, urban functions and urban characteristics were exhibited by places no larger than agricultural settlements, but without them feudalism as a system

[30] Harold Carter, *An Introduction to Urban Historical Geography*. London: Edward Arnold, 1983, 34–5.

[31] This dual perspective is the analytical heart of Hohenberg and Lees's analysis of European urbanization. 'The Central Place System is rooted in the stability of the land and its tillers. A neat geometric mosaic of graduated centers structures the commercial, administrative, and cultural needs of a region and eventually integrates regions into a unified nation . . . By contrast, the Network System testifies to the mercurial force of movable wealth and universal ideas. If the links among its cities could be described mathematically, it would be with topology rather than Euclidian geometry . . . Our own preference is to retain the two models as complementary ways of looking at interurban relationships and at the complex process that is urbanization.' Hohenberg and Lees, *The Making of Urban Europe*, 69–71.

would not have been possible. As Frederic Cheyette has shown, the rural world was remade in the obscure period from the fifth to the tenth centuries. The dispersed habitations of the kind that had been characteristic of the Roman agricultural world, from petty farmsteads to great villas, disappeared, to be replaced by a network of nucleated villages with organized fields. New sites were settled to unprecedented levels of density. The main effect of this development was to deflect European agriculture from the migrant, pastoral, wild-grass economy that had characterized the countryside before the fifth century. But a secondary effect was to provide potential nodes of urban development.[32]

The growth of towns from this proto-town basis occurred hand in hand with the growing wealth and population of the countryside in early medieval Europe, From this perspective, there was no single moment 'at which either "pre-urban" fortresses or "pre-urban" trading places became towns'. The growth of towns is thus better accounted for within larger explanations about the confluence of demographic, political, military, ecclesiastical, and economic factors that shaped the development of the feudal mode of production more generally,[33] though, of course, once urban growth was set into motion, it contained elements that were self-reinforcing.

To be sure, with the exception of Venice, the earliest feudal towns had little or no formal independence. 'Nevertheless any town was by its nature well-fitted to make the most of the opportunities for autonomy which medieval methods of government and judgement gave to all local communities.' When these opportunities were seized, as they were in the eleventh to the thirteenth centuries, the collective activities of townspeople did not need special authorization within the framework of feudal law and social, political, and economic relations:

Once townspeople had the common interests, the confidence, and the influence to negotiate with their rulers or with anyone else, then

[32] Frederic Cheyette, 'The Origins of European Villages and the First European Expansions', *Journal of Economic History*, 37 (Mar. 1977).

[33] Reynolds, *Kingdoms and Communities*, 160–1.

they could do so on whatever subject they wanted, asking for confirmation of their customs, restriction of their dues, or even, if they were ambitious enough, for entirely new privileges. What would limit the success of any town community, whether it worked through a guild or through its normal assembly, would not be its lack of formal constitutional machinery or legal standing, but its lack of political and economic muscle.[34]

In short, autonomous, self-governing towns with local and long-distance trading functions, and centres of craft production, were different from other local communities only in the degree of their independence and freedom of action, but not in kind. It would be a matter of anachronistic teleology if we viewed this corporate quality of the town as separate from the larger framework of feudalism. Like the system's other corporate entities, towns were whole worlds with a local order characterized by the fusion of property and sovereignty.[35]

If towns can be seen as external capitalist agents within feudalism only by reading history backwards, and by imposing later definitions of economic activity on to uncomprehending contemporaries, what cannot be excluded by the rejection of the Sweezy–Postan position is the possibility that in the long compass of historical change *feudal* towns may have incubated a capitalist challenge. In a moment, we will see that I think this was the case, but not in the way associated with the 'external' position. It is just this double aspect of urban centres that justifies Merrington's characterization of the autonomy of the feudal town as having 'internal externality'. 'It is wrong', he concluded,

to interpret the 'freedom' of the medieval towns in a one-sided, unilateral sense outside the feudal context which both determined the 'externality' of this freedom of merchant capital and defined its limits. The town's autonomy was not that of a 'non-feudal island' (Postan); its freedom and development as a corporate enclave was not 'according to its *own* propensities' as in Weber's historicist formulation. It was grounded on and limited by the overall parcellization of

[34] Ibid., 164, 168.
[35] A nice summary discussion of the fusion of comital administration and vassal service can be found in Keen, *Pelican History of Medieval Europe*, 54–5.

sovereignty, based on *the coincidence of political and economic relations of subordination/appropriation* which defined the feudal mode. It was the existence of this corporate urban autonomy as a 'collective seigneur' within a cellular structure based on sovereignty 'in several degrees' that precisely encouraged the fullest development of merchant capital in the medieval town. Hence urban 'capitalism' was both internal and external to the feudal mode—or, more precisely, the former was the *condition* for the latter.[36]

But what was the relationship of this merchant capitalism, where capitalists (the 'people who specialize in the accumulation, purchase, and sale of capital')[37] did not themselves employ wage-workers or directly organize production, to later capitalism, where capitalists took direct control over production? Was there a movement along a straight line, or, as in Pirenne's metaphor, was capitalist development marked 'by a series of separate impulses not forming continuations one of another, but interrupted by crises'? This history, he insisted, 'resembles a staircase, every step of which rises abruptly above that which precedes it'.[38] But if it was like a staircase, what was the importance of its urban steps?

III

The relationship between the merchant capitalism of feudal towns, the post-feudal mercantilism headquartered in the political capitals of absolutist regimes, and the industrial capitalism of factory cities was emphatically not one of a movement along a straight line. The feudal town was not the lineal ancestor of the early modern city, nor was the early modern city the lineal ancestor of the industrial-capitalist city. Any such thought has been decisively rebuffed by Jan de Vries's reconstruction of European urbanization in early modern Europe. On the basis of a data set he constructed of all

[36] Merrington, 'Town and Country', 78.

[37] Tilly, *Coercion, Capital*, 17.

[38] He continues: 'We do not find ourselves in the presence of a gentle and regular ascent, but of a series of lifts.' Henri Pirenne, 'The Stages in the Social History of Capitalism', *American Historical Review*, 19 (Apr. 1914), 515, 495.

cities in Western Europe from 1500 to 1800 with populations greater than 10,000, he was able to fill in the gap between the medieval city and the industrial city and to show that the long-term expansion of European cities was neither direct nor unbroken. There was no gradual and benign process of urbanization hand in hand with a steady development of capitalism culminating in the 'great towns' studied by Engels that were created *de novo* in the late eighteenth and early nineteenth centuries.[39]

The pattern on the ground was discontinuous. The medieval period produced a legacy of between 3,000 and 4,000 towns.[40] Through the sixteenth century, these administrative and trading centres had been growing at roughly the same pace, and had remained small. As an urban system, these locations had

---

[39] Jan de Vries, *European Urbanization 1500–1800*. London: Methuen, 1984. The data base de Vries created is a major achievement in its own right. It takes the form of providing estimates of population in 50-year intervals for all 379 cities that had at least 10,000 people at any time between 1500 and 1800. This statistical base provides the possibility of moving significantly beyond conjecture in identifying objects of explanation in the development of the European city. For a critical comment on setting the lower limit at 10,000, see Jack Goldstone, 'Cities and Social Change', *Sociological Forum*, 2 (Winter 1987).

In a thoughtful review, Paul Wheatley points out that de Vries's attempt to locate the city as a sector within a wider urbanized society, and to study urban–rural interactions in a regional framework with attention to larger-scale processes, is a strategy that has been pursued to good effect in the study of urban hierarchies outside Europe. Paul Wheatley, 'European Urbanization: Origins and Consummation', *Journal of Interdisciplinary History*, 17 (Autumn 1986). Notable examples are Robert Redfield, *The Primitive World and its Tranformations*. Ithaca, NY: Cornell University Press, 1953; Gilbert Rozman, *Urban Networks in Ch'ing China and Tokugawa Japan*. Princeton, NJ: Princeton University Press, 1973; Rozman, *Urban Networks in Russia, 1750–1800, and Premodern Periodization*. Princeton, NJ: Princeton University Press, 1976; Paul Bairoch, *De Jericho à Mexico: Villes et économie dans l'histoire*. Paris: Gallimard, 1985; and G. William Skinner (ed.), *The City in Late Imperial China*. Stanford, Calif.: Stanford University Press, 1977. Hohenberg and Lees's magisterial overview of European urbanization draws in part from the work of Skinner on central places.

[40] De Vries, *European Urbanization*, 69.

utilized virtually all the available topographical places that had the capacity to perform these functions within the conditions of feudalism. Between the sixteenth and late eighteenth centuries, this stock of towns provided the field of play for an increasingly heterogeneous and stochastic urbanization.

Seen as a whole, the pattern of medieval urbanization was one of relatively stable, evenly growing systems, especially in northern Europe. Most towns—some 3,000 of the total of 3,267 towns in northern Europe in 1330—were local marketing centres with fewer than 2,000 residents. Intermediate towns of between 2,000 and 10,000 people accounted for most of the rest; these tended to have administrative as well as market functions. Fewer than 50 towns had populations larger than 10,000, with the largest oriented more to overseas than local trade, and these averaged just over 19,000 residents.[41]

Then, in the seventeenth century, some cities emerged from the pack to dominate north-west Europe, so that by the middle of the eighteenth century a new urban hierarchy was in place. The period 1500–1750 thus represents a coherent moment of selective and concentrated urban growth in which mammoth new Baroque capitals and mercantile centres developed which concentrated royal authority and the organization of national and overseas commerce, rivalling in size the large city-states of Florence, Venice, and Milan,[42] and signifying a shift in the geography of hegemony in Europe. At the same moment, thousands of smaller cities either did not grow or declined. By contrast, in the century after 1750 urban growth concentrated disproportionately in smaller, older cities, and in new small industrial cities; the biggest urban centres grew only sluggishly. De Vries labels this pattern 'urbanization from below'. Yet another shift took place by the middle of the nineteenth century. Then, led by the expansion of such cities as Manchester in England, urban growth was led once again by giant and rapidly growing concentrations of people and functions,

[41] These estimates are those of Norman Pounds, *An Historical Geography of Europe, 450 B.C.–A.D. 1330*. Cambridge: Cambridge University Press, 1973, 358. His estimates are discussed in Hohenberg and Lees, *The Making of Urban Europe*, 51–5.

[42] In 1490, Florence had 297,000 inhabitants, Milan 337,000, and Venice 357,000. Tilly, *Coercion, Capital*, 48.

but this time they were associated more with capitalist production than with political and trading activities, though the older mercantile cities resumed very rapid growth as well.[43]

This complicated urban pattern constrains various understandings of the epochal changes at work in late feudalism and beyond; it suggests puzzles that must be solved, and it hints at various possible lines of explanation. These, we shall see, have the double effect of introducing an urban-spatial element into Marxist specifications of the transition from feudalism to capitalism and of exposing the limits of attempts to account for this epochal change without extending the meaning of the transition from feudalism to include the genesis of centralized national states. Without such an extension, it is not possible to understand the role of late feudal and early modern European cities as cause and effect.[44] How is it possible to pursue

[43] De Vries, *European Urbanization*, chs. 6 and 7, and 255–60. If this was the variegated trajectory of city growth over time, there was also a radical shift in these centuries in the location of city development. The first part of the 17th century witnessed a decisive shift away from the Mediterranean and away from a multi-centred city system towards a system with a single centre in north-west Europe. For a discussion, see Charles Tilly, 'The Geography of European Statemaking and Capitalism Since 1500', Center for Studies of Social Change, New School for Social Research, New York, Working Paper No. 4, Jan. 1985.

[44] The following discussion is certainly not complete. If we understand the making of modern Western society not just in terms of the transition from feudalism to capitalism, but in particular also in terms of state-making and the development of an international geopolitical system of competitive national states, then a host of issues not considered here, such as the role of war and the military, diplomatic relations, and the conquest of colonies, are quite fundamental. Here my purpose is much more limited: to sketch the connections between urban development and the European modernity, and in so doing to comment on key themes in Marxism's first project of epochal transformation. For a suggestive discussion of the issues of epochal transition from a macrosociological perspective that argues that 'neither feudalism nor capitalism, if they are used as general periodizations of European history, would be merely economic labels', and thus counsels against their use in understanding the dynamism of Europe after 1500, see Michael Mann, *Sources of Social Power*. The citation is from pp. 375–6.

If, as Michael Mann writes, 'capitalism and the national state

this course in a way that is consistent with the empirical challenges posed by the urban portrait of de Vries?

IV

Underneath and underpinning this story of discontinuous urbanization and the dynamic interrelationship of cities with the development of both capitalism and centralized states was a profound shift in the relationship between property and political authority. If we understand feudalism not simply as a system of production but as 'an articulation of state and economy',[45] then we are better able to focus on the dual character of the 'transition from feudalism to capitalism', which entailed fundamental changes to the nature of the state, the character of the economy, and the relationship between the two.

With regard to states, the tense dualism of sovereignty and suzerainty was resolved in favour of the former. A particular kind of state, the national state, emerged from the pack of alternative types to become the dominant form. With regard

---

formed a loose but coordinated and concentrated alliance' in post-feudal Europe, and if we understand that 'real-life capitalism, the form of economy that actually triumphed for a time over Europe and the whole globe, actually presupposed, and embedded within itself, other forms of power, especially military and political power' (446, 495), then we must also ask, with Charles Tilly, 'how the dominant patterns of coercion and accumulation affect the actual experience of living in cities, and to what extent the character of cities determines those patterns of coercion and accumulation'. Charles Tilly, 'Since Gilgamesh', *Social Research*, 53 (Autumn 1986), 410. Unfortunately, the lively debates about the transition from feudalism to capitalism have taken place in isolation from the literature on mercantilism. As a consequence, the issues of the consolidation of national states and the interrelationships between the making of states and the making of modern capitalist economies have been obscured unnecessarily. I was first stimulated to think about the separation of the transition and mercantilism literatures by Margaret Somers. A suggestive discussion can be found in Charles Tilly, 'Space for Capital, Space for States', *Theory and Society*, 15/1–2 (1986).

[45] Gintis and Bowles, 'State and Class', 35.

to the economy, the dualism of private property and suzerainty likewise was resolved in favour of the former. The articulation of state and economy was now based on a decisive separation between concentrated sovereignty and property.

The feudal coincidence of the two was thus sundered in the era of mercantilism. The state simultaneously asserted its absolute right to property by dissolving the cell-like units of feudalism that had property rights[46] and divested itself of all rights to property except those that were directly concerned with governance and rule. With this split, capitalism was truly born. Governments now had a (near and growing) monopoly over the use of violence and the collection of payments for protection, and they supplanted the juridical activities of the lords as well; at the same time, governments offered protection for those with property and, over time, the prospect of participating in state institutions of representation and governance. The state now stood aside from the private economy while also intervening in the economy on its—and its own— behalf.[47] The result was a robust synergism of state and

[46] 'The break in the fusion of suzerain state and manorial economy effectively withdrew from the hands of the landlord class its traditional means of ensuring the reproduction of its position of social dominance. The first step in this direction was the communation of services, which deprived the lord of political leadership at the site of feudal production. The refusal of traditional Marxist theory to recognize a political structure *within* the site of production has led to a general underestimation of the importance of this change.' Gintis and Bowles, 'State and Class', 41.

[47] See Frederic Lane, 'The Role of Governments in Economic Growth in Early Modern Times', *Journal of Economic History*, 35 (Mar. 1975). Lane develops a model in which he treats governments in early modern Europe as enterprises seeking to maximize their own profits: 'When government has secured a monopoly in using violence and collecting payments for protection, it can raise prices above the cost to it of producing the protection it provides; that is, it can collect in taxes more than is needed to police its territory and defend it against attack from outside. Viewed as an economic enterprise, a government which seeks to maximize its profits can use its monopoly to set the price of its products above the amount that the government spends to produce it. It can in this way take from those whose property rights it protects much of the society's surplus protection. This "take" by the government I call tribute, for it is useful to have a word to designate the difference between the cost of producing

commerce under the auspices of mercantilist principles and practices. The prospects of state and capital proved mutually confirming. The spheres of sovereignty and property, however intertwined, and whichever dominated at a given moment, were now independent, their relationships contingent.

This split had many ramifications. It was certainly fundamental to capitalist accumulation, for as 'the state divested the appropriating class of direct political powers and duties not immediately concerned with production and appropriation', it left them with 'private exploitative powers purified, as it were, of public, social functions'. From this vantage-point, capitalism represented the privatization of the political power that inheres in property, while the new state emerged 'with an unprecedented *public* character'. Inside the workplace, capital was triumphant; outside the workplace, capital lacked the prerogatives that economically dominant classes had under feudalism.[48]

This division also profoundly affected the development of cities not only as points in a web of urban-based relationships, but as places with distinctive forms and social relations arrayed in space. With the demarcation of property and sovereignty, the state and the private economy became the two main instruments shaping the configuration of urban space. We shall soon see that the balance between them, like the development of post-feudal urbanization, was discontinuous and uneven. In tracing this historical process we will make our way back to the nineteenth-century industrial cities explored by Engels.

If cities were marked by the new relationship of mercantile capitalism and the state that placed the powers of property and sovereignty in separate realms, in turn they performed key tasks in the shaping of the new states and the new capitalism of early modern Europe.

The towns of feudalism, especially after 1300, played a partially contradictory role from the perspective of the post-

---

protection and the price charged for it; that is, the difference between the protection's costs to its producers and to its consumers' (12).

[48]   Wood, 'The Separation of the Economic and Political in Capitalism'.

feudal epoch. On the one hand, they were testing grounds of what might be called new social technologies of power and commerce, which were most fully realized only later under absolutism and mercantilism. On the other hand, the most important feudal features of the towns—their high degree of autonomy, their regulated economies, and their juridical and substantive fusion of power and property—helped deflect the further development of the political and economic innovations they pioneered to locations (both rural and urban) outside their confines.

Feudal towns were incipiently mercantile. They provided protected and regulated economic environments for the elaboration of increasingly robust craft production and for the extension of networks of trade beyond the confines of the local region. The very success of medieval agriculture and increases in rural productivity made it possible for the towns to become more weighty corporate actors within feudalism. As they became so, they also became internally better integrated units of economic activity, much as the national state was to become in the era of absolutism and mercantilism. More and more as feudalism developed, the increasingly capable towns, and the merchants within them, elaborated new forms of commerce that heralded future mercantile patterns.[49]

Like the national state two centuries later, the towns, through municipal legislation and control over citizenship, reinforced the corporate character of their economic activity. The units of market competition were not just individual merchants, but the towns themselves, which sought to enforce their monopolistic privileges against the countryside and

---

[49] Pirenne, 'Stages in the Social History of Capitalism', 508–9. Writing about the feudal towns of the 14th century, Pirenne took note of the ambitious reach of the largest: 'Documents abound which attest the existence in the great cities of men of affairs who hold the most extended relations with the outside world, who export and import sacks of wool, bales of cloth, tuns of wine, by the hundred, who have under their orders a whole corps of factors or "sergeants" (servientes, valets, etc.), whose letters of credit are negotiated in the fairs of Champagne, and who make loans amounting to several thousands of livres to princes, monasteries, and cities in need of money.'

against rival towns. In these ways, some of the urban centres within feudalism provided laboratories for the working out of techniques and practices of economic production and exchange within a protected political framework. As such, they provided a history and an experience of a dynamic repertoire that was later elaborated on a much larger scale.

The feudal town was also a political incubator. Although their self-governing features were an instance of the corporate insulation made possible within feudalism more generally, and although the townspeople needed no new political theory to assert their autonomy because the towns already possessed the legal capacities of corporations, the right to self-government was especially important to city-dwellers engaged in commerce:

The *bourgs* and old episcopal towns round which the new urban societies grew up had been ruled in the past by bishops or noble landlords, who had little or no understanding of problems which had everyday urgency for commercial men, the judgement of questions of contract and debt, the regulation of wages and prices, and conditions of labour and sale.[50]

Hence, towns struggled, frequently with success, to enlarge their political autonomy within the dependent framework of feudalism.

These struggles came at a moment when the royal monopoly over trade and markets, which had reached its peak in the tenth and eleventh centuries, was becoming increasingly difficult to sustain. As markets became more specialized, as the scale of trade increased, and as regulations became more specific and were elaborated in new areas of activity, centralized control became less and less feasible. The devolution of control over trade to local communities put the regulation of commerce in the hands of those who managed it on a daily basis.

Thus, by the late twelfth century, the development of feudal towns had produced a 'revolution' in government, characterized by more independence for long-established towns and comparable autonomy for newly founded urban areas, as well

---

[50] Keen, *Pelican History of Medieval Europe*, 92.

as major advances in the technology of public administration and in the scope of government activities. Public authority in the towns over commerce and daily life deepened and broadened. Local governments concerned themselves with the attempt to secure privileges to trade outside their own walls and with the terms of trade within them. To these ends, as the towns gained a greater capacity to govern their own affairs, new institutions and rules of governance were fashioned.[51]

The right to the liberties of the town were granted to all its citizens (a status ordinarily obtained by people who had resided in the town for a year and a day and who contributed dues to the community), who participated in the town's assemblies, which, in larger towns, had been replaced by councils by the thirteenth century. Some towns based their patterns of representation on wards, others on occupational crafts. In virtually all, a class-privileged political élite dominated the affairs of the town, more often than not without controversy about basic principles. Within this agreed frame, vigorous conflicts concerned with economic interests and the use, or misuse, of government were endemic.

The vigour of this city politics reflected the importance and complexity of the activities of municipal governments: law courts and judicial proceedings; the regulation of industry and trade (including the fixing of tolls, the setting of maximum wages, hours of work, and terms of apprenticeship, control of prices, proscriptions of cartels, rules ensuring that goods were brought to the open market, and the inspection of weights and measures); the construction and maintenance of public works; the attempt to secure public health; and the raising of revenue through direct taxation.[52]

It was precisely the combination of commercial and political innovation within the confined compass of these towns that,

---

[51] There was a great deal of variation in this pattern in different parts of Western Europe, as Reynolds details in *Kingdoms and Communities*, 168–80, but there were also enough similarities to warrant my presentation of these developments in a collective singular voice.

[52] This portrait is drawn from a variety of sources, the most important of which for me have been Reynolds, *Kingdoms and Communities*, ch. 6, and Dodgshon, *The European Past*, ch. 6.

on a small scale, anticipated the mercantilist–absolutist future, and provided models on the ground for it. Yet, paradoxically, the concentrations of power and merchant capitalism that followed the feudal epoch were located elsewhere, outside these prototype urban centres. Why this lack of continuity?

The answer lies within this very paradox. The insularity and self-sufficiency of the towns made them adversaries of kings and princes who sought to reassert the prerogatives of states, a process that culminated in the development of highly centralized, bureaucratic, absolutist (or constitutional) regimes in the sixteenth and seventeenth centuries. Where cities were strongest, along the trade routes from the Mediterranean to the North Sea, they succeeded well into the eighteenth century in resisting the attempt of centralized states to dominate them. These important exceptions aside, cities lost their autonomy: 'where postfeudal monarchs and their armies could dominate them, cities were turned into agents of centralization by princes intent on binding the territories of the realm ever more tightly to the crown.'[53] The older cities became sources of capital for the process of state-building. Thus the growth of absolutist and constitutional states came at the expense of the prerogatives of the city.[54]

There is some historical irony here because the late medieval town helped provide the capital resources required by the state-builders. Indeed, this is the pivot of Tilly's explanation of why it was that some states were able to lead in the creation of national states, which from the seventeenth to the nineteenth centuries eventually became the dominant form of

[53] Hohenberg and Lees, *The Making of Urban Europe*, 170. See also Nell, 'Economic Relationships in the Decline of Feudalism', 331–46. A portrait of one of the more interesting, and complex, cases of city–state relationships is detailed by Marjolein t'Hart, 'Cities and Statemaking in the Dutch Republic, 1580–1680', unpublished paper, 1987.

[54] A useful discussion of the strategic game between merchants and the state can be found in Edgar Kiser, 'The Formation of State Policy in Western European Absolutisms: A Comparison of England and France', unpublished MS, Apr. 1986. Kiser is interested in the potential autonomy of the state, and he turns the debate over whether absolutist states were autonomous into a discussion of variability.

state throughout Europe. Locating war and war-making capacity at the heart of the statist enterprise, Tilly traces three different ways rulers sought to secure the resources needed for these activities. In areas like Brandenburg and Russia, where there was little urbanization, and thus little by way of concentration of capital, rulers built their own direct and massive structures to extract resources directly from their populations. In areas like the Italian city-states and the Dutch Republic, where concentrations of capital in highly autonomous cities were far more developed than comparable state capacity, rulers made compacts with capitalists to provide resources without the need to create strong, centralized state structures. But in the areas we have been focusing on, especially in France, England, and Prussia, there was something of an intermediate situation in the balance between the resources of merchant capitalists in the towns and the capacity of the monarchy. There, rulers both built their own extractive bureaucracies and made compacts with capitalists, to be sure, but they 'spent more of their effort . . . on incorporating capitalists and sources of capital directly into the structures of their states'. This they did by such mechanisms as systems of representation, as in Parliament; by the appointment of merchants to key positions within state treasuries; and by striking bargains with capitalists by establishing coherent rules of transaction that protected property in exchange for the ability of the state to tax the surplus for its own purposes.[55] Unlike those that followed the 'coercion-intensive' path to state-building, these states were based on the resources of a new capitalism and a clear split between sovereignty and property. And unlike those that followed the 'capital-intensive' path, these states built capable, centralized state apparatuses.

These national states put an end to the parcellized sovereignty that had been the hallmark of feudal rule. They collected sovereignty and political capacity, and concentrated them in central places. There, in capital cities, courts and professional bureaucracies of finance, justice, and military and diplomatic affairs were concentrated. London, Amsterdam, Paris, Madrid, Lisbon, and half a dozen other cities reached an

---

[55] Tilly, *Coercion, Capital*, 30.

unprecedented size; by the late sixteenth century each had a population of at least 100,000, in some instances reaching 250,000. The impact of the absolutist monarchies in the creation of a new, differentiated urbanization was astonishing. Madrid, for example, was a town with only a few thousand residents when the Habsburgs made it the capital of their empire in 1561, but, as de Vries observes, 'supported by nothing more than government employment, this centrally located city grew to 65,000 by 1600 and 170,000 by 1630'.[56]

The pace of state formation outran the process of economic integration. With the elaboration of rule capable of penetrating large territories, imposing order on them, and extracting resources from them, a new framework for economic development and competition in an emerging world trading system was created, with north-west Europe at its core. From then to the present, capitalism, both merchant and industrial, has made its history predominantly within a *national* scaffolding.

It was within this new context that the European economies found solutions to the profound and multidimensional economic crisis of the seventeenth century.[57] Just as political

[56] Jan de Vries, *Economy in Europe in an Age of Crisis, 1600–1750.* Cambridge: Cambridge University Press, 1976, 151. He continues: 'Paris and London possessed more varied functions, it is true, but their administrative and attendant social roles were central to their explosive growth. In the mid sixteenth-century, Paris had some 130,000 and London 60,000 inhabitants. They were already by far the largest cities north of the Alps. By 1650, both were approaching the half million mark—unprecedented in western Europe ... When the Danish King Frederick III assumed absolute powers in 1660, Copenhagen was a city of 23,000 inhabitants. A century later it numbered 93,000.' For useful discussion of the political theory of state formation, and, in particular, of the development of conceptions of the state as might, power (might tempered by law), and authority (power as legitimate), see Alexander Passerin d'Entrèves, *The Notion of the State: An Introduction to Political Theory.* Oxford: Oxford University Press, 1967.

[57] For a summary discussion, see de Vries, *Economy in Europe*, esp. ch. 1. A useful overview of European economic history from the late medieval period to the 19th century is William N. Parker, 'The Pre-History of the Nineteenth Century', in Parker, *Europe, America and the Wider World: Essays on the Economic History of Western Capitalism*, Cambridge: Cambridge University Press, 1984, i.

power and sovereignty grew more concentrated, so did merchant capital. The dense regulatory environment of the medieval town and the particularism of local protectionism and controls had produced profound barriers to the elaboration of trade on a larger scale. Mercantilism, as economic doctrine and economic practice, as Eli Heckscher stressed in his unsurpassed treatment, was above all an instrument of unification. Within the framework provided by the state, the level at which industry and trade were regulated shifted upward from the towns. The tools of regulation were those that had been pioneered successfully and tenaciously by them; but the *locus* was now at the centre, under the aegis of the state in the new political capitals. In this way, the rigidities of economic regulation were overcome by the creation of much larger and more flexible economic units, which coincided with the boundaries of states.[58]

The state and the new economy were mutually supportive. In the massive Baroque capitals, wealth and power went hand in hand. 'Behind every successful dynasty stood an array of opulent banking families', and elaborate patterns of trade as well as control over the agricultural production of the countryside. Likewise, 'successful state-building and empire-building activities plus the associated tendency toward the concentration of urban population and government expenditure, offered the private economy unique and invaluable opportunities to capture economies of scale'.[59] These cities, in short, by virtue of their location in a world trading system whose centre of gravity had shifted to the north and west, served as sites for mercantile activity, on the one hand, and as fulcrums for state activity, on the other.

The nationalization of the economic policies and techniques of the feudal towns, together with the growth of state power and political administration, account for the growth of the

---

[58] Eli F. Heckscher, *Mercantilism*, 2 vols., trans. from Swedish by Mendel Shapiro. London: Allen and Unwin, 1935. For a more recent textbook treatment, see Peter Kriedte, *Peasants, Landlords and Merchant Capitalists: Europe and the World Economy, 1500–1800*, trans. from German by V. R. Berghan. Leamington Spa: Berg Publishers, 1983.

[59] De Vries, *Economy in Europe*, 242–3.

capital cities as the most visible products of the new interdependence of state and economy. This state-centred mercantile
order was also a boon to the Atlantic ports, including Hamburg, Liverpool, and Cadiz, and to such naval centres as
Portsmouth and Toulon. At the same time, the older medieval
towns became less and less hospitable as profitable locations
for craft production, especially when artisans produced not for
direct sale but for regional or international markets. Handicraft
production for local markets continued in the older, small
cities, where guild regulation continued to hold sway. But,
stymied by these pre-capitalist barriers to market-driven patterns of investment and exchange, and by the increasingly
defensive posture of urban guilds under stress (in late feudalism guilds elaborated ever more complicated regulations, not
to exploit new possibilities but to secure their prerogatives),
investors seeking to create enterprises to produce goods for
export fled to the peripheries of feudal cities to operate in
unregulated zones. Innovation moved to the margins, near, but
free from, urban-feudal controls. These new enterprises low-
ered wages, cheapened their products, and established new
techniques of production. In this way, they undercut traditional urban industries. Not surprisingly, many towns sought
to proscribe this development, ultimately without success.[60]

Students of this proto-industrialization, characterized by
production in homes and workshops outside the older urban
centres, have focused mainly on rural production. In part for
this reason, R. A. Butlin has argued against the use of the
term; as he notes, industrial development before the industrial
revolution took place on different scales in quite different
types of locale, including smaller cities.[61] Hohenberg and Lees
likewise argue against a too stark portrait of division between
production in the older medieval towns and production in the
countryside. They argue, rather, that there was a discontinuity
between urban places as well, with the conditions for domestic
production for export having been available in urban centres

[60] For a treatment of these issues, see Dodgshon, *The European
Past*, 259–69.
[61] R. A. Butlin, 'Early Industrialization in Europe: Concepts and
Problems', *Geographical Journal*, 152 (Mar. 1986).

as well as rural locations. Although the dominant trend was toward rural production, urban locations were preferred when fabrication required a good deal of capital, close supervision by entrepreneurs, and the need to adapt quickly to market trends. They thus conclude that proto-industrialization 'flourished best not as town *or* country, but as a complementary system involving both rural and urban places and the various elements of a regional urban hierarchy'.[62] Later, towards the beginning of the nineteenth century, both the countryside and small cities, as well as their (semi-) proletarian populations, were available as locales of the new capitalist industrialization in the age of the industrial revolution.

V

Engels surveyed the condition of the English working class at the vital early moment of the formation of recognizably modern working classes in Western capitalist societies. More and more people came to fill places in the economy character-ized by a lack of ownership or control over the means of production or over the labour power of others. Regional and national capitalist labour markets inserted the great majority of these workers into wage contracts unsoftened by the older bonds of Tory paternalism and mutual obligation. In this epoch, a language of class grew up alongside, and in some instances supplanted, the older discourse of trades. The eight-eenth-century world of 'class struggle without class' existed no longer.[63]

[62] Hohenberg and Lees, *The Making of Urban Europe*, 130.

[63] Over more than a decade now, the most important work on 'objective' class relations within capitalism has been provided by Erik Olin Wright; see esp. his *Classes*. London: New Left Books, 1985. There, he elaborates on John Roemer's conceptualizations of exploi-tation to develop a framework for class analysis in feudal, capitalist, and socialist societies. Karl Polanyi made the fashioning of a national labour market in England in the 1830s, both marked and promoted by the New Poor Law of 1834, the hallmark of *The Great Transfor-mation*. Boston: Beacon Press, 1944. On the issue of working-class meaning systems, see the fine collection of essays by Gareth Stedman Jones, *The Language of Class*. Cambridge: Cambridge University

But it was not proletarianization as such that was new when Engels wrote *The Condition of the English Working Class*. A century earlier, roughly half the population of Europe already earned wages from the sale of their labour power.[64] What was unprecedented was the location and density of proletarianization. Capital and labour concentrated in new kinds of urban spaces.

We have seen how in early modern Europe, there had been a dramatic shift in the *locus* of urbanization from the Mediterranean Sea to north-west Europe,[65] and the cities that grew most rapidly were ports and political capitals. The mercantile intertwining of the growth of international trade and the development of centralized, capable national states proved the main impetus to urban development in the two and a half centuries after 1500. For nearly a century from the 1750s, there was virtually no growth of consequence in these cities. Rather, new smaller towns joined the urban stock at a great pace. Such an extensive and assertive period of town-building had not occurred since the development of a network of walled towns within feudalism. Now, urbanization in the countryside, with the ruralization of textile manufacturing, had a symbiotic tie

---

Press, 1983; and on 18th-century paternal relations, see E. P. Thompson, 'Eighteenth Century English Society: Class Struggle Without Class?', *Social History*, 3 (May 1978).

[64] Charles Tilly, 'Demographic Origins of the European Proletariat', in David Levine (ed.), *Proletarianization and Family Life*. New York: Academic Press, 1984.

[65] 'At the beginning of the fourteenth century, only some 40% of the cities with populations of more than 20,000 were in the western European countries with access to the Atlantic (Germany, Belgium, France, the Netherlands, the United Kingdom). More than half of them were in these countries by the start of the eighteenth century. Italy was by far the greatest loser; it had more than a quarter of all of the larger European cities in 1300, but its share had dwindled to one-seventh by 1700. What is more, the largest cities were now located in the North.' Paul Bairoch, *Cities and Economic Development: From the Dawn of History to the Present*. Chicago: University of Chicago Press, 1988, 140–1. In 1500 Italy had 21 cities with populations greater than 20,000; in 1700, 22. By contrast, the countries in Western Europe with access to the Atlantic Ocean had 41 such cities in 1500 and 70 by 1700.

to the emergent mechanized industrial economy. Later, in the nineteenth century, these proto-industrial centres, as well as towns created *de novo*, burgeoned into massive factory cities. Concurrently, the great political and mercantile centres of Europe cast their stagnation aside under the impact of the deepening of capitalist industrialization and its spatial extension.[66] By the end of the century, urban ways of life that for all previous human history had been exceptional in the industrial countries were becoming the norm.

It is impossible to overstate the radical quality of the urban break of the nineteenth century. As Mark Girouard has recently observed, 'two hundred years ago or so it was possible to see the whole of any city in the world, without having to go several thousand feet up in an aeroplane to do so. One could see London from Highgate, Rome from Monte Mario, or Paris from Monmartre.' Big as they were, these cities had familiar qualities:

a forest of roofs, with towers, domes or spires breaking out of it, but a forest with edges, an island with water or green fields visibly flowing up to its shores. This was what people expected a city to be, and it was not so very different from the medieval city with its spires and towers rising from behind a circuit of walls. The walls had gone for the most part, the cities had grown, but the human eye could still encompass them.

The unprecendented growth of the older political capitals and financial centres and the burgeoning of new factory cities put an end to this familiarity. In the great cities—London, Paris, Berlin, New York—by the end of the nineteenth century, 'one could climb a hill, but one no longer saw the whole city, one saw a forest that had no edges, no obvious shape, no clarity, often, because of the smoke that billowed out of it, or the fog or haze that engulfed it'. Factory cities like Engels's Manchester represented an even starker break with the urbanism of the past; they turned the familiar urban conventions upside down:

Even in great commercial centres like Amsterdam or London, the skyline was still presided over by the towers and domes of churches

[66] De Vries, *European Urbanization*.

and public buildings; the warehouses, impressive as they were, did not dominate the city. In Manchester factory chimneys far outnumbered church towers, eight-storey mills towered over squalid little houses, opulent warehouses, some of them as large as the mills, were grander and bigger than the town hall.[67]

William Wylde's famous 1851 painting of the city—a belching wasteland of smokestacks dwarfing familiar landmarks—not only defined popular imagery but identified a space from which all who could would seek to escape to new suburbs like Victoria Park, that were located still, as Engels put it, 'in free, wholesome country air'.

Just these dramatic features of mid-nineteenth-century

[67] Mark Girouard, *Cities and People: A Social and Architectural History*. New Haven, Conn.: Yale University Press, 1985, 344–5, 258. The Wylde painting is reproduced on pp. 260–1. In the earliest stages of industrialization, factories were set up in already existing stables, barns, and mills. But with the development of the steam engine, and the liberation from water sources of power, the size of enterprises grew and buildings were constructed with their specific use as factories in mind. With exception of locations where an effort was made to mask the usage of these structures by disguising their exteriors, a new, utilitarian kind of building, highly distinct from the traditional urban fabric, and separate in space and in scale from housing areas, made its appearance. The radical rupture in the character of these cities went hand in hand with the profound transformations inherent in mechanization. Most obviously, this industrialization transformed the character of work, but not this alone. It made labour more abstract, more divided from conceptualization, less skilled, less industry-specific. It dramatically accelerated productivity, making the introduction of further machinery more likely. It promoted the concentration of capital and the intensification of labour. It changed the social division of labour, and it introduced a new kind of periodicity to capitalist crises. As a result of the variable rate of technical change, mechanization helped produce uneven development in different regions and spaces, and it transformed the economics of location. As Ross Thomson has observed, 'capitalist production was no longer tied to streams for power or to rural locations of production as the putting out system had been. Location came to be more determined by cost of transporting inputs and the product and by external economies or diseconomies of urban locations.' Ross Thomson, 'Industrialization and Capitalist Class Structure', unpublished discussion paper, Committee on Historical Studies, New School for Social Research, New York, Proseminar on Class Formation, Nov. 1984.

urbanization seized Engels's attention in the 1840s. In early modern England only London, which had achieved a population of 500,000 by 1700, was a highly concentrated urban area. In that year, the next largest city numbered only 20,000. Two hundred years earlier, in 1500, London had had a population of just 50,000. It was the only city to experience significant growth in pre-industrial England. London prospered and grew as a political capital, as a national and international market, as the entrepôt for Britain's extensive network of trade, as an artisanal manufacturing centre specializing in luxury goods such as coach-building, watch-making and jewellery, and as the provider of services to its rapidly growing populace.

London began to lose its relative share in manufacturing in the eighteenth century to the proto-industrial centres in the north and midlands. Local manufacturers moved their trades to these new centres of production 'either to escape the strict craft regulation of the capital or to seek cheaper food and fuel, lower wages and rents, or closer proximity to raw materials'. Thus, London shoe-making moved to Northampton in the 1730s and 1740s; framework knitting moved from Shoreditch and Norton Folgate in London to Leicester, Derby, and Nottingham.[68]

Yet London continued to grow in the eighteenth century, having become the financial centre and the most robust port of Western capitalism. Especially after the Peace of Paris in 1763 and the extension of the country's political as well as economic reach, London was crowded with trading ships and all the ancillary activities needed to sustain the country's global imperatives. London also became the key distribution centre for the entire country, with England's largest cattle market, fish market, fruit and vegetable market, and markets in other commodities.

By the mid-nineteenth century, London had yet new sources of growth: the renewal of specialized manufacturing trades, such as printing, clothing, and silk in the city's core, organized in small shops on the model of the domestic system, and the

---

[68] George Rude, *Hanoverian London, 1714–1808*. London: Secker and Warburg, 1971, 28–9.

establishment of metal and textile factories and warehouses on the periphery. In just the half century from 1800 to 1850 the population of Greater London grew from just over 1.1 million to 2.7 million; by 1900, Greater London numbered more than 6.5 million residents.[69]

Not just London, but a congeries of new 'great towns', transformed England's industrial and geographical landscape, led by the dramatic growth of Leeds, Birmingham, Liverpool, and Manchester. Smaller towns in the industrializing regions also grew robustly. Even after villages like Marsden in the West Riding of Yorkshire and nearby Rotheram, Milnrowe, Ogden, Huddersfield, and similar proto-industrial villages had become established woollen and worsted textile centres in the seventeenth and eighteenth centuries, their residents had continued to farm as well. The textile industry continued to expand so that by the end of the eighteenth century it had achieved something of a coequal status in the villages' economic base. Textile production was none the less an integral aspect of essentially rural and, to a considerable degree, isolated settlements. Manufacturers maintained an interest in land. Often, they turned to textile production to compensate for insufficient returns from farming. Still, settlement patterns were relatively sparse and the countryside dominated the towns. Most woollen and worsted production took place on the basis of the domestic system.[70]

Throughout most of the eighteenth century, woollen production on this basis was dispersed widely in textile villages

[69] J. B. Harley, 'England *circa* 1850', and J. T. Coppock, 'The Changing Face of England: 1850–*circa* 1900', in H. C. Darby (ed.), *A New Historical Geography of England after 1600*. Cambridge: Cambridge University Press, 1986. A useful (and well-illustrated) overview can be found in J. David Lloyd, *The Making of English Towns*. London: Victor Gollancz, 1984.

[70] David Woodhead, 'Marsden 1690–1750: A Dual Economy', *Old West Riding*, 5 (Summer 1985); H. C. Prince, 'England *circa* 1800', in Darby, *A New Historical Geography*. For a portrait of Yorkshire's much earlier pattern of urbanization, see R. B. Dobson, 'Yorkshire Towns in the Late Fourteenth Century', *Publications of the Thoresby Society*, 59 (pt. 1, 1983); and for early modern England, see John Patten (ed.), *Pre-Industrial England: Geographical Essays*. London: Dawson, 1979.

in Essex and Suffolk, Gloucestershire and Wiltshire, Somerset and Devonshire, as well as the north. By the end of the century, the manufacture of woollen and worsted goods employed more English workers than any other industry. Nearly half of the country's production was exported.

The boom continued after the turn of the century, but the character of the industry changed considerably. With the introduction of machines for spinning yarn and a concomitant increase in the amount of capital needed to invest in the new technology, the spatial characteristics of woollen and worsted production altered, albeit gradually. By mid-century, hand-weaving by domestic workers who lived in villages spread across the landscape was being supplanted by factory workers using mechanical looms concentrated in the bulging towns. Even in this industry where industrialization proceeded more slowly than in cotton or in iron, coal, and steel, the old style of production could not keep up, except in specialized, high-quality products. No longer did, or could, most manufacturers and workers combine textile production with agriculture. With the shift to steam power, there was a massive accelera-tion in rates of investment, the concentration of capital and workers, the tranformation of small villages into towns, and of towns into cities. In just the five years between 1833 and 1838 'the number of woollen mills in the country increased from an estimated 129 to a reported 606. By 1850 the figure was 880.' No longer was the industry spread across the English landscape. Spinning fell into decay and pauperism increased in many of the country's proto-industrial villages. Even within Lancashire the new capitalism imposed itself unevenly. In the first half of the century, the population of its cotton and woollen districts tripled, but the more rural north increased by just some 50 per cent.[71]

---

[71] Alan Harris, 'Changes in the Early Railway Age', in Darby, *A New Historical Geography*; John K. Walton, *Lancashire: A Social History, 1558–1939*. Manchester: Manchester University Press, ch. 6. For a discussion of the concentration of the population of the county, see R. Lawton, 'Population Trends in Lancashire and Cheshire from 1801', *Transactions of the Historical Society of Lancashire and Cheshire*, 114 (1962). This essay contains useful data for Manchester. In his work on Lancashire, Michael Anderson usefully distinguishes

The extraordinary urbanization of England both in London and in provincial industrializing towns presaged the urban revolution that was soon to transform the landscapes of Europe and the United States.[72] While the contours of any specific city were in some considerable measure a product of local particularities of topography, location within transport networks, the structure of the building industry, the pace of expansion, and the preferences of political élites, among other factors, there was nevertheless a very great resemblance between them. Both the older cities—whose pre-industrial core coexisted with, and imposed limits and an order upon, the new urban development that was necessarily oriented to the city centre as a point of reference—and the cities built in more haphazard and unplanned ways, without such a given point of reference for industrial capital, could be distinguished

---

between three types of production system with regard to the ties between family units and work. In undifferentiated purely domestic systems of production, he writes, 'the family and economic systems were superimposed in a way not dissimilar to that . . . for farmers in rural areas'. In semi-differentiated systems, there was more of a separation between the two, but it was not complete. In this rudimentary type of factory production, employers recruited their main employees but then left it to them to hire and pay assistants. 'Thus family heads may recruit and employ children or kin, and also others, under their surveillance and economic control.' Last is the differentiated system of factories where the ties between family and work are broken by the shift in the control of labour entirely to the employer. Michael Anderson, *Family Structure in Nineteenth Century Lancashire*. Cambridge: Cambridge University Press, 1971.

[72] For this reason, English urbanization commands the same theoretical as well as empirical status that Marx ascribed to English industrial development in *Capital*. Bairoch (*Cities and Economic Development*, 243) puts the point this way at the start of his chapter on 'The City and the First Phases of the Industrial Revolution in England': 'From the socioeconomic point of view, of the three major turning points in the evolution of human societies (the other two being the Neolithic revolution and the break with the past at the start of the sixteenth century), the Industrial Revolution unquestionably left the deepest mark. And yet for five to eight decades England alone underwent this momentous change. England being the cradle of the Industrial Revolution, an inquiry into the relations between the birth of the Industrial Revolution and urbanism in that country seems in order.'

from pre-industrial urban settlements by the market-driven mechanisms of their expansion, their distinctive organization of space by function, their social geographies, and the new roles and responsibilites assumed by local governments in shaping the built-environment of these cities and managing the consequences of their social relations. With all the differences and local peculiarities that divided one city from another, there were common, recurring patterns. Just as Engels foretold, it was the new spatial pattern of industrial Manchester, the great hinge between past and future, that proved characteristic:

The pattern which had been pioneered in Manchester was to be repeated, with variations, all over the world. Cities (or interested parties within cities) promoted a communications network of railways and/or steamer lines, of which their city became the nexus ... An industrial and manufacturing zone grew up on the edge of the city, with a large immigrant population of workers to go with it. In the centre, trade and services also boomed, land values rose and the residents were often pushed out into their neighbourhoods ... In the middle of the city the scale of everything steadily increased. Grand new buildings appeared: town halls, law courts, public libraries, museums, colleges, art galleries, hotels, department stores, covered markets, railway stations, theatres, exchanges, banks and insurance offices. Existing streets were widened and new ones opened (although not usually on a sufficient scale in either case). If the city in question was a national capital, a whole hierarchy of new national government buildings was superimposed on the local ones.[73]

[73] Girouard, *Cities and People*, 269. The older capital cities that had been created as great urban centres in the age of absolutism and mercantilism were marked by great individual character. By contrast, the new industrial cities were very much alike. In the industrial age, the great capitals, likewise, came to be more alike in their reorganization of space, often involving large-scale planned rebuilding of the central city, slum clearance, and railway schemes, and in the character of their peripheral expansion. For discussions of the individuality of European capital cities, see the collection of short essays by Abram de Swaan *et al.*, Capital Cities as Achievements. Amsterdam: Centre for Metropolitan Research, University of Amsterdam, 1988; and Donald Olsen, *The City as a Work of Art: London, Paris, and Vienna.* New Haven, Conn.: Yale University Press, 1986.

Whether created *de novo*, as with Chicago, Pittsburg, Roubaix, or Oberhausen; on the foundations of older villages or small cities, as with Lille, Saint-Étienne, or Essen; on the outskirts of existing major cities, as with the suburban extensions of Brooklyn, Vienna, and Paris; near coalfields, or at the nexus of railway lines, the new industrial towns were characterized by the organization of production in factories employing hundreds of people working machinery powered by water or steam, by broadly common solutions to such problems as sanitation and food and energy supply, by a similar social geography and process of division into zones of work and residence, by distinctive social classes, by class-specific forms of housing, and even by a tendency for better housing to be built to the west, and housing for the working class to the east, which, most frequently, lay downwind of the new factory districts. This new kind of city

was larger in population, more specialized in function, and it lacked that intimate relationship with surrounding rural areas which had been so important a feature of the pre-industrial town . . . The new industrial town, whether or not it grew out of a small country town, was superimposed upon the landscape, built in styles that were eclectic and international and of concrete and brick of no particular origin.[74]

---

[74] Pounds, *An Historical Geography of Europe*, 119. The older great cities, such as London, Paris, and Vienna, accommodated the new with the old as persistent older patterns of work and living coexisted with the new manufacturing impulse. Nevertheless, they were neither unaffected nor unchanged. Pound's chapter on 'Urban Development in the Nineteenth Century' is the best compact statement available on European urbanization in the 19th century, with particularly useful country-by-country surveys that cover France, the Low Countries, Germany, Poland, Scandinavia, Switzerland, the Habsburg Empire and the Balkans, Italy, Spain, and Portugal. An exceptionally important and pioneering study of Vienna is summarized in Elisabeth Lichtenberger, *Die Wiener Altstadt: von der mitterlalterlichen Burgerstadt zur City*. Vienna: Franz Deuticke, 1977. See also Paul White, *The West European City: A Social Geography*. London: Longman, 1984. White's point is that European urbanization was rather different from that of the New World and from the British example because of the more historically layered character of continental cities. In my reading, however, he demonstrates the more profound similarities stemming from the pivotal impact of industrialization, and the rapid

These cities were a constitutive part of the assertive capitalism of the age of classic liberalism, individualism, and *laissez-
faire*, less as cause than as consequence.[75] By contrast with the
development of the large political capitals in early modern
Europe, in the urbanization of the nineteenth century, as John
Merrington has put it, the 'dominance of the town is no longer
externally imposed: it is now reproduced as part of the accumulation process'.[76] The tempo and character of the burgeoning industrial cities were inseparable from the investment
decisions of capitalists, who searched for locations with the
fewest constraints and the greatest natural and social advantages. Industrialization concurrently transformed capitalism
and the cities. Technological invention sought to overcome
bottlenecks of labour supply, marketing, and transport, and to
accelerate the speed of production. City invention was a quest
to find locales appropriate for this concentrated, insistent,
mechanized capitalism. Whereas urbanization before mechanization was mostly concerned with administrative, commercial, craft-related, and religious matters, now manufacturing
became the pre-eminent feature. Building factories and work-

---

expansion, marked by the taking down of city walls, in mid-19th-
century Brussels, Geneva, Stockholm, Vienna, Barcelona, Madrid, and
Paris, amongst others. For the United States, see the overviews by
Michael P. Conzen, 'The American Urban System in the Nineteenth
Century', and John P. Radford, 'The Social Geography of the Nine-
teenth Century US City', in *Geography and the Urban Environment:
Progress in Research Applications*, 4 (1981), as well as the splendid
case study by Elizabeth Blackmar, *Manhattan for Rent, 1785–1850*.
Ithaca, NY: Cornell University Press, 1989.

[75] Of course not entirely without cause. Especially after the first
moments of the industrial revolution, cities helped promote and
diffuse innovation, opened paths to economic mobility, enhanced the
flexibility of labour markets, hastened the monetization of society,
and provided built-forms for the circulation of capital. See the quite
thorough review of this issue in Bairoch, *Cities and Economic
Development*, as well as his convincing conclusions (250 ff.), and the
balance sheet he draws up on p. 345.

[76] John Merrington, 'Town and Country in the Transition to
Capitalism', 88. Even such new city institutions as urban newpapers
became integral to the functioning of the new capitalism, as they
were used to publicize local markets.

ing-class housing came to be the two main aspects of the construction of urban centres.

These cities also broke radically with the traditional pattern linking city to countryside. With the growth of nineteenth-century industrial cities, the countryside became more rural. The high proportion of industrial workers who had lived and worked in rural areas in 1800 almost disappeared during the nineteenth century. As a result, the divide between city and country grew more stark, a change of great economic and social consequence. The goods produced in cities were intended far more for spatially extended markets than for local hinterlands, and industrial labour became almost entirely urban. Moreover, this change also entailed profound social transformations. 'For dating from the nineteenth century, at least,' Paul Bairoch observes,

industry meant wage labor, and the proportion of wage earners employed in trade increased at this time as well. The rural world of the nineteenth century, on the other hand, was dominated by small independent farmers. Thus one of the distinctive features of life in the traditional economies of the West was reversed: in the nineteenth century the urban world was in many respects less free than the rural world.[77]

But, as we shall see, this contraction of freedom at the workplace proved to be only part of the story. For, not without irony, outside their workplaces, in their homes and communities, working-class people achieved a new kind of independence, free from the authority and surveillance of their employers.

Here, in *these* revolutionary cities—unprecedented in scale, function, social geography, and mix of freedom and unfreedom—the new working classes tried to make sense of industrial capitalism. In so doing, they became historical subjects. How, and what kind, are the topics to which I now turn.

[77] Bairoch, *Cities and Economic Development*, 270.

6 Working Classes Map the City

FOR Marxism, the main issues of social theory within the industrial phase of capitalism focus on the formation of working classes. This subject is best treated, in significant measure, as an urban one. The spatial requirements of industrial capitalism shaped nineteenth-century cities: their patterns of growth, interconnections, built-environments, and social geographies. In turn, the experience of such cities, and attempts to make sense of their properties, were decisive elements in the early histories of Western working classes.[1]

The cost to Marxism of its neglect of cities is especially pronounced with regard to these issues. People live in spaces that are the products of specific relationships between the natural environment and human creativity. In these constructed spatial worlds, which are necessarily distinctive as to time and location, they experience, interpret, and fight about the social order.[2] The interaction of people with this 'real

[1] A useful, suggestive, attempt along these lines is R. S. Neale, 'Class and Urban History: The Historian's Task', in his collection of papers, *Writing Marxist History: British Society, Economy and Culture*. Oxford: Blackwell, 1985. I have been instructed by this hortatory essay's treatment of the underexplored links between urban and class history, in particular by Neale's emphasis on the ties between structure and agency; the ways in which property relations shaped the physical form and human relations of cities; phenomenal questions concerning how it felt to live in these urban places; the contingent relations of economy and culture; and the ways in which urban development forces a modification of simple Marxist class models. I confess to being less enamoured of Neale's focus on model-building, and his substitution of a five-class model for leaner Marxist approaches.

[2] 'Social systems have to reproduce themselves in a material world. Whether we see this materialism as having a constitutive or merely an incidental role in their formation, no societal system can gloss the need to interlace itself with the real world, and, in the process, to organise itself spatially ... To interact with the world ... is to

world', that is, with the spatial dimensions of their lives, must be a constitutive element of any social theory concerned with transactions of structure and agency, at least as a mediating element between large-scale social processes and social activity and consciousness.[3] How much more so for Marxism, whose structures and agents have determinate names, and whose capitalism and contending social classes have been astonishingly and powerfully urban.

If any good social theory will profit from making space integral to an understanding of the structuring of social relationships, it is even more manifest that it is not possible to pursue adequately questions of working-class formation in the nineteenth century without an urban-geographical dimension. Class formation is a process concerned with experience in a double sense: experience of the world and learning to act within and on it. No one meets with capitalism in general or directly engages the abstract commodity form whose very essence is that it is fetishized. Capitalism is lived in particular locations at particular times. In the nineteenth century, the experienced world of the new working classes was primarily

---

incorporate a space specificity into social process, to tie it down to specific areas of space . . . In having to be place specific, to reify itself, societal organisation has to commit itself to a particular form in a particular place, transforming a world of choice into one of decision and closed possibilities.' R. A. Dodgshon, 'Geographical Change: A Study in the Marching Time or the March of Time?', *Society and Space*, 5 (June 1987).

[3] Some, but only a distinct minority, and a marginal minority at that, of orientations in social science give to space and place a constitutive role: 'one thinks, in particular,' John Agnew notes, 'of French social geography; French electoral sociology; the *Annales* school of social history; American regional sociology, in the fashion of the "North Carolina School"; American political sociology in the "group-ecological" tradition of Key; and, perhaps above all, historical and cultural geography, and American cultural anthropology.' By contrast with these minority currents, the 'theories of social organization and social change that have been dominant in Western, particularly American-influenced, social science since the Second World War have had no or only a limited role for a concept of place'. John A. Agnew, *Place and Politics: The Geographical Mediation of State and Society*. Boston: Allen and Unwin, 1987, 25. He treats the causes of the devaluation of space as he sees them in ch. 5.

urban. These 'shapes on the ground' were integral to the new class-based 'shapes in society';[4] the analysis of working-class formation is in significant measure the study of how working people constructed images and mental maps of the remarkably innovative spatial terrains in which they found themselves forced to work and to live. At issue were the terms and content of places of work and residence in each of the meanings of 'place' stressed by John Agnew: '*locale*, the settings in which social relations are constituted . . .; *location*, the geographical area encompassing the settings for social interaction as defined by social and economic processes operating at a wider scale; and *sense of place*, the local "structure of feeling"' that defines the emotive sensibilities people develop about the different spatial settings of their lives.[5] It was in the construction of these mappings that the lived experiences of a class-structured society were named. How they were, and with what consequences for collective activity, are central, variable, issues of class formation.

By not moving in and through the built-environments produced by the spectacular urbanization of the nineteenth century, where working-class individuals and families fashioned their daily engagements with capitalism, Marxism created cardboard working classes ('in themselves') who, in ways, times, and places difficult to specify, were expected to overcome the very barriers to class consciousness and collective activity inherent in capitalism. When they did not, excuses were fashioned for them: the aristocracy of labour, patriarchy, ethnic heterogeneity, élite social control, state repression, and so on. In this approach to class formation the substantive

[4] David Cannadine, 'Residential Differentiation in Nineteenth Century Towns: From Shapes on the Ground to Shapes in Society', in James H. Johnson and Colin Pooley (eds.), *The Structure of Nineteenth Century Cities*. London: Croom Helm, 1982.

[5] Agnew, *Place and Politics*, 28. He explicitly, and suggestively, argues for the relevance of a place perspective for the analysis of class in order to overcome its reification 'as a thing or a universal geist that moves people to act in certain ways'. Such is the promise when place is understood 'as the geographical context or locality in which agency interpellates social structure' (41, 43). Political behaviour and collective assertion, moreover, are always place-specific.

content of working-class lives and orientations remain pain-
fully underexplored, let alone analysed comparatively.[6]

The new urban Marxism of the 1970s and 1980s has been
important precisely because of its attempts to put an end to
the tradition's urban and spatial elisions. It did so initially by
focusing on how space is integral to capitalist accumulation,
and by locating twentieth-century social movements within
the sphere of capitalist consumption and reproduction. But in
its present-mindedness, this work has trod very little on the
path Engels forged in his early work.[7] We have seen, by
contrast, how more recently the works of Manuel Castells and

---

[6] These ideal working classes have existed exclusively inside the
heads of theorists who tend to forget Irving Howe's aphorism, 'The
working class is a reality, the proletariat an idea.' Irving Howe, 'Sweet
and Sour Notes: On Workers and Intellectuals', *Dissent* (Winter
1972), 264.

If it is a central theme of this chapter that the project of social
theory within Marxism must impel an incorporation of urban-spatial
themes into the heart of considerations of structure and agency, so, it
is clear, the omission of these concerns from other epistemic communities has also been costly. Commenting on recent work in urban
history, only some of which has been Marxist or Marxisant, Kathleen
Conzen observes: 'Paradoxically, the new urban historians, much as
they have wished to eschew the specifically urban, have been forced
time and again in their quest for generalization to confront the
independent influence of both city role within the urban system and
the peculiar character of local development upon the social phenomena under observation . . . the new urban history may thus be forcing
urban historians willy-nilly to the long-avoided examination of the
urbanization process itself. It is, finally, at this point that the essential
link with the city-building and governance concerns of the "other",
more traditional urban history should also become more evident once
again, for in those decision-making processes lies the ultimate source
of persistent local characteristics, the fundamental arena in which
structure and culture interact.' Kathleen Neils Conzen, 'Quantifica-
tion and the New Urban History', *Journal of Interdisciplinary History*, 13 (Spring 1983).

[7] An overview that thoughtfully demonstrates these features of the
literature is Kieran McKewon, *Marxist Political Economy and Marxist Urban Sociology: A Review and Elaboration of Recent Developments*. London: Macmillan, 1987. Grounded mainly in critiques of
the work of Manuel Castells and Jean Lojkine, the book's main
contribution is to advocate the development of micro-level analysis
within urban Marxism.

David Harvey have sought to confront directly questions of structure and agency through spatial analysis, but also how the results of their efforts have been counter-intentional: either Marxism must be jettisoned as a privileged social theory or the varied and messy reality discovered in close empirical analysis must be tidied up to fit into its traditional aspatial categories. These attempts by Castells and Harvey to enlarge Marxist social theory by the incorporation of things urban effectively brought it to definitive conclusions, if by different routes. By these roads, the pairing of Marxism and the city as a promising aspect of Marx's third project of social theory came to a dead end.

What Marxist social theory badly requires but has never secured is the systematic inculcation of an urban-geographical imagination into the analysis of working-class formation.[8] Such an effort, an example of which I wish to sketch in this chapter, entails three related steps: a specification of the structural determinants of city growth and development; a presentation of the spatial configurations characteristic of these new spaces; and a systematic, contingent, and comparative account of how the new working classes made sense of these spaces in the different Western countries.[9]

I

At the time Engels wrote *The Condition of the Working Class in England*, he thought the formation of a class-conscious

---

[8] A recent exception to this generalization is the collection of essays edited by Nigel Thrift and Peter Williams, *Class and Space: The Making of Urban Society*. London: Routledge and Kegan Paul, 1987. This is a very good anthology, and I return to it, and especially to a very illuminating essay by Craig Calhoun, below in Chapter 7. In spite of the volume's manifest plea for a tight linkage between urban space and class formation, the various essays on the 19th century disappointingly do not take up the urban form as integral to their analysis, nor do they tackle the issue of comparative analysis except in a single paired comparison of Sheffield and Leeds by Thrift.

[9] Since capitalism after the separation of sovereignty and property developed within national frames, it makes sense to expect national variations in working-class formation.

working class to be something of an automatic process. We know, in retrospect, that he was wrong. There is no ineluctable path from the life situations of working people in capitalist cities to their emergence as a group sharing anti-capitalist dispositions with a willingness and capacity to act against the social order. Class formation is not something that occurs as a quantitative matter, more or less. It is a contingent process whose terms and content vary from place to place.

The congested terminology of class itself places obstacles in the way of understanding this process. As an aid to description and explanation, I have argued elsewhere that it is useful to distinguish between four levels or layers of class.[10] The first is class within the structure of capitalist development, the level of class Marx analysed in *Capital*. This is a model of empty places within the mode of production. By contrast, class at the second level of ways of life concerns how actual people live within determinate patterns of life and social relations. Class, here, refers to the features of the organization of social exist-ence, at work and off work. At a third level, that of cognitive and linguistic dispositions, class refers to the ways people come to represent their lived experiences and how they consti-tute a normative guide to action. I mean this in the sense that Bourdieu uses his concept of *habitus* 'as a structured and structuring structure [that] produces systems of schemes gen-erating classifiable practices and works, and systems of schemes of perceptions and appreciation'.[11] As actors, members of a class are constituted only within a given cultural order and its

[10] A fuller discussion may be found in Ira Katznelson, 'Working Class Formation: Constructing Cases and Comparisons', in Ira Katz-nelson and Aristide Zolberg (eds.), *Working Class Formation: Nine-teenth Century Patterns in Western Europe and the United States*. Princeton, NJ: Princeton University Press, 1986, 13–22.

[11] Pierre Bourdieu, *Distinction: A Social Critique of the Judgement of Taste*, trans. Richard Nice. London: Routledge and Kegan Paul, 1984, 171. He writes: 'Because different conditions of existence produce different habitus—systems of generative schemes applicable, by simple transfer, to the most varied areas of practice . . . the habitus is not only a structuring structure, which organises practices, but also a structured structure: the principle of division into logical classes which organises the perception of the social world is itself the product of internalization of the division into social classes' (170).

distinctive set of preferences, cognitions, and possibilities.[12] These class dispositions are not simply mirrors or reflections of class realities; they are plausible and meaningful responses to circumstances. In turn, these dispositions grounded in language and symbols constitute significant cultural resources which structure the repertoire of working classes at the fourth level of class, that of collective action. People who share dispositions may or may not act together in pursuit of common objectives. A class may be said to exist at this fourth level when its members act self-consciously through movements and organizations to affect society and the position of the class within it. Just as working-class dispositions have varied considerably from country to country, so too have patterns of working-class collective action:

Class formation, from this perspective, may be thought of more fully and more variably as concerned with the conditional (but not random) process of connection between the four levels of class. The specification of four levels of class allows us to keep the advantages of defining class formation in terms of outcomes while providing a more elaborated and variable object of comparative historical analysis. The content of each of the four levels of necessity will vary from society to society; no level need be understood or analyzed exclusively in class terms; and the connections between the levels are problematical and conditional.

Questions about the content of each level and about the connections between the levels of class constitute the very heart of the analysis of class formation. A precise (but not too narrow) charting of class formation, based on a contingent, but not undetermined

---

[12] I have found very suggestive the discussion of these issues by Scott Lash and John Urry, 'The New Marxism of Collective Action: A Critical Analysis', *Sociology*, 18 (Feb. 1984). For an important critique of the methodological individualism of Jon Elster's treatment of class, focusing on his avoidance of ideological issues and their autonomy and his view of classes as comprised of individuals who may or may not engage in collective action, see Charles Taylor, 'Formal Theory in Social Science', *Inquiry*, 25 (1980), 139–44. For a compatible critique, grounded in the monological and dialogical categories of Jurgen Habermas, see Claus Offe and Helmut Wiesenthal, 'Two Logics of Collective Action: Theoretical Notes on Social Class and Organizational Form', in *Political Power and Social Theory*, 1 (1980), 67–115.

approach to the relationship between these levels, and the attempt to develop macrocausal hypotheses about variations in class formation are the interrelated tasks that follow from this approach.[13]

In this formulation, class formation is not a specific outcome (as, say, in formulations about revolutionary consciousness), nor is it an all or nothing matter. Rather, the two sets of variation in disposition and collective action at the third and fourth levels of class constitute twin objects of analysis of variations in working-class formation: Under what conditions will class-based understandings of social life experienced at the second level of class develop? Will these be limited to workplace relationships and to the terms of the demands working people put to their employers, or will they encompass other arenas of social and political life? Under what conditions will working people assert their claims against their employers or their landlords or the state or against other targets within or outside legitimate systems of interest representation?

It will be my claim that the history of working-class formation in the first moments of the creation of modern working classes can be understood in a fresh way in terms of the representation of urban space and of the development of forms of collective action appropriate to these namings. Reading the new city in an effort to make its contours and social relations legible, thus reducing chaos to pattern, constituted a central challenge for the working people who had to live and labour in its precincts. How they mapped the city in a search for intelligibility and coherence constitutes the key mediation between structure and agency in nineteenth-century working-class history. In taking note of the centrality of economic, class representations in the nineteenth century (which, at the time, provided 'the matrix around which all others are organized'), art historian T. J. Clark contrasts the epoch's bourgeois certainties—signified by such grand and ambitious projects as the development of Nash's Regent Street in London, Baron Haussmann's rebuilding of Paris, and, later, that great iconographic expression of bourgeois assertion, Vienna's Ringstrasse—to the great flux of working-class terminologies that

---

[13] Katznelson, 'Working Class Formation', 21–2.

spanned the indeterminate conception of 'the people' and the theoretically thick notion of 'the proletariat'.[14] Understanding the challenges, choices, and determinations of this historical effort to represent the experiences of working-class life constitutes the main subject of this chapter.[15]

By way of a comparative illustration, I take up the cases of working-class formation in nineteenth-century England and the United States. Many treatments of this subject have been marked by disappointment. English historiography has been concerned to explain what is (mistakenly) seen as the 'exceptionalism' of working-class reformism and moderation when the making of the English working class is compared to Continental experiences. American historiography has taken up an even more basic kind of 'exceptionalism': as compared to the English and Continental cases class understandings seem limited to labour relations, and not even a moderate working-class political organization on the model of the Labour Party has ever come into existence.[16] In both instances

[14] T. J. Clark, *The Painting of Modern Life: Paris in the Art of Manet and His Followers*. New York: Knopf, 1984, 7. 'More economically than any other single source, the great forum built along Vienna's Ringstrasse, with its monuments and its dwellings, gives us an iconographic index to the mind of ascendant Austrian liberalism.' Carl E. Schorske, *Fin-de-Siècle Vienna: Politics and Culture*. New York: Knopf, 1980, 27. For a discussion of the bourgeois certainties of the period and the ways in which the 'age of capital' has troubled Marxist historians, see Gareth Stedman Jones, 'Society and Politics at the Beginning of the World Economy', *Cambridge Journal of Economics*, 1 (Mar. 1977).

[15] See William Sharpe and Leonard Wallock (eds.), 'From "Great Town" to "Nonplace Urban Realm": Reading the Modern City', in Sharpe and Wallock, (eds.), *Visions of the Modern City: Essays in History, Art, and Literature*. New York: Heyman Center for the Humanities, Columbia University, 1984. The term 'battlefield of representation' comes from David Harvey's review essay of Clark's *The Painting of Modern Life*, 'The Representation of Urban Life', *Journal of Historical Geography*, 13 (July 1987).

[16] I take up these issues in Ira Katznelson, 'Working Class Formation and the State: Nineteenth Century England in American Perspective', in Peter Evans, Dietrich Rueschemeyer, and Theda Skocpol (eds.), *Bringing the State Back In*. Cambridge: Cambridge University Press, 1985. This chapter is based in part on that essay. For a treatment of the German working class along broadly similar lines,

historians have searched rather more for explanations of what has not happened than for what has.

Here, instead, I want to show, first, how both the English and American working classes experienced capitalism through broadly similar transformations in city space; second, how new divisions in nineteenth-century urban space posed fundamental challenges to the formation of class-based dispositions; and third, how integral the character of each country's state was in bringing about variations in 'classness' in each of the cases. In particular, I want to look at why it was that in the United States a split consciousness came to divide the working class: as labourers at the workplace and as members of ethnic groups or residents of this or that territory in their residential communities, whereas in England 'class' joined rather than divided the realms of work and off work. In England, working-class political leaders directed demands at workplace employers and, away from work, at the state in the same broad class terms, whereas in the United States they pressed their demands in different terms in each arena. I argue that these dissimilarities in class understanding and activity primarily involved differences not at the place of work but at the place of residence, and that the main source of this variation was the political context created by state authorities who shaped how the place of residence was understood by the new urban working classes. As before, in assaying the linkages between capitalist development and working-class formation, I want to demonstrate both the capacity of a spatialized Marxism and its limits.

In short, my subject is what might be thought of as the 'hidden agenda' of the city; my aim is to reveal and expose the

---

see Geoff Eley, 'Combining Two Histories: The SPD and the German Working Class Before 1914', *Radical History Review*, 28–30 (1984). A variant of the traditional Marxist historiography on American exceptionalism, based on the cumulative defeats of the American working class at key moments of struggle, can be found in the interesting article by Mike Davis, 'Why the U.S. Working Class is Different?', *New Left Review*, 123 (Sept.–Oct. 1980). A fine article that asks, 'Just how "natural" is the relationship between trade unionism, labour, and socialism?' is Jean Smith, 'Labour Tradition in Glasgow and Liverpool', *History Workshop*, 17 (Spring 1984).

making, meaning, and uses of urban space in order to strengthen Marxist social theory, and, in this way, to evaluate and transcend the choices offered by Castells and Harvey. In pursuit of these aims, I wish to make two critical connections regarding the relationship of urban-spatial development and class formation: between cities as points in a larger urban-economic network and cities as forms with distinctive internal spatial configurations; [17] and between these configurations and the creation of collectivities whose bases of imagery, identity, and organization are constituted not only in time but in space.

If an urban consciousness was an inherent part of the history of class formation, what character would it assume? What perceptual filters to process and screen information would working people develop in relation to the fundamental trans-formations in social geography they experienced? How wide-ranging would they be? If cities concentrated capitalism's new working classes, would the propinquity of working-class indi-viduals and families in their residential areas promote or impede class-based collective action? Answers to these ques-tions for specific working classes depend, in the main, on the ways they came to understand, talk about, and act within the new divisions separating work and home.[18]

[17] For a discussion of this linkage, see Charles Tilly, 'The Urban Historian's Dilemma: Faceless Cities or Cities Without Hinderlands', University of Michigan, Center for Research on Social Organizations, Working Paper No. 248, Oct. 1981.

[18] I am well aware that the terms 'work' and 'home' may promote a gendered mystification in that they imply that domestic labour in the home is not work. I emphatically do not mean this. The home, as Elizabeth Blackmar rightly insists, 'remained a workplace; housework was still an essential part of securing and maintaining a living'. In her attack on the perspective, such as my own, that stresses the separa-tion of workplace and home in 19th-century cities, Blackmar con-flates two issues that are best kept separate. She writes that according to interpretations stressing this spatial disjuncture, 'as men found employment in expanding workshops, factories, stores, and offices, housing lost its economic function and became a "sphere" set apart from productive relations'. Elizabeth Blackmar, *Manhattan for Rent, 1785–1850*. Ithaca, NY: Cornell University Press, 1989, 110. This punch-line does not logically follow. It is quite possible to stress the significance to men and to women of the profound spatial reorgani-zation of cities that created separate place-realms for the performance

II

Undergirding this analysis of class formation are the claims
that the new industrial capitalist cities in England, the United
States, and the other Western countries did in fact experience
a powerful spatial reorganization that divided the spaces where
people worked for wages from the residential communities
where they lived (and where women performed unpaid
domestic labour); that this split segregated the social classes
from each other; and that it produced fine-grained differentia-
tions between members of social classes based on income and
styles of life, including the consumption of housing. It was
these changes on the ground that compelled new readings of
the city.

---

of wage labour and the functions, including domestic labour, of
family life without denying the economic significance of unpaid
labour, the specificity of the experience of women, or the importance
of the realm of housing (the subject of Blackmar's excellent work) as
an economic component of major significance in modern capitalism.
I utilize the language of separation of work and home self-consciously,
with these caveats in mind, because it was a common, emblematic
feature of all modern capitalist cities. It established the basis for
fundamental puzzles about class and society and about the linkages
between these realms. And, in my view, it sharpens the questions we
can ask not only about class, but also about gender.
    A critique along lines similar to that of Blackmar, that explicitly
but sympathetically criticizes my earlier work for its neglect of
gender, is Martha A. Ackelsberg, 'Women's Collaborative Activities
and City Life: Politics and Policy', in Janet Flammang (ed.), *Political
Women: Current Roles in State and Local Government.* Beverly
Hills, Calif.: Sage Publications, 1984. I accept the criticism that I
have had too little to say about gender. I reject the notion that the
stress on the physical, geographical, and social split between workplace and residence makes such an analysis difficult. To the contrary,
it suggests research, much of it in fact taken up fruitfully by a growing
feminist literature, that treats the implications of this split from the
perspective of women, examining the way women and their families
have joined and managed the two realms. This body of scholarship
has engaged the key political issue I have addressed in some of my
own work: namely, how an emancipatory politics can be forged across
this great divide of work and home.

These claims about the facts of spatial reorganization, which are the premiss of my comparative and contingent analysis of working-class formation, are contested, so I will dwell on them, with a special stress on the English case. Though I plan below to contrast American with English patterns of class formation, most of my discussion of spatial reorganization will focus on English cities, in part because they were the first to grow in the dramatic fashion of Manchester, in part because there was a much more developed existing urban system, which leads to questions about how much in fact changed between old and new, and in part because the very idea of fundamental social and spatial change there has been called into question.

In a leading instance, Patrick Joyce takes some pains to deprecate the significance of the separation of work and residence and segregation between the classes. He insists that the factory town of the mid- to late nineteenth century 'retained more of the village than it acquired of the city. Understood as the "walking city" the factory town grew by cellular reproduction, the town slowly absorbing factory neighborhoods in its expansion.' Until the introduction of tramways and bicycles at the turn of the century, 'the link between home and work remained firm until these severed it'.[19]

Joyce concludes his discussion of the residential community with a caution. The impersonality and class segregation of the twentieth-century city is too often read back into the nineteenth century so that we forget just how unlike they were.[20]

---

[19] Patrick Joyce, *Work, Society, and Politics: The Culture of the Factory in Late Victorian England*. New Brunswick, NJ: Rutgers University Press, 1980, 118–19.

[20] In this reminder of the danger of reading back modern patterns into the past, Joyce echoes geographer David Ward, who stresses that from a 20th-century perspective the social geography of English and American cities in the 19th century was one of comparatively weak patterns of spatial differentiation as compared to the patterns that came later. David Ward, 'Victorian Cities: How Modern?', *Journal of Historical Geography*, 1/2 (1975). The debate between this position and the one I adopt here, on the side of the social geographers and historians who have stressed differentiation and segregation, is reviewed in Richard Dennis, *English Industrial Cities of the Nineteenth Century: A Social Geography*. Cambridge: Cambridge Univer-

As words of prudence, these imprecations are well taken, but for the purposes of a consideration of the separation of work and home in nineteenth-century cities, understood in terms of their own specificity, they miss key points of material change and social experience. Writing about the industrial revolution more generally, William Sewell has observed:

What now appears as the hesitant beginnings of a long and slow development seemed to be a major departure to contemporaries: Even a very few steam engines or blast furnaces or spinning mills could make a powerful impression on people who had never seen them before. From their point of view, modern industry was a distinctive feature of their age; theirs was an industrial society as no previous society had ever been.[21]

---

sity Press, 1984, and in Cannadine, 'Residential Differentiation'. Cannadine concludes his review of the debate by arguing that subjective distance between the classes was greater than objective differences on the ground. This is both correct and misleading. Correct, because from a 20th-century perspective the actual degree of differentiation was not nearly as great as it was to become, yet subjective social divisions were considerable. Misleading, because, as I note below, from a more immanent time perspective the objective changes were great indeed.

[21] William H. Sewell, *Work and Revolution in France: The Language of Labor from the Old Regime to 1848*. Cambridge: Cambridge University Press, 1980, 143. For discussions of pre-industrial patterns concerning the integration of work and home, see Frank E. Brown, 'Continuity and Change in the Urban House: Developments in Domestic Space Organization in Seventeenth Century London', *Comparative Studies in Society and History*, 28 (July 1986); Catharina Lis, *Social Change and the Labouring Poor: Antwerp, 1770–1860*. New Haven, Conn.: Yale University Press, 1986; John Langton, 'Residential Patterns in Pre-Industrial Cities: Some Case Studies from Seventeenth-Century Britain', in John Patten (ed.), *Pre-Industrial England: Geographical Essays*. London: Dawson, 1979; Jeremy Boulton, *Neighbourhood and Society: A London Suburb in the Seventeenth Century*. Cambridge: Cambridge University Press, 1987. W. J. Smith, 'The Architecture of the Domestic System in Southeast Lancashire and the Adjoining Pennines', in S. D. Chapman (ed.), *The History of Working Class Housing: A Symposium*. Newton Abbot: David and Charles, 1971; and J. G. Timmins, *Handloom Weavers' Cottages in Central Lancashire*. Lancaster: University of Lancaster Centre for North-West Regional Studies, Occasional Paper No. 3, 1977.

So with the spatial concomitants of industrialization. What mattered not at all to contemporaries was the degree of difference between the nineteenth- and twentieth-century city; impressed on their lives and consciousness was the new urban form which introduced patterns of separation between work and residence not just for the wealthy, as had been the case in mercantile cities, but for the majority. In some towns, places of work and residence may have been only a short walk away; but they were places *apart*, and except in the case of employer-provided housing (by best estimates only a small fraction of working-class housing even in single-factory towns) workers came to cluster in communities separate from the *locus* of wage work, separate from other social classes, even separate from workers with different Weberian class attributes. This multiple revolution in space and in social segregation, even if somewhat inchoate, incomplete, and interlaced by older craft patterns characterized by the conjoining of work and residence within cross-class households, was the central phenomenal feature of the remarkable large-scale urbanization of nineteenth-century England.[22]

In Liverpool, for example, which, with Manchester, was one of the two great towns of industrializing Lancashire, by the mid-nineteenth century the upper and middle classes 'who could afford to do so had moved from their place of work or business into areas on the outskirts of the town or even beyond

---

[22] The unevenness of the pace and scale of urban segregation is remarked on by Richard Dennis: 'It is clear that the spatial segregation of status groups did not begin suddenly in 1800, but the awareness of segregation, the attitudes toward it and the scale at which it occurred did all evolve during the century. Early nineteenth century forms of social segregation, vertically within buildings and horizontally between front-street and court dwellings, had, by mid-century, evolved into segregation by streets or estates, although these effects were still often too detailed to show up clearly in analyses at the scale of enumeration districts. Only in the largest cities, such as Manchester, or at the extremes of status—middle-class suburb and immigrant slum—were homogeneous social areas of the type expected by contemporary urban theory to be found.' Richard Dennis, 'Stability and Change in Urban Communities: A Geographical Perspective', in Johnson and Pooley, *The Structure of Nineteenth Century Cities*, 256.

it into adjacent townships'. Their residential areas in new suburban rings were divorced from both the work and residence places of workers. Within the heart of the city there were 'distinctive zones of different economy and society'. Lawton has found that 'in the Liverpool of 1851 there was a well-marked zoning'. Dividing the city into eight areas, he shows with great clarity how Liverpool's space had come to be sorted out into spatial divisions of the classes from each other, and within the working class into districts differentiated by rates of immigration, ethnicity, durability of employment, command of skill, and wage levels.[23] In a complementary treatment Treble has shown how much of the housing constructed in early nineteenth-century Liverpool was built explicitly for wage workers in working-class neighbourhoods, and how this process of building and development, together with trickle-down features of housing inheritance from the middle classes who were purchasing new environments, created a stratified mix of types of working-class housing: cellars, lodging houses, converted multi-occupation tenements, back-to-back court-system dwellings, and single-family terraced housing.[24] For the vast majority in Liverpool and other industrializing cities workshop houses were the places of domicile of the past. This older pattern did continue to exist in many places, to be sure. Burnett's history of working-class housing notes that

In many parts of the country where domestic industry was carried on, especially in the domestic textile areas of the Midlands and the North, houses survived from the pre-factory age, and continued to be built at least until the middle of the century, which combined the functions of home and workshop. The handloom-weavers of Yorkshire and Lancashire, the hosiery-knitters of Nottinghamshire, Coventry, Macclesfield and Spitalfields, the nail-makers of Birmingham

[23] R. Lawton, 'The Population of Liverpool in the Mid-Nineteenth Century', *Transactions of the Historical Society of Lancashire and Cheshire*, 197 (1955), 93, 94. See also Colin G. Pooley, 'Choice and Constraint in the Nineteenth Century City: A Basis for Residential Differentiation', in Johnson and Pooley, *The Structure of Nineteenth Century Cities*.

[24] James H. Treble, 'Liverpool Working Class Housing, 1801–1851', in Chapman, *History of Working Class Housing*.

and district, shoe-makers, glove-makers, straw-plaiters and other local craft-workers scattered throughout the country used their homes as workrooms as had their ancestors for generations before.[25]

But this pattern, he observes, was, by mid-century, in rapid, unmistakable decline; indeed, given the transformations in the country's markets and system of production, 'the ultimate separation of work from home was a condition precedent to the development of a decent home life for the vast majority of industrial workers'.[26]

These new urban spatial forms were not only characteristic of the larger towns and cities,[27] but of such smaller towns as

[25] John Burnett, *A Social History of Housing, 1815–1870*. Newton Abbot: David and Charles, 1978, 79.

[26] Ibid., 81. Such transformations have been documented carefully for city after city in England. Pritchard, for example, has treated the spatial transformation of Leicester, where, in 1840, the integration between work and residence was still very tight; by 1870 it had been shattered, and a modern form of spatial organization had developed. Vance has done the same for Birmingham, Prest for Coventry, Trowell for Leeds. Olsen, Wohl, Sheppard, and a good many others have shown how even in London, where craft production survived as the dominant form throughout the nineteenth century, there was a 'systematic sorting-out of London into single-purpose, homogeneous specialized neighbourhoods', an increasing crowding of the working classes into wholly separate residential areas, and, overall, a large-scale separation of work and home. R. M. Pritchard, *Housing and the Spatial Structure of the City*. Cambridge: Cambridge University Press, 1976; James E. Vance, Jr., 'Housing the Worker: Determinative and Contingent Ties in Nineteenth Century Birmingham', *Economic Geography*, 43 (Apr. 1967); John Prest, *The Industrial Revolution in Coventry*. Oxford: Oxford University Press, 1960; F. Trowell, 'Speculative Housing Development in the Suburb of Headingly, Leeds, 1838–1914', *Publications of the Thoresby Society*, 59 (pt. 1, 1983); Donald J. Olsen, 'Victorian London: Specialization, Segregation, and Privacy', *Victorian Studies*, 17 (Mar. 1974), 267; A. S. Wohl, 'The Housing of the Working Classes in London', in Chapman, *History of Working Class Housing*; Francis Sheppard, *London 1808–1870: The Infernal Wen*. London: Secker and Warburg, 1971; Harold Pollins, 'Transport and Social Divisions', in Ruth Glass (ed.), *London: Aspects of Change*. London: McGibbon and Kee, 1964.

[27] These various changes can be traced through a series of articles about a medium-size city, Nottingham: Anne Bosworth, 'Aspects of Middle Class Life: The Park Estate, Nottingham, 1841–1881', *Journal of Regional and Local Studies*, 5 (Spring 1985); Ken Brand, 'The Park

Chorley, in Lancashire, which has been the subject of a very careful case study by A. M. Warnes, who charted its development between 1780 and 1850, when its population grew from 4,200 to 12,750. Noting that 'little has been written until recent years about the consequences of rapid urbanization and industrialization on the internal structure of towns', and that 'the geographical changes following the setting up of the first large-scale employing units have been neglected', he takes three 'snapshots' of Chorley—in 1780, 1816, and 1850.[28] Before 1780 Chorley was an agricultural township, serving the market and commercial functions of its rural environment. The town's growth began to accelerate around 1780 as a result of the growth of the weaving trade stimulated by the mechanization of spinning. Even so, its landscape continued to be defined by its pre-industrial functions: 'nowhere had large employing units been formed; most people still lived at or immediately adjacent to their place of employment.' Between 1780 and 1816 the town's population increased by 50 per cent to 6,000, a growth stimulated mainly by new employment in early, small textile mills. At this date factories and clusters of houses around them became part of the town's topography, but most of the growth of the textile industry can be accounted for more by the enlarging of existing workshops than by their replacement by factories. With respect to patterns of settlement, the broadest conclusion that can be reached, based on available town records, maps, and an unusually detailed Vestry Committee Survey, is that 'residential location was still to a great extent determined by the location of employment and not usually by the social differences among the population'. Never-

---

Estate, Nottingham: The Development of a Nineteenth Century Fashionable Suburb', *Transactions of the Thoroton Society of Nottinghamshire*, 88 (1984); S. D. Chapman, 'Working-Class Housing In Nottingham During the Industrial Revolution', *Transactions of the Thoroton Society of Nottinghamshire*, 67 (1963); and Christopher Weir, 'The Growth of an Inner Urban Housing Development: Forest Fields, Nottingham, 1883–1914', *Transactions of the Thoroton Society of Nottinghamshire*, 89 (1985).

[28] A. M. Warnes, 'Early Separation of Homes from Workplaces and the Urban Structure of Chorley, 1780–1850', *Transactions of the Historical Society of Lancashire and Cheshire*, 212 (1970), 106.

theless, the 1816 social geography of the town was rather more complicated than that of 1780. A somewhat more differentiated pattern had developed, characterized by a better defined commercial core, a more rapid pattern of growth in outlying parts, and scattered but discernible clusters of settlements associated with specific new occupations, including calico works and cotton-spinning factories.[29]

By 1850, the town had been radically transformed. In the years since 1816 Chorley had become a factory town. Hand-loom weavers, once the majority of the working population, were reduced to under 10 per cent of the work-force. Using enumerators' books from the 1851 census, Warnes estimates that 'over one half of the economically active were engaged in branches of the textile industry that necessitated a journey to work'. Further, he finds not only that there was a dramatic shift from domestic employment, but that 'by 1851 the proximity of home and workplace was breaking up, at least for certain sections of the workforce', and 'the conditions for a recognizable pattern of social segregation were beginning to develop'.[30]

It is important, just as Joyce cautioned, not to overstate the modernity of this pattern. Only a negligible number of workers (about 4 per cent) lived more than a mile (1.6 kilometres) from their work; and over half of the 1,813 people Warnes examined lived within a quarter of a mile (0.4 kilometres) of their workplace. Of the two in three workers who no longer laboured where they lived, the majority only had to move short distances to overcome the separation. 'Nevertheless, there is no doubt that the average distance travelled to work had sharply increased since 1816, not only because more workers lived away from their work but also because of the increasing variety of employment.' Indeed, in a striking finding, Warnes reports that 'the newer the factory the less close were the locations of residence of its workers'.[31]

---

[29] Ibid., 111, 119.

[30] Ibid., 122, 120.

[31] Ibid., 132. With the diversification of workplaces, there may have been a reduction of commitment by workers to a particular factory or employer, and a diversification of family employment in different factories. These changes tended to increase the average

The spatial consequences of the extinction of the handicraft system in Lancashire, like the dissolution of household production more generally in the industrial revolution, were numerous and fundamental. With the exception of company towns, where factory masters held sway over the totality of working-class life, the role of capitalists was constricted to the workplace, freeing workers to live without direct supervision in their residential areas. This new freedom (undergirded, over time, by the enlarged rights of liberal citizenship) was the concomitant of a new division between markets for labour (now elaborated on a regional, and national, scale) and markets for housing (that operated on a more local scale). In the workshop structure of employment and residence the two had moved to the same market rhythm. With the sundering of this link, residential communities not only came more and more to be shaped by speculation and the strategies of builders and landlords, and stratified by income and styles of life; they also came to be environments which people of all social classes sought to define, shape, and control. It was in these new environments that working-class people created new institutions, new relationships, new patterns of life.[32]

The contingent connections between these social and spatial changes in capitalist cities and patterns of working-class formation have long been neglected, by Marxist and non-Marxist scholars alike. Most studies of class and class formation

---

distance of family members from work. Residential differentiation based on occupation was being replaced by a 'tendency for those with similar incomes, educational levels, or other status variables, to congregate in limited parts of the town'. Paradoxically, belonging to certain occupations (spinners, printers, and bleachers) made such a divorce between occupation and residence possible. Warnes, 'Early Separation of Homes from Workplaces', 133. A parallel discussion may be found in T. C. Barker and J. R. Harris, *A Merseyside Town in the Industrial Revolution: St. Helen's, 1750–1900*. Liverpool: Liverpool University Press, 1954.

[32] Not only working-class people, of course. Think of Dickens's portrayal of the clerk John Wemmick in *Great Expectations*. Welsh observes that 'nowhere in literature is the modern segregation of hearth and city, of personal life and business, so sharply and consciously drawn'. Alexander Welsh, *The City of Dickens*. Cambridge, Mass.: Harvard University Press, 1986.

have not taken territorial arrangements into account. To incorporate space, however, is not to *solve* questions about the specificities of working-class history, or working-class 'exceptionalism' in this or that setting, only to *refocus* them. Whether the development in nineteenth-century cities of autonomous, segregated working-class districts facilitated the political consciousness and mobilization of workers on a class basis proved radically contingent. It is plausible, as Richard Harris has noted, to hypothesize that the separation of work and home and the segregation of residential areas by class (in both the Marxist and Weberian senses) may sustain political insularity by reducing contact between the classes, thus making the class structure opaque from the vantage-point of the residential community. But it is just as convincing to propose that residential differentiation may heighten the possibilities of developing dispositions based on class understandings, as well as the probabilities of political mobilization on a class basis, by increasing opportunities for contact between members of the same class.[33]

Cannadine concludes his reflections on the state of work on urban space and class formation in a pessimistic frame of

[33] Richard Harris, 'Residential Segregation and Class Formation in the Capitalist City: A Review and Directions for Research', *Progress in Human Geography*, 8/1 (Mar. 1984). The contradictory features of working-class residential segregation are also taken up by Cannadine, ('Residential Differentiation', 244 ff., and esp. 246), who also raises the question of whether class conflict and class collaboration may not in fact shape spatial structures, thus reversing the causal arrows of Harris's questions, and by Daunton, who insists that the 'social meaning of the pattern of social segregation is rarely considered, although it is by no means self-evident. The nature of physical form must be interpreted in the light of contemporary culture and society. It could indeed be argued that a high level of social segregation could result in the formation of a strong sense of class identity in self-sufficient working class communities. On the other hand, a sense of distance could imply a lack of knowledge and experience of other classes and a lower level of conflict than was possible where social segregation was not well developed . . . The precise meaning attached to the use of space does not emerge as a self-evident truth from the maps of historical geographers.' M. J. Daunton, *House and Home in the Victorian City: Working-Class Housing 1850–1914*. London: Edward Arnold, 1983.

mind. Observing that 'on the basis of the research at present available, we have no coherent body of theory concerning the links between spatial segregation and social class', he ruminates aloud both about whether this connection is significant, and, even if it is, whether the connections are not too complex and difficult to describe to make this focus rewarding.[34] To the contrary, I think this linkage is fundamental; if anything, his focus, like that of Harris, on the relationship between spatial segregation, on the one side, and class conflict and collaboration, on the other, is too limited. For the prior question to that of militancy is that of the existence of class itself as a category of social description and action.

Comparisons between the American and English experiences—so similar in the objective structuring of space in capitalist cities yet so different in the character of class dispositions and patterns of collective action—are instructive here. Consider, first, the shared features of the reorganization of city space. Cannadine himself has carefully shown, despite differences between landownership patterns and the character of land law in the two countries, that the broad determinants of spatial patterns were remarkably similar. In American cities, 'as much as in England, topography and the economic substructure of the urban community took precedence in determining how the land was utilized'.[35] Indeed, of all the Western industrializing countries, the urban-spatial histories of the United States and England in the nineteenth century came to be most alike after the initial difference of much lower patterns of urbanization in the early American Republic.

In the nineteenth century, Michael Conzen observes, 'the urbanisation of the United States "caught up" with that of Western Europe, starting from a decidedly modest base'. In 1800, London was second only to Peking in city size; that year, Philadelphia, the largest American city, ranked just 119th, and New York 133rd. By 1900, after a century of phenomenal growth in the American urban system as a whole, New York

---

[34] Cannadine, 'Residential Differentiation', 247, 248–9.

[35] David Cannadine, 'Urban Development in England and America in the Nineteenth Century: Some Comparisons and Contrasts', *Economic History Review*, 33 (Aug. 1980), 324.

was outranked only by London; Chicago was the world's fifth largest city; and of the top fifty cities the United States accounted for seven and Britain for six.[36] Most American cities, unhindered by a pre-industrial built-form, developed to the tempo of capitalist development and market forces, producing a less mediated character to urban growth and social geography. By 1840, the United States had a coherent urban system, with great port cities and industrial towns; by 1880, this network spanned the continent.

As things worked out, the relative *tabula rasa* of the American landscape facilitated a non-intentional mimetic process in which 'a set of principles, first worked out largely in Britain, was taken to a logical conclusion'. The spatial form and social geography of American cities followed the logic first spelled out by Engels, but was reinforced by the less mediated character of American urban development. Thus, John Radford notes, 'While the streetcar system of Leeds was encumbered by municipal constraints and somewhat muddled demand factors, that of Boston evolved in bursts of growth related directly to the quantitative forces of the national economy, the urban land market, and rate of in-migration.' As in England, a robust urban-based industrialization impelled shifts in land use and in the relations of labour and housing markets. With the advent of factory industry came the 'physical and psychological separation of work and residence [that] led to the development of a housing market distinct from the market for productive land, and thence to functional districting, a functional hierarchy, urban sprawl, and working class residential

[36] Michael Conzen, 'The American Urban System in the Nineteenth Century', in D. J. Herbert and R. J. Johnson (eds.), *Geography and the Urban Environment*. London: John Wiley, 1981, 296. A useful overview of the American experience is provided by Patrick O'Donnell, 'Industrial Capitalism and the Rise of Modern American Cities', *Kapitalistate*, 6 (Fall 1977). A consideration of the Canadian experience, stressing that in contrast to US cities, Canadian cities were more likely to be founded on the frontier, as an aspect of statist policies of seeking outposts to stake out national claims, is Gilbert A. Stetler, 'The Political Economy of the City-Building Process: Early Canadian Urban Development', in Derek Fraser and Anthony Sutcliffe (eds.), *The Pursuit of Urban History*. London: Edward Arnold, 1983.

areas', as well as the expansion of a service-oriented central business district.[37] By mid-century, even in New York, the city most constrained by earlier spatial patterns, the landscape, Elizabeth Blackmar concluded, 'lost its association with the conditions of independent proprietorship, and houses no longer sheltered and integrated trade and domestic labor. Though the proprietary house and shop persisted as a residual form . . . the vast majority of New York households had moved onto the cash nexus of wages and rent.' Shelter, now separate from the wage workplace, was distributed by a pattern of neighbourhood formation that was class-based.[38]

The relationship between capitalist industrial development and the transformations of the material and spatial character of daily life, at work and away from work, was mediated on both sides of the Atlantic (indeed, throughout the industrializing capitalist world) by fundamental transformations in the treatment of land and housing, by the instantiation of new kinds of markets to regulate both, and by the emergence of new sets of social actors—landlords, tenants, and solicitors, among others—who played key roles in the operation of these markets. The dynamics of the new urban markets for land and housing depended on an artificial scarcity, the result of concentrated ownership, 'the structure of the competitive housing market and particularly the purchasing power that permitted [the middle and upper classes] to claim particular blocks for their exclusive use', and, with proletarianization, the reduced capacity of working people to acquire and own property.[39]

In short, there was a fundamental shift in the assignment of land and in the mechanisms to secure it. As James Vance points out in his classic essay, in medieval cities land ownership had been mainly functional, with a concomitant permissive attitude to the encroachment of public space. The key spatial unit of work and residence was the household. Save for institutional buildings such as churches, town halls, and

[37] John P. Radford, 'The Social Geography of the Nineteenth Century US City', in Herbert and Johnson, *Geography and the Urban Environment*, 258, 281–2.

[38] Blackmar, *Manhattan for Rent*, 250.

[39] Ibid., p. 104.

guildhalls, the town was characterized by very little morphological differentiation. Such geographical differentiation as existed was produced by occupational clustering. Vance's main argument, against this background, is to show that with the 'treatment of urban land as a source of income, which came in with the general conceptual baggage of the capitalist system as it developed', city space was transformed in a fundamental way. 'If land assignment had been primarily social during the Middle Ages, it became primarily economic during the time of mercantilism and industrialism.'[40]

As capitalism entered the industrial epoch, the concept of the land–rent gradient that pointed toward the highest economic use by introducing a profit motive into land use and housing was already established. With the explosion in the demand for land for factories as well as for working-class housing, this market logic accelerated the processes of segregation of both uses and social classes. Less and less were people provided with shelter within the framework of an integrated household economy. Housing became a personal and family matter in the market-place, thus 'any distinctions among men could not fail to be reflected in the housing provision'.[41] Now, housing and labour markets separated. The provision of housing became a matter independent of the provision of work. A person's choice of the type and location of housing was dictated by the individual's or the family's ability to pay rent. In this 'capitalist assignment' of housing, there developed a close relationship in market and social terms between housing districts and finely graded distinctions of social class. There was also a logic to the circulation of housing, as those with means captured new, more attractive housing locations, abandoning their former quarters to those with the next highest rent-paying capacity.[42]

[40] James E. Vance, Jr., 'Land Assignment in the Precapitalist, Capitalist, and Postcapitalist City', *Economic Geography*, 47 (Apr. 1971), pp. 101, 102, 106, 115, 107.

[41] Ibid., p. 112.

[42] Blackmar presents a number of vivid case studies of this process of capture and filtering in ante-bellum New York (Blackmar, *Manhattan for Rent*). There was an internal relation between the growth of the scale of cities and their internal form and social geography. In the

Supporting this set of market developments was the severing of the linkage between labour and housing markets. Working with both American and English case study materials, Vance shows decisively how 'probably few events in economic history have had more fundamental effect on the shape of the city than the physical parting of the residence from the workplace'. With the breaking of these ties, it was possible for workplaces to cluster separately from home places, for clear hierarchies of land usage to develop, for distinctive flows of capital to circulate in industrial and real-estate sectors, and, above all, for there to be a massive change in the scale of cities by 'the detachment of the housing function from the strictures of "productive location"'.[43]

---

process of increasing segregation of the city, the development of the city went hand in hand with the development of capitalist accumulation in shaping the form of the city. Dodgshon makes the point this way: 'If we are forced to select a single factor which, more than any other, nurtured the growth of a price-fixing market in urban land, then a case can be made out for seeing the scalar growth of towns as a more potent influence on both the unshackling of urban rents and on their subsequent character and movement ... Sustained scalar growth affected urban land-markets in two ways. First, it pressurised and, ultimately, collapsed any residual restraints on the customary control of land prices. Second, through the sheer numbers that now made up the urban community, it created an imperative for new expressions of social differentiation. Class differences provided this basis, sorting large numbers into simpler categories of meaning, a system compatible with the large impersonal nature of the industrial town and the divorce of interest between capital and labour.' Robert A. Dodgshon, *The European Past: Social Evolution and Spatial Order*. London: Macmillan, 1987, 332–3. Also, for a discussion of the relationship between the expansion of the built-up area of the city and its internal restructuring, see the concise overview by H. Carter, 'Towns and Urban Systems 1730–1900', in R. A. Dodgshon and R. A. Butlin (eds.), *An Historical Geography of England and Wales*. London: Academic Press, 1979.

[43] James E. Vance, Jr., 'Housing the Worker: The Employment Linkage as a Force in Urban Structure', *Economic Geography*, 42 (Oct. 1966), 307. Vance points out that the provision of housing became divorced mentally from the establishment of mills and shops later than it came to be divorced functionally. Only then was there a true generalized housing market independent of the housing market in which housing no longer was an adjunct to work (309). A comple-

The shift from a situation in which people's employment determined where they lived to the situation of a generalized housing market was no simple, once and for all matter. In industrial city after industrial city undergoing the transformation from household to factory production, and from artisanship to a proletarian working class, a multiplicity of intermediate stages could be found. The landscape was not coherent; it was layered, its parts moved to different rhythms. None the less, the robustness and directionality of the pattern was clear: the constant change and expansion in the scale at which market mechanisms operated. Given the pace of change, 'we can regard the "ideal" landscape created by free markets as a chimera, a state to which conditions worked but never reached, before the innate volatility of markets changed the target'.[44] But even with (perhaps especially with) this gathering of a market-driven urbanization of pace and scope, the proletarianization of the work-force and the establishment of housing markets went hand in hand: 'The creation of a proletariat was accompanied by the creation of the residential quarter ... This was the watershed of housing generalization.'[45] With this shift, the residential area came to be what Vance labels a conscious environment, with specific criteria of choice; with this shift, the geography of the city became social as much as economic. Housing became 'a school of social

---

mentary essay to the work of Vance that provides a significant overview is Michael Ball, 'The Development of Capitalism in Housing Provision', *International Journal of Urban and Regional Research*, 5 (June 1981).

[44] R. A. Dodgshon, 'Geographical Change', 186. Elsewhere, he writes: 'long before such adjustments had reached anything like completion or had created a price-efficient landscape, that is, one that yielded the highest rent under a given set of market conditions, these conditions had moved inexorably forwards or backwards. Instead of a single coherent system of spatial order, we are faced with a patchwork of incomplete adjustments, each oriented towards a particular conjunction of market circumstances, some—like anciently-formed rocks—bearing the mark of a past magnetic north, but all bearing testimony to the innate tendency of markets to turn eventually.' Dodgshon, *The European Past*, 317.

[45] Vance, 'Housing the Worker: Determinative and Contingent Ties in Nineteenth Century Birmingham'.

intercourse'[46] between individuals and families sharing more than an occupation or a trade. *What this new sharing was to be called, how it would be identified—by class categories of one or another kind, by territorial namings, by ethnic or religious solidarities—came to be a pivotal puzzle of nineteenth-century class formation.*

Only with the joining of an autonomous labour market by an autonomous housing market were the distributive mechanisms of working-class life in industrial capitalist society in place. Land, housing, and labour, as well as capital, had been referred to the market, and were now ordered by it. At this point it is possible to speak of a society determined in the first instance by its economic relationships, and shaped by economic rather than cultural, political, or social values.[47] This moment, suspended, as it were, between a past of regulated mercantile markets and a future of statist inverventions to organize markets and mitigate their distributional effects, was precisely the time of the birth of modern working classes. Through the mechanisms of the markets for labour and shelter, working people in the city were forced to face capitalism, unprotected.

Marxism, of course, has pursued this confrontation, but lacking an urban-spatial dimension, it has done so unarmed. What has been missing has been the linkage between the economic system and the social and spatial specificity of the structuring of working-class lives. With the shift from family to factory production, and from integrated to functionally and socially segregated city space, working-class experiences changed in many dimensions: in the timing of the day, in the

---

[46] Lion Murard and Patrick Zylberman, 'Industrial City and Mass Mobilization', unpublished MS, Social Science Research Council Seminar on Mass Values, Nuffield College, Oxford, 3–6 July 1979. In this essay, grounded in the work of Foucault, Murard and Zylberman stress the new dialectic between intimacy and mass sociability in industrial cities, as well as dominant and middle-class fears of contact with the working classes and the poor. A new discourse on housing stressed contagion, frequently in the language of public health and sanitation, rather than communication.

[47] This, of course, is a central insight of Karl Polanyi in *The Great Transformation*. Boston: Beacon Press, 1944.

character of the family and the meaning of home, in the features of organizational life, and in relationships with the state and other social classes.[48] Workers engaged in factory production had to schedule their days to include short or long journeys to work;[49] in families with more than one wage-

---

[48] In the discussion of these issues, I draw on Allan Pred, 'Production, Family, and Free-Time Projects: A Time-Geographic Perspective on the Individual and Societal Change in Nineteenth Century U.S. Cities', *Journal of Historical Geography*, 7 (Jan. 1981).

[49] Critics of the view that the separation of work and home was meaningful in the mid-19th century like to stress that most journeys to work were short. In San Francisco in 1860, for example, the mean distance travelled to work by industrial workers was less than half a mile (0.8 km), with the modal commuting distance between a quarter and half a mile (0.4–0.8 km). Even twenty years later, a majority of workers lived under a mile (1.6 km) from their place of work. Pred, however, rightly reminds us not to impose a modern sense of distance on these figures: 'Factory and large-scale shop workers . . . had to allocate a portion of their time to resources for movement. The factory or large-scale shop employee was apt to spend at least 15 minutes, and perhaps an hour or more, going to and from work, for regardless of whether he or she had to journey as little as one or two blocks, or as much as a mile or more, it almost always had to be done on foot.' Public transport, until the late 19th century, was mainly the preserve of the middle and upper classes. As late as 1880 only 17 per cent of the work-force of Philadelphia commuted to work by street-railway. Of course, with the cheapening of public transport and its development as mass transport, the separation in space between work and home could grow (it was greatest at first for the middle and upper classes), but that frequently did not mean that the time spent in commuting actually went up. The San Francisco data are from Robert A. Elgie, 'The Development of San Francisco Manufacturing, 1848–1860', unpublished MA essay, Department of Geography, University of California, Berkeley, Calif., 1966, and the Philadelphia figure is from Roger Miller, 'A Time-Geographic Assessment of the Impact of Horsecar Transportation on Suburban Non-Heads of Households in Philadelphia, 1850–1860', unpublished Ph.D. dissertation, Department of Geography, University of California, Berkeley, Calif., 1979. Both are cited in Pred, 'Production, Family, and Free-Time Projects', 13–14, from which the citation also comes. There is a discussion of how differentiation antedated the transport revolution in English cities too in Colin G. Pooley, 'Choice and Constraint in the Nineteenth-Century City: A Basis for Residential Differentiation', in Johnson and Pooley, *The Structure of Nineteenth Century Cities*, 202–3 and 222.

earner, this produced new challenges of co-ordination, providing yet a new element to the time-discipline of modern capitalism. Family life became centred on home and neighbourhood, more bounded as a domestic emotional institution. Gender roles sharpened, as did the divide between paid and unpaid labour. Male wage-earners were often absent when key family activities had to be performed. There was now a clearer break between work and leisure, or 'free' time. As work and home divided into increasingly autonomous spheres, new kinds of organizations sprang up specific either to wage work (unions) or to working-class residential communities (friendly societies, working men's clubs). The state appeared in working people's lives where they laboured as the (potential or actual) regulator of hours and conditions of employment, and where they lived as the regulator of public space, the provider of services, and the definer of the rights of citizenship. Less and less face to face, relationships between the social classes came increasingly to be structured within and across formal organizations. Each sphere of life—at work and away from it—was now characterized by its own distinctive patterns of organization and interaction.

With these alterations, working-class people were confronted by new situations and choices about how to map the city. Writing about the United States, geographer Allan Pred has argued that in the face of the split between work and home industrial workers were presented with the option of selecting 'only one of two broad noneconomic institutional project types: those defined by institutions organized by fellow laborers of the same occupation; and those defined by institutions oriented toward individuals of the same ethnic or religious background'. He observes, further, that 'occupationally and ethnically oriented institutions were usually, but not always, mutually exclusive', and he speculates that

The relationship between the demands of production projects, residential location, and participation in free-time projects defined by occupationally and ethnically oriented institutions is very likely critical to an understanding of both specific instances of labor unrest and the more general failure of the American working-class to organize itself politically.[50]

[50]   Pred, 'Production, Family, and Free-Time Projects', 35.

In this way, Pred provides an urban-spatial explanation for the most basic puzzles of American working-class formation: the stark split between the ways workers think, talk, and act at work and when they are away from work at home in their residential communities. On the whole, American workers have acted on the basis of the shared solidarities of class at work, but on those of ethnic, religious, and territorial affinities away from work:

The links between work and community conflicts have been unusually tenuous. Each kind of conflict has had its own separate vocabulary and set of institutions: work, class, and trade unions; community, ethnicity, local parties, churches, and voluntary associations. Class, in short, has been lived and fought as a *series of partial* relationships, and it has therefore been experienced and talked about only as one of a number of competing bases of social life.[51]

It is this system of values, ideas, organizations, and practices that constitutes the core of what is distinctive about the American experience of working-class formation.

Pred's attempt to account for this outcome by a social–spatial explanation is welcome but unconvincing: welcome, because it directly connects the puzzles of working-class agency to their everyday-life experiences in time and space in a way that traditional Marxism has not; unconvincing, because other working classes, including the English, experienced just these social–spatial transformations, with very different results. In England, class came to define the terms of speech and action of working-class people both where they worked and where they lived. Clearly, very similar objective spatial circumstances could produce divergent patterns of class formation.

Think for a moment about fraternal orders. In her meticulous survey of the American case, Mary Ann Clawson shows how widespread membership in such organizations was for working people in the nineteenth century, and concludes that 'the existence of the local lodge as a focal institution of working class communities diverted energy and resources away from the formation of more autonomous working-class

[51] Ira Katznelson, *City Trenches: Urban Politics and the Patterning of Class in the United States*. New York: Pantheon Books, 1981, 19.

institutions'. Locating these organizations within the nexus of the split between workplace and community life, she finds that 'to the extent that the resources and identification of working class men were incorporated into fraternal orders and other community organizations, those resources could be diverted from the potential construction of autonomous class-based social and cultural institutions'.[52]

Like Pred, Clawson treats this as a given, almost a truism in the face of the objective spatial split between work and home. Yet it was precisely such organizations in working-class residential communities in England as those whose effects on class consciousness she describes for the United States that provided the institutional basis for a more holistic understanding of class that transcended the divisions of work and home. English working-class community-based organizations were integral parts of a network of values and organizations that, in stark contrast to the American pattern, reflected and promoted the view that class pervades all social relationships, not just those at the workplace. Or, to take another institutional example, whereas historians of American neighbourhood and political party life have long been impressed by the combination of sociability and political action of local party machines oriented to limited, particularistic goals on the basis of ethnic and territorial identities, the same dual role of leisure and instrumental activity characterized Chartist meetings in working men's clubs, friendly societies, and public houses.[53] Whereas such activities underscored a divided working-class consciousness in the United States, they helped promote a more global consciousness of class in England, what Eric Hobsbawm has called 'high classness'.[54]

---

[52] Mary Ann Clawson, 'Fraternal Orders and Class Formation in the Nineteenth-Century United States', *Comparative Studies in Society and History*, 27 (Oct. 1985), 674, 695.

[53] In his discussion of Nottingham pubs, Rowley writes of annual dinners held to 'commemorate the birthday of Tom Paine, enlivened by radical songs, toasts, and recitations', and, more generally, of heavy drinking during business meetings. J. J. Rowley, 'Drink and the Public House in Nottingham, 1830–1860', *Transactions of the Thoroton Society of Nottinghamshire*, 79 (1975), 76.

[54] E. J. Hobsbawm, 'From Social History to the History of Society', *Daedalus*, 100 (Winter 1971), 20–45.

Further, quite unlike the American patterns, where even early trade unions developed meeting places at or very near the places of work they sought to organize, English trade union branches, many secret and illicit, met in working-class neighbourhoods. The organization of industrial disputes was often based in pubs, and their landlords frequently acted as strike co-ordinators or union treasurers. Many unions were identified with specific public houses, and some important Chartist pubs were also prominent meeting places for industrial and political organizers. Friendly societies, the main self-help community organizations of English workers, also gathered in ale houses. Intensely local in character, many of these societies were trade unions by other names that sought to protect their funds and their members from legal recriminations.[55]

The quality of the 'trade union consciousness' created by this compressed set of working-class organizations in the residential community was obviously rather different from the 'trade union consciousness' that came to prevail in the United States, where from the earliest moments of trade union history labour unions were disconnected from other institutions and locations of working-class life and political activity.

History, Edward Thompson reminds us, knows no regular verbs.[56] Whereas American historiography, when it has

[55] P. H. J. H. Gosden, *The Friendly Societies in England 1815–1875*. Manchester: Manchester University Press, 1961. For a treatment of French working-class formation that likewise stresses the importance of locality-based neighbourhood institutions, see the case study of Toulouse by Ronald Aminzade, who, writing about Second Republic and Second Empire France, stresses the importance of '"free social space" in which workers could find refuge from the dominant culture and its values of hierarchy and possessive individualism' to explain the development of a vibrant and militant consciousness of class. 'The social networks of informal working-class gathering places, including cafes, taverns, cabarets, dancehalls, theaters, and circuses, played a key role in the growth of working-class consciousness.' Ronald Aminzade, *Class, Politics, and Early Industrial Capitalism: A Study of Mid-Nineteenth Century Toulouse, France*. Albany, NY: State University of New York Press, 1981, 94, 82.

[56] 'For historical explanation discloses not how history *must* have eventuated but why it eventuated in this way and not in other ways; that process is not arbitrary but has its own regularity and rationality; that certain kinds of event (political, economic, cultural) have been

touched on urban space, has been quick to see in the spatial division of work and home the sufficient explanation for the pattern of divided working-class dispositions and patterns of collective action, the English case is a reminder that just such spatial patterns can be the framework for a very different working-class reading of capitalism and the city. And whereas English historiography has been concerned to explain the gradualist and reformist tendencies of the working class, on the assumption that this represents a departure from the norm of a militant class consciousness,[57] the American case is a

---

related, not in any way one likes, but in particular ways and within determinate fields of possibility; that certain social formations are not governed by "law" nor are they the "effects" of a static structural theorem—but are characterised by determinate relations and by a particular logic of process.' E. P. Thompson, *The Poverty of Theory and Other Essays*. London: Merlin Press, 1978, 242.

[57] This broad cultural pattern has been identified by Pelling as a combination of political and social 'conservatism, associated however with a profound sense of class consciousness and quite commonly a marked sense of grievance'. Henry Pelling, 'Then and Now: Popular Atttitudes Since 1945', in Pelling (ed.), *Popular Politics and Society in Late Victorian Britain*. London: Macmillan, 1968, 165. In a kind of mirror image, much German scholarship on social democracy has assumed that English reformism is the 'natural' pattern, and that the more radical moments of SPD history demand explanation as aberrations. A thoughtful review is provided by Geoff Eley and Keith Nield, 'Why Does Social History Ignore Politics?', *Social History*, 5 (May 1980). In this essay, they highlight an important problem in Marxist treatments of England as the paradigmatic case of class formation which, by taking classness for granted as the inevitable outcome of a working class within industrial capitalism, focuses on variations in militancy as something of an all or nothing matter divorced from the actual content of the society's discourses, organizations, and competing capacities of classes. The result, they observe, is an imitation by Marxist historiography of the liberal 'intellectual schematization—if workers go on the barricades they are "revolutionary", if they do not they are "reformist" or "integrated"'—a perspective that 'misses the realities that drive workers to action or condemn them to inaction'. In accepting this dichotomy much Marxist historiography has appended it to the assumption that a formed working class would 'naturally' develop in certain ways, and in the absence of such developments historians should search for a 'theoretical alibi' for the working class as a whole. The most common of these approaches within English Marxism has been that of the 'labour aristocracy'.

reminder that the issues of the degree and kind of working-class activity are distinct subjects of inquiry and that the construction of class as a category of social action across the divide of work and community is a conditional matter that demands explanation.

III

The sharpest differences between the early development of the English and American working classes were not at the place of work but at the place of residence. In both countries, neighbourhood solidarities provided bases for working-class organization, and for at least an inchoate awareness of potential political capacity. And in both, working people constructed tools where they lived to respond to the bewildering environments in which they now found themselves. While the forms assumed by local working-class organizations in the two societies were virtually identical, their rhetorical, dispositional, and institutional contents diverged radically.

Thus, one way to think about this comparative problem of working-class formation is to inquire about why both trade union and political agitation were pressed into the institutions of the residential community in England, but not in the United States. In the voluntary associations created in their relatively autonomous communities, separated from work and thus from the surveillance of their employers, English workers learned to put claims to their employers and to the state using a rhetoric and idiom of class.

What accounts for this divergent development? Here, the tools of Marxist social theory prove insufficient. A structural account of capitalist development, even when joined to a materialist analysis of the making and remaking of urban space and its social relations, is not capable of accounting for the divergent trajectories of class formation. On its own, Marxism reaches an impasse about a subject vital to its own social-theoretical (and political) project—the making of modern working classes. Even in the hands of a master like Edward Thompson, who has produced unsurpassed work on the subject, it has not proved possible for Marxism within its own analytical tradition to do better than work with the formula that class formation lies at the junction of determination and consciousness, which assumes that once a working class is 'made' by the impact of external conditions, the people sharing this fate will 'make themselves' into a class capable of affecting history. The single-country focus of *The Making of the English Working Class* allows Thompson to adopt this soft, but still teleological, version of the structural 'class in itself–for itself' model, and, in this way, to avoid the question of whether the movement from the experience of class society to class dispositions and activity in all spheres of life is necessary, likely, or entirely contingent; nor is he compelled to present an ordered causal account of the process that produces such an outcome.[58] Although Thompson's approach 'fits' the English case, it inhibits comparative analysis because, as the American example shows, it takes for granted that which must be explained.[59]

If Marxism provides unsurpassed tools for understanding the making of capitalist cities at the moment of their formation as embodiments of the logic and demands of accumulation, and if a historical materialism of city space working within the framework of Marxist social theory can account for the most

[58] Nor, for that matter, does the great volume of work by social geographers on the spatial patterns of 19th-century cities, most of which focuses on England. Its focus has been to explain the material underpinnings of the high classness of the English working class as if it were the automatic effect of the new industrial and spatial changes of capitalist development. See e.g. Richard Dennis, *English Industrial Cities in the Nineteenth Century: A Social Geography*. Cambridge: Cambridge University Press, 1984, and the collection of essays edited by Johnson and Pooley (*The Structure of Nineteenth Century Cities*).

[59] E. P. Thompson, *The Making of the English Working Class*. London: Victor Gollancz, 1963. As Gareth Stedman Jones points out, in England, 'equations between social and political forces have been only too easy to make because much of modern English political history has generally been thought to coincide with class alignments, and because, at the level of everyday speech, one of the peculiarities of England has been the pervasiveness of the employment of diverse forms of class vocabulary'. Gareth Stedman Jones, *Languages of Class: Studies in English Working Class History, 1832–1982*. Cambridge: Cambridge University Press, 1983.

fundamental alterations to the spatial worlds of everyday life for working-class people, an immanent and enclosed Marxism cannot solve its most important social-theoretical problem: the contingent and variable making of working-class subjects within capitalist societies. We have already seen how Castells's understandable impatience with this limitation caused him to abandon the Marxist framework in his analysis of contemporary social movements and how Harvey dealt with this impasse by forcing phenomenally non-class manifestations of an urban consciousness into the procrustean bed of the divide between capital and labour.

My proposal is different. It is that Marxism be simultaneously enriched by the incorporation of a spatial imagination and by an open posture toward the second great large-scale process of post-feudal modernity, the making of modern national states. As we shall soon see, the ways working classes read the city were deeply informed not only by patterns of capitalist development inscribed in space but also by their experience of how state formation, citizenship and the franchise, and public policies shaped and penetrated urban spatial and social relationships. At issue is not, as some recent formulations would have it, the relative capacity of economy-centred versus state-centred explanations.[60] Rather, I wish to explore how they can be made to work together, in this instance to advance solutions to the problem of differential class formation so basic to Marxism itself.

This problem of class formation is fundamental not only in terms of working-class responses to structural developments but because it defines the very character of the identity of the actors who, by their language and activity, have constituted and reconstituted the contours of capitalist societies. What I have suggested so far is that we can best approach the early history of working-class formation through the city, by asking not only about the relationships of people and the urban form but also 'What are the social meanings of the spatial patterns

---

[60] For an example, see Theda Skocpol, 'Bringing the State Back In: Strategies of Analysis in Current Research', in Evans, Rueschemeyer, and Skocpol, *Bringing the State Back In*.

and forms we see?'[61] The task of making sense of the new industrial cities was unavoidable, for just the reason suggested by Clifford Geertz: 'Reading the signs in urban sprawls (something nearly as difficult for the inhabitants of them as it is for external observers) is a necessity for anyone who would not get lost in them, left adrift—baffled, clumsy, angry, and powerless.'[62] It is my claim that the most important differences in readings of the newly fragmented city spaces of industrial capitalism can be accounted for by differences in state-related factors.

A focus on the state as a major source of variation in patterns of class formation in the English and American cases immediately confronts an important feature of social science literature on the state, the tendency to lump these countries together under the rubric of the Anglo-American 'weak state'.[63] Most treatments of the 'weak' state in the United States, from de Tocqueville's *Democracy in America* to treatments such as Samuel Huntington's analysis of the diffusion of the Tudor polity,[64] root the American experience in the British for the obvious historical reasons. In this largely persuasive line of analysis, Britain is understood as the aberrant case of state-building in early modern Europe. The Glorious Revolution of 1688, though radical from a Continental perspective, ratified the traditional prerogatives of Parliament against those of an absolutist alternative. Sovereignty was defined not by a confla-

---

[61] Elizabeth Blackmar, 'Re-Walking the Walking City: Housing and Property Relations in New York City, 1780–1840', *Radical History Review*, 21 (Fall 1979), 131.

[62] Clifford Geertz, '*Toutes Directions*: Reading the Signs in an Urban Sprawl', unpublished MS, 1988.

[63] Peter Nettl's seminal essay proposing that stateness be treated as a variable favourably cites Marx for observing that the United States and England were excluded from the 'necessity of violent overthrow of the state because there was no state as such to overthrow'. In neither country is the state 'instantly recognizable as an area of autonomous action', and, in both, the law, rather than being an enumeration of the state, has a great deal of autonomy. J. P. Nettl, 'The State as a Conceptual Variable', *World Politics*, 20 (July 1968), 577, 584.

[64] Samuel P. Huntington, *Political Order in Changing Societies*. New Haven, Conn.: Yale University Press, 1968.

tion of the civil and the civic within the state but in terms of representation, and, ultimately, a system of political parties linking state and society through electoral mechanisms. Although English sovereignty crystallized in a single representative body, indicating a pattern of centralization very different from the American federal system where sovereignty ultimately resided in 'the people', both countries shared a very clear contrast with the state patterns of Continental Europe. These states, unlike those of Prussia or France, did not have a monopoly of access to technical, professional information. Furthermore, for reasons Barrington Moore explains, 'England's whole previous history, her reliance on a navy instead of an army, on unpaid justices of the peace instead of royal officials, had put in the hands of the central state a repressive apparatus weaker than that possessed by strong continental monarchies.'[65] Colonial America, of course, shared in and inherited these characteristics of the British state, whose crown bordered on an abstraction, and which was relatively undeveloped as an autonomous entity demarcated from civil society.[66]

Although one might be tempted to point to an apparent correlation between strong states and militant working classes in Europe and to the seeming correlation between weak states and reformist tendencies within the working classes of England and the United States, the consequences of the weak states in both England and the United States compared with the absolutist and bureaucratic regimes of the Continent are not self-evident. Propositions along these lines would have to depend on caricature to the point of distortion. Continental

[65] Barrington Moore, Jr., *Social Origins of Dictatorship and Democracy: Lord and Peasant in the Making of the Modern World.* Boston: Beacon Press, 1966, 444.

[66] See Kenneth Dyson, *The State Tradition in Western Europe.* New York: Oxford University Press, esp. 36–44 and 186–202. The common existence of porous states based on obeisance to the law and on notions of consent may be invoked to explain some shared features of the English and American political experiences, including their permeable bureaucracies and their constitutional quietism. The very elusiveness of these states has tended to put fundamental constitutional questions of order and organization beyond politics.

working classes have hardly displayed a uniform propensity for revolutionary or proto-revolutionary activity, just as the English working class has known moments of militant contention and American workers have challenged capital at the workplace with great courage and at high risk and cost.

If it is difficult to move directly from an assessment of a given state as strong or weak to statements about revolutionary versus reformist working-class orientations to the regime, so it is even more difficult to make this kind of causal claim if we want to explain whether class, as a category of understanding and action, joined the spheres of work and community or was limited to the sphere of work. Kenneth Dyson, for one, has tried to tread this path of analysis for England. Its weak state, in his view,

helped to cement polarization in the industrial and political systems . . . Accordingly, the experience of a relatively 'unbridled' capitalism gave it a bad reputation, created a powerful and isolated working class culture, and undermined willingness to cooperate both in industry and in politics. Britain acquired a peculiar class structure: the obstinacy and distrust associated with attitudes of 'them' and 'us' were not directed at the state but at bastions of privilege and exclusiveness associated with society.[67]

The American experience, however, where 'us' and 'them' distinctions based on class were mainly restricted to employer–employee conflicts at the workplace, appears to belie this line of argument.

But appearances can be deceptive, for if we inquire about the precise organizational forms that the 'weak state' took in England and the United States; if we examine the different clusters of political rights the two working classes possessed in the early industrial period; and if we explore the effects these differences had on the content of working-class organizations located where workers lived, we shall be able to make more persuasive connections between the characteristics of these states and their activities and divergent patterns of class formation.

The most important political right in the nineteenth century

[67] Ibid., 249–50.

was, of course, the right to vote. What is striking about the familiar discussions of the franchise and class is how they avoid the questions of classness that concern us here. The quick extension of the franchise to males in the United States (virtually all adult males could vote by the early 1830s) and the much more protracted expansion of the right to vote in England (only one in five adult males composed the eligible electorate after reform in 1832, one in three after 1867, and only two in three even after 1886) are central to explanations of the differences between a divided and a global classness. But the impact of the variation in political rights on classness was not a direct or simple one. To understand it we have to take up the franchise in combination with another key difference between the two countries concerning the organization of the state: that of federalism versus a unitary state.

However diffuse the concept and reality of the state were in Britain, in the United States they were more so. Although he was insufficiently sensitive to the differences between these two 'weak' states, Nettl recognized the point. 'In England', he wrote, 'it would be on the whole difficult to find an agreed definition [of the state] at all, while in the United States, the word had a precise but totally different meaning *in contradistinction* to its European meaning—namely the residual area of regional government and territory.'[68] The diffuse organizational character of the American state took much of the charge out of the issue of franchise extension, for there was no unitary state to defend or transform. Once suffrage restrictions were lifted (in tandem with other democratizing reforms such as an increase in the number of public offices and in the regularity and frequency of elections), the United States had the world's first political system of participatory federalism.

Within this framework of state organization and democratic political rights, new kinds of political parties with a mass base were constructed. These political organizations, reaching into virtually every ward and neighbourhood in the country, brought together the spatial, ethnic, religious, and political identities of the various subgroups of the American working class. This act of organization and social definition took place

[68] Nettl, 'The State as a Conceptual Variable', 577–8.

where workers and their families lived. It created direct links between the political system and voting citizens, who were organized into politics on the basis of many identities but rarely those of class as such. This pattern created an institutional and participatory structure that was set apart from the organizations workers created to put their demands to their employers.

American participatory federalism was not just a system of voting based on intensely local solidarities. It was also a system of governance, taxation, and delivery of services. Partisan identifications based on territory and ethnicity made good sense of a city politics that delegated fiscal capacity and distributive resources to local government and party officials. This period saw the introduction of professional police forces, the bureaucratization of municipal charity and poor relief, and the establishment of public school systems, as well as a massive programme of publicly licensed construction. Political parties focused on the connections between these services and the various neighbourhoods of the city. Local politics became a segmented and distributive politics of community. In this politics, workers appeared in the political arena not as workers but as residents of a specific place or as members of a specific (non-class) group. Although there were many class-related economic issues on the national and state political agendas, including internal improvements, tariffs, control of banking, and slavery, the process of voting was for most urban workers insulated from these concerns, because it was focused elsewhere. By contrast with the United States, the interplay of state and class in England was radically different in each of the respects I have noted. The unitary English state concentrated distributive public policies at the centre. Quite unlike the federal government in the United States, Parliament and Whitehall took on major new responsibilities for social policy and the regulation of working conditions. Factory inspection, and poor law and public health reform, directly affected working-class life. Such parliamentary legislation, moreover, brought bureaucracies into being that were charged with carrying out the law, which in turn provided an impetus for the further expansion, and centralization, of the state. The growth of the central government was staggering. In 1797 most of the 16,000 employees on the central government payroll were customs, excise, and post office personnel. By 1869 this number had grown to 198,000, reflecting the new activities undertaken by the administrative agencies of the state. For the nineteenth century as a whole, public expenditure grew fifteen times in real terms.[69]

If patronage and property were the two hallmarks of the pre-nineteenth-century civil service, by mid-century patronage had been sacrificed to 'save the main pillar, property'.[70] The professionalization of governmental administration, a process that marked the period from 1830 to 1870, further focused attention by members of all social classes on the centre of the state apparatus in London. As Parliament and Whitehall took on new responsibilities for social policy and the regulation of working conditions and as they reorganized their affairs to rationalize the enforcement of regulations and the delivery of services, they potently reached into and affected working-class life, at the workplace but especially in the residential community. Each new parliamentary act and each new wave of administrative expansion and reform focused ever more

[69] Harold Perkin, *The Origins of Modern English Society*. London: Routledge and Kegan Paul, 1969, 123–4. The two main poles of a lively historiographical debate about this dramatic expansion of the state are the view that this growth was mainly the result of the initiatives of humanitarian and Benthamite civil servants and parliamentarians, and the view that it was the result of dominant class efforts to defuse class-based opposition to industrial capitalism. For discussions, see Oliver MacDonagh, *Early Victorian Government, 1830–1870*. London: Weidenfeld and Nicolson, 1977; Paul Richards and R. A. Slaney, 'The Industrial Town and Early Victorian Social Policy', *Social History*, 4 (Jan. 1979); Robert D. Storch, 'The Policeman as Domestic Missionary: Urban Discipline and Popular Culture in Northern England, 1850–1880', *Journal of Social History*, 9 (Summer 1976); D. C. Moore, 'Political Morality in Mid-Nineteenth Century England: Concepts, Norms, and Violations', *Victorian Studies*, 13 (Sept. 1969); John Milton-Smity, 'Earl Grey's Cabinet and the Objects of Parliamentary Reform', *Historical Journal*, 15 (Mar. 1972); Henry Parris, 'The Nineteenth Century Revolution in Government: A Reappraisal Reappraised', *Historical Journal*, 3 (Mar. 1960); and David Roberts, 'Jeremy Bentham and the Victorian Administrative State', *Victorian Studies*, 2 (Mar. 1959).

[70] Perkin, *Origins of Modern English Society*, 310.

sharply the attention of the working class on the state and its activities.

From the perspective of members of the English working class, the state that they confronted was not a 'weak state'. The comparative intensity of the tie between the working class and the central state was powerfully reinforced by the second aspect of what Harold Perkin has aptly called the nineteenth-century 'battle for the state': the struggle for the franchise.[71]

Just as the services and the regulations of government penetrated working-class life and thus reinforced class identities at the place of residence as well as at the workplace, so the demand by English workers for the right to vote could have been constructed on no other basis than that of class, for the working class was excluded on explicit class criteria. Only with universal suffrage, Heatherington wrote in the *Poor Man's Guardian* in December 1831, would 'the term *classes* merge into some comprehensive appellation, and no bloodshed will ensue'.[72] Although working-class reform organizations before and after 1832 were local in organization, unlike American political machines they directed their claims of citizenship to the centre; that is, to Parliament.

One effect of the interplay between the state and workers where they lived was the creation of a common fault-line, based on class, in all parts of English society. English working-class voluntary associations turned outwards in two respects. Rather than reinforcing local particularities based on intra-class differences of territory, income, or craft, they linked the activities and sensibilities of workers to each other across these lines. Furthermore, they joined to the concerns of the residential community the class issues of political participation, public policy, and trade unionism. In this respect, the Chartist movement provided the most important post-1832 concretization and deepening of these tendencies, which con-

[71] Ibid., 308–19.
[72] Cited in Patricia Hollis (ed.), *Class and Class Conflict in Nineteenth Century England*. London: Routledge and Kegan Paul, 1973, 80.

trast so sharply with the role played by neighbourhood-based working-class voluntary organizations in the United States.

Chartism provided the unifying pivot of working-class dispositions and organization. The Chartist movement took a working class that had oscillated from the turn of the century between economic and political action and fused both in a national network of community-based associations. For some two decades, Chartism created a distinctively English global consciousness of class harnessed not only to the campaign for votes, but to poor law agitation, trade unionism, factory reform, Owenite socialism, an unstamped press millenarianism, and machine-breaking.

In all these activities Chartism reflected the great diversity of the working class in a period of radical change in conditions. Where there was a substantial number of artisans, Chartist associations tended to stress the values of self-help and independence. Where handloom weavers predominated the form and content of agitation tended to be more strident. Where domestic industry predominated, workers were more likely to seek allies and guidance from middle-class reformers.[73] But overall, there were consistent themes to Chartism: the attempt to build an independent political voice for labourers based on class understandings, and the regular elaboration of links between economic problems and political representation. At its most vigorous, Chartism swallowed up other working-class movements, and gave them a common definition. Its key feature, J. F. C. Harrison has argued, was 'its class conscious tone and temper ... Chartists of many shades of opinion emphasized that their movement was concerned to promote the interests of working men as a class.' They 'assumed the need for class solidarity and their leaders talked the language of class struggle'.[74]

From the point of view of the historiographical *problematique* of gradualism, Chartism seems to be another instance of working-class reformism. From the vantage-point of the American comparison, the important feature of Chartism is its

[73] J. F. C. Harrison, *The Early Victorians, 1832–1851*. London: Weidenfeld and Nicolson, 1971, 156.

[74] Ibid., 157.

scope and depth as a class institution and its posing of a democratic, egalitarian alternative to the existing political and economic order based on a class analysis. The People's Charter was not just a political document but a coherent class-based set of demands connecting all spheres of society.[75] This orientation was reflected at the level of organization. Unlike American political parties which were class-specific in the neighbourhood but were otherwise inter-class institutions, the Chartist 'party' was entirely independent of the Tories and Whigs, and, over time, Chartists drew away from middle-class allies.

If Chartism disconnected the working class from other classes, it joined the political to the economic aspirations of workers, and it was affected as a movement by economic conditions and struggles. The dominant classes and politicians who successfully managed to use the state to deny workers the vote in 1832 tried to crush trade unions both before and after. As a consequence, it was possible for Chartism to become the common core of the working class and to impose itself as the common sense of a holistic rather than a divided kind of class consciousness, in tandem with a trade unionism quite different from its American counterpart. Just as the absence of political citizenship pressed political agitation into the autonomous institutions of working-class localities, so the state's stance with respect to union activity produced relatively weak unions and compelled workers to bring their workplace organizational efforts into the relatively protected space of the residential community.

The Combination Acts of 1799 and 1800, in existence for a quarter of a century, made early trade union organization very risky and drove labour activity underground, to the pubs and friendly societies of hospitable neighbourhoods. Even after the

---

[75] 'Implicit in the Charter', Tholfsen has written, 'was both a demand for the transformation of the structure of politics and the broader principle that working men ought to exercise control over every aspect of their lives ... What set Chartism ideologically apart from middle-class liberalism ... was the conviction, often only tacit, that class was the crux of the problem of progress and justice.' Trygve Tholfsen, *Working Class Radicalism in Mid-Victorian England*. New York: Columbia University Press, 1977, 85.

Acts were repealed, the state used common law to interdict strike activity. After 1825 trade unions were harassed though not legally suppressed; unions as such were no longer unlawful, but action in restraint of trade was. The Combination Act of 1825 did not by itself make strikes illegal, but it left to judicial opinion whether a strike was in restraint of trade. This legal situation did not prevent the development of unions; on the contrary, there was an explosion of public unionization attempts, sometimes on a grand scale, in the late 1820s and 1830s. But the fact that 'after 1825 the common law was invoked against trade unions to an unprecedented extent' produced a situation that compelled unions to keep their planning and activities as secret as possible, hidden from the authorities in community-based associations.[76] Moreover, the legal climate of repression, combined with the pressures on union activity provided by the operation of business cycles, made unions especially fragile institutions. At moments of economic depression the state could leave to economic forces the role of restraining unions, but when the cycle proved favourable and unions grew more bold, the state could invoke the doctrine 'to the effect that any overt positive action by groups of workers was likely to be a wrong in the nature of Conspiracy, even where the strike was quietly conducted'.[77]

In the United States, the relatively mild character of state repression against trade unions made a clearly defined, public, workplace-based organization of workers possible. There, too, workers were liable for combinations under the common law; but in the American federal system there was no national legislation nor central direction to anti-union prosecutions. Charges brought in one locality were not brought in another. Prosecutors found convictions difficult to obtain in a system of trial by peers rather than magistrates. American unions were buffeted by economic crises throughout the nineteenth century and in the century's later decades were faced with a wave of public as well as private attempts to repress labour

[76] D. F. McDonald, *The State and the Trade Unions*. London: Macmillan, 1960, 23.

[77] Gerald Abrahams, *Trade Unions and the Law*. London: Cassell, 1968, 28.

organizations. In the early period of working-class formation, however, the problems that unions had with the law were quite secondary. In times of economic prosperity workers were not on the whole inhibited from joining unions. In the middle 1830s, for example, a high proportion of workers, some two in three in New York City, belonged to unions that organized openly in the workplace.[78]

As a consequence of the comparatively repressive legal climate in England, organized labour was too fragile to provide an independent basis for action against capital. Quite unlike the picture painted by Dyson of an English working class in the context of a weak state directing its fire against capital rather than the state, English workers were pushed out of the arena of work into politics and into the residential community at the same time. Although the trade unions never joined Chartism as such as unions, 'the greater number of trade unionists declared for the Charter'.[79]

The organizational form of the American and British states, and their constitutional and public policies with regard to political rights, in short, had very different consequences for the political content of local working-class associations and for the naming and meaning of the residential spaces of the working classes of the two countries. In the United States, political agitation for the vote was unnecessary, and the community provided the location for the organizations at the base of cross-class political parties which appealed to voters by mobilizing the non-class solidarities of religion and ethnicity grounded in territory. Unions, in turn, were permitted a public, separate existence. In their embrace, the American working class was formed as labour.

Not so in England, where only the institutions of the residential community were available to workers to put

[78] See the discussion in Katznelson, *City Trenches*, ch. 3.
[79] Peter William Slosson, *The Decline of the Chartist Movement*. London: Frank Cass, 1967 (first pub. 1916), 46. See also David Jones, *Chartism and the Chartists*. London: Allen Lane, 1975; and Brian Brown, 'Industrial Capitalism, Conflict, and Working Class Contention in Lancashire', in Louise Tilly and Charles Tilly (eds.) *Class Conflict and Collective Action*. Beverly Hills, Calif.: Sage Publications, 1981.

demands both to employers and to the state. Pressed together by the exigencies of law, repression, state organization, and public policy, the locality-based voluntary organizations fused the separate facets of working-class life into a common, deeply felt, consciousness of class.

This holistic political culture outlasted the period of Chartist agitation. Cautious, gradualist, and reformist, to be sure, the English working class after 1848 continued to exhibit a striking independence and lack of deference.[80] Autonomous workers' institutions imbued with a solidaristic impulse, if also a pragmatic one, continued to be created in working-class communities. Late nineteenth-century trade unions and socialist organizations did not have to start afresh, nor did they have to confront as barriers the kind of fragmented classness that so frustrated efforts to create labour and socialist political parties in the United States at the turn of the century.

The combination of gradualism and classness that distinguished the English working class from *both* its American and its Continental counterparts solidified into a distinguishable and enduring pattern in the 1850s, when new accommodations were fashioned between the autonomous institutions of the working-class community and the wider society. As John Foster has stressed, this was a process that played itself out at the urban level. While it is possible to discern broad national patterns to the liberalization of British society in the 1850s, problems of social and cultural control were, at their base, matters of local relationships. Order had to be restored and re-created in town after town where people laboured and lived. The crux of the matter was the grant of autonomy and capacity to indigenous institutions of workers (most importantly, by the withdrawal of direct repression), and the extension of the role workers could play in party life and the factory, in implicit exchange for a new attitudinal and behavioural conformity. Friendly societies, working men's clubs, public houses, and non-conformist churches were given legal and symbolic space in which to function. Liberal and Conservative Party leaders

---

[80] For discussions, see Tholfsen, *Working Class Radicalism*, and H. I. Dutton and J. E. King, 'The Limits of Paternalism: The Cotton Tyrants of North Lancashire, 1836–54', *Social History*, 7 (Jan. 1982).

incorporated men of working-class origin into party life, on terms that allowed them to continue to promote traditional radical concerns for a limited working day and mass suffrage, but only within the framework of regular politics.[81]

Radical strains from the past could persist in this political world, but only in so far as they were adapted to new shared limits regarding what was possible in a short time-span, and legitimate political activity. Working-class institutional autonomy was recognized in exchange for a restricted universe of political and economic expression, but, in contrast to the United States, one still based on global understandings of class. In these terms, workers' institutions were sufficiently autonomous to be agencies of genuine class self-development; but sufficiently part of the regime to be effective agencies of social order and a degree of social change. It was this inheritance and this tradition that the English working class carried as baggage into the second industrial revolution.

IV

This comparative exercise suggests further puzzles, approaches, propositions, and ways to extend this kind of analysis. The first point to make is to underscore its historicity. This moment of early working-class formation came at the time of maximum autonomy for capitalist, and urban, development from other macrostructures, most notably the state.[82] For this reason, Marx's attempt to develop social theory

[81] John Foster, *Class Struggle and the Industrial Revolution: Early Capitalism in Three English Towns.* London: Weidenfeld and Nicolson, 1974. See the critiques of Foster by D. S. Gadian, 'Class Consciousness in Oldham and Other North-West Industrial Towns, 1830–1850', *Historical Journal*, 21 (Mar. 1978), and Gareth Stedman Jones, 'Class Struggle and the Industrial Revolution', *New Left Review*, 90 (Mar.–Apr. 1975). The classic treatment of working-class reformism, of course, is Walter Bagehot, *The English Constitution.* London: Collins, 1971.

[82] Writing about the late 19th century, Rodger takes note of the end of this bounded period of urban development: 'The proliferation of public health statutes, the development of limited housing improvement schemes and their ultimate translation into town

which identified the logic of capital, and its immanent requirements, as the basis of politics, culture, ideology, and, by
implication, space and social geography, resonated with the
situation on the ground. Further, Marx's choice of England for
illustrative material lent the issue of working-class formation
a simplicity and directionality that in other settings and times
could not be sustained. We have seen how even in the hands
of a historian as skilled as Edward Thompson the selection of
the English case has made it possible for Marxism to make
unwarranted assumptions about the available repertoire of
working-class dispositions and collective activity within capitalism. It could thus limit its questions about class formation
to those about the timing of militancy and revolutionary
behaviour rather than focusing on the quite broad sets of
alternatives working people possessed in relation to how
capitalism might be represented, supported, and challenged.

Even within the privileged period for traditional Marxist
social theory, a focus on cities and space highlights contingency in the connections between working-class materiality
and meaning and it forces an encounter with the significance
of the state. The spatial segregation by function and by class
imposed on cities and towns by the imperatives of capitalist

---

planning projects, the legislative intrusion of central government,
supplemented by the adoption of local byelaws, all successively
influenced and distorted the operation of the land market. From a
relatively unfettered position in the mid-nineteenth century, with
the price mechanism wholly responsible for clearing the market and
allocating land to its various uses, the market became increasingly
adulterated by institutional interference, albeit undertaken for
enlightened, though sometimes misguided, reasons.' Richard Rodger,
'Rents and Ground Rents: Housing and the Land Market in Nineteenth Century Britain', in Johnson and Pooley, *The Structure of
Nineteenth Century Cities*, 68. This essay contains a useful comparison of Scottish and English urban land and housing markets, as does
Rodger, 'The Invisible Hand: Market Forces, Housing and the Urban
Form in Victorian Cities', in Fraser and Sutcliffe, *The Pursuit of
Urban History*. On the subject of the erosion of urban *laissez-faire*,
see also Anthony Sutcliffe, 'The Growth of Public Intervention in the
British Urban Environment During the Nineteenth Century: A Struc-
tural Approach', in Johnson and Pooley, *The Structure of Nineteenth
Century Cities*.

accumulation as well as markets for land and housing proved, in the case materials of the comparative terms and contents of English and American working-class formation, to have been a contextual rather than a causal variable, with the main differences accounted for by state-connected factors of organization, repression, political incorporation, and public policy.[83]

We should remember, too, that even within this special moment of capitalist and class development, the urban-spatial experience of the great majority of English and American workers and their families was by no means universal. Many working people, in settings as diverse as mining communities, agricultural settlements, and the garment industry neighbourhoods of great cities did not experience the separation of work and home common to industrial cities. When workplaces and residential communities were tightly intertwined, the 'classness' of politically relevant dispositions tended to be more holistic and intense, and militant political action proved more likely. Such was especially the case when the unity of work and community was conjoined to a situation of political exclusion, but even in the United States the conjoining of the two spheres proved a necessary condition for both urban and agrarian socialist party success, and for populist movements of subordinate groups.

If the separation of work and home in industrializing cities broadened the range of possibilities regarding working-class dispositions and collective action that had been envisaged by Marxism, the spatial processes of urbanization also had the effect of complicating the class structure of modern capitalism. The second level of class—that of ways of life within capitalist society—refers to the experiences of working people not only at work but at home and in their residential communities. The growing disengagement of this realm from the workplace, as well as the autonomy of generalized housing markets, made the class structure more complex. First, it fragmented the working class understood in Marxist terms along Weberian,

---

[83] For essays on these themes as they concerned French and German, as well as American, patterns of working-class formation in the 19th century, see Katznelson and Zolberg, *Working Class Formation*.

market-based lines. As the capacity to purchase residential environments became increasingly independent of the functioning of labour markets, a gradational hierarchy of desirable neighbourhoods embodying different styles of life developed, at once making less sharp the divide between bourgeoisie and proletariat and producing divisions of a new kind between people who met all the Marxist criteria (however precisely defined) for membership in the working class. Second, it provided a material basis for the development of dispositions and patterns of collective action based on territory, ethnicity, religion, race, recency of immigration, and other non-class criteria. Mappings of the city that gave a place of privilege to these bases of affiliation were constructed on the basis of the new social geography of the city. Third, it ushered in the creation of new sets of actors—lawyers who handled the conveyancing of property, housing inspectors, health visitors, fire, police, and sanitation workers, collectors of property taxes, planners, and speculative builders, among others— whose tasks were those of organizing and managing the new housing markets and the character of life within the residential areas of the city. These individuals did not fall neatly into the class-structural categories of Marxism, but rather formed an important city and neighbourhood based aspect of the development of new middle classes.

With the transformations of city space the scope of politics broadened considerably. Politics came to be concerned not only (indeed, one might say less and less) with the issues that pit labour and capital in direct confrontation, but also with matters distinctively urban: housing, zoning, property taxes, rent controls, the regulation of construction, transportation schemes, slum clearance, policing and the regulation of public space, schooling, sanitation, fire protection, water (and, later, gas and electricity) supply—in short with the law, policies, infrastructure, and services of cities characterized by divisions between work and residence and by the segregation of social classes and groups.[84] The content of this new politics, how-

---

[84] An excellent consideration of these themes is provided by Avner Offer, *Property and Politics, 1870–1914: Landownership, Law, Ideology and Urban Development in England.* Cambridge: Cambridge

7 Remapping the City

WE have seen how the making of class categories that shaped the identities, motives, and actions of early working classes proved far more contingent than Engels foresaw,[1] and how the ways in which class emerged as a coherent marker and guide for working people may be understood in terms of how working classes mapped the capitalist city. Taking this approach, it is possible to make sense of why in some circumstances, but not all, class came to define the identities of political and social actors beyond the workplace, in the residential community and the home. So, too, an urban-spatial imagination can assist in addressing other significant puzzles for Marxism with regard to class and class conflict. At no time since the early nineteenth-century history of working-class formation have working classes fulfilled their scripted role as agents of fundamental social change in the theory's drama of transition to socialism. In the late twentieth century, moreover, as capitalism is manifestly being restructured on a global scale, the relative significance of class categories themselves is in question. An engagement of Marxism with the city can shed some light on these problems by helping us to understand why militancy in the full Marxist sense has existed only in the realm of theory and by giving us a vantage-point from which to consider current patterns of class and group formation.

[1] 'The ideological struggle is a struggle *about* class before it is a struggle *among* classes.' Adam Przeworski, 'Proletariat Into a Class: The Process of Class Formation from Karl Kautsky's *The Class Struggle* to Recent Controversies', *Politics and Society*, 10/1 (1980), 371.

I

By not embarking on the journey linking city space, capitalist development, and class formation, Marxism denied to itself a critical dimension in the material analysis both of the target it wished to confront and of the class it expected to be the agent of this successful engagement. This point is best understood if we think again about the content of the second of the four levels of class, that of the social organization of society experienced as ways of life within the various capitalist countries.

There is a fateful compression at the heart of Marxist social theory. Because exploitation, the extraction of surplus value from the proletariat by the bourgeoisie, is the key antagonistic and dynamic feature of class relations and the most important macro-analytic characteristic of the 'laws of motion' of capitalism at the first level of class analysis, that of the structure of capitalist economic development, Marxism has yielded to the temptation at the second level to focus almost exclusively on the capitalist workplace. The most common Marxist approaches conflate these two levels and treat the abstract logic of capitalism and the site of the workplace together as 'the economy', the 'base' of capitalist social, political, and ideological relations. Whether they work by deduction or induction, virtually all Marxist approaches to social class develop definitions and categories based on an analysis of the technical and social relations of production; such is the case where class is treated abstractly, as in such categories as productive and unproductive labour, or where class is understood more concretely in terms of the attributes of people within the active labour force.

There are many costs to this analytical strategy. One, which I have noted elsewhere, is the elimination 'in one stroke [of] a series of important questions about the connections between key aspects of capitalist accumulation and national economic histories on one side and the organization of labor markets and workplaces on the other. As any student of capitalist industrialization knows, the growth and expansion of capitalism has proved capable of fostering many different kinds of workplaces and work.'² A second cost, more central to the analysis here, has been the suppression of the off-work characteristics of social organization. Nineteenth- and twentieth-century industrial capitalism has been in the main an urban capitalism. Cities have concentrated working classes. Even when we define the working class in Marxist terms as a group composed of individuals who work for wages within capitalist work-places and labour markets and are located in positions of subordination within the hierarchies of businesses and firms (and if we leave aside the puzzle of the class position of those who do not enter a labour market to sell their labour power for a wage), we do well to remember that they also live in particular kinds of residential areas where they are enmeshed in the economic (as well as social, political, and cultural) relations of housing, domesticity, and consumption of both private and public goods. Like sites of work, these places are also the products of the dynamics of capitalist development operating at the first level of class. Although living places and housing markets have not been shaped and determined by capital alone, of course, there have been important features common to cities in capitalism, including those of social geography, because these cities have been organized princi-pally to accommodate the requirements of capitalism as a dynamic system of growth and expansion.

Enmeshed in the social and political relations of cities, working-class people have experienced the urban face of capi-talism. They have done so not only in the structurally and spatially segregated world of work, but at home and in com-munity life in the realm of residence. By engaging with the city to confront the various dimensions of the social organiza-tion of class at work and away from it, Marxism can better address its disappointments about the working class. Down this road, Marxism can better understand why its most cher-ished expectations of revolutionary consciousness have never

² Ira Katznelson. 'Working Class Formation: Constructing Cases and Comparisons', in Ira Katznelson and Aristide Zolberg (eds.), *Working-Class Formation: Nineteenth Century Patterns in Western Europe and the United States*. Princeton, NJ: Princeton University Press, 1986, 16.

been more than plausible in theory, and, more positively, how today Marxism might be rescued from intellectual obsolescence while it discovers a new modesty.

Marxist social theory has sought to do more than understand day-to-day life within capitalism or make sense of determination and of structure and agency as analytical challenges. For Marx himself, the project of social theory capable of analysing specific whole capitalist societies nestled within his ambitious project of comprehending and shaping epochal change. Specifically, Marx sought to provide the means to account for variation, history, and agency because he understood that capitalism's tendencies to crisis would be of historical moment only if they could connect to the self-conscious behaviour of subjects in specific situations. Thus, social theory about capitalism was meaningful to Marx, and to committed Marxists, because it promised to contribute to the transition from capitalism to socialism.

There have been times in the twentieth century when the structural crises of capitalism seemed to provide Western working classes with opportunities to ditch the system. Nowhere were these possibilities realized. Instead, each such instance has proved to be one of capitalist restructuring marked by the discovery of new paths of accumulation, and by the creation of new social knowledge and public policy capable of reinvigorating the economic system. In this process of capitalist renewal, Western working classes have been reconciled to capitalism and have given allegiance to it. With the recurrent failure of the proletariat to perform its imputed historical task, capitalism has come to be punctuated by crises, not by Crisis.

Classical Marxism did not anticipate this disjunction between structural opportunities and missing agency. Western Marxism, by contrast, has attempted for the past 100 years to make sense of its recurring political defeats. Hankering after the missing proletariat, Marxists have been concerned to understand its painful absence.

In this respect the writings of Marx are of little assistance. Whether because he ran out of time as the fragmentary section at the end of the third volume of *Capital* suggests, or because he took the various issues of class formation for granted,

Marx's theoretical work makes no allowance for the existence of a class structure without class struggle in the full sense. Even in his brilliant probes of 1848 and 1871 in France, which are certainly not stories of the triumphant overcoming of capitalism, Marx treats these insurgencies as dress rehearsals for more fundamental changes to come. Like the rest of his corpus, these writings do not anticipate the possibility that once modern working classes accommodated to the existence of capitalism they would forgo efforts to overthrow the mode of production.

Because this issue has proved so fundamental to the politics of the late nineteenth and twentieth centuries, western Marxists have sought to fill in Marx's silences. They have done so either by providing increasingly complex structural elaborations of the two-class structure that underpins Marx's logical account of capitalist accumulation, as in the scholarship of Erik Olin Wright, or by writing richly textured histories of national working classes in the manner first produced by Edward Thompson.

These important bodies of work can only partially illuminate the core Marxist puzzles of class because they do not fully break with the 'class in and for itself' problematic. However softened, it is just this teleological trajectory that is open to question. Assuming good mappings of class structures and good historical understandings of the dispositions and actions of working-class people, we are still stuck with the fact, using Thompson's language, that the tie between the social being of working classes and their social consciousness has proved not only more contingent than expected with regard to the very existence of class as a global category but capable of supporting a robust consciousness of class without a concomitant 'revolutionary consciousness' (even where, as in England, the working class was formed on the basis of holistic understandings of class). Further, the very crises and restructurings of capitalism in the absence of working-class efforts to create socialism have called into question the durability of class as a basis of naming and representing the core groups of capitalist society. Thus, the absence of coherent and persuasive accounts of the problematic linkages between 'social being' and 'social consciousness' is not only the weakest feature of the treatment of structure and agency in Marxist social theory but is itself a source of political debilitation.

Certainly the history of the West in the past century and a half has been marked by deep conflicts based on class on both sides of the work–home divide. Class has also provided the structural and discursive basis for the organization of working people into political parties and trade unions. Yet, ever since Engels ventured into Manchester in the 1840s to discover the first working class with the potential to become a proletariat, not a single Western working class has fulfilled this role. Nowhere today is capitalism in danger of being supplanted by socialism. There have been such moments, the most recent of which spanned the beginning of the Great Depression to the years following the Second World War, but they passed. Today, class struggle in the full classical usage of the term does not exist, except, perhaps, in working-class assaults on what little remains of the 'socialism' of Marxist-Leninist-Stalinist systems.

Equally painful to Western Marxism has been the growing lack of confidence about the capacity of traditional class categories themselves to describe social reality in settings where for some time class did provide the common sense of everyday social and political life. This distress manifests itself in laments for 'the forward march of labour halted'; in post-Marxist discourse theory, which makes class relations a contingent and provisional semiotic; and in a shift in considerations of agency from working classes to new social movements.

The twin vexations of the absence of a proletariat willing to act for socialism and challenges to the ability of class categories to chart capitalist politics and society have produced a profound crisis for Marxist scholars. Of course, Marxists have understood the need to come to terms with these analytical challenges, and they have tried to do so: by seeking impediments to class consciousness in gender and patriarchy, labour aristocracies, ethnicity and race, repression and social control; in the bribery that comes with prosperity; in the cultural hegemony of capitalism, and in other such causes. Each of these has been a genuine and important feature of the histories of working classes, but what continues to be defective is the undergirding logic which insists that the 'natural' process of class formation has been impeded by key mediating factors that have deflected it. A second strategy has focused on the class structure itself, especially the rise of a middle class. This has been the pivotal problem of the most interesting treatments of this kind, and in this way has been a mirror image of the criticisms mounted against Marxism for its obsolescence by non-Marxist sociology and social theory.[3] But if the complications of class structure are now organic to capitalism, can a class strugggle based on the idea of struggle between the two basic classes of bourgeoisie and proletariat be countenanced? A third response has been to explain the debilitations of working-class history in particular times and places as histories of defeat by the dominant classes or as betrayals by the leadership stratum of the working class, but usually without a comparative or theoretically-constructed frame of reference, and thus without an answer to the puzzle of why it is that this pattern recurs across all the cases. A fourth strategy has been to argue that the organizational, ideological, and programmatic features of the dominant social democratic and reformist politics that has engaged the working classes as a political project within Western Europe and North America contain their own powerful logic of compromise and social integration. Much in this account is persuasive, but much with respect to the problem of proletarian reticence at moments of capitalist crisis is also tautological.

The continuing relevance Marxism has as a guide to late twentieth-century capitalism rests on its capacity to address its disappointments about the working class more persuasively than it has to date. In Chapter 6 I tried to show how a respatialized and permeable Marxism could discern reasons for partial as opposed to holistic patterns of early working-class formation. In this chapter, I tackle the problem for Marxism of the historical absence of class struggle in the full Marxist

[3] A significant variant of this strategy is the location of sources of working-class consent within production itself, understood as an ideological and political, as well as economic, process. See Michael Burawoy, *Manufacturing Consent*. Chicago: University of Chicago Press, 1979; and Burawoy, *The Politics of Production*. London: Verso Books, 1985.

sense, and I examine the contingent relationship linking the recession of working-class identities as ways of organizing, understanding, discussing, and acting on contemporary capitalism and recent changes in the urban built-environment.

II

The drawing of lines in space between the social classes within the new social geography of the capitalist city in the nineteenth century helped assure the residential propinquity of members of the working class as well as their isolation from other classes. From the later years of the century to the First World War, the patterning of space in these cities crystallized in an unambiguously modern form characterized by a more stark division of work and home (whose distances grew with the accessibility of public transportation to the working classes),[4] segregation of city space by class, and a growing

___

[4] In some accounts, it was the revolution in transportation technology that was the primary driving force behind the reorganization of city space in the 19th century, rather than the dynamics of capitalist accumulation and the tandem operation of newly distinctive housing and labour markets. I find this unpersuasive. As we saw in Chapter 6, the dynamics of separation predated the late 19th-century accessibility of public transport to all social classes. Indeed, as Dennis stresses, against a simple technological determinism, investments in transportation making more distant journeys to work possible only made sense once the process of separation of work and home was already under way: 'Once intra-urban transport exists, and especially once there is competition between rival railway companies, or between independent bus, tram, and waggonette operators, it is reasonable to argue that innovations are adopted in anticipation of greater profits, or to prevent the erosion of profits by competitors. But to explain initial investment in public transport we have to understand why investors put their money into something new, rather than something proven.' Noting that alterations to urban structure preceded changes in transportation, Dennis continues: 'The implication is that transport services *facilitated* urban growth and change, they *permitted* suburbanisation, segregation and the separation of residence and workplace beyond walking distance, but they did not *initiate* change.' Richard Dennis, *English Industrial Cities of the Nineteenth Century: A Social Geography*. Cambridge: Cambridge University Press, 1984, 110–11. Where the new technologies of

differentiation of housing as a result of the operations of autonomous housing markets.[5] This solidification of patterns which had only achieved a partially modern format in earlier decades had a contradictory relationship to working-class formation. On the one hand, it corroborated the different specific mappings of the city crafted earlier by working classes making sense of their new social and spatial realities. *Both* the partial *and* the holistic understandings of class were reaffirmed in this new milieu by the ways existing patterns of talk and organization had already made sense of the new divisions in space. Materiality and meaning proved mutually confirming.[6] On the other hand, with the elaboration of new networks made possible by the nationalization of labour markets, the

---

transportation, especially railways, had the greatest impact was less in creating a new urban social geography than in demanding quite radical transformations to accommodate their routes, central city terminals, and sites adjacent to them. In terms of transportation as such, the greatest impact of railways was in reducing barriers to trade and communications between cities, rather than in shifting patterns of commutation within cities and their suburbs. See also John Kellett, *The Impact of Railways on Victorian Cities.* London: Routledge and Kegan Paul, 1969; Harold Pollins, 'Transport Lines and Social Divisions', in Ruth Glass *et al.*, *London: Aspects of Change.* London: McGibbon and Kee, 1964; and esp. John P. McKay, *Tramways and Trolleys: The Rise of Urban Mass Transportation in Europe.* Princeton, NJ: Princeton University Press, 1976. McKay stresses how 'the scope and content of change in European urban transport long lagged behind burgeoning industrialization and urbanization', and the importance of decisions by public authorities as well as private investment in the making and extension of public transport in cities.

[5] Even for those social geographers who wish to stress the premodern character of mid-19th-century cities, this period unambiguously marks the hegemony of these spatial patterns. See three essays by David Ward: 'Victorian Cities: How Modern?', *Journal of Historical Geography*, 1/2 (1975); 'Environs and Neighbours in the "Two Nations": Residential Differentiation in Mid-Nineteenth Century Leeds', *Journal of Historical Geography*, 6/2 (1980); and 'The Place of Victorian Cities in Development Approaches to Urbanization', in John Patten (ed.), *The Expanding City.* London: Academic Press, 1983.

[6] I take up this theme in Ira Katznelson, *City Trenches: Urban Politics and the Patterning of Class in the United States.* New York: Pantheon Books, 1981, ch. 3.

growing sense that working classes shared a community of fate that transcended given localities, and significant advances in communications and transportation, the ties between class and space grew more complicated and tentative.

It is by coming to grips with this double process that I think we can best readdress the haunting puzzle of how to account for the fact that nowhere—in spite of the elaboration of strong union and political party organizations that challenged both the terms of life in capitalism and rhetorically announced for socialism—have working classes, whether characterized by a divided or holistic consciousness, become politicized in the revolutionary manner classical Marxism took for granted. Once the fundamental struggles about capitalist control had been settled to the detriment of artisans experiencing a devaluation of their labour, social conflict ceased to be about the most fundamental question in Marxist social and political theory, the transformation of the mode of production. From a Marxist perspective, the battles between the social classes became secondary: no longer about the existence of capitalism as such, but about conditions of life within the capitalist epoch.

In a cautionary essay, Krishan Kumar argues persuasively that this break in working-class history must call into question facile evolutionary accounts that assume a high degree of continuity between the working classes of artisans at the moment of the birth of class and the working classes of unskilled and semi-skilled factory labourers at the end of the nineteenth century. The most radical battles were fought by the first; a reformist pattern of integration characterized the second: 'a politicised working class, comparable to that which existed before 1850, has never again been seen in the kingdom.'[7]

But why should the shift from an artisanal to a proletarian

---

[7] Krishan Kumar, 'Class and Political Action in Nineteenth-Century England: Theoretical and Comparative Perspectives', *Archives Européennes de Sociologie*, 24/1 (1983), 18. For a discussion of the break between early and late 19th-century working classes, see also Eric Hobsbawm. 'The Making of the Working Class 1870–1914', in Hobsbawm, *Worlds of Labour: Further Studies in the History of Labour*. London: Weidenfeld and Nicolson, 1984.

character necessarily defang the working class? Kumar argues that the new proletariat could not get very far without forging alliances across class lines, but his own evidence that artisans also fought their struggles with important allies undercuts this point.

A start toward a better explanation is provided by Craig Calhoun's account of 'Class, Place, and the Industrial Revolution'. The premiss of this paper is a critique of the sharp divide in Marx's work between his treatment of class struggle in his logical account of capital accumulation and in his delineation of social theory. The former sees such struggle as inherent in the abstract relations of capitalism at work; the latter assumes a translation of this imperative into specific times and places. Missing in each, Calhoun avers, is both a spatially specific treatment of the city and an organizational analysis that insists that the mechanisms and scale necessary for the working class to confront capitalism must be more than a series of local systems. Without such a capacity, he insists, class struggle in the full Marxist sense is not possible.

Thus, the centrepiece of Calhoun's essay is the joining of an organizational to a spatial analysis of class formation. Unlike treatments of working-class formation that leave place considerations out, Calhoun underscores the significance of local community-based relationships for the development of nationally distinctive features of classness during the first industrial revolution. The direct, face-to-face, social relationships within segregated working-class residential areas facilitated trust and solidarity that in some circumstances came to be based on class understandings. Yet, he argues, even where a global classness on the English model defined working-class readings of the city and capitalism, the localism of class understandings hindered the capacities of workers to engage with capital effectively at just the moment when workers were most willing to challenge the fundamental premiss of the capitalist mode of production. 'To be salient in the class struggle engendered by capitalism,' Calhoun insists, 'classes—bourgeoisie, proletariat—must be organized at the same level as capital accumulation.' At this early moment, such translocal organization was achieved more readily by members of the bourgeoisie, who were smaller in number and possessed more resources, than by the dispersed urban working classes who, enclosed within their factories and residential communities, were inhibited from confronting capitalism as a system that transcended the experiences of this or that local area.[8] While the local spatial environment provided workers with affective bases of support, unlike the workplace the residential community did not include 'the enemy to be confronted nor was it composed of a sufficiently broad network of relationships to reach all those concerned'.[9] Hence a first historical paradox: just when beleaguered artisan communities were most willing to challenge the prerogatives of capital they lacked the transportation and communications infrastructure to do so in a manner that confronted the indirect, translocal features of capitalism as a mode of production; 'in the early nineteenth-century, class struggle, at least the struggle of bourgeoisie against proletariat, which Marx proposed, was impossible.'[10]

From the perspective of the organizational problems of co-ordination and communications, class struggle in the full Marxist sense did become possible only in the late nineteenth century. Just as classical Marxism paid little attention to actual working-class people outside their places of work, so, too, Marx and Engels had little to say about the organizational dimensions of class outside specific workplaces. 'One result of this is that as classes are deduced from the economic theory, their collective action is presumed to follow simply from rational recognition of common interests.' Calhoun stresses, instead, how important it is to see that 'classes become important social bases for collective action when society is knit together through large-scale systems of indirect relationships'.[11] In the late nineteenth century, trade unions with a

---

[8] Craig Calhoun, 'Class, Place and Industrial Revolution', in Nigel Thrift and Peter Williams (eds.), *Class and Space: The Making of Urban Society*. London: Routledge and Kegan Paul, 1987, 51.

[9] Thus, Calhoun argues, since classes 'are too large and widely dispersed to be mobilized on the basis of direct interpersonal relationships . . . Large-scale organization of indirect relationships becomes essential.' Ibid., 53, 59–60.

[10] Ibid., 54.

[11] Ibid., 56. In a suggestive discussion, Calhoun argues that the

national scope and political parties contesting for power at the centre became just such organizational vehicles. As such, these institutions cannot be understood simply as the products of class formation but as mechanisms for the making and remaking of class (and, of course, of other social categories).[12] Direct face-to-face relationships, whether in factories or in residential communities, Calhoun stresses, cannot by themselves 'give the class collective agency'. He insists that

For these collectivities to provide the basis for sustained, effective insurgencies their members must be linked to each other through some mediating agency. Trade unions work in this way for their members, and are thus in direct line of development of class struggle (as Marx thought) and not necessarily to be distinguished from a more revolutionary class consciousness (as Lenin suggested). Trade unions and working-class political parties do vary in the extent to which they *represent* loosely organized constituents, or *organize* those constituents for direct participation in action (the latter comes much closer to Marx's conceptualization of class struggle). In either case, this sort of mobilization differs significantly from that which is based on direct relations such as those of the local community. Moreover,

---

modern state provides the archetype for the development of indirect social-organizational ties between members of the working class. 'Over a period of hundreds of years,' he writes, 'the development of absolutist and eventually parliamentary states reduced the role of personal control and co-ordination in favour of formal organizational structures. The direct, personal relations of domination characteristic of both feudalism and the cities which grew in late medieval Europe were replaced by the indirect relations of bureaucracy', and, one might add, of citizenship. The state, moreover, not only was a model for the indirect manifestations of class in organizations but was a key 'part of the process that produced them. It not only made a broader organization of markets possible, but it sundered the autonomy and unity city life had maintained in both economic and political spheres. Aside from differences in content, this made possible a transformation of the scale of state functioning. States became simultaneously more permanent, more efficient and more powerful . . . Whatever the reasons, though Marxists have debated the relationship between state and party at length, they have not considered that it might be much like that between state and citizenry.' Ibid., 58–9.

[12] This theme has been the centrepiece of Przeworski's many writings on this theme. See esp. his *Capitalism and Social Democracy*. Cambridge: Cambridge University Press, 1985.

it depends on a level of communications and transportation infrastructure which had not been developed prior to 1840.[13]

With the radical diminution in the costs of transaction between dispersed working-class communities by the elaboration of national railway and telegraph networks, the institutions of national trade unions and political parties became possible. But with this development there emerged a second historical paradox: at just the moment when class struggle in the full Marxist sense achieved its necessary infrastrucure, it came to be shackled by the organizational imperatives of the new working-class institutions of union and party. As formal organizations enmeshed in the possibilities for gains made feasible by the permissive rules of democratic political regimes, unions and parties pursued class interests in ways that were inherently short term and limited, whatever their rhetorical commitments to more fundamental social change. If 'these organizations are necessary to the co-ordination of action at the same level at which capital and political power are centralized', they are 'distinct from the classes they represent'. Parties and unions engage these classes only in partial and role-specific ways. They have their own reproduction imperatives. Apart from the activists who staff and run them, they 'appear as non-essential consumer goods rather than an essential part of life'. Participation in such organizations lacks the vibrant intensity of social movements based on direct face-to-face relationships. Indirect class struggle is thus 'a *part* of capitalism—or at least capitalist democracy'.[14]

I find this analysis suggestive but incomplete. While Calhoun, like Kumar, focuses on the disjuncture between the working classes of the early and late nineteenth century, and thus on the distinction between localized and direct versus national and indirect patterns of collective action, he considerably understates the integral connections between the local and national, the direct and indirect. Nor does he closely examine the ties between early nineteenth-century mappings of the city, with their resulting alternatives of partial or global classness, and later 'modern' patterns of class organization.

[13] Calhoun, 'Class, Place and Industrial Revolution', 60.
[14] Ibid., 64–7.

Missing, too, is any comparative sense of the differing potentials of the new forms of organization depending on their linkage to older patterns of reading the city.[15]

Once again, consider Chartism. Calhoun treats this massive class-based movement as a transitional one, because of the way it joined the residential communities of workers, the union organizations that were embedded within them, and an emergent national infrastrucure made possible by improved road transport. By transitional, he means a pattern coming to an end, not one heralding the future. For, in his view, the national-organizational level was soon to overwhelm the local.

This is not persuasive. There was no simple transition from the local urban setting of class politics to national organizations and networks. If capitalism, as Calhoun stresses, was translocal and abstract, and thus needed to be confronted on comparable terms by working-class contestants, it also remained deeply and inherently experiential and local; it is impossible to conceive of cross-class confrontations outside the lived worlds of workers and their families.

Not surprisingly, the city level has remained a constitutive aspect of modern working-class politics. It was certainly integral to the new unions and political parties Calhoun wrongly counterposes to locality-based relations. While their national scope was a genuine innovation, it is important not to lose sight of the fact that their very existence as organizations depended on their federated character. Unions are based in specific workplaces, and parties in constituencies, and these are community-specific. Unions and parties interpret the daily lives of working people where they work and live. Indeed, if union and party organizations had not become integral to these urban experiences they would have had no capacity to recruit and mobilize followers. Just as Calhoun is right to

[15] To be sure, Calhoun is not entirely silent about these questions. He is sensitive to the enduring significance of face-to-face relationships but tends to dichotomize between conflicts based on these community-based relationships, which he sees mainly in terms of a vulnerable populism, and conflicts based on translocal class organizations. The most satisfactory of his discussions linking the local and the national is that of Chartism, which I comment on in the discussion that follows immediately.

reject the notion of class as an abstract rather than an organizational matter, so it is necessary to insist that the organizational aspects of class have been grounded in the materiality of the city, thus in the ways cities have been mapped and remapped by working classes under the spatial and organizational conditions that confront them.

But, given earlier nineteenth-century mappings of the city, workers could not respond to these challenges just as they pleased. The available repertoire of late nineteenth- and early twentieth-century working-class collective action in different countries was informed and limited by the patterns of working-class formation that had developed earlier in the nineteenth century. The scope of union aspirations; their ties to political parties; the very existence of various labour, social democratic, and socialist political parties; their representations of capitalism, and their capacities to mobilize followers all depended in considerable measure on the outcomes of the first period of working-class formation. The choices available to English working-class organizations in the later years of the century were different from those open to unions and parties in the United States. There the earlier split consciousness of the working class, reproduced in the ordinary politics of the early and middle years of the century and by the intensification of the divisions in space between work and home in urban life, directed unions to the path of a restricted, if militant, workplace labourism that eschewed party politics; at the same time it directed parties to the path of mobilizing workers on the basis of non-class identities. In this context, the foundation of a political party like the Labour Party, if not excluded a priori, was made very difficult. American efforts along these lines proved remarkably unsuccessful in spite of the intensification of capitalist exploitation and the existence of advanced forms of the infrastructural conditions stressed by Calhoun. The content of the organizational revolution, in short, was in considerable measure determined by the terms in which the early separations of work and community had been talked about and fought about.

The existing differences between the United States and England became even more pronounced as a result of the demographic transformation of the American working class by mass immigration from southern and eastern Europe after the

1870s. Entering an urban world in which the place of residence was constructed in linguistic and organizational terms as separate from the place of work, the newcomers rapidly gave a more pronounced ethnic twist to city neighbourhoods while they joined their lot to transethnic labour–management struggles in the factories.

Two important studies of Detroit at the turn of the century, with their different emphases, capture this reassertion of older patterns of class formation in an age of new working-class organizational capacity, and show quite clearly the character of the new urban situation and the challenges they posed for working-class re-readings of the city. The first, Olivier Zunz's *The Changing Face of Inequality*, by focusing on neighbourhoods, homes, and housing markets, argues that the ever-growing separation between the factories and the residences of the working class made it possible for ethnic neighbourhoods to become 'the spatial anchor of the communities, the primary colors of the urban quilt'; immigrant areas thus became relatively autonomous environments. The working class, fragmented by ethnicity and by place, resisted the homogenizing forces of the second industrial revolution. 'Because ethnic bonds remained so strong during the industrialization process, the American social structure remained free from the threat of organized class conflicts despite extreme inequality of conditions.'[16] The immigrant neighbourhoods were not just the product of the desire of the newcomers for propinquity, but of migration chains that pulled kin and acquaintances together, as well as common occupations and income levels. Moreover, as Kathleen Conzen observes, once an area secured an ethnic character it became less attractive to non-group members with equal or higher status. 'Thus the locations of jobs and cheap housing, combined with the degree of heterogeneity of the group, strongly influenced the extent of residential concentration.'[17] The extent of this concentration was determined by

[16] Olivier Zunz, *The Changing Face of Inequality: Urbanization, Industrial Development, and Immigrants in Detroit, 1880–1920*. Chicago: University of Chicago Press, 1982, 178, 5.

[17] Kathleen Neils Conzen, 'Immigrants, Immigrant Neighborhoods, and Ethnic Identity: Historical Issues', *Journal of American History*, 66 (Dec. 1979), 610.

the character of journeys to work. The more independent the location of the workplace from that of the residential neighbourhoods, the more likely it was that cross-ethnic workplaces could draw their work-forces from different, ethnically distinctive areas.[18]

The second study, Richard Oestreicher's *Solidarity and Fragmentation*, examines the same immigrant working class only to find a robust pattern of working-class consciousness and collective action, especially in the 1880s, in spite of the important differences of ethnicity and neighbourhood stressed by Zunz. Working-class solidarity competed with these fragmenting features of the city's life, and, from time to time, proved the dominant shaper of working-class dispositions. 'In a contradictory social environment, there was always an inner tension in which the extent of class consciousness was a function of concrete opportunities for its expression. Where such vehicles, e.g., the Knights of Labor, thrived, class consciousness increased; when they did not, it declined.'[19]

These very different accounts of working-class Detroit tell two aspects of the same tale. Whereas Zunz draws our attention to the ways in which a pre-existing pattern of class formation provided a crucible for the forging of a keen localized ethnic identity and sociality, Oestreicher shows how the same individuals engaged the labour side of the divide between work and home. If ethnicity, as Zunz rightly insists, mitigated class consciousness in the demanding Marxist sense, and provided the main basis for participation in political party life, it did not prove incompatible with a quite enthusiastic participation in the American labour movement. Just as in England in this period, labour organizations utilized heretofore unavailable transport and communications technologies to build unions and federations of unions that joined together widely dispersed union locals. And, just as in England, there was a good deal of tension within the labour movement about the desirability of building on the base of workplace affiliations to enter the

---

[18] Zunz, *The Changing Face of Inequality*, 178–83.
[19] Richard Jules Oestreicher, *Solidarity and Fragmentation: Working People and Class Consciousness in Detroit, 1875–1900*. Urbana, Ill. University of Illinois Press, 1986, p. xviii.

domain of party politics as labour. However, whereas in England this problem was resolved in keeping with older patterns and experiences in favour of the founding of a new kind of political party grounded in the union movement, in the United States, after the rapid collapse of the Knights of Labor in the 1880s, the bread-and-butter unionism of the American Federation of Labor (AFL), which refused to commit the labour movement to political engagement, emerged as the hegemonic form of trade unionism by the end of the century. Because the AFL was convinced of the futility of socialist and other third-party political activism, it sought to protect its sphere of action by taking on only those conflicts it thought it could win.[20] In this way, not only were the older split readings of the city reinforced, but so too were the most integrative and least militant features of working-class life at work and at home. The labour movement focused on the most skilled and on battles for better wages and terms of work; in the neighbourhoods, the differentiation of workers by ability to rent and purchase housing was interpenetrated by ethnic definitions of space and party politics. The result, Oestreicher argues, was a mixed picture of high levels of intra-class ethnic antagonisms, which coexisted with impressive cross-ethnic solidarities:

the workers who fought police on behalf of streetcar workers, the stove workers who refused to patronize a saloon selling scab bread, the Italian stonecutters who honored the stonecutters' picket lines, the Polish street laborers who called for equal division of available street work, the working-class theater goers who refused to patronize boycotted theaters in 1899 all demonstrated that the concept of solidarity had been effectively communicated to workers of many trades and nationalities.[21]

It is noteworthy that each of these instances of class-conscious collective action cited by Oestreicher was work-related. Continuous with the mid-nineteenth-century readings of the city,

---

[20] For a sympathetic discussion of the choices made by the AFL, see Richard Oestreicher, 'Urban Working-Class Political Behavior and Theories of American Electoral Politics, 1870–1940', *Journal of American History*, 74 (Mar. 1988).

[21] Oestreicher, *Solidarity and Fragmentation*, 229.

the American working class continued to be formed as a class, but class understood only as labour.

In spite of enduring differences in patterns of class formation, there were, nevertheless, important shifts in the character of urban relations that were shared by the English and American working classes at the turn of the century which challenged them both to re-read the city, and to do so in ways that reduced significantly the prospects of militancy in the Marxist sense. These changes concerned the structuring of city space and a new role for the state on the urban scene.

Capitalist cities continued to grow dramatically and to become increasingly intertwined with each other as points of accumulation and exchange. As they grew, the ambiguities of form that have recently produced debates between social geographers about the extent of the modernity of the early industrial city gave way to an intensification of the various spatial separations that had earlier interlaced the cross-class and mixed land-use patterns inherited from household-based production arrangements. This clarification had a contradictory aspect in both countries, carrying with it powerful impulses that on one side sharpened the immediacy and intensity of class and that on the other significantly diminished the prospects of militancy.

One of the deepening features of city space concerned the spatial divisions between working-class and non-working-class residential areas. With this working out of by now long-standing trends came the increasing autonomy of working-class neighbourhoods and institutions and thus 'the mutual insulation and repulsion of the classes',[22] their organizations, and their ways of life. The divisions between 'us' and 'them' that had also grown more prominent with the creation of large-scale factories and their hierarchical organization of production now became more visible away from work as well.

Concurrently, the operation of housing markets, over time, came to divide the working class into distinguishable subgroups that occupied quite different parts of the city, characterized by diverse standards of housing and amenities.

---

[22] Kumar, 'Class and Political Action', 41.

This intra-class stratification established new bases of difference and meaning within the working class.

In the United States, this pattern of working-class spatial differentiation was complicated by the much more varied ethnic heterogeneity, but both countries—indeed all the industrialized Western capitalist countries—shared in this reorganization of city space. The English case is a reminder that ethnic divisions in American cities reinforced this *common* spatially grounded differentiation between working-class groups by their ability to purchase residential environments. Indeed, as Zunz carefully demonstrates, the steady working out of this market and status-driven process restructured the character of American ethnic neighbourhoods to produce something of a convergence with English arrangements. Whereas in Detroit in the 1880s ethnicity as a principle of spatial segmentation was sufficiently strong to bring together in ethnic enclaves members of ethnic groups who had quite different market attributes, by the 1920s, except for blacks who remained pressed together by racial segregation, the socio-ethnic geography of the city had altered. Members of ethnic groups now sought housing appropriate to their incomes and styles of life. As a result, neighbourhoods took on more of a cross-ethnic aspect even as they became more homogeneous in market terms.[23] Poles, Irish, Italians, Jews, and other white ethnic groups increasingly came to live side by side in areas stratified by the housing market. With these changes in working-class communities, the link between residential patterns and ethnic identity grew less direct. Initially, Conzen notes, the emergence of ethnicity as a central category of meaning and action in the United States depended on common residence. This concentration was necessary at this first stage to support the development of locality-based ethnic organizations. But with shifts generated by the continuing operation of autonomous housing markets, ethnicity became despatialized as it steadily lost its place-specific underpin-

---

[23] See the discussion of the new social and spatial cleavages of early 20th-century Detroit in Zunz, ch. 13. He speculates that these changes in living space made the development of a new industrial class consciousness less difficult to achieve.

nings. With this change, ethnicity began to be transmuted into something more cultural and symbolic; which, in turn, later in the twentieth century, has crystallized into the formal solidarities of national interest groups.[24]

These changes on the ground in cities occurred at exactly the same time as the nationalization of the infrastructures of class emphasized by Calhoun. The organizations of union and party were able to tap into a spatially rooted, thus magnified, consciousness of class that helped them overcome barriers to solidarity and collective action. Yet, the new spatial divisions within the working class helped limit their political horizons by deflecting them into new areas of concern. As a result, at the very moment when the capacities of the working class were enhanced by their new translocal institutions, though limited in goals by their organizational imperatives, working-class resources were also tempered and channelled by intra-class spatial divisons.

As new housing markets functioned, geographer David Ward observes, 'the increased internal differentiation of the residential patterns of the city' divided the working class

into smaller sub-cultures each with its own small-scale versions of success ... Expectations were formulated in terms of minor gains in income and status rather than as a reorganisation of society as a whole ... As older bases of status disappeared and as income discrepancies between the skilled and unskilled diminished, the more prosperous and secure manual workers sought a more emphatic definition of their place in society by moving to residential quarters housing people with similar occupations and incomes ... *social differences were increasingly calibrated on a spatial order rather than one of external appearance* ... For the upwardly mobile segments of the working class, a new address with generally recognised social associations, provided a new but emphatic basis of their rising places in society.[25]

There is something of a resemblance between this perspective and the most familiar account by English Marxists, that of the 'labour aristocracy', for the failure of the working class to be more militant. Work in this tradition has examined

---

[24] Conzen, 'Immigrants, Immigrant Neighborhoods', 612 ff.
[25] David Ward, 'Victorian Cities: How Modern?', 148. Italics added.

wages and conditions of work (including the divide between craft and factory workers), and the distinctions in world-views between leaders and followers in labour unions and political parties, as well as urban neighbourhood differentiation—the focus I find most congenial—to find a fault-line dividing the working class. The analytical pay-off is an understanding of how the 'aristocracy' sold out a working class otherwise prepared to do battle with capital. As Henry Pelling has observed, 'It is an essential feature of the Marxist theory of the labour aristocracy that this supposedly small section of the working class was conservative in politics and imposed its conservatism upon working class institutions, thereby concealing, but by no means eliminating the underlying militancy of the mass of workers.'[26]

The labour aristocracy approach has elusive qualities. As a number of critics have noted, micro-level treatments of relations of craft and manual workers in specific industrial settings and of workers in residential areas indicate just how inexact the term 'labour aristocracy' is and how difficult it is to specify locations where aristocrats of labour actually confronted and contained a more radical mass of workers. Contrary to expectations of the theory, empirical evidence, especially for the late nineteenth century, suggests that 'it was the more prosperous workers who were the more politically militant and radical, while the lower ranks displayed either apathy or conservatism'.[27] Correct though this criticism by Pelling may be, it

[26] Henry Pelling, 'The Concept of the Labour Aristocracy', in Pelling, *Popular Politics and Society in Late Victorian Britain*. London: Macmillan, 1968, 41. Rooted in an article by Engels in 1885 that sought to explain why his expectations of the 1840s had not been borne out, and in Lenin's treatment of imperialism, the concept of a labour aristocracy was introduced into contemporary historical scholarship by Eric Hobsbawm. For the development of the concept, see Friedrich Engels, 'England in 1845 and 1885', in the collection of works by Marx and Engels, *On Britain*. Moscow: International Publishers, 1934, 67, 99; and E. J. Hobsbawm, 'The Labour Aristocracy', in Hobsbawm, *Labouring Men*. London: Weidenfeld and Nicolson, 1964.

[27] Pelling, 'The Concept of the Labour Aristocracy', 56. See also the telling criticisms made by H. F. Moorhouse in 'The Marxist Theory of the Labour Aristocracy', *Social History*, 3 (Jan. 1978), and 'The Significance of the Labour Aristocracy', *Social History*, 6 (May 1981).

misses the point that it is the undergirding theoretical apparatus of the 'labour aristocracy' position that is its deepest flaw. While right on the mark in looking at both organizational and spatial determinants of a lack of militancy, the refusal of this approach to break with the view that the working class is immanently revolutionary produces a rather idealist imputation of blame. Instead, with Calhoun and with Ward, we would do better to focus on how the organizational and spatial features of working-class life entirely undercut the possibilities for classically Marxist class consciousness and militancy. The organizational imperatives enmeshed leaders and followers, and the new spatial design of cities established new issues, concerns, and family mobility strategies that divided workers from each other in a finely graded way, not a small privileged group from a seething mass that it managed to restrain and sell out.

This portrait of the working class is an ideological construction, rather different, if in some ways drawing on, the complex interplay between inherited systems of meaning and collective action from an earlier moment of class formation, the new translocal features of working-class unions and party organizations, and the deepening segregation of city space in conjunction with the differentiation of neighbourhoods by subclasses with differential access to housing. It was this combination that produced an enhancement of the capacity of working classes to confront capital at work and away from work, to join their senses of grievance in both domains, and to mobilize resources of organization and solidarity in both spheres in pursuit of their aims; but it also produced a situation that limited the horizons and aspirations of the working classes as wage workers, as citizens, and as members of a class-based civil society. In this way, the indirect and face-to-face dimensions of class worked in tandem to minimize the prospects that the working class would act as a proletariat that confronted capitalism as a whole, with the goal of supplanting it with a new, socialist mode of production.

If important shifts in social geography provoked new readings of class and capitalism, so, too, did the fact that the shaping of city space was no longer the privilege of capital working with a high degree of independence. The manifestly

more important role of the state in shaping urban environments impelled members of the working class to address issues
of work and home not only as workers confronting capitalists
in labour and housing markets, but as citizens confronting the
state and emergent political issues about land, the urban
environment, and municipal services.

The new capitalism of the second industrial revolution no
longer accorded to capital the autonomy that had characterized
the first. *Laissez-faire* as prescribed by the political economists
proved insupportable, for the sphere of democratic politics
engendered movements to tame the cycle of boom and bust
and to mitigate the harsh operations of the market-place.
Further, as capitalism grew in scale and reach at both the
domestic and international levels, the state moved to organize
the very terms of the functioning of markets themselves—
through regulation, tariff and tax policy, and imperial assertion. As integral aspects of this changing tapestry of the
relations of state and capitalism, governments in cities moved
to shape and reshape space within the field of tension established by the conflicting claims of accumulation and citizenship. City growth became less and less a matter of the direct
imposition of the logic of capital and more and more the
product of planned state interventions. Road-building, slum
clearance, the provision of sanitation and water infrastructures, and the like became politicized, and objects of
attention for all the various social classes.[28] The dominant
classes understood the explosive potentialities of a concen-

[28] For a narrowly focused, but revealing discussion see Colin G.
Pooley, 'Housing for the Poorest Poor: Slum-Clearance and Rehousing
in Liverpool, 1890–1918'. *Journal of Historical Geography*, 11 (Jan.
1985). For different vantage-points on this set of issues, see the
discussion of tax abatements and tax policy in the rebuilding of
Vienna in Carl E. Schorske, *Fin-de-Siècle Vienna: Politics and Culture*. New York: Knopf, 1980, ch. 2; for the organization of the
politics of property see Avner Offer, *Property and Politics,
1870–1914: Landownership, Law, Ideology, and Urban Development
in England*. Cambridge: Cambridge University Press, 1981; and for
an elaboration of urban planning as a discourse and a set of practices
see Anthony Sutcliffe, *Towards the Planned City*. Oxford: Basil
Blackwell, 1981, and Richard Fogelsong, *Planning the Capitalist City*.
Princeton, NJ: Princeton University Press, 1986.

trated and disaffected urban working class, and they were reminded forcefully of that potential not only by such dramatic events as the Paris Commune but by recurring urban protests, demonstrations, and riots rooted in the networks and solidarities of residential communities. In these circumstances the class-segregated city became a quite terrifying object for the middle and upper classes, who were uncertain about what the 'dangerous classes' would do next. As a product of a 'mixture of fear, bad conscience and goodwill . . . the conditions of the working classes, especially in big cities, [became] a major subject of concern in the mid-Victorian years'.[29]

Though the relationship between these urban issues and other union and party concerns varied from time to time and from place to place, nowhere could the new organizations of the working class successfully mobilize workers without attention to these questions; they became integral to the new class understandings. More generally, the connections between the more intimately local and the more experience-distant national-organizational levels defined the terms and content of working-class political life. The city did not cease

[29] Mark Girouard, *Cities and People: A Social and Architectural History*. New Haven, Conn.: Yale University Press, 1985, 356. In part as a consequence of the work of the 1884–5 Royal Commission on the Housing of the Working Classes, which found that the private sector, even when augmented by building trusts and philanthropic associations, was unable to meet the pressing need for decent working-class housing, Parliament in 1890 passed the Housing of the Working Classes Act, which enlarged the capacities of local governments to construct housing. This and other such national policy developments went hand in hand with the modernization of local government, represented most dramatically by the creation of the London County Council to replace the mish-mash of private vestries and the Cities of London and Westminster that had previously been responsible for local government. The result was a new politicization of local issues, the contesting of seats by Fabian socialists and social Liberals at municipal elections, the emergence of municipal socialism as a feature of working-class mobilization, and the creation of new local instrumentalities to affect the daily lives of workers, especially in the area of housing. Public housing also became a major focus of attention on the Continent, where cities also became the sites, as in the well-known case of Vienna, of an assertive and successful socialist party politics.

to be significant, as Calhoun implies, only different in its importance.

The failure of Western working classes to act as revolutionary proletariats during the most profound crisis of modern capitalism in the Great Depression was not the result of mediating factors that interposed themselves between a class-conscious working class and the collective expressions of their militancy. Rather, the very organizations workers required to confront capital limited their politics, and the very spatial patterns that divided workers from the dominant classes fragmented their life experiences and aspirations. In the interconnections between working-class organizations and local relations, the barriers to a revolutionary Marxist project became insurmountable. Workers were thus capable of an assertive class perspective during the 1930s and 1940s, but seen through the lenses of Marxist expectation this politics of class was a politics lacking in class struggle.[30]

III

The relationship of Marxism and the city stands today on unsure ground. Now it is the politics of class itself that is in question. The class identities and actors so central to Marxism have receded as the basis of individual dispositions and strategic group activity in the cities that have been the most important *loci* for class formation under capitalism. Cities themselves, moreover, no longer seem very well defined. Clear boundaries between city and country are hard to find in the face of a formless, sprawling urban pattern. It is reasonable to think these developments are connected, but how?

In discussing this question, I draw on and assess a lively discussion within the new urban Marxism on the persistence

---

[30] Capitalism did not survive this moment unchanged. Under the impact of a working-class politics the transactions between the state and the capitalist economy and between the state and its citizens altered significantly to provide for a more assertive role for the state in organizing capitalist markets and, through the welfare state and redistributive public policies, to mitigate the market apportionment of wealth, income, and services.

and character of the city and on arguments about the troubled status of class and class struggle in today's capitalism. Given the vast expanse of these subjects, it is not my intention to offer more than a sketch of an approach that joins these issues together, overcoming the old, unwelcome division, and that shows that some of the more persuasive answers can still be found in an engagement of Marxism with the city.

I proceed by examining two of the most significant attempts to show how changes to cities and urban space affect contemporary patterns of class formation, those of Mark Gottdiener and Eric Hobsbawm. They show how recent complex transformations of urban social geography go a long way towards helping us account for why it is that the class categories of traditional Marxism are losing their grip at the centre of the capitalist world; but they do so, I argue, in ways that are not entirely satisfactory.

Their work is grounded in ideas about changes to cities that they share with a large number of urban-oriented Marxists who have been attempting to make sense of the restructuring of capitalism in the closing decades of this century. If the issues of domestic capital accumulation and local social movements filled the pages of the initial renewal of interest by Marxists in the city in the 1960s and 1970s, today the overriding topic in the relevant journals and books is the reorganization of capitalism, and with it the transformation, some think the elimination, of the city as a distinctive kind of space. And if Engels was the key initiator of Marxist work on cities, as well as its missed chances, Lefebvre has re-emerged as the progenitor of appropriate work on the new capitalism because of his insistence that we shift attention from the city as a determined and bounded place to a more fluid conception of space.[31]

If there is no single version of capitalist, and urban, restructuring in these largely (but not, we shall see, entirely) persuasive discussions, there are common threads.[32] Capitalism has

---

[31] Mark Gottdiener, 'Space as a Social Force of Production: Contribution to the Debate on Realism, Capitalism, and Space', *International Journal of Urban and Regional Research*, 11 (Sept. 1987).

[32] The literature on the restructuring of capitalism is immense.

become more globalized and interdependent. The internationalization of production and finance have gone hand in hand. Large-scale 'Fordist' manufacturing has declined while services, design-intensive industries, and high-technology production have become increasingly significant both in structuring the economy and in shaping its social relations. In this dual process of deindustrialization and reindustrialization capital and labour have become more specialized and mobile. The circuits of capital move more swiftly and are less anchored in specific places. A profound technological revolution in microelectronics has transformed communications, and has made information, not goods, the key commodity of advanced capitalism. Production is more oriented to process than to product. The disarticulation of work from place has grown so stark that an American insurance company serving customers in the United States can process their claims in a remote Irish village.[33] Decentralization and flexibility in labour as well as capital markets are new hallmarks of the economy. Governments underwrite these developments by subsidies of defence budgets, corporate research and development, transportation

---

Some of the best of this work has been provided by Manuel Castells and David Harvey. Castells has been particularly concerned with rapid shifts in communications and with technological transformations. Harvey, within a framework that treats recent changes as evidence confirming Marx's statement in the *Communist Manifesto* that it is a hallmark of capitalist change that 'all that is solid melts into air', adopts the language of the French Regulation school to chronicle a shift from the Fordist regime of post-war accumulation to a new regime of flexible accumulation. Harvey is particularly concerned to understand the connections between these changes to capitalism's base and the bewildering shifts of experienced time and space and their cultural representations in post-modernism. I return to these themes below. See Manuel Castells, *The Informational City*. Oxford: Basil Blackwell, 1990; Castells, 'High Technology, Economic Restructuring, and the Urban–Regional Process in the United States', in Castells (ed.), *High Technology, Space, and Society*. Beverly Hills, Calif.: Sage Publications, 1985; David Harvey, *The Condition of Postmodernity*. Oxford: Basil Blackwell, 1989.

[33] Sandra Barwick, 'Sleepy Castleisland Enjoys Home Comforts in the Global Office: A US Insurance Company has Set Up a Claims Office in an Irish Market Town', *Independent*, 30 Aug. 1988, 4.

infrastructures, and competitive bidding for the location of new industries and plants. In the most ambitious interpretations, these trends are thought to constitute an entirely new stage in the development of capitalism.[34]

The new capitalism is transforming the organization of territory and the spatial division of labour. The great metropolises—London, New York, Tokyo, Paris, Berlin—are in the midst of a shift from centres of manufacturing to centres of knowledge. Outside these giant cities, large manufacturing centres are declining in scale and significance. Space is being reshaped. New configurations of work and home are literally plonked in the middle of nowhere, located at key points of communication and transport created by high-speed motorways and airports, as the real-estate industry converts the rural landscape to office, production, and living uses. Areas come to be known by such signifiers as Route 128 in Massachusetts or the M4 corridor west of London. Places with existing built-forms are put at a competitive disadvantage, as they are burdened by the fixed arrangements of older forms of manufac-

---

[34] For discussions and representative examples of this literature, see Saskia Sassen, *The Mobility of Labor and Capital: A Study in International Investment and Labor Flow*. Cambridge: Cambridge University Press, 1988; Doreen Massey, *Spatial Divisions of Labour*. London: Macmillan, 1984; Erica Schoenberger, 'From Fordism to Flexible Accumulation: Technology, Competitive Strategies and International Location', paper presented at the Conference on Technology, Restructuring and Urban/Regional Development, International Sociological Association, Dubrovnik, Yugoslavia, June 1987; Alan J. Scott, 'Flexible Production Systems and Regional Development: The Rise of New Industrial Spaces in North America and Western Europe', *International Journal of Urban and Regional Research*, 12 (June 1988); Peter Hall and Ann Markusen (eds.), *Silicon Landscapes*. Boston: Allen and Unwin, 1985; N. S. Dorfman, 'Route 128: The Development of a Regional High Technology Economy', *Research Policy*, 12 (1983); Michael Piore and Charles Sabel, *The Second Industrial Divide*. New York: Basic Books, 1984; John Urry, 'Class, Space and Disorganized Capitalism', in Keith Hoggart and Eleonore Kofman, *Politics, Geography and Social Stratification*. London: Croom Helm, 1986; Scott Lash and John Urry, *The End of Organized Capitalism*. Cambridge: Polity Press, 1987; and the excellent collection of essays in Alan J. Scott and Michael Storper (eds.), *Production, Work, Territory: The Geographical Anatomy of Industrial Capitalism*. Boston: Allen and Unwin, 1986.

turing and by the costs of unionized labour. With the exceptions of those at the nodes of international finance, services, and trade, cities wither from disinvestment and abandonment. Capitalism now grows either in 'enclaves within older manufacturing regions, or . . . [in] a series of areas that hitherto largely coincided with the extensive geographical margins of capitalist industrialization'.[35]

Grounded in Lefebvre's conceptions of space, the most theoretically ambitious and self-consciously Marxist elaboration of these themes is Mark Gottdiener's *The Social Production of Urban Space*. Much as Engels in the 1840s sought out the most advanced spatial example of the new industrial capitalism in Manchester, so Gottdiener premisses his book on today's equivalent of the 'shock city': the dispersed spatial arrangements of the United States in the 1970s and 1980s. Gottdiener's premiss is that the traditional city, whose hallmark has been the concentration of capital, production, people, and power, has ceased to be a generative force:

Urban life has become portable and, thus, so has the 'city'. In place of the compact city form which once represented a historical process years in the making, we now have a metropolitan population distributed and organized in ever expanding regional areas that are amorphous in form, massive in scope, and hierarchical in their scale of social organization.

This new spatial morphology represents not a continuation of older patterns, but a radical break, with profound significance

[35] Scott, 'Flexible Production Systems', 179. For discussions, see Thierry Noyelle and Thomas Stanback, *The Economic Transformation of American Cities*. Totowa, NJ: Rownan and Allanheld, 1984; Peter Hall 'Technology, Space, and Society in Contemporary Britain' and Annalee Saxanian, 'Silicon Valley and Route 128: Regional Prototypes or Historic Exceptions?', in Castells (ed.), *High Technology*; Manuel Castells, 'High Technology and Urban Dynamics in the United States', and John D. Kasarda, 'Economic Restructuring and America's Urban Dilemma', in Mattei Dogan and John D. Kasarda (eds.), *A World of Giant Cities: The Metropolis Era*. Beverly Hills, Calif.: Sage Publications, 1988; and Christopher B. Leinberger and Charles Lockwood, 'How Business is Reshaping America', *Atlantic*, 258 (Oct. 1986); and Michael Peter Smith, *City, State, and Market: The Political Economy of Urban Society*. Oxford: Basil Blackwell, 1988.

for all aspects of economics, politics, culture, and society, not least for the character and meaning of class and class struggle. Above all, the new polynucleated growth is characterized by deconcentration, 'the massive regional dispersal of people, commerce, industry, and administration along with the contemporary restructuring of such regions into multicentered realms—sprawling for miles and miles and located everywhere in the country, especially in those areas once thought immune from urban development'.[36]

Gottdiener upbraids both mainstream ecological and recent Marxist approaches to urban development for not treating this new spatial configuration head-on and for not recognizing that the city can no longer be considered an object of analysis, but only a part of the larger process of spatial reorganization.[37] Urging a return to the production of space perspective of Lefebvre, Gottdiener seeks to develop theory appropriate to capitalism's new spatial situation. He asserts that recent spatial changes must be understood as informed by the structural nexus of the emergence of the global corporation, the interventionist state, and the acceleration of technical innovation. These developments have a distinctly capitalist twist in 'the progressively more footloose nature of industry', the more fluid flow to the circuits of capital, the fractionization of capital and labour, and the uneven development that 'represents both a process of capital accumulation and a competitive relation between different fractions of capital'. Within 'late capitalism' the key agency undergirding these processes is provided by interests and conflicts that revolve around the distribution of land and property. This sector is now 'the

[36] Mark Gottdiener, *The Social Production of Urban Space*. Austin, Tex.: University of Texas Press, 1985, 4, 5, 9.

[37] More fundamentally, Gottdiener rejects Marxist treatments of spatial forms as containers of social processes and as manifesting more fundamental material relations in favour of a perspective that gives to space itself a constitutive status at the intersection of a multiplicity of social processes during the 'late' phases of capitalist development including, but not limited to, the accumulation process. Space is socially produced at the intersection of economic, ideological, administrative, and political processes, and thus has a multiple ontological status.

leading edge of capitalist restructuring in space'. No longer entirely or even principally private, the property sector often combines 'public–private coalitions which also include elements of organized labor and which support themselves through local bureaucracies deeply dependent on growth'. These growth networks—their interests, activities, politics—produce the new spatial relations by connecting the characteristics of the political economy and the volitions of actors capable of changing the organization of space. In the United States, this shift has entailed the deconcentration of housing and workplaces in existing metropolitan areas and the shift of people and production to the sunbelt of the South and Southwest. Gottdiener concludes that 'the production of space has occurred in the main not because of economic processes alone but, more specifically, because of a joint state–real estate sector articulation which forms the leading edge of spatial transformations'.[38]

Gottdiener connects these dramatic changes to issues of class formation. Under these new conditions, he argues, what is at issue is not how working classes map the city, but the absence of a city to map and the absence of a working class to map it. In his view, the new decentralized organization of space has transformed social relations on the ground to the profound detriment of class solidarities or, indeed, any single, coherent vision of the social structure.

He sees a great paradox at work. The acceleration of communication and the dissemination of information and the dramatic extension of transportation routes, especially roads (car ownership has penetrated quite deeply into the various Western working classes), have more radically severed the relationship between work and home than at any time in the past—thus divorcing class based on labour force experiences from class based on locality. At the place of residence, these changes have produced an ever-finer segregation of the population for whom the determination of where to live is shaped mainly by the operation of highly autonomous housing markets. The result has been a contraction of social and political horizons. 'The spatial segregation of social groups', Gottdiener

[38] Gottdiener, *Social Production*, 199, 200, 209, 222, 227–8, 241.

writes, 'has liberated the vast majority of the population from responsibility for the less advantaged, because the former no longer live in close proximity to the latter.' Even more important, he argues, local space, bereft of streets and public areas, has contracted primarily to isolated single-family homes. In such circumstances, in effect, the residential community disappears. 'Neighbors become increasingly estranged through a lack of common experiences, despite the superficial appearance of civility between them, as the personalized network of commuters replaces the localized community of the past, with its once dense social relations.' Space becomes abstract. It loses its tangible markers. Place-specific social relations and cultures attentuate, even disappear. 'Local communities are transformed into privatized domains devoid of street interaction, with limited services and limited use of public space.'[39] If the nineteenth-century revolution in settlement space provided a material underpinning for working-class fraternal, instrumental, and political organizations, the new spatial patterns, by changing the experiences of everyday life, have reduced possibilities for class dispositions and collective action at just the moment when the infrastructural barriers to class formation identified by Calhoun, and discussed earlier in the chapter, have been overcome decisively.

Though Gottdiener's avowed aim is the writing of a new Marxist urban theory appropriate to the novel conditions of abstract space and the shattering of familiar urban forms, his Lefebvrian path takes him to the point of abandoning the project of Marxism and the city. Hobsbawm, by contrast, reaches conclusions rather similar to those of Gottdiener with regard to the fate of the working class from within far more traditional Marxist ways of working. His approach reasserts the structural vitality of Marxist analysis and extends it through an analysis of city space to account for the indeterminate patterns of class and group formation that currently obtain. For Hobsbawm, the current crisis of class is grounded in basic shifts in the experienced worlds of capitalist societies that have eroded the material and spatial bases of working-class dispositions and collective action.

[39] Ibid., 285–6, 289–91.

Hobsbawm first attempted to account for the crisis of class within Marxism without any reference to cities and space. His 1978 Marx Memorial Lecture, 'The Forward March of Labour Halted?', took the form of an elegy for the British labour movement. Except for a voluntaristic coda, the talk was something of a reluctant and deeply regretful farewell to the predictable, if limited, labourist politics of the cloth-cap, mainly male, manufacturing working class. The Left now had to face the reality of the collapse of working-class agency despite the increasingly dismal structural situation of capitalism. 'My conclusion is that the development of the working class in the past generation has been such as to raise a number of very serious questions about its future and the future of its movement. What makes this all the more tragic', he continued, 'is that we are today in a period of world crisis for capitalism.'[40]

Although Hobsbawm upbraided the Labour Party for choices badly made, the weight of his argument was that the march had been halted less by developments in the realm of subjectivity and organization than in the realm of class as an objective way of life. The 'common style' of working-class life that had developed in the late nineteenth century and which flourished until the middle of the twentieth century could not survive technological and sectoral transformations in the organization of work, rising standards of living, and demographic changes in the work-force that introduced divisions based on gender and nationality. It was the challenge of these changes that the trade unions and the Labour Party had failed to meet.

Perhaps because it was written from quite traditional Marxist premises about the privileged place of production and of the manufacturing working class, Hobsbawm's lecture elicited howls of anguish from the Left for its negative reading of the historical role of the working class and its immense scepticism about the capacities of Marxism as social and political theory

[40] Eric Hobsbawm, 'The Forward March of Labour Halted?', and commentaries by Raymond Williams, Robin Blackburn, and Tony Benn, among others, in Martin Jacques and Francis Mulhern (eds.), *The Forward March of Labour Halted?* London: Verso Books (in association with *Marxism Today*), 1981, 18.

to cope with shifts in the social organization of contemporary capitalist societies. His talk, moreover, antedated the assertive ideological conservatism of the Thatcher governments at home, the widespread disarray of left-wing political parties and trade union movements elsewhere in the West, and the collapse of avowedly Marxist regimes in East and Central Europe. The persuasive power of Marxism has eroded even further under the pressure of these developments. If, earlier in the twentieth century, Marxism had to face the situation of class without class struggle, now it has to confront the prospect of capitalism without class.

With the exception of a brief reference to the nineteenth-century working class as a collection of separate localized communities, Hobsbawm's talk devoted no attention to cities and their social geography. Likewise, the many rejoinders to the lecture had a good deal to say about the character of the labour force, specific industries, and the sociology of work, but nothing about the experience of the working class away from work. The debate thus had something of a partial quality, as if members of the working class lived and experienced capitalism, and found ways to resist integration within its embrace, either without reference to place or exclusively in the realm of work.

It was Hobsbawm himself who shifted the debate about the decomposition of class in late twentieth-century capitalism to the theme of 'Labour in the Great City' in his 1986 Herbert Gutman Memorial Lecture, virtually the only attempt by someone working outside the framework of the new Marxist urban studies, but within Marxism, to connect issues of city space to contemporary working-class formation. In this second formulation of the halting of the working-class march, capitalist cities numbering in the hundreds of thousands and millions—'a giant concentration of workers'—were regarded as conditions of working-class consciousness and movements. 'Clearly, without the existence of class-specific residential concentrations such organizational triumphs' as working-class mobilizations and massive voting for left-wing political parties 'would have been much more difficult, or even impossible'. It was the segregation of the working class, carried to extremes in large-scale tenement blocks, that concentrated activists and followers in a distinctively proletarian milieu. In these places, housing and rents joined workplaces and wages as key issues of working-class political consciousness. 'Actual social movements were particularly likely to flare up in the "towns within cities", where wages, rent, community feeling and class organization coincided.'[41]

I turn later to what I think are shortcomings in this argument which reduce the pay-off of this engagement with the city for Marxism. None the less, Hobsbawm's essay is important for the manner in which it treats the city and its social–spatial relations as necessary, if not sufficient, conditions for class-based dispositions and patterns of collective action. By bringing these matters to the fore, Hobsbawm challenged Marxism—theoretically and politically—to confront the implications of late twentieth-century spatial change for the very existence of class as a meaningful political category within advanced capitalism. In the nineteenth century it was plausible for Engels to think that the urbanization that concentrated capitalist power and production by also concentrating the working class would help organize the agents of capitalism's transformation.[42] Changes in the social geography of capitalist cities at the end of the twentieth century, Hobsbawm insisted, have dashed even diluted expectations of a class conscious proletariat.

Hobsbawm argued that the separation between work and home has grown to such an extent that there is today an insufficient basis in city space to sustain an integrated working-class politics at work and away from it. Suburbanization has decentralized cities, and they have become deindustrialized as manufacturing and service work have found new locales outside the city. The commuting patterns of the working class have been extended, snapping 'the links between day and night, or between the places where people live and those where they work, with substantial effects on the potential of labour organisation'. Inner cities have come to be

[41] Eric Hobsbawm, 'Labour in the Great City', *New Left Review*, 166 (Nov.–Dec. 1987), 43, 47.

[42] This is the theme of a neglected article by Nigel Harris, 'Urban England', *Economy and Society*, 3 (Aug. 1974).

peopled increasingly by 'the miscellaneous poor, the unskilled, the socially marginal and problematic, the ethnic and other minorities of whatever kind'. Further, urban renewal, road-building, and central business district redevelopment have broken up the traditional working-class neighbourhoods. 'The effect of all this on labour movements in the great city has been to deprive them of their former cohesion.' Now that 'the labouring population of the great city is returning from the status and consciousness of a "proletariat" to that of the pre-industrial and miscellaneous "labouring poor" . . . labour movements are losing, or have lost, . . . much of that class identification of working people as such which used to give them force, and a sense of collective power.'[43] The solidaristic politics of class has been replaced by the much more frag-mented politics of minorities seeking coalitions.

IV

Gottdiener and Hobsbawm suggestively connect up issues that too frequently in the history of Marxism have been considered separately. Each in his own way, however, does so in a manner that insufficiently apprehends the complex layering of changes to the city now under way and that links spatial to class analysis in too unmediated and unidirectional a way.

Both are impressed by the range and intensity of urban–spatial transformations; rightly so. None the less, there is something unsettling about Hobsbawm's generalizations about the impact of alterations to the cityscape on class formation from the experience of a small number of 'great' cities, Gottdiener's confident reasoning about the end of the city, and the now hegemonic portrait of city change within urban Marxism, with their shared assurance about the timing of change and the way they simplify current trends to the material and spatial base of urban life.

Surely some scepticism is in order with regard to the urban literature's account of the abruptness of transition in the regime of accumulation and the character of cities. After all,

---

[43] Hobsbawm, 'Labour in the Great City', 48, 49.

not many people share the privilege of living at a moment said to be as pivotal as ours, and even fewer have so quickly understood the profound qualities of such transformations just as they were happening. In accounts such as Gottdiener's of transition to a new stage in the history of capitalism and its organization of space, the crisis of spatially agglomerated 'Fordist' capitalism is said to have become manifest, with great suddenness, in the early to middle 1970s. The various elements of 'post-Fordism' are presented as having come together in a sufficiently robust way to define a new regime of accumulation only since the oil shock of 1973 and the recession of 1974–5.

'Such profound transitions to new forms of economy, society and culture', Nigel Thrift usefully reminds us, 'usually take longer, are more complex, and are more conservative than commentators of the time, who fix on the new, tend to realise.' The watershed shift to industrial capitalism in nineteenth-century England—the most dramatic such stepwise change within a compressed time and place yet to occur—was no simple matter of the new instantly supplanting the old. 'Victorian Britian,' Thrift observes, 'the paradigm of the shift to industrial capitalism, has been revealed by social and economic historians as the heyday of the horse as well as steam power, of hand power as well as mechanical power, and of a services-oriented South East England as well as an industrial North.' If older forms of production and space are now being supplanted, they will continue to count, if in a new context and in new ways. It makes little analytical or political sense simply to shift attention to the newer forms of social being as if they did not maintain dense relationships with the older ones.[44] Likewise, ways of understanding the new situation

[44] N. J. Thrift, 'New Times and Spaces? The Perils of Transition Models', *Society and Space*, 7 (June 1989), 127–8. Thrift also warns against some other dangers in this mode of analysis. One pitfall is that 'of simply making the wrong choice about the key elements of the model, leading to a blinkered approach about what is going on. Thus some commentators have fixed upon flexible production systems as the touchstone of current change. Of course, flexible production has led to important changes in certain industries . . . but it is certainly legitimate to ask if it is the most important process at work.

necessarily draw on traditional languages and tools of comprehension. The formation of group and class dispositions under new circumstances can hardly happen as if the past did not exist.

The literature on recent changes to urban spatial structures stresses discontinuities, but, as Norman and Susan Fainstein argue, their most important qualities are at least as much characterized by substantial continuities with earlier moments of the development of capitalist cities. The Fainsteins do not question the post-1973 production and spatial restructurings of Western capitalism, but they sensibly underscore both that such reorganizations in response to impasses and bottlenecks are endemic to the history of capitalism, and that the mechanisms identified by analysts of recent changes to account for industrial and spatial restructuring—'the devalorization of fixed capital; geographical disaggregation of the integrated firm; the flight of industry to areas with lower factor costs; absentee ownership; the entry of new states into the capitalist core; new international divisions of labor; and the increased importance of service-and-control employment within the occupational structure'—are long-familiar hallmarks of capitalist development.[45]

Indeed, in our examination of the role of cities in early modern Europe, we have seen how the search for economic locations on the peripheries of established spaces and regula-

---

What if the assumption implicit in many commentators' accounts, that the important trigger of change must be found in the productive sphere, is wrong? Changes during the 1980s can perhaps be described equally well as the result of the growth of fictitious capital combined with restructuring of financial and commercial capital, the redistribution of income, a massive consumer binge fuelled by easy credit, and an associated engineering of class and consumption.' An ambitious attempt to develop a more varied, supple, cautious, and contingent model of restructuring is A. Warde, 'Industrial Restructuring, Local Politics and the Reproduction of Labour Power: Some Theoretical Considerations', Society and Space, 6 (Mar. 1988).

[45] Susan S. Fainstein and Norman I. Fainstein, 'Technology, the New International Division of Labor, and Location: Continuities and Disjunctures', in Robert Beauregard (ed.), Economic Restructuring and Political Response. Urban Affairs Annual, xxxiv. Newbury Park, Calif.: Sage Publications, 1989, 24.

tions has been a recurring and fundamental feature of modern Western economies. Decentralization and the search for a greater scope for innovation in relatively peripheral places, marked by a leapfrogging in technology, transportation, organization of the firm, and financial practices, were certainly the hallmarks of the nineteenth-century industrial revolution. Now, as then, Dodgshon observes, existing industrial complexes and regions have something of 'the nature of a cul-de-sac, a trajectory of commitment that offers finite possibilities and diminishing returns'.[46] Entrepreneurial capital, seeking enhanced opportunities, tries to find them in new, less bounded places. From this vantage-point, the tensions between fixed and circulating capital—between the build-up of concentrated areas to capture specific advantages of location and the tendency to find new, less-fettered possibilities—provide crucial mechanisms for capitalism to maintain its revolutionary character. Further, this movement of capital in space in search of advantages continues to have the effects we have already observed in nineteenth- and early twentieth-century cities: transformations in the connections between the worlds of work and home, the division of cities into working and residential zones, and ever-finer distributions of space by income and housing quality.

Gottdiener has created a new teleology of space, in which the linear trend from concentration to deconcentration is inexorable. There are two main problems with this view. Why assume that a given reconfiguration of production and space will necessarily extend its reach everywhere, or, when it does diffuse, that it will have equal effects in each location on space, civil society, culture, politics, and the formation of collective identities and behaviour? Such patently was not the case with the industrial revolution; why now? The significant changes under way in the organization of economic activities and urban space in the capitalist countries of the West are hardly uniform or one-dimensional. The older

---

[46] R. A. Dodgshon, 'Geographical Changes: A Study in Marching Time or the March of Time?', *Society and Space*, 5 (June 1987), 190. See also Dodgshon, *The European Past: Social Evolution and Spatial Order*. London: Macmillan, 1987, chs. 9 and 10.

Fordist industrial areas are not simply disappearing in a headlong rush to a flexible regime of accumulation; far more typical are attempts by firms to take advantage of the shift in class forces between capital and labour to preserve Fordist patterns in a more globalized and competitive climate. While there is a new diversity in forms of production and labour markets, in the older industrial regions these have not added up to a new regime of accumulation. A multi-layered complexity, not an emergent homogeneity, characterizes the current situation.[47]

Another difficulty in Gottdiener's argument is that his portrayal of current changes is deliberately overdrawn. If the dynamic reorganization and layering of space defines what may in fact be a critical branching moment, modern capitalism has remained decidedly urban. Of the host of new centres of living and production that have sprung up, the vast majority concentrate living and working, even if in privatized, sprawling ways that are jarring to residents of older, more dense cities. Cities in the familiar form have not disappeared, nor, on recent trends, are they likely to, even if they are undergoing significant alterations in form and function. The trend of deconcentration, in short, has been accompanied by the counter-trend of urban concentration.[48] The nodal points of the American polynucleated landscape stressed by Gottdiener are rarely situated 'nowhere', but either within, near, or in functional relationship with, city settlements. Jacksonville, Houston, Denver, Los Angeles, San Diego, Seattle, to name just a few of the most robust centres of growth in the United States, are cities that, like their older counterparts, concentrate people, culture, capital, and power, even if their agglomera-

[47] I have been impressed by the careful review of R. Hudson, 'Labour Market Changes and New Forms of Work in Old Industrial Regions: Maybe Flexibility for Some but not Flexible Accumulation', *Society and Space*, 7 (Mar. 1989).

[48] 'A suburban office boom is matched by a downtown office boom, and the expansion of "planned communities" in the suburbs is paralleled by the pullulation of fashionable residential and recreational playgrounds downtown.' Neil Smith, review of Mark Gottdiener's *Social Production, American Journal of Sociology*, 92 (Sept. 1986).

tions, especially on their outer fringes, have many features that make them appear unrooted in historical space. In these cities and their metropolitan areas, as well as in Boston, New York, Chicago, and other urban centres in the East and Midwest, there can be found a complex and dense patchwork of land uses, housing patterns, types of workplace, and linkages to regional, national, and global economies. High technology intersects older patterns of labour-intensive manufacturing and services. Housing markets appear as ordered and as chaotic. Diversity and predictability compete.[49]

Overall, there is no evidence of a rush away from cities as *loci* of living. On the contrary, if the industrial revolution entailed a ruralization of the countryside, by stripping it of non-agricultural functions, the combination of new communications and transportation technologies, as well as the immense growth in the productivity of agriculture, has now made it possible for the countryside to urbanize. If we examine trends in urbanization since the Second World War in North America and Western Europe, we find a steady increase in the population living in towns and cities side by side with a slowdown in the rate of urbanization as compared to the nineteenth-century period of city-building. Bairoch argues that this trend is less a flight from the city as a *locus* of living and working than a diffusion of city living and 'a certain harmonization of levels of urbanization'.[50] The average size of cities has not grown, but the number of people living in cities, or in metropolitan areas with integral and interdependent ties with central cities, has continued to grow (whether suburban land is included in legal definitions of cities is more a juridical matter than a substantive one of spatial arrangements or ways of life). In spite of recent examples of dispersion, the twentieth century has continued to intensify as an urban century. As Bairoch observes:

[49] For a discussion of contemporary Los Angeles along these lines, see Mike Davis, '*Chinatown*, Part Two? The "Internationalization" of Downtown Los Angeles', *New Left Review*, 164 (July–Aug. 1989).

[50] Paul Bairoch, *Cities and Economic Development: From the Dawn of History to the Present*. Chicago: University of Chicago Press, 1988, 220.

Around 1800 less than 3% of the total population of developed countries lived in cities with populations of more than 100,000. By 1900 the proportion had risen to 14%, approaching 50% in 1980. In the most highly developed countries, the proportion is even in the order of 60%, and in 1980 there were in the developed world as a whole some 110 cities with populations of more than 1 million.[51]

If it is not the demise of cities that characterizes the present moment, what does seem to distinguish it is a multiplicity of urban forms, a speed-up of change, and a reduction in the share of the landscape that is not urban in some extended sense of the term. This new urbanization is highly contradictory in character, mixing centralization and decentralization, a more decisive break between work and residence and new ways of joining these spheres together, a growing homogeneity of space and an enhanced importance of place-identities and competition between places for economic resources. The conclusion of Susan and Norman Fainstein is apt: 'In general, we may say that these forces are reducing the technical necessity for a particular form of urban development, rather than imposing an emergent type.'[52] Reinvigorated traditional cities, suburban sprawl, and new agglomerations in formerly peripheral areas are developing simultaneously. There has been a change in the new division of labour between cities, with some, usually where major universities are located, becoming centres of research and development, others providing concentrations of headquarters and associated legal and banking services, others manufacturing goods with new technologies, others specializing in white-collar information processing, others as border entrepôts, yet others as retirement centres.[53] In the giant cities like New York and Los Angeles, all of these activities may take place, but in most there is a layering of functions within a hierarchy of economic activities. Urban business people and government officials search for ways to make their specific locales successful 'growth machines', and the strategies they

[51] Ibid., 226.

[52] Fainstein and Fainstein, 'Technology', 25.

[53] This classification of emergent cities is drawn from Harvey Molotch and John R. Logan, 'Urban Dependencies: New Forms of Use and Exchange in U.S. Cities', Urban Affairs Quarterly, 21 (Dec. 1985).

adopt in pursuit of this goal (and in pursuit of the effort to make growth seem value-free) have a formative role in shaping the character of local politics, social movements, and conflicts.[54]

From this perspective, we are not witnessing the end of the city, but a proliferation and diversification of city-types. The new contingencies of economic and social organization in space certainly include the outcome identified by Gottdiener, but not as the exclusive or inevitable end-point of current technological, public policy, and investment trends. The new complicated and highly variable patterning of space in late twentieth-century capitalism has thus created a situation in which for some individuals and families 'space *in toto* has been socialized through the annihilation of space by time',[55] and by the replacement of the city as a physical entity by an abstract spatial landscape in which propinquity counts for very little; but for others, still the very large majority, diverse kinds of physical cities remain the location of the pressing features of everyday life.

V

In the face of challenges to the viability of class as the dominant form of collective identity and action, Hobsbawm and Gottdiener sought to find alternative bases of challenge to advanced capitalism. Hobsbawm ended his 1978 lecture on a hortatory note. While the barriers to the resuscitation of working-class parties and movements are formidable, 'there is no reason for automatic pessimism', for even if men and women must act in 'circumstances that history has provided for them and within its limits . . . it is they who *make* their history'. But, he counselled,

[54] The treatment of the city as a 'growth machine' is the centre-piece of the important work on urban development and property relations by John R. Logan and Harvey L. Molotch, *Urban Fortunes: The Political Economy of Place*. Berkeley, Calif.: University of California Press, 1987.

[55] Kevin Cox, 'Review Essay', *Political Geography Quarterly*, 3 (Jan. 1984), 81.

if the labour and socialist movement is to recover its soul, its dynamism, and its historical initiative, we, as Marxists, must do what Marx would certainly have done: to recognize the novel situation in which we find ourselves, to analyse it realistically, and concretely, to analyse the reasons, historical and otherwise, for the failures as well as the successes of the labour movement, and to formulate not only what we would want to do, but what can be done.[56]

The second lecture provided content to these goals by advising the supercession of old-fashioned political appeals based on class by a return to what Edward Thompson, in his discussion of the eighteenth century,[57] labelled class struggle without class: 'Now that we are in some ways reverting to a version of the "city crowd" politics of the pre-industrial days of the "lower orders" and the "labouring poor",' Hobsbawm asks, 'would it not be logical to revert also to the populist politics of those days?'[58] In this, Hobsbawm counsels a fundamental rethinking of the practical and discursive bases of collective identities and activities. Similarly, Gottdiener proposes to refocus socialist strategy on struggles to democratize the various features of lived experience, but his farewell to class is even more emphatic. 'The new political agenda organized around what can be called the sociospatial praxis', he argues, 'can make progress only through a clean break with past notions which focus on some abstraction called the working class.' Moreover, this new politics will require a break with place-specific organization and understanding in favour of building networks of people to counteract the currently dominant growth strategies. To be viable analytically and politically, Marxism, he counsels, must now leave the city and the working class as relics of times past.[59]

Hobsbawm's project of re-reading the city in pre-industrial fashion and Gottdiener's prescription for a post-class politics follow in rather too assured a way from their underlying analyses of the city, both of which are only partial accounts of

[56] Hobsbawm, 'The Forward March', 18, 19.
[57] E. P. Thompson, 'Eighteenth Century English Society: Class Struggle Without Class?', Social History, 3 (May 1978).
[58] Hobsbawm, 'Labour in the Great City', 51.
[59] Gottdiener, Social Production, 272.

changes in particular, not necessarily representative, kinds of urban space. Further, Gottdiener and Hobsbawm arrived at quite similar strategic conclusions by very different means. The resemblance in their calls for a politics that differs from one of class and class struggle should not obscure the irreconcilable features of their analyses. Gottdiener severed while Hobsbawm tightened the ties binding place, social geography, dispositions, and collective action. Neither approach is quite satisfactory. Each is worth a closer look.

Because of the complex layering of time and space in the urban situation of older city forms that refuse to expire and new patterns of urbanization whose contours have yet to be established, and because the pace of change seems ever more rapid, the relevant distances more encompassing, and the line between city, suburb, and country out of focus, the relationship between space and place seems out of kilter to residents and to analysts of the city. Not since the late nineteenth century has urban life been so bewildering, even threatening. The contingent qualities of spatial change, the emergent jumble of mixed forms of old and new, homogeneous and marginally differentiated, cities, and the compression of time and space that has taken place under the impact of massive changes in technology, transport, and communications make it difficult for people to get a coherent grip on urban reality. Cycles of building and rebuilding occur much more rapidly. Familiar landscapes alter. Boundaries between city and country blur. Information diffuses quickly. The pace of life quickens. Ephemerality, fragmentation, and plasticity have become hallmarks of the age.

We have seen how, at a similar moment of bewildering transformations to time and space at the turn of the century, differentiation theory sought to apprehend the new features of the city but in fact redescribed them without locating urban change within a social process framework. A parallel impulse to make plasticity internal to social theory is at work today. Once again it is tempting to mimic the bewilderment of the situation on the ground.

By the time Gottdiener concludes his provocative analysis of the effect of large-scale processes on cities and space he arrives at a place very similar to Laclau and Mouffe, whose

Hegemony and Socialist Strategy makes sense of the erosion of class dispositions and behaviour and the new plurality of social movements by setting aside the social-theoretical tensions of structure and subject in favour of a virtually un-anchored, free-wheeling agency. Recoiling from essentialism, they abjure strong structural-causal accounts (leaving some room for weaker ones, acknowledging that 'between total determination and partial limitation there is a whole range of intermediate possibilities'), especially Marxist ones which ascribe a privileged position to a working class with objective interests in anti-capitalist struggles:

What is now in crisis is a whole conception of socialism which rests upon the ontological centrality of the working class, upon the role of Revolution, with a capital 'r', as the founding moment in the transition from one type of society to another, and upon the illusory prospect of a perfectly unitary and homogeneous collective will that will render pointless the moment of politics.[60]

Their solution is surgical: the excision of the leading position of the working class, and of class structures and categories, from the project of socialism.[61] In their rendering, actual

---

[60] Ernesto Laclau and Chantal Mouffe, *Hegemony and Socialist Strategy: Towards a Radical Democratic Politics*. London: Verso Books, 1985, 2. See also Laclau and Mouffe, 'Post-Marxism Without Apologies', *New Left Review*, 166 (Nov.–Dec. 1987), 94, 96, 104.

[61] The disappointingly orthodox rejoinder to Laclau and Mouffe by Ellen Wood reasserted the strong determinism of traditional Marxist base–superstructure social theory, and, in this way, confirmed Laclau and Mouffe's portrait of the baleful features of Marxist analysis as requiring the simplification and reduction of agency to structural necessity. Ellen Meiksins Wood, *The Retreat from Class: A New 'True' Socialism*. London: Verso Books, 1986. See also Norman Geras, 'Post-Marxism?', *New Left Review*, 163 (May–June 1987); Laclau and Mouffe, 'Post-Marxism Without Apologies'; Norman Geras, 'Ex-Marxism Without Substance: Being a Real Reply to Laclau and Mouffe', *New Left Review*, 169 (May–June 1988). In the first of his essays, Geras upbraids Laclau and Mouffe for giving 'a caricatured and impoverishing account of what Marxism is ... In a nutshell, Marxism is defined by Laclau and Mouffe in the most uncompromis-ingly necessitarian or determinist, most rigidly economistic, and—if one must—most simplifyingly "essentialist" terms; and then dis-missed for being determinist, economist, "essentialist"' (48). There is some merit to this charge, but, in the circumstances, it is beside

historical working classes are understood not as having been formed by multi-levelled processes of materiality and meaning, but exclusively in terms of meaning and the discursive construction of collective identities, almost as if this were wholly a voluntary matter. The result, as Przeworski has put it, is 'a radical indeterminism in which everything is possible and hence the success of political projects is exclusively a matter of will'.[62] Gottdiener differs from Laclau and Mouffe in his acceptance of a special role for the working class within capitalism, but only before recent transformations to production and space. Now that spatial relations have become abstract and generalized, he too thinks the choice of social identities and strategies has become a matter of open selection from competing possible discourses. Gottdiener's materialism becomes an anti-materialism; it is precisely the dissolution of place in favour of more generalized and abstract space in the

---

the point because it misses the radical quality of the critque of Laclau and Mouffe. For them—and this is a perspective that demands to be taken seriously—the achievements of Marxist writing have been gained in spite of the strong tendencies of the theoretical apparatus of Marxism to reductionism and determinism. The best Marxist work modifies or disposes of some of the core assumptions of the work of Marx. My own approach to their critique is to insist on distinctions between different projects in the work of Marx, and to distinguish aspects of his work where the system of analysis is logically closed and those aspects that are better viewed as open and speculative hypotheses. I am fully in accord with Laclau and Mouffe when they rail against the hubris of a totalizing Marxism; I am in disagreement with their solution, which amounts to a departure from any kind of materialist or realist perspective, whatever its provenance. I think it should be a matter of some regret that Geras chose to pursue his own critique in an incredibly nasty fashion, impugning the personal motivations of Laclau and Mouffe as opportunists seeking after fashion and fame. Not only is this ridiculous and offensive, but it has shifted the character of debate about their work away from issues that matter. Wood's work, while also polemical, is responsible. The problem with her book is its wooden reiteration of old truths as if their restatement amounted to a refutation of Laclau and Mouffe's position or to a coherent way to confront difficulties in Marxist social theory and class analysis.

[62] Adam Przeworski, 'Class, Production and Politics: A Reply to Burawoy', *Socialist Review*, 19 (Apr.–June 1989), 96.

manner of Lefebvre that effectively makes this unbounded voluntarism possible.

If Gottdiener now opts for unconstrained agency, Hobsbawm's lectures overtilt the other way, as people appear as the bearers of social, structural, and spatial properties. Welcome as Hobsbawm's turn to the city was, his analysis treats the connection between urban social geography and class consciousness in a manner that withdraws independence and autonomy from agency in favour of structural and spatial determinations of working-class dispositions and patterns of collective action. We have seen, however, that capitalist cities of the nineteenth century sharing in key spatial features were mapped by working classes in quite diverse ways. Why should we think only one possible mapping is currently available?

In a critique of Laclau and Mouffe marred by tendentious personal attack, Norman Geras asserts that their discursive theory that 'turns its back on Marxism will quickly reach its limits, limits continually recreated by capitalism and class',[63] rather than open up to alternative identities with the capacity to become bases of systemic challenge. These are not mutually exclusive options.

As the social geographies of cities change and diversify, older mappings of the city prove insufficient. Because of the new range and complexity of the urban-spatial situation, not because discursive choices are commanding and open in principle, issues of class (and group) formation have come to the fore once again with a plurality of solutions. These are not indeterminate, however. They are limited and shaped both by characteristics of urban life, now much more complex and varied than before, and by the imperative that patterns of group and class formation must still map actual urban spaces in ways that make sense of them. There is no a priori reason why class and non-class categories cannot be put to use in such mappings. In some settings, class identities may recede in importance; in other very similar ones they may grow in significance. It is this variability in relationship to the social and spatial organization of cities that must now be confronted.

We do well to recall, moreover, that the process of making

---

[63] Geras, 'Post-Marxism?', 80–1.

sense of cities is not only constrained, as Hobsbawm reminds us, by such material and spatial characteristics as the relationship of work and home and demographic settlement patterns, but that it is also informed by existing urban mappings. These, like all representations of social reality, possess the capacity to outlive the particular conditions of their creation. For this reason, holistic class mappings of the current situation in English cities remain more likely than in equivalently structured American ones.

Thus, both Gottdiener and Hobsbawm can be faulted for eliding some vital issues that pivot on the contingent but not unconstrained relationship of city space and class formation. Because the spatial conditions underpinning working 'classness' have altered considerably, the formation of social-structural identities is once again at a formative state with prospects that cannot be determined directly either by treating space as the unmediated outcome of capitalist development or by treating the dispositions of city residents as the unmediated outcome of spatial configurations. Urban mappings are uncertain because the material world they map is complex, because alternative coherent ways of reading the situation on the ground make a good deal of sense, and because past urban and class representations can still be adapted to fit the new spatial realities. Consider just a limited number of possible alternatives: given the formative power of capitalism in shaping urban space, it is still plausible to map the city in holistic class terms. Given the heightened importance of fragmented housing markets and political jurisdictions, it makes sense to map the city in Weberian class terms as divided between areas distinguished by residents' fine-grained capacities to consume in the market-place. And given the ever more stark divide between work and home, a divided pattern of class formation on the traditional American pattern provides yet another possible way to map the new spatial situation. If the new spatial complexity has ushered in a new battle of urban representations, we have learned from past equivalent moments that the situation on the ground alone will not decide it.

If Hobsbawm shares in the limitations of a Marxism that moves too reflexively from material conditions to their representation, Gottdiener's attempt to transcend the materiality of city space is at least as problematical as the direction taken by the differentiation theorists of a century ago. An alternative approach of the kind sketched in earlier chapters, that seeks to understand the causal grounding of urban-spatial change and the ways these have been mapped, continues to commend itself. The large-scale processes of capitalism and national states continue to be the fundamental determinants of urban-spatial arrangements. These are structural matters grounded in systemic relationships that have an objective existence independent of any claims to know or to speak of them. In turn, individuals and collectivities continue to experience these processes in actual places of residence and work. How they do so, and with what effect on the composition of structures and spaces, remain central and pressing questions.

To the extent that Marxist social theory wishes to contribute to an understanding of the current kaleidoscope of urban classes, groups, and social movements, it can best do so by learning from the shortcomings of the episodic engagement of Marxism with the city, and from the ways a more open and respatialized Marxism has been able to address such basic puzzles as the transition from feudalism to a world of capitalism and states, divergent patterns of working-class formation, and the acquiescence of Western working classes in capitalism. In so doing, two questions which classical and most Western Marxism have long considered resolved would be approached agnostically: the degree to which economic determinations as understood by Marxist theory possess the privilege of primacy, and the extent to which phenomena in specific historical settings that lie outside the confines of the process of capitalist accumulation are superstructural in G. A. Cohen's demanding sense of the term. 'After so many failed prophecies, is it not in the interest of [Marxism] to embrace complexity, be it at some sacrifice of its claim to predictive power?'[64]

[64] Albert O. Hirschman, 'Rival Interpretations of Market Society: Civilizing, Destructive, or Feeble?' *Journal of Economic Literature*, 20 (Dec. 1982), 1483. Where I have inserted 'Marxism' in brackets, Hirschman's text says 'social science'. I think he will forgive this liberty.

Select Bibliography

ABRAMS, P., and WRIGLEY, E. A. (eds.), *Towns in Societies: Essays in Economic History and Historical Sociology*. Cambridge: Cambridge University Press, 1978.

AGNEW, J. A., *Place and Politics: The Geographical Mediation of State and Society*. Boston: Allen and Unwin, 1987.

BAIROCH, P., *Cities and Economic Development: From the Dawn of History to the Present*. Chicago: University of Chicago Press, 1988.

BLACKMAR, E., *Manhattan for Rent, 1785–1850*. Ithaca, NY: Cornell University Press, 1989.

BRAUDEL, F., *Capitalism and Material Life, 1400–1800*. New York: Harper and Row, 1973.

CANNADINE, D., 'Residential Differentiation in Nineteenth Century Towns: From Shapes on the Ground to Shapes in Society', in J. H. Johnson and C. G. Pooley (eds.), *The Structure of Nineteenth Century Cities*. London: Croom Helm, 1982.

—— 'Urban Development in England and America in the Nineteenth Century; Some Comparisons and Contrasts', *Economic History Review*, 33 (Aug. 1980).

CASTELLS, M., *The City and the Grassroots: A Cross-Cultural Theory of Urban Social Movements*. Berkeley, Calif.: University of California Press, 1983.

—— *City, Class and Power*. London: Macmillan, 1978.

—— *The Urban Question: A Marxist Approach*. London: Edward Arnold, 1977.

DENNIS, R., *English Industrial Cities of the Nineteenth Century: A Social Geography*. Cambridge: Cambridge University Press, 1984.

DE VRIES, J., *European Urbanization: 1500–1800*. London: Methuen, 1984.

DODGSHON, R. A., *The European Past: Social Evolution and Spatial Order*. London: Macmillan, 1987.

ENGELS, F., *The Condition of the Working Class in England*, trans. W. O. Henderson and W. H. Chaloner. Stanford, Calif.: Stanford University Press, 1968.

FAINSTEIN, N., and FAINSTEIN, S., 'Technology, the New International Division of Labor, and Location: Continuities and Disjunctures', in Robert Beauregard (ed.), *Economic Restructuring and Political*

Response. Urban Affairs Annual, xxxiv. Newbury Park, Calif.: Sage Publications, 1989.

GINTIS, H., and BOWLES, S., 'State and Class in European Feudalism', in C. Bright and S. Harding (eds.), *State-Making and Social Movements*, Ann Arbor, Mich.: University of Michigan Press, 1984.

GIROUARD, M., *Cities and People: A Social and Architectural History*. New Haven, Conn.: Yale University Press, 1985.

GOTTDIENER, M., *The Social Production of Urban Space*. Austin, Tex.: University of Texas Press, 1985.

GOULDNER, A., *The Two Marxisms: Contradictions and Anomalies in the Development of Theory*. New York: Seabury Press, 1980.

GREGSON, N., 'On Duality and Dualism: The Case of Structuration and Time Geography', *Progress in Human Geography*, 10 (June 1986).

HALL, P., and MARKUSEN, A. (eds.), *Silicon Landscapes*. Boston: Allen and Unwin, 1985.

HARLOE, M. (ed.), *Captive Cities: Studies in the Political Economy of Cities and Regions*. London: John Wiley, 1977.

HARRIS, R., 'Residential Differentiation and Class Formation in the Capitalist City: A Review and Directions for Research', *Progress in Human Geography*, 8 (Mar. 1984).

HARVEY, D., *The Condition of Postmodernity*. Oxford: Basil Blackwell, 1989.

—— *Explanation in Geography*. New York: St Martin's Press, 1979.

—— *Limits to Capital*. Chicago: University of Chicago Press, 1982.

—— *Social Justice and the City*. London: Edward Arnold, 1973.

—— *Studies in the History and Theory of Capitalist Urbanization*, 2 vols. Baltimore: Johns Hopkins University Press, 1985.

HILTON, R. (ed.), *The Transition from Feudalism to Capitalism*. London: New Left Books, 1976.

HOBSBAWM, E., 'Labour in the Great City', *New Left Review*, 166 (Nov.–Dec. 1987).

HOHENBERG, P. H., and LEES, L. H., *The Making of Urban Europe, 1000–1950*. Cambridge, Mass.: Harvard University Press, 1985.

HOLTON, R. J., *Cities, Capitalism and Civilization*. London: Allen and Unwin, 1986.

JOYCE, P., *Work, Society, and Politics: The Culture of the Factory in Late Victorian England*. New Brunswick, NJ: Rutgers University Press, 1980.

KATZNELSON, I., *City Trenches: Urban Politics and the Patterning of Class in the United States*. New York: Pantheon Books, 1981.

—— and ZOLBERG, A. (eds.), *Working Class Formation: Nineteenth*

Century Patterns in Western Europe and the United States, Princeton, NJ: Princeton University Press, 1986.

KERN, S., *The Culture of Time and Space, 1880–1918*. Cambridge, Mass.: Harvard University Press, 1983.

LASH, S., and URRY, J., 'The New Marxism of Collective Action: A Critical Analysis', *Sociology*, 18 (Feb. 1984).

LEFEBVRE, H., *Du rural et de l'urbain*. Paris: Anthropos, 1970.

—— *Le Droit à la ville*. Paris: Anthropos, 1968.

—— *La Pensée marxiste et la ville*. Paris: Casterman, 1972.

—— *La Production de l'espace*. Paris: Anthropos, 1974.

—— *La Révolution urbaine*. Paris: Gallimard, 1970.

LOGAN, J. R., and MOLOTCH, H. L., *Urban Fortunes: The Political Economy of Place*. Berkeley, Calif.: University of California Press, 1987.

MASSEY, D., *Spatial divisions of Labour*. London: Macmillan, 1984.

MCKEWON, K., *Marxist Political Economy and Marxist Urban Sociology: A Review and Elaboration of Recent Developments*. London: Macmillan, 1987.

MERRINGTON, J., 'Town and Country in the Transition to Capitalism', *New Left Review*, 93 (Sep.–Oct. 1975).

MUMFORD, L., *The City in History*. New York: Harcourt, Brace, and World, 1968.

—— *The Culture of Cities*. New York: Harcourt Brace, 1938.

MURRAY, P., and SZELENYI, I., 'The City in the Transition to Socialism', *International Journal of Urban and Regional Research*, 8 (Mar. 1984).

OESTREICHER, R. J., *Solidarity and Fragmentation: Working People and Class Consciousness in Detroit, 1875–1900*. Urbana, Ill.: University of Illinois Press, 1986.

OFFER, A., *Property and Politics, 1870–1914: Landownership, Law, Ideology and Urban Development in England*. Cambridge: Cambridge University Press, 1981.

PELLING, H., *Popular Politics and Society in Late Victorian Britain*. London: Macmillan, 1968.

PICKVANCE, C. G. (ed.), *Urban Sociology: Critical Essays*. London: Methuen, 1976.

PRED, A., 'Production, Family, and Free-Time Projects: A Time-Geographic Perspective on the Individual and Societal Change in Nineteenth Century U.S. Cities', *Journal of Historical Geography*, 7 (Jan. 1981).

REYNOLDS, S., *Kingdoms and Communities in Western Europe, 900–1300*. Oxford: Oxford University Press, 1984.

SASSEN, S., *The Mobility of Labor and Capital: A Study in Inter-*

national Investment and Labor Flow. Cambridge: Cambridge University Press, 1988.

SAUNDERS, P., *Social Theory and the Urban Question.* London: Hutchinson, 1981.

SCOTT, A. J., and STORPER, A. (eds.), *Production, Work, Territory: The Geographical Anatomy of Industrial Capitalism.* Boston: Allen and Unwin, 1986.

SMITH, M. P., *City, State, and Market: The Political Economy of Urban Society.* Oxford: Basil Blackwell, 1988.

SMITH, N., *Uneven Development: Nature, Capital, and the Production of Space.* Oxford: Basil Blackwell, 1989.

SZELENYI, I., 'Structural Changes of and Alternatives to Capitalist Development in the Contemporary Urban and Regional System', *International Journal of Urban and Regional Research,* 5 (Mar. 1981).

TABB, W., and SAWYERS, W. (eds.), *Marxism and the Metropolis,* 2nd edn. New York: Oxford University Press, 1984.

THRIFT, N., and WILLIAMS, P. (eds.), *Class and Space: The Making of Urban Society,* London: Routledge and Kegan Paul, 1987.

TILLY, C., *Coercion, Capital, and European States,* AD 990–1990. Oxford: Basil Blackwell, 1990.

VANCE, J. E., 'Housing the Worker: Determinative and Contingent Ties in Nineteenth Century Birmingham', *Economic Geography,* 43 (Apr. 1967).

—— 'Housing the Worker: The Employment Linkage as a Force in Urban Structure', *Economic Geography,* 42 (Oct. 1966).

WARD, D., 'Victorian Cities: How Modern?', *Journal of Historical Geography,* 1/2 (1975).

WARDE, A., 'Industrial Restructuring, Local Politics and the Reproduction of Labour Power: Some Theoretical Considerations', *Society and Space,* 6 (Mar. 1988).

WILLIAMS, R., *The Country and the City.* New York: Oxford University Press, 1973.

WIRTH, L., 'Urbanism as a Way of Life', *American Journal of Sociology,* 44 (July 1938).

ZUNZ, O., *The Changing Face of Inequality: Urbanization, Industrial Development, and Immigrants in Detroit, 1880–1920.* Chicago: University of Chicago Press, 1982.

Index

Abrahams, Gerald 249
Abrams, Philip, *Towns in Societies* 5–8
absolutism 161, 163, 176, 183, 186, 240–1
action, collective *see* collective action
Adams, Robert McCormick 166
agency, concept of *see* Marxist concepts
Agnew, John 205
agriculture 173–4, 183, 189, 196
Althusser, Louis 38, 59–60, 65, 75, 117
American Federation of Labor (AFL) 275
Amsterdam 1, 12, 187, 193–4
Anderson, Perry 27–8, 73, 75, 88, 162–5, 169
Antwerp 12

Bairoch, Paul 202, 299–300
Balibar, Étienne 59
Berlin 13, 19, 193, 286
Birmingham 145, 196, 218
Blache, Vidal de la 1
Blackmar, Elizabeth 226, 227, 239–40
Boston 225, 299
Bourdieu, Pierre 208–9
Bowles, Samuel 165, 167–9, 180
Bradford, Yorks 147
Braudel, Fernand 170
Brandenburg 187
Brazil 32
Brooklyn 200
Burgel, Gallia et al. 94–6
Burnett, John 218–19
Butlin, R. A. 190

Cadiz 190
Calhoun, Craig 17, 267–72, 278, 280, 282–3, 290
Calvino, Italo, *Invisible Cities* 8–9
Cannadine, David 154, 205, 223–4

capital:
    accumulation 48, 54, 62–4, 82–3, 97, 102–3, 107–10, 182, 253–4
    circulation of 108–12, 121–3, 131–3, 285
    finance 108–12
    urban concentration of 12, 24–5, 30, 36, 163–4, 187
capitalism:
    and coercion 165, 170, 181, 187
    crises in 48, 54, 94–5, 110, 121, 153, 159, 260, 291
    Fordist 285, 295–6, 297–8
    internationalization of 192, 284–8
    and labour interaction *see* class conflict
    restructuring of 95, 260–4, 284–90, 295–8
    and state formation 132–3, 180, 186–90, 192
    as system of production 28, 33–4, 36, 47, 53–4, 107
    urban nature of 20–1, 24–5, 30, 91, 120–7, 163–4
Carlyle, Thomas 21
Carter, Harold 172–3
Castells, Manuel 41–2, 98–9, 140, 142, 206–7, 213, 239
    City Class and Power 115
    La Question urbaine 37–9, 93–4, 100–3, 112–15, 136
    The City and the Grassroots 39–40, 115, 119, 134–9
Castilla 134
Chartism 151, 234, 235, 246–8, 250–1, 271
Cheyette, Frederic 174
Chicago 9, 13, 200, 225, 299
Chicago School of Sociology 18, 20–1, 23, 100, 112–13
Chorley, Lancs 220–1
Christendom and the Church 165, 169, 173
churches in cities 20, 226, 251

cities:
  and capital accumulation 97,
    102–3
  capitalist nature of 20–1, 24–5,
    30, 91, 120–7, 163–4
  and concentration of capital 12,
    24–5, 30, 36, 163, 187
  continuity in 296–8, 307
  de-urbanization of 292–4
  defined 2–4, 135–6
  disorientation in 9–11, 16–22, 26,
    38, 237, 303
  diversity in 176–80, 298–301, 306
  feudal 12, 25, 29, 160–4, 169–76,
    182–90
  growth of 11–22, 29, 146–7,
    176–80, 187–8, 193–6, 224–5
  industrial 193–6, 198–202, 224–5
  origin of 172–6
  as political centres 11–13, 24–5,
    29, 106, 178, 184–8, 192–3
  present and future 283–98, 303,
    306–8
  Roman 173
  structure of 148–52, 198–202,
    217–21, 224–6
  see also urban analysis; urban
    development; urbanization
Clark, T. J. 210–11
class 74, 262–3
  landlord 109, 226
  middle 247–8, 255, 263
  working 13, 15, 35, 36, 148–51;
    organizations 151, 232, 233–4,
    237, 238, 251; see also parties,
    political; trade unions
class conflict:
  in Marxist theory 36, 41, 46–7,
    52–5, 58, 73, 137–8
  non revolutionary 95, 125,
    259–64, 265–83, 290–1
  realignments of 40, 100, 114,
    125–6
  see also collective action;
    militancy; proletariat, formation
    of
class consciousness 61, 65, 122, 130,
  151–2, 251, 261, 274
class formation 125, 127–9, 152–3,
  203–56
  in a changing world 283–94,
    306–8
  ethnic aspects 272–3

  USA and England compared
    211–12, 233–56, 272–8
  see also collective action;
    movements, social
class segregation 34, 148–52, 200,
  214–30, 253, 264
  homogeneity of subgroups 15,
    273, 276–8, 280, 289–90
Clawson, Mary Ann 233–4
clubs, working men's 151, 232, 234,
  251
coercion and capital 165, 170, 181,
  187
Cohen, G. A. 84–5, 308
collective action 121, 130, 134
  classless 115, 135, 138, 233–5,
    255, 292–3
  spatial aspects of 267–83, 288–90,
    292–4, 301–8
  see also class conflict; class
    formation; movements, social
colonialism 32
Combination Acts 248–9
commodity fetishism 65–7
communications 110, 267–8, 270,
  274
  and modern technology 274,
    285–6, 289, 299
community identity see
  consciousness
consciousness:
  class 61, 65, 122, 130, 151–2, 251,
    261, 274
  urban 11, 121–2, 125–30, 213,
    223, 239
consumption, collective 113–15,
  117, 136
Conzen, Kathleen Neils 273, 277
Conzen, Michael 224–5
Coventry 218
credit systems 110, 131–2
Croce, Benedetto 71
Cuba 32

Danzig 1
De Vries, Jan 176–80, 188–9
  European Urbanization 29
Délégation à l'Aménagement du
  Territoire et à l'Action
  Régionale (DATAR) 96
Denver 298
Derby 195

determination, causal see Marxist
    concepts
Detroit 273–4, 277
Devon 197
division of labour 13, 20, 31–4, 172
Dobb, Maurice 161
Dodgshon, R. A. 165, 166–7, 229,
    297
Durkheim, Émile 6–7, 10, 16–17, 21
Dyson, Kenneth 242, 250

ecology, human 23–4
Engels, Friedrich 31–3, 86, 145–56,
    268, 284, 293
  in Manchester 140, 143–52, 199,
    262, 287
  The Communist Manifesto 34–6
  The Condition of the Working
    Class in England 30, 140,
    143–56, 191, 195, 207–8
  The German Ideology 34
  The Housing Question 34, 36
England 145–8, 168, 187
  class formation in 211–12,
    233–56, 272–8
  as model for study of capitalism
    50–1, 72, 75–6, 159, 253
England, urbanization in 145–56,
    198, 217–21
Essen 200
Essex 197
ethnicity, in USA 272–5, 277–8
Eurocommunism 115
Europe, urbanization in 198
exploitation, of labour 73–4, 258,
    272

Fainstein, Norman and Susan 296,
    300
Febvre, Lucien, A Geographical
    Introduction to History 1
federalism 241, 243–4
feudalism 12, 157–91
Florence 178
Fordism 285, 295–6, 297–8
Foster, John 251
Fourier, Charles 48
France 94–6, 145, 168, 187, 241, 262
  see also Paris
franchise 242–3, 246
Frankfurt School 59
friendly societies 151, 232, 234, 235,
    248, 251

Gay Movement, Los Angeles 135,
    138
Geertz, Clifford 240
gender, in social movements 135,
    232, 291
Geneva 1
Geras, Norman 306
Germany 145, 168
gesellschaft and gemeinschaft
    16–18
Giddens, Anthony 87–8, 90–1
Gintis, Herbert 165, 167–9, 180
Girouard, Mark 193–4, 199, 282
Glasgow 40, 134
Glorious Revolution (1688) 240
Gottdiener, Mark 284, 294–5
  The Social Production of Urban
    Space 287–90, 297–9, 301–8
Gouldner, Alvin, The Two Marxisms
    58–61, 65, 68–9
Gramsci, Antonio 68–71
guilds 25, 163, 169, 172, 190, 227

Hadjimchalis, Costis 31
Hamburg 190
Harloe, Michael, editor, Captive
    Cities and City, Class and
    Capital 116–17, 118
Harris, Richard 223, 224
Harrison, J. F. C. 247
Harvey, David 117–19, 140, 142,
    206–7, 213, 239
  Consciousness and the Urban
    Experience 41, 119–34
  Explanation in Geography 103–4
  Social Justice and the City 7–8,
    37–8, 93, 99–100, 104–8
  The Limits to Capital 107–12,
    123, 127, 131–2
  The Urbanization of Capital
    38–9, 41, 131
  and urban analysis and Marxism
    98, 99–103, 103–12, 119–34
Haussmann, Baron Georges 120,
    123, 124–5, 210
health, public 133, 244
Heckscher, Eli 189
hegemony, concept of 71, 73, 81,
    88–9
Hirschman, Albert O. 308
Hobsbawm, Eric 83–5, 234, 284,
    290–5, 301–3, 306–8
Hohenberg, P. H. 186, 190–1

316 Index

Holton, R. J. 162
homosexual movements 135, 138
housing 15, 20, 113, 124, 218–21
  in Manchester 146, 149–51
  market in 225–30, 254, 259, 265
  as political issue 255, 292–3
Houston 298
Huddersfield, Yorks 196
humanism 97, 101
Huntington, Samuel P. 240

immigration 22, 272–5
imperialism 110
industrialization 97, 146–9, 190–1,
  192–202, 214–220
  and deindustrialization 285
  and proto-industrialization 164,
    190–1, 193
  and reindustrialization 285
industry, location of 201–2, 285–9,
  296–7
information, theory of 95
International Sociological
  Association, Research
  Committee on Urban and
  Regional Development 116–18
investment 52, 103, 108–12
Ireland 285
Isaac, Jeffrey 89
Italy 69–70

Jacksonville 298
Joyce, Patrick 215, 221

Kearns, Gerry 128
Keen, Maurice 184
Kern, Stephen, *The Culture of Time
  and Space* 11
Knights of Labor 274, 275
Kolakowski, Leszek 43
Korsch, Karl 59
Krieger, Leonard 60–1, 70, 76
Kumar, Krishan 266–7, 270, 276

labour:
  aristocracy of 205, 278–80
  and capitalist confrontation *see*
    class conflict
  division of 13, 20, 31–4, 300
  exploitation of 73–4, 258, 272
  force 48, 110, 113, 123, 153
  market in 230, 265, 285
Labour party 211, 272, 275, 291

Laclau, Ernesto, *Hegemony and
  Socialist Strategy* 87, 88–90,
  303–6
Lacq-Mourenx, France 96
Lamarche 117
Lancashire 197, 218, 222
land, use of 106, 108, 110, 124–5,
  224–8, 288–9
landlords 109
landscape, urban 41, 108, 148–51,
  193–4, 286–8, 298
law, and capitalism 77–9, 133, 181,
  185
Lawton, R. 218
Lebas, Elizabeth, editor, *City, Class
  and Capital* 118
Leeds, Yorks 147, 196, 225
Lees, L. H. 186, 190–1
Lefebvre, Henri 93–103, 126, 139,
  284, 287–8, 290, 305–6
  La Pensée marxiste et la ville 37,
    93
  Le droit à la ville 37
  La Révolution urbaine 37, 93
Leicester 195
Lille 200
Lima 40
Lisbon 187
Little, David 49–53, 83, 128, 155
Liverpool 145, 147, 190, 196, 217–18
location of industry 201–2, 285–9,
  296–7
Lojkine, Jean 117
London 12, 13, 147, 187, 193–4, 286
  development of 195–6, 198, 210,
    224–5
Los Angeles 298, 300
Lubasz, Heinz 158
Lucerne 1
Lukács, Georg 59, 61, 101, 126, 130
  History and Class Consciousness
    65–8
Lukes, Stephen 57–8

M4 corridor 286
Macclesfield 218
McDonald, D. F. 249
Madrid 40, 135, 138, 187–8
Maine, Sir Henry 16
Manchester 194, 199, 217
  development of 13, 145, 147–8,
    178, 196, 215

Engels in 140, 143–5, 147–52, 262, 287
Mann, Michael 169
Martins, Mario Rui 32, 35, 101–2
Marx, Karl 29–37, 45–64, 92, 260–1, 268
  Capital 31–2, 34, 49–53, 56, 60–2, 82, 108–9, 127–8, 208
  and France 262
  Grundrisse 31–2, 34, 60
  his model of capitalist economy 48–55, 64, 75–6
  his social theory 55, 64, 68, 72–3, 76–7, 81, 86, 90, 260
  his theory of history and change 46–7, 49, 64
  as historian 56, 58, 60–1, 64–5, 70–1, 76
  The 18th Brumaire 61
  The Class Struggles in France 61
  The Communist Manifesto 34–6
  The German Ideology 34
  see also Marxism
Marxism:
  closed 41, 61–4, 76, 128–32, 165
  critical 59–61, 63, 65, 101
  dichotomies in 58–61
  and new urban analysis 9, 93–134, 141–3, 155–6, 283–94, 301–8
  scientific 59–61, 65–8
  urban analysis limited 27–42, 207
Marxist concepts 43–91
  of base and superstructure 55–9, 66, 71–2, 77–86
  of capital accumulation 48, 54, 62–4, 82–3, 97, 102–3, 107–10, 182, 253–4
  of causal determination 56–7, 59, 61, 70, 79–86, 90
  crises in capitalism 48, 54, 94–5, 110, 121, 153, 159, 260, 291
  of 'laws of motion' in capitalist economy 55, 62, 64, 81, 258
  of structure and agency 53–8 *passim*, 64–8, 73, 86–90, 128–9, 139–40, 141–2, 262, 304–6; and Harvey 105, 128–9, 139–40; and Lefebvre 97, 102
  transformation of capitalism by class conflict 36, 41, 46–7, 52–5, 58, 73, 137–8
Marxist regimes 30–1, 34, 292
Merrington, John 175–6, 201

Mesopotamia 166
Mexico 166
Milan 178
militancy 224, 253–4, 276, 279–80
  see also class conflict; proletariat, formation of
Milnrowe, Yorks 196
mode of production:
  capitalist 48, 55, 84–5, 121–2
  in Marxist theory 28, 33–4, 36
monarchy 165–8, 187
Moore, Barrington 241
Mouffe, Chantal, *Hegemony and Socialist Strategy* 87, 88–90, 303–6
movements:
  social 38, 40, 103, 112, 114–15, 118, 133, 134–40; ethnic 135, 272–5, 277–8; homosexual 135, 138; and women 135, 232, 291; *see also* class formation; collective action
Mumford, Lewis 91, 161
  The Culture of Cities 2–4
Murrard, Lion 229–30
Murray, Pearse 34

Nash, John 210
Nettl, Peter 240, 243
new towns 95–6
New York 9, 13, 193, 286, 299, 300
  development of 224–5, 226
  trade unions 250
Northampton 195
Nottinghamshire 147, 195, 218

Oberhausen 200
occupational associations 25, 38
  see also guilds; trade unions
Oestreicher, Richard Jules, *Solidarity and Fragmentation* 274–5
Ogden, Yorks 196
Olives, José 117

Paris 12–13, 135, 187, 193, 200, 286
  Commune 40, 41, 125–6, 134, 282
  Peace of 195
  rebuilding of 111, 120, 122–5, 130, 210
Park, Robert 20

parties, political:
  in England 46, 247–50, 269–72, 280, 291–3; Labour 211, 272, 275, 291
  links with urban social movements 103, 114–15, 133, 136, 262
  local base of 262, 268–70, 271
  in USA 234, 243–4, 248–50, 272, 274–5
Peking 224
Pelling, Henry 279
Perkin, Harold 245, 246
Philadelphia 224
Pickvance, C. G.(ed), *Urban Sociology: Critical Essays* 117
Pirenne, Henri 161, 172, 176
Pittsburg 200
Pol Pot 30
Polanyi, Karl 106–7, 131
population, urban 145, 148, 162, 176–8, 202, 299–300
ports 29, 186, 190, 192, 195
Portsmouth 190
Postan, M. M. 161, 175
Pounds, Norman 200
power, steam 197, 200, 216
Pred, Allan 232–4
profits 48, 52, 54
proletariat, formation of 66–7, 145, 153, 191, 211, 229, 262, 280
  see also class conflict; militancy
property 133, 168, 182, 245, 288–9
property development 117
Proudhon, Pierre-Joseph 48
Prussia 187, 241
Przeworski, Adam 305
public houses 151, 235, 248, 251

Radford, John 225–6
railways 200, 270
Rawls, John 105
reading rooms 151
reformism 236, 241, 247, 266
rent 106–12, 124, 227
revolution *see* class conflict
Reynolds, Susan 166, 171–5
Ricardo, David 33, 48
Roman Europe 173–4
Rome 193
Rotherham, Yorks 196
Roubaix, France 200
Russia 95, 187

St Louis 9
Saint-Étienne 200
San Diego 298
San Francisco 40, 134, 135, 138
Santiago 40, 135
Saunders, Peter, *Social Theory and the Urban Question* 6–7, 36
Schumpeter, Joseph 111
Seattle 298
Second International 30, 31, 70
segregation:
  class *see* class segregation
  functional 149–51
separation of workplace and home *see* workplace and home
Seville 12
Sewell, William 216
Simmel, Georg 10, 18–21, 24, 121, 131
  Social Differences 19
  The Philosophy of Money 19
Slosson, Peter William 250
Smith, Adam 33, 48
  The Wealth of Nations 160
socialism 30, 151, 153
Soja, Edward W. 31
Somerset 197
sovereignty 163–5, 167–71, 175–6, 180–2, 187, 240–1
space:
  and Marxist theory 35–6, 40–1, 93, 105–12
  post Marxist theories of 92–140, 290
  reshaping of 283–90, 296–301, 303
Spain 40, 134, 135, 138, 187–8, 190
state:
  centralization 187, 243–5
  formation of 6, 11, 24, 132–3, 239–52; national 85, 166, 178–9, 180–1, 186–90, 192
  as instrument of capitalism 130–4
  intervention 113–14, 181–2, 244, 280–2
  as target 119, 212
Stedman Jones, Gareth 66–7, 86
Stinchcombe, Arthur L. 40
structuration theory 87–8
Suffolk 197
suzerainty 167, 180

Sweezy, Paul 161–2, 163, 175
Szelenyi, Ivan 34

technology, advanced 95, 285–7,
    289, 299
textile industry 192, 196–7, 218–19,
    220–1
Thatcher, Margaret 292
Therborn, Goran 59
Third International 30
Thompson, Edward 235–6, 261, 302
    An Open Letter to Leszek
        Kolakowski 43–5
    and Marxism 43–5, 59–61, 72–80
    Poverty of Theory 59–61, 65,
        73–6, 79
    The Making of the English
        Working Class 72, 74, 152–3,
        237–8, 253
    Whigs and Hunters 77–9
Thrift, Nigel 295
Tilly, Charles 163, 165, 186–7
    Big Structures, Large Processes,
        Huge Comparisons 16–17, 24
Tocqueville, Alexis de, Democracy
        in America 240
Toennies, Ferdinand 10, 20
    Community and Association
        16–17
Tokyo 286
Topalov, Christian 76–7
Toulon 190
trade unions 135, 151, 232, 279–80,
    291–2
    clandestine 232, 235, 237, 246–52
    links with urban social
        movements 103, 114–15, 262
    nationally organized 268–72, 280
    in USA 272, 274–5
transformation, revolutionary see
    class conflict; militancy;
    proletariat, formation of
transportation:
    and collective action 264, 268,
        270–1, 274
    and journeys to work 15, 150–1,
        217, 231–2, 274
    and modern technology 286, 289,
        299
    and urban development 15, 110,
        112, 113, 133, 225
Treble, James H. 218
Trimberger, Ellen Kay 75

urban analysis 1–9, 15–27
    differentiation approach 4, 16–27,
        96, 100
    limited in classical Marxism
        27–42
    and new urban Marxism 9,
        93–140, 141–3, 155–6, 283–94,
        301–8
urban development 11–22, 95–8
    change in 288
    early industrial 9–11, 13–15, 28–9
    in England 145–56, 198
    from feudalism to capitalism
        12–13, 157–202
    Marx on 34–5
    new towns 95–6
    planning 95, 105, 117, 133
    and state intervention 280–2
    see also cities
urbanism 20–2, 96–8, 105
urbanization 101, 107, 176–80,
        195–202
    and anti-urbanization 30–1, 34
    and de-urbanization 292–4
    in England 145–52, 195–8, 217–21
    new 299–300, 303
    in USA 198, 224–6
USA 12, 25, 27, 152
    class formation in 211–12,
        233–56, 272–8
    ethnicity in 272–5, 277–8
    political parties and trade unions
        in 234, 243–4, 248–50, 272,
        274–5
    urbanization in 198, 224–6

Vance, James 226–9
Venice 1, 174, 178
Vera Cruz 134
Vienna 111, 200, 210
Vilar, Pierre 47
voluntarism 59, 61, 66–7

Ward, David 278, 280
Warnes, A. M. 220–1
Weber, Marianne 9–10
Weber, Max 6–7, 9–10, 97, 116, 161,
        175
    The City 12–15, 24–7
Williams, Raymond:
    Marxism and Literature 79–84
    The Country and the City 11
Wiltshire 197

Wirth, Louis 20–2, 100, 121
Wolf, Eric 83
Wood, Eileen Meiksins 54–5, 170
workplace and home:
  and class formation 212–13,
    232–44, 272
  journeys between 150–1, 215,
    215–17, 231
  linkages 106, 151, 154, 218–19,
    220–1, 254
  separation of 10, 13–15, 124, 129,
214–56, 264; contemporary 285,
  289, 293–4, 297
workplace, and modern technology
  in 285–7
Wright, Erik Olin 261
Wylde, William 194

Zunz, Olivier, *The Changing Face of
  Inequality* 273–4, 277
Zurich 1
Zylberman, Patrick 229–30